Y0-DBX-518

Directory of Computer Conferencing in Libraries

Supplements to Computers in Libraries

1. Essential Guide to dBase III+ in Libraries
Karl Beiser
ISBN 0-88736-064-5 1987
2. Essential Guide to Bulletin Board Systems
Patrick R. Dewey
ISBN 0-88736-066-1 1987
3. Microcomputers for the Online Searcher
Ralph Alberico
ISBN 0-88736-093-9 1987
4. Printers for Use with OCLC Workstations
James Speed Hensinger
ISBN 0-88736-180-3 1987
5. Developing Microcomputer Work Areas in Academic Libraries
Jeannine Uppgard
ISBN 0-88736-233-8 1988
6. Microcomputers and the Reference Librarian
Patrick R. Dewey
ISBN 0-88736-234-6 1988
7. Retrospective Conversion: A Practical Guide for Libraries
Jane Beaumont and Joseph P. Cox
ISBN 0-88736-352-0 1988
8. Connecting with Technology 1988: Microcomputers in Libraries
Nancy Melin Nelson, ed.
ISBN 0-88736-330-X 1989
9. The Macintosh ® Press: Desktop Publishing for Libraries
Richard D. Johnson and Harriett H. Johnson
ISBN 0-88736-287-7 1989
10. Expert Systems for Reference and Information Retrieval
Ralph Alberico and Mary Micco
ISBN 0-88736-232-X 1990
11. EMail for Libraries
Patrick R. Dewey
ISBN 0-88736-327-X 1989
12. 101 Uses of dBase in Libraries
Lynne Hayman, ed.
ISBN 0-88736-427-6 1990
13. FAX for Libraries
Patrick R. Dewey
ISBN 0-88736-480-2 1990
14. The Librarian's Guide to WordPerfect 5.0
Cynthia LaPier
ISBN 0-88736-493-4 1990
15. Technology for the 90's
Nancy Melin Nelson, ed.
ISBN 0-88736-487-X 1990
16. Microcomputer Management and Maintenance for Libraries
Elizabeth S. Lane
ISBN 0-88736-522-1 1990
17. Public Access CD-ROMS in Libraries: Case Studies
Linda Stewart, Kathy Chiang, & Bill Coons, eds.
ISBN 0-88736-516-7 1990
18. The Systems Librarian Guide to Computers
Michael Schuyler and Elliott Swanson
ISBN 0-88736-580-9 1990
19. Essential Guide to dBase IV in Libraries
Karl Beiser
ISBN 0-88736-530-2 1991
20. UNIX and Libraries
D. Scott Brandt
ISBN 0-88736-541-8 1991
21. Integrated Online Library Catalogs
Jennifer Cargill, ed.
ISBN 0-88736-675-9 1990
22. CD-ROM Retrieval Software: An Overview
Blaine Victor Morrow
ISBN 0-88736-667-8 1992
23. CD-ROM Licensing and Copyright Issues for Libraries
Meta Nissley and Nancy Melin Nelson, editors
ISBN 0-88736-701-1 1990
24. CD-ROM Local Area Networks: A User's Guide
Norman Desmarais, ed.
ISBN 0-88736-700-3 1991
25. Library Technology 1970-1990: Shaping the Library of the Future
Nancy Melin Nelson, ed.
ISBN 0-88736-695-3 1991
26. Library Technology for Visually and Physically Impaired Patrons
Barbara T. Mates
ISBN 0-88736-704-6 1991
27. Local Area Networks in Libraries
Kenneth Marks and Steven Nielsen
ISBN 0-88736-705-4 1991
28. Small Project Automation for Libraries and Information Centers
Jane Mandelbaum
ISBN 0-88736-731-3 1992
29. Text Management for Libraries and Information Centers: Tools and Techniques
Erwin K. Welsch and Kurt F. Welsch
ISBN 0-88736-737-2 1992
30. Library Systems Migration: Changing Automated Systems in Libraries and Information Centers
Gary M. Pitkin , ed.
ISBN 0-88736-738-0 1991
31. From A - Z39.50: A Networking Primer
James J. Michael
ISBN 0-88736-766-6 1992
32. Search Sheets for OPACs on the Internet
Marcia Henry, Linda Keenan, Michael Reagan
ISBN 0-88736-767-4 1991
33. Directory of Directories on the Internet
Ray Metz
ISBN 0-88736-768-2 1992
34. Building Blocks for the National Network: Initiatives and Individuals
Nancy Melin Nelson
ISBN 0-88736-769-0 1992
35. Public Institutions: Capitalizing on the Internet
Charles Worsley
ISBN 0-88736-770-4 1992
36. Directory of Computer Conferencing in Libraries
Brian Williams
ISBN 0-88736-771-2 1992
37. Optical Character Recognition: A Librarian's Guide
Marlene Ogg and Harold Ogg
ISBN 0-88736-778-X 1991
38. CD-ROM Research Collections
Pat Ensor
ISBN 0-88736-779-8 1991
39. Library LANs: Case Studies in Practice and Application
Marshall Breeding
ISBN 0-88736-786-0 1992
40. 101 Uses of Lotus in Libraries
Robert Machalow
ISBN 0-88736-791-7 1992
41. Library Computing in Canada: Bilingualism, Multiculturalism, and Transborder Connections
Nancy Melin Nelson and Eric Flower, eds.
ISBN 0-88736-792-5 1991
42. CD-ROM in Libraries: A Reader
Susan Adkins, ed.
ISBN 0-88736-800-X 1992
43. Automating the Library with AskSam: A Practical Handbook
Marcia D. Talley and Virginia A. McNitt
ISBN 0-88736-801-8 1991
44. The Evolution of Library Automation: Management Issues and Future Perspectives
Gary M. Pitkin, editor
ISBN 0-88736-811-5 1991
45. Electronic Information Networking
Nancy Nelson and Eric FLower, eds.
ISBN 0-88736-815-8 1992
46. Networking Information: Issues for Action
Elaine Albright, ed.
ISBN 0-88736-823-9 1992
47. Windows for Libraries
Dan Marmion
ISBN 0-88736-827-1 1992
48. CD-ROM Periodical Index
Pat Ensor and Steve Hardin
ISBN 0-88736-803-4 1992
49. Libraries, Networks, and OSI
Lorcan Dempsey
ISBN 0-88736-818-2 1992
50. Unix-Based Network Communications
D. Scott Brandt
ISBN 0-88736-816-6 1992
51. The Role of Libraries in a National Research and Education Network
Charles R. McClure
ISBN 0-88736-824-7 1992
52. Using Windows for Library Administration
Kenneth Marks and Steven Nielsen
ISBN 0-88736-829-8 1992
53. Electronic Collection Maintenance and Video Archiving
Kenneth Marks, Steven Nielsen, and Gary Weathersbee
ISBN 0-88736-830-1 1993
54. An Internet Primer for Librarians and Educators
Elizabeth Lane and Craig Summerhill
ISBN 0-88736-831-X 1992
55. Directory to Fulltext Online Resources 1992
Jack Kessler
ISBN 0-88736-833-6 1992
56. Campus-Wide Information Systems and Networks: Case Studies in Design and Implementation
Les Lloyd, ed.
ISBN 0-88736-834-4 1992
57. DOS 5.0 for Libraries
Karl Beiser
ISBN 0-88736-835-2 1992
58. Wide-Area Network Applications in Libraries
Gregory Zuck and Bruce Flanders
ISBN 0-88736-841-7 1992
59. Information Management and Organizational Change
Gary M. Pitkin, ed.
ISBN 0-88736-842-5 1992
60. The Infosphere Project: Public Access to Computer-Mediated Communications and Information Resources
Thomas M. Grundner and Susan E. Anderson
ISBN 0-88736-843-3 1992

Directory of Computer Conferencing in Libraries

Brian Williams

Meckler
Westport · London

Library of Congress Cataloging-in-Publication Data

Williams, Brian K., 1938 -
Directory of computer conferencing in libraries / Brian Williams.
p. cm. -- (Supplements to computers in libraries ; v.36)
Includes bibliographical references.
ISBN 0-88736-771-2 (alk. paper) : $
1. Library information networks--United States--Directories.
2. Computer conferencing--United States--Library applications--Directories. 3. Communication in library administration--United States--Data Processing--Directories. 4. Communication in library science--United States--Data Processing--Directories. 5. Libraries--United States--Communication systems--Automation--Directories.
6. Telecommunication in libraries--United States--Directories.
I. Title. II. Series.
Z674.8.W55 1992
021.6'5025'73--dc20 91-39968
CIP

British Library Cataloguing-in-Publication Data

Williams, Brian
Directory of computer conferencing in libraries.
I. Title
004.608

ISBN 0-88736-771-2

Meckler Publishing, the publishing division of Meckler Corporation,
11 Ferry Lane West, Westport, CT 06880.
Meckler Ltd., 247-249 Vauxhall Bridge Road,
London SW1V 1HQ, U.K.

Printed on acid free paper.
Printed and bound in the United States of America.

Contents

1. Introduction to Computer Conferencing

In 1985, a small nonprofit organization of community energy groups and agencies in Northern California, the Energy Network, decided to try to computerize some of their board meeting functions. They were a good candidate for such a move as their constituents ranged over a territory of about 400 miles in length. As one of the original proponents of such an experiment, I was chosen as Conferencing Coordinator. In that capacity I evaluated the available options, chose a system, set up the conferences, ran them, and produced a monthly newsletter of the conference material. In the process of experimenting with the medium, the Energy Network eventually had conferences on three different conferencing systems: Confer at Wayne State; Econet, now defunct; and IGC, who took over Econet. In 1987, I established conferencing for another group, the Online Librarian's Microcomputer Users Group, also on Confer at Wayne State. I have also participated in conferencing, as a user, on many of the other public conferencing systems available at this time.

In the course of preparing previous papers on this subject I interviewed many of the authors and developers of conferencing software for basic details of the history of conferencing that had never been published. I was struck by the fact that much development of conferencing software has been done, for the most part, in isolation. Typically, a developer of one system had never looked at another to build on the best features of the available systems, but had, as is so often the case with computer software, gone his own way. As a librarian, I looked for information management tools in these information systems, but what was there was generally behind development taking place in online literature searching, for instance. Thus, it seemed that information on conferencing should be more widely available for several reasons: to encourage communication between developers, to stimulate development based on the best features of the available software, to stimulate development of information management tools in conferencing as well as other features, and to give the consumer of these products some information upon which they could base selection decisions. As important as all of these objectives might be, I found in putting this material together the objectives could not possibly be met at the same time in any reasonably sized monograph. Fortunately, I believe other works, either recently published or in press at this time, help to cover parts of the subject. I recommend the interested reader to John Quarterman's *Matrix* for an overview of computer communication networks and some history and specifics of conferencing systems.

The present work is an attempt to:

- provide an introduction to computer conferencing for the uninitiated
- provide data for a comparison of conferencing software and services
- provide some basic general information on accessing systems via vari-

ous networks
- provide a basic set of resources that can be used to obtain more information

The first part of the book is a general introduction to conferencing, its history, structure, and vocabulary. It is not meant to be exhaustive, but rather to give the reader who is not acquainted with this type of communication an introduction and some perspective.

The second part is a survey of the major conferencing software used today and the main conferencing systems using that software. Any survey such as this will be out of date to some extent within a few months of its publication as new systems and software emerge, and changes are made to existing systems. Nevertheless, it has been my experience that the changes in the last three or four years have not been qualitative as much as quantitative, and so perhaps it is not too unrealistic to expect the descriptive data to be relevant for a few more years.

Not every piece of software that could be categorized as conferencing is included. Software needing to be accessed with considerable additional expense was not included, unfortunately, and software I am not aware of yet has also not been included, obviously. In the world of computer software, it is very difficult, at any one time, to say with certainty that you know about every package that could be reasonably included in some category. I believe this is especially true of the bulletin board category.

More and more bulletin board systems are including conferencing in their list of features and deserve to be included in a survey of conferencing software. There are a few bulletin board packages reviewed, but not as many as some might argue deserved consideration. I am sympathetic to these arguments, but feel the real future in conferencing software development is going to be in additional features in the major packages and not the bulletin board softwares catching up with what conferencing has already been providing for the last five years. That doesn't mean this more powerful software will have to be running on a UNIX mainframe. More and more conferencing software packages will be made available in fully featured versions for smaller machines with multiuser operating systems.

In some cases such as COM, VAX Notes, and Notepad, notably, I was not able to get access to a system running the software. In those three cases other resources have been used to ascertain some of the details of the software.

There is no attempt to list all the purchasers or licensees of any package. If I have the approximate number of customers, I have included that, but a list of names would be so inaccurate in a few months I elected not to try and include it. It should be pointed out that in many cases the software is installed on hundreds of machines all over the world, many in academic environments but also many in corporate environments. Most of the descriptive information about a software package is given in the section dealing with that package. In the survey of systems using that package, however, only the modifications and customized features of the software are given in detail. Refer to the sections on the software for the broader picture of software features.

The systems covered in the book have limitations similar to those the software has, unfortunately. There are undoubtedly some systems, which should have been included but aren't for reasons like those mentioned previously. Nevertheless, the systems included are the major ones and give a good representation of what is available at this time. Systems are sometimes included because they are good examples of the application of a particular piece of conferencing software. Mostly they are included, however, because they are considered to be ones the reader might want to know about and use. Bulletin boards tend not to be available over networks and so are only practical for a small region of users. This lessens their importance from my perspective. Inclusion in this review is determined by a weighted product of significance in the conferencing environment, significance to librarians, and accessability. The conferencing on CompuServe, Delphi, and Genie, for instance, in my humble opinion, is not as interesting as that on the WELL, IGC, and many other smaller systems. This is true because the information content is more of the bulletin board type and the use of conferencing, per se, is not as sophisticated.

I confess this is subjective and due to relatively small changes in a specific environment. For instance, a system like Echo in New York does not have network access at present. Chances are, however, that within a few years not only will they have such connections but also that conferences on many of the Caucus systems, of which Echo is one, will be distributed and access to any one topic will be possible from a variety of systems. Distributed conferencing is a feature presently being developed for several major software packages and already installed on the APC network, beginning with the IGC system in San Francisco. I have tried to anticipate these changes by including these systems when it seemed likely they would be regarded as major systems in the near future.

A few examples of online educational systems are included. In some cases, these systems are good examples of existing conferencing software and in others they are simply bulletin boards without strong conferencing features. They deserve a book of their own as this phenomena is growing rapidly and needs to be developed with the standard set of educational resources, including librarian support. In the language of ERIC descriptors it is called Distance Learning. I don't believe this term defines the online aspect as distinct from the classic correspondence course, so I am calling it online education. It takes various forms, but can be found to be offering courses, and other educational support, at every level, from elementary to doctorate programs. Time is spent on this subject primarily to stimulate the library profession to become involved with this educational phenomenon, but one feature in particular deserves to be pointed out. These systems are among the first to recognize that supporting documents need to be online and to be delivered to the student electronically. As librarians are at present, or soon will be, facing the complexities of electronic document delivery, we may be able to watch these educational systems for some clues to the problems involved.

A survey was distributed to each system coordinator. A copy of the survey is included in the appendix. In general, in addition to the details the survey solicits, I tried to include an example logon to the system, a list of the available conferences so that the reader could get an idea of the scope and depth of the system, and a few help screens or other examples of the online system illustrating the system's uniqueness. In some cases, a more extensive list of system commands is included in this section as that system uses unique software, which is not generally distributed. I have also included a few references to the system in print if those could be found and were not simply press releases.

As a rule, downloaded material that is reproduced verbatim is reproduced in a smaller serif type font so that it can be distinguished from text that I produced. In some cases the downloaded text is annotated to point out certain features and in some cases other text is really downloaded, but heavily edited by me. This is particularly true of excerpts of manuals.

The Usenet's Netnews is included as a conferencing system because of its size and significance rather than because of its set of conferencing features (see Appendix). The discussion of whetherNetnews is a real conferencing system or not is simply not addressed in this book as, regardless, it is a significant computerized information resource, and that is the broader picture needing to be addressed. The Bitnet Listservs and Internet FTP's are also included for the same general reason. Netnews is included along with a short description of rn, the main software package used to access Netnews , but the Fidonet is not included. Fidonet is less of a conferencing system than Netnews is, even though it is sometimes hard to say exactly how much that is! This might be arbitrary, but I choose to draw the line there.

Internet and Bitnet have particular potential for online services. Any conferencing resource that is accessible via Internet for logon, for example, with TCP/IP compatibility is given special notice. I think those Internet accessible resources are especially valuable and I believe that the greatest change in the conferencing environment will be the increase in systems accessible over the Internet. It is, of course, possible to send mail to many systems that simply send and receive mail with an Internet connection several times a day, but are not available for logging on via that connection. Therefore, it is important to keep in mind that an Internet address may be useful for sending mail to someone on some particular system, but that same address cannot always be used for access to that system's conferencing. The point is, if a system is accessible via Internet, then the network costs have been absorbed by some other entity in the network structure and not, usually, by the end-user. Therefore that online connection is, in effect, free for the end-user. As online networking costs can be a very big percentage of a system cost, the availability of systems over the Internet is going to substantially lower the access costs to conferencing, and other online resources for that matter. This should make more and more conferencing available to a wider and wider audience, as the Internet becomes more available over the next few years. An increase in use can only be a stimulant to the development of better software.

A short section on computer networks is intended to give the user an overview of the main public computer networks. In my experience, there is much ignorance of the basics of these networks and their out-dial services in particular. This is a nontechnical introduction to those things. Bitnet and Internet are included for obvious reasons. Telenet is now part of US Sprint and has been renamed SprintNet; it is referred to that way.

The appendixes include supplemental information that is too long to include in the text itself, but I believe it is very useful for the beginning conferencing user. Much of this material is available online via the Internet, in particular, but I feel it is helpful for it to be pulled together in print in one place for the beginning network user. There are several of the classics on Internet and Bitnet use for instance.

The list of resources is intended to be a quick reference to phone numbers and addresses of the main participants in computer conferencing and networks. A few references to published information are included in each section for quick reference. All of these references are also included in the bibliographic section at the back of the book. The bibliography is selective. There is already a very large body of work on conferencing. Much of the work done has been sponsored by the government and so has produced the typical plethora of reports. A list of everything would be very boring. What is included is representative of the work that has been done and what seems to be most meaningful. Even so, it is a long list and growing. The format is ANSI.

Bibliography

Quarterman, John S. *The Matrix: Computer Networks and Conferencing Systems Worldwide.* 12 Crosby Drive, Bedford, MA 01730: Digital Press; 1990.

Williams, Brian. Teleconferencing — What, Why, How? *Proceedings of Small Computers In Libraries Conference*, 1986.: 197-201. Westport, CT: Meckler; 1986.

______,The Online Librarian's Microcomputer User Group: Teleconferencing by and for Librarians. *Proceedings of Small Computers In Libraries Conference*, 1987. Westport, CT: Meckler; 1987.

Read 5-2-92 @ Starbuck's, Oak Pk.

2. Definition and Description of Computer Conferencing

Computer conferencing, also called computer-mediated conferencing or computer teleconferencing, is communication between people that is input through remote terminals or microcomputers to a central computer where the information is organized and distributed to the participants. There is a continuum of electronic computer-based communication from electronic mail through bulletin boards to computer conferencing.

An electronic mail system takes a message entered from a remote terminal to a central computer, usually over a data network like SprintNet or Tymnet, and holds the text of the message there on the system for the recipient to pick up, alerting them that there is mail for them when they logon next. Messages can be sent to more than one person at a time, and the transaction can be very fast.

Bulletin boards, on the other hand, are not for private, one-to-one, communication, only, but for the posting of public bulletins for all to read and comment on. The bulletins posted on an online bulletin board system are like 'open letters' to whoever happens to pass by the bulletin board.

Teleconferencing usually includes both these communication modes, public and private, but goes further in organizing the material that is posted around a certain topic. Typically the computer conference is about something specific. All the public communications of the conference and the participants are dealing with this subject. The subject can be broad and subdivided, but typically more control is exercised over the material in a conference than on a bulletin board system. Typically, also, the computer conference has more developed indexing, searching, and text manipulation subroutines. It is not possible to draw definite lines between bulletin boards and conferencing systems. They share many features, and bulletin boards are developing quickly toward more complex communication media. As a general rule, however, bulletin board communication is a chronological stream of items about different subjects interwoven together over time. Bulletin board topics are not broken down as finely as conferencing topics and the communication is more informal. Early conferencing software, EIES and Participate, for instance, in some ways appears more similiar to bulletin board software today, than conferencing software such as Confer and Caucus. It is a thin line, subject to interpretation, and constantly changing.

The metaphor for computer conferencing is the real-time face-to-face department meeting. The topics of a computer conference are agenda items of the department meeting. It might be possible to conduct some of the meeting business on the department bulletin board, but not much of it. It is very similar electronically. Online bulletin boards can do some of the communication for the people involved, but the computer conference is a better medium for a discussion as opposed to announcements. The use of this analogy to the real-time face-to-face meeting is not meant to imply computer conferencing should not be thought of as a completely new type of communication medium. As conferencing software moves away from the reference to the face-to-face meeting, we will see a change in the features of computer conferencing. Nevertheless, computer conferencing needs to fulfill as many of the objects of the face-to-face meeting as possible as a starting point.

The term teleconferencing is used for all types of meetings over a distance. The most common form of this is the phone conference. A similar sort of meeting can be conducted over short wave radio, such as the PeaceSat network across the South Pacific. This medium allows somewhat normal phone communication, extended to more than one party at a time. The meetings are synchronous, the material of the meeting being sent and received at the same time.

Video conferences are also synchronous. They extend the medium to include a picture along with the voice, allowing the meeting to have almost the same dimensions of medium as a regular meeting, except over larger geographical areas.

Computer conferencing, however, is most often asynchronous, or spread out in the time dimension as well as the geographical one, without all the participants being there at the same time. Input is typically typed in at a remote terminal. Typing substitutes here, rather clumsily, for speaking, at least at this point in the technological development. There can be synchronous computer meetings, and these are a necessary part of certain organizational processes. Most of the material, however, is simply posted on the system for the participants to comment on, or add to, whenever they have time to logon or at a schedule that has been predetermined.

"...the three most important values of the system were its time independence, the availablity of hard copy, and the ability to enter one's message without interruption." (Vallee, p.37) A study done by Knowledge Industry Publications, Inc., of teleconferencing users of all types reported users perceived the main advantage of teleconferencing to be the savings on travel time to meetings and conferences. This seems natural; it was the main incentive for the Energy Network also. As we continued to use the system, however, other advantages become equally as important. The time dimension, for instance, provides a very flexible communication medium, we can work on problems as they fit into our schedules, and still the information exchange is fast and complete. As these systems develop there seems to be more text processing capability developed for the joint production of material. This material might then go into the normal streams of publication, but eventually we will see it remain in the electronic form and be quoted as such. One common use of the teleconferencing material is to go to a newsletter to be circulated to members of the relevant organization. With the use of a microcomputer and newsletter preparation software, this is a great way to generate material for a publication.

Conferencing Features

The typical conferencing system might have some of the following features:

- microcomputer-based front end
- terminal support for several terminal types
- command-driven interface with submenus
  - user control over interface
- online help
  - context-sensitive help screens
  - support-oriented conferences
  - online manual
- user configurable
  - availablity of high-level script language
  - settings for page size, type of prompt, etc.
- online membership directories
- electronic mail
  - standard electronic mail capabilities
  - receipt of mail delivery
  - control of message until delivery
  - X.400 compatibility
- asynchronous online meetings
  - control of meeting membership
  - acknowledgement of new material
  - input of new material from the keyboard
  - uploading of new material in ascii format
  - batch downloading of new material
  - "hooks" for remote operation
  - ability for user to edit and delete own material
  - audit trail of user activity
  - user polling (voting)
  - indexing or table of contents generation
  - searching for strings in text
  - retrieval of material by date, author, subject, or keyword
  - display of item headings only

- synchronous online meetings
- text editor
- accessory text material management
    - joint authorship software
    - tickler files
    - calendars
- accessory graphics files management
- accessory database management
- accessory binary file management
    - uploading and downloading binary files
    - ability to execute object files
- distributed conferencing
- access to NewsNet
- access to other online services
    - newswire services
    - online databases

Not all of the above features have been recognized as important, and certainly none of the current systems have them all. There are probably just as many features that are not on this list that will become standard or desirable as this medium becomes more widely used and a more diverse user base makes demands on it. Let's discuss some of these in detail:

• Front end packages (frends) for systems are just beginning to become available. There is one called Bizlink for Participate, which the Participate developers are working to enhance. Caucus and EIES2 are developing front ends. There is a hypercard front end for Cosy. These packages run on the microcomputer at the user's end and automatically perform the mechanics of connecting and retrieving any new material, log off and present the new material, take any input offline, then reconnect and upload the new material. Or they do something like that, depending on the package. At least they make the interaction shorter and hopefully easier. Coconut has a front end that provides the DOS user with a graphics interface to that software with pull-down menus for the various functions. Coconut will also run in a non-graphics mode for the rest of us. In most cases they are extras and not required for access, but in the case of Online America, for instance, they are required.

• The user interface has improved radically over the last fifteen years, but most systems still befuddle the unwary at certain points in a session. It is not at all uncommon to hear a user say it has taken him or her several months to get comfortable with the commands of a system. I might have said that myself in some cases.

• Most systems have good context-sensitive help available at every prompt. In addition they should have conferences set up for the user to ask questions and topics for the practice sessions of users. It is also convenient to have online help available, as on the WELL, at an address like "support." There should be a set of read-only topics or items giving the basic information about the system, who runs it, what it runs on, some history, who is the staff, etc. The manual should be available online in a searchable form. Not knowing what to do next is one of the most frustrating things in the world. Help and a "way out" should always be right there where you need it.

• The electronic mail and editing facilities on the system should be as standard as possible with a full set of features. The systems that use UNIX mail and the UNIX editors available as an option are a step in the right direction. UNIX mail, although easy enough to use and fairly complete, does not have all the features that should be there, for instance automatic delivery notification. Some of the mail subsystems on conferencing systems are superior to it, in my opinion. On the other hand, there are other mail packages for the UNIX platform and software that are sure to be constantly upgraded. The UNIX editors are superior to the editors on most conferencing systems, in my opinion.

• Not all systems allow easy uploading of text into items, responses, or mail messages. Kermit, or some other protocol, should not be necessary for such transfers. Almost all communication programs have a simple text upload function for this and systems should have been designed to accept this type of upload of any size file.

• Very few systems have a built in routine to go through all the new material without stopping in between items or conferences. This should be available so that the material can be collected and then processed offline. In fact, ideally, this batch collection should be automatically put into a special file for you and then, if desired, mailed to your main electronic mail box each day, much like the Bitnet Listserv forums. You probably should be able to mail responses back as well.

• There should be standard "hooks" inserted into the software so that a user can search through several different conferencing systems without having to know each system's own command language. This is similar to the problem of having many different library catalog systems available on the Internet. One does not want to have to know the details of each one to search them all. The "hooks" would allow another software package to do that interfacing for you.

• The polling features that some systems have developed are fascinating. They allow one not only to solicit a response from users, but also allow the responses to be anonymous, allow built in statistical analysis of the response, allow multiple choice type responses, allow different types of voting, and more. These would be valuable in many situations, especially if widely available. In an educational system they would greatly facilitate testing of the audience.

• Sophisticated keyword indexing of entries is almost nonexistant. VAX Notes seems to have the best indexing features. From an information management perspective, keyword indexing of each public response should have been built in long ago. It is a glaring deficiency of the conferencing system we have today. On any reasonably sized system, BIX or the WELL, say, you will see information repeated over and over again in different conferences in response to users who cannot find the information that they are looking for. Obviously they need index and retrieval routines. The extra storage and cpu cycles that retrieval and indexing would require might be a legitimate deterence in some small systems, but in all cases it is a questionable tradeoff. This material should be indexed just like articles in the Dialog databases, or something as effective for retrieval.

• High-level scripting languages, macros, are somewhat available in conferencing software today. Macros are available in almost all microcomputer packages today, they should be available in conferencing packages as well. Access to UNIX scripts should be available on the systems running on the UNIX operating system.

• Joint authorship software should be available. It allows a group of people to work collectively on one document, managing the various input and deletions. This would really help grant writing, for instance, even in-house. I only know of one system that makes it available at this time, Cignet in Seattle. It has in the past been available on other systems, but those, Augment, and Genie (Portland), are not still available as far as I can discover at this time. There are joint authoring packages available without conferencing, of course.

• Database management has become available on some systems. In most cases this is an interface with an available DBMS package, Foxbase for Caucus, for instance.

• Distribution of conferencing is becoming more common. In distributed conferencing items and responses are running on more than one system at the same time. A network of some kind connects the two systems and the material is automatically transported between the systems. This is already being done on the APC systems and VAX Notes. For instance, on the APC systems IGC in San Francisco and Greennet in England, new material is exchanged every hour. Distributed conferencing is currently being developed on Caucus, CoSy, and EIES2.

• More and more systems are recognizing the importance of being on the Internet or having other gateways to other services. Both the WELL and IGC have or are planning for Internet access in the near future. Confer at Wayne State and University of Michigan is available via the Internet. MicroUsers, a conference for LITA (Library and Information Technology Association of the American Library Association) members using Confer at University of Michigan, can thus be accessed using telnet via the Internet. Netnews, already distributed over the Internet, can provide an exisiting base of conferencing material, so that the critical mass required to build up interest in the conference's material is not so hard to achieve. All conferencing systems should have some UUCP connection to send and recieve mail over the Internet.

Applications

Here are a few specific applications that conferencing has or might be successfully used in.

Crisis Management

Several of the original conferencing systems were developed and used for crisis management. The ability to draw expertise from a wide geographical area in a short time, get good response time, and keep a record of the transactions is obviously a major advantage in such situations.

Remote Management

In cases where the management of a project is widespread, such as a scientific experiment involving several labs, a board of directors of a large corporation, heads of libraries in a network, some meeting functions, or premeeting functions, can be accomplished or enhanced with a conferencing system.

Problem Solving

Certain types of problems can be best addressed with a group of experts who will probably not be located on one spot. For instance, automation managers from different libraries could help each other with the typical problems of microcomputer support via a conferencing system. This has been effectively demonstrated with the Pacs-L Bitnet listserv forum where problems of networking CD-ROMs in libraries are frequently discussed.

Community Communications

Conferencing available to a regional public, such as the PEN system of Santa Monica, can increase public awareness of details of governmental processes and use conferencing to establish some voice in planning. Libraries connected to such systems will find themselves playing an active role as information providers, as the Santa Monica library is doing already. Libraries are the logical location for the placement of terminals for access to such systems for those who do not have terminals at their homes. For academic communities, conferencing can be the vehicle for posting general information on services and soliciting feedback. In the typical college and university setting, conferencing can be used effectively to augment office hours.

Education

Online education has become a large subclass of conferencing systems. Obviously, the conference can quite easily model itself after the classroom and much sociological study is being done at this time on that environment. Some of the online systems in existence at this time support teacher activities and some directly emulate classroom experience. There are accredited programs through the doctorate degree for those who cannot be in residence in the location of a school with the program that they would be able to or willing to take part in. Many of these systems are delivering documents used in the classroom online. An online library will become necessary as a support for these activities.

Entertainment

Much of the traffic on the systems like Bix and the WELL is typical of the discussions at the local coffee shop. They can be very educational, but most of it is within an entertainment context, probably the best educational environment, for that matter.

In-house

In-house conferencing, for any organization, can facilitate work group meeting and document preparation. General organization information, schedules, and calendars can be made available. Outside expertise and consulting can be brought in more easily and less expensively.

Selection of a Conferencing Solution

There are four possibilities for a person or group wanting to have access to computer conferencing. First, there is the possibility that one only wants to participate on one of the public conferences available. The conferencing available on CompuServe, Delphi, Bix, the WELL, and many others are the most available to the public, with the exception of regional systems, if they are available. With these systems you simply want to participate in the ongoing conferences available with a simple subscription to the service. Access to these systems is facilitated by their having data network addresses, so there is no long distance phone bill associated with their use for those close to a network node.

For those who want to have their own conference, they will either purchase the software from the producer and mount it on their own computers, or arrange for the conference to be set up on a vendor's computer. In the second case, there are businesses with this service and in some cases universities with conferencing software running available to those with contracts with the university. One in particular is Wayne State, which has the Confer conferencing system available to people associated with the school and non-profit organizations from the outside who contract with Wayne State. To get access to this central computing facility, they should be available via a network such as Tymnet, SprintNet, or the Internet.

Until recently most of the teleconferencing software was written for mainframe computers. Now there are packages for microcomputers. It is possible for these to be mounted on your in-house micro, just as you would a bulletin board. Ideally one would want these on a multiuser operating system with several phone ports and hardwired input.

In the descriptive material that follows, information has been distilled from many published sources as well as online. Some of the more general works that are helpful for this examination are listed below in the bibliography for this section.

"When such systems become widespread, potentially intense communication networks among geographically dispersed persons will become actualized. We will become the Network Nation, exchanging vast amounts of both information and social-emotional communications with colleagues, friends, and 'strangers' who share similar interests, who are spread out all over the nation. Ultimately, as communication satellites and international packet-switched networks reach out to other cities and villages around the world, these social networks facilitated by computer-mediated communications will become international; we will become a 'global village' whose boundaries are demarcated only by the political decisions of those governments that choose not to become part of an international computer network. An individual will, literally, be able to work, shop, or be educated by or with persons anywhere in the nation or in the world." (Hiltz, p.xxix)

Bibliography

Hughes, C., G. Cook, J. McGrath. *A Survey of Computer-Mediated Communications: Computer Conferencing Comes of Age.* (Office Information Systems; Nov. 9, 1987) Stamford, CT: Gartner Group, Inc;1987.

Hiltz, Starr Roxanne and Murray Turoff. *The Network Nation: Human Communication via Computer.* Reading, MA: Addison-Wesley; 1978.

3. Survey of System Software

3.1 HISTORY

The first conferencing software is usually considered to have been the EMISARI system set up by Murray Turoff, amoung others, at the Office of Emergency Preparedness in 1970. (Hiltz, p. 47) It was based on the Delphi concept of group process decision making and was essentially a tool to facilitate the delphi process over a distance and with a central computer to record the process and help with some quantitative work. "In 1972 there was a community of less than 100 people who had been exposed to computer conferencing, most of them inside goverment, and a few hundred who had used electronic mail in some form, most of them in the military." (Vallee, p.xi)

Ideas from the EMISARI experience went into the development of EIES, which was sponsored by the National Research Foundation at New Jersey Institute of Technology in 1977. The principle motivation of the National Research Foundation was in how such a communication system could help with scientific processes. The EIES development, along with the Control Data Corporation's program PLATO, inspired the development of FORUM. FORUM became the Institute for the Future's PLANET in 1975 leading to Infomedia's Notepad in 1978. Another EIES derivative was Participate by Harry Stevens introduced on the Source in 1980.

COM was also influenced by EIES and PLANET when it was developed in 1977 for the Swedish National Research Institute. In turn, COM influenced COSY developed at the University of Guelph in 1983. (Quarterman, p. 410) In parallel development, in 1975 Bob Parnes was writing Confer at the Wayne State University computer center, which inspired Picospan and Caucus.

PLATO was the basis for VAX Notes in 1980 and also the first version of the software the IGC system used; now it has been updated. PLATO was written with the ability to transport communication between systems, distributed systems, built in. VAX Notes became an official product of DEC in 1986 with a distributed conferencing system. IGC began in 1984, and pretty well stabilized by 1986. IGC become the most successful distributed system with distributed conferences around the world in 1987 or 1988 with conferences distributed to England's GreenNet. Usenet Netnews began in 1980.

All the early software was written for large computers and most were tied to proprietary operating systems, like Confer on MTS. Today's development is 180 degrees from that, with a few exceptions. Most of the revision of the original packages includes both portability and the downsized requirements for hardware. This is possible for two reasons, one, the smaller and less expensive hardware, 80386-based for instance, is just as powerful for most functions. Secondly, multiuser operating systems are available for the smaller machines, such as various versions of UNIX.

Bibliography

Hiltz, Starr Roxanne and Murray Turoff. *The Network Nation: Human Communication via Computer.* Reading, MA: Addison-Wesley; 1978.

Quarterman, John S. *The Matrix: Computer Networks and Conferencing Systems Worldwide.* 12 Crosby Drive, Bedford, MA 01730: Digital Press; 1990.

Vallee, Jacques. *Computer Message Systems.* New York, NY.: McGraw-Hill; 1984)

3.2 SURVEY

3.2.1 Caucus

Metasystems Design Group, Inc.
2000 North 15th Street, Suite 103
Arlington, VA 22201
(703) 243-6622 (voice)

Caucus was created by Camber-Roth and is marketed and supported by Metasystems Design Group Inc. and a network of distributors in the United States, Europe, and Japan. Caucus licensees include a wide variety of organizations including major corporations, small businesses, government agencies, and educational institutions. It resembles Confer in many respects because it is based on that software, without some of Confer's special features, such as polling.

Hardware / OS Requirements

Caucus 2.1 is available for most of the popular operating systems and LANs, including UNIX, Primos, VMS, AOS, Xenix, Novell, and 3Com. Computers being used as hosts for Caucus networks include DEC, Hewlett-Packard, Prime, Sun, Data General, AT&T, IBM, NCR, Gould, Unisys/Sperry, and Plexus.

Costs

Caucus Support Services

The current pricing schedule for Caucus support services is available from Metasystems Design Group as of September 1988.

Note: The figures in this schedule reflect modular pricing. Tailored support packages comprised of these basic services can be designed for your particular organization or Caucus application.

I. Custom technical support

A.	custom installation	$4,900
B.	custom configuration	$2,500
C.	custom macros	$4,200
D.	upgrades and enhancements	$2,400
E.	phone and online support	$2,400
F.	custom user guide	$1,500

Description of the Software

The basic structure in Caucus is a "conference" and a single Caucus "host system" can contain many different conferences, some open to anyone having access to the system, others open only to selected persons.

Each conference on a Caucus host system contains group discussions that are called "items" and appended "responses." Anyone can add an item, to be seen by everyone else. These responses are automatically tagged with the name of the responder.

Each item is given a number, starting with 1. To get started, look at the first item by typing "SHOW ITEM 1" when AND NOW? appears. Caucus will show you the body of the item and all of the responses that people have added to the item, and then will ask if you'd like to add a response.

AND NOW? (enter MENU, a command, or ? for help)

At the "AND NOW?" prompt in the command mode, Caucus expects you to tell it what to do. There is a menu interface available that can be selected at this point, otherwise, you must type a command and press <RETURN>.

Here are some examples:

Verb	Object	Instance	Modifiers
SHOW	RESPONSES	NEW	
LIST	ITEMS	ALL	BRIEF
SHOW	PERSON	John Smith	
SHOW	MESSAGE	5-10	PRINT
ADD	PSUBJECT	"Neat Items"	
SETSCREENSIZE	60		
FORGET	ITEMS	16-20	

These are the most frequently used Caucus commands:

STOP exit Caucus

HELP	get help on Caucus usage
SHOW	show the text of an object (such as items or responses)
LIST	briefly list an object (such as messages or subjects)
SEND	send a private message to a person
CHANGE	change the text of an object you put into Caucus
JOIN	switch to a different conference

The remaining commands are used less often:

ADD	add a new object
DELETE	delete an object permanently
FORGET	instruct Caucus never to tell you about an item
FREEZE	stop discussion on an item
SEARCH	search items or responses for a set of words
SET	customize Caucus the way you like it
STATUS	tell you where you are, and what you've seen

When typing a command, you can use any unique short form of the command. For example, you can shorten "CHANGE" to just "CH." The first four letters of a command is always sufficient. One or two letters work unless another command begins with the same letters.

Many Caucus commands (SHOW, LIST, ADD, DELETE, and CHANGE) act on objects. Those objects are:

ITEMS	an entire discussion item
RESPONSES	the responses to an item
MESSAGES	private messages to and from other people
PERSON	people in the conferences
OSUBJECTS	item subject categories created by the organizer
PSUBJECTS	personal subject categories you create

Some Caucus commands (SHOW, LIST, CHANGE, and DELETE) require that you give a specific instance of the object.

For the objects ITEMS, RESPONSES, and MESSAGES, you must specify a range of item or message numbers. A range can be any one of the following:

a number	(like 17)
a, b	(like 17, 19)
a-b	(like 10-13, which is the same as 10, 11, 12, 13)
THIS	the item you were just looking at
LAST	the highest numbered item or message
ALL	all of your messages, or all of the items
NEW	messages, responses, or items beyond the highest you've seen
FRESH	anything that was new when you entered the conference today

UNSEEN	items that are not new that you haven't seen
FORGOTTEN	items that you FORGOT
AUTHOR	"smith" all items added by person Smith
TITLE	"results" all items with the word "results" in the title
OSUBJECT	"fun" all items the organizer filed under the subject "Fun"
PSUBJECT	"good" all items you filed under subject "good"

For the objects PERSONS, OSUBJECTS, and PSUBJECTS, the specific instance must be either a name or the word "ALL". For example:

SHOW OSUBJECT "Apple"

displays the full name of all organizer-defined subject categories containing the word "Apple," along with the list of items filed under each subject.

LIST PERSON ALL

displays an alphabetized list of the names of ALL the people in this conference.

Modifiers effect the way a command is performed. The Caucus modifiers are:

Modifier	Relevant Command	Action
PASS	SHOW	doesn't prompt you for response or reply
BRIEF	LIST	displays one-line descriptions
PRINT	SHOW, LIST, HELP	prints text on the computer's printer
LIFO	SHOW	shows responses backwards (last in first out)
>output	SHOW, LIST, HELP	puts text in file "output"
>>output	SHOW, LIST, HELP	appends text to end of file "output"
<input	SEND, ADD	reads text from file "input"

These are some examples of commonly used Caucus commands:

SHOW MESSAGES NEW	look at all your new messages
SHOW RESPONSES NEW	look at all the new responses
SHOW ITEMS NEW	look at all the new items
SEND	send a message to someone
JOIN LIST	see the list of other conferences
SHOW MESSAGES 1-5 PASS	look at messages 1 through 5 w/o pausing
DELETE MESSAGES 2-4, 6	delete my messages 2, 3, 4, and 6
SEARCH ITEMS ALL FOR "compute"	search the whole conference for "compute"
LIST ITEMS BRIEF AUTHOR "Smith"	briefly list Smith's items
LIST ITEMS BRIEF TITLE "pc"	list items with "pc" in the title
CHANGE PSUBJECT "Good" + ITEM THIS	add this item to my private "good" list

This is not a full list of Caucus commands, just a sample.

All Caucus commands, prompts, and help screens are contained in a master dictionary file in standard ASCII text, which the system manager can tailor with any text editor — or translate into another language, e.g., French, German, etc. A single Caucus host can support multiple dictionaries and each user can select any dictionary available on the host. Also, each Caucus conference can be tailored by the conference "organizer" who can edit the conference "banner" that is seen by participants each time they log on. The conference organizer also controls the participant access list (open or private) and manages the conference subject index.

Text Editing

The editor for Caucus can be set to any editor on the operating system, ie. the standard UNIX editors, but it also comes with one. Here is the editor's main help screen:

You are now using the CAUCUS text editor. You can use this editor to make changes to any text that you entered. (For example, to fix typing mistakes). Each line of your text is given a line number. The editor has several commands, each of which works on a line or range of lines of your text. (For example, to see the first twenty lines of your text, you would type SHOW 1 20). Examples of the commands are shown below:

SHOW 5 10	(displays lines 5 through 10, with line numbers.)
VIEW 5 10	(displays lines 5 through 10, without line numbers.)
DELETE 2 4	(gets rid of lines 2 through 4)
ADD 6	(lets you add more text between lines 6 and 7.)
STOP	(stop using the text editor)
SEARCH 2 8	(searches lines 2 through 8 for a word or string.)
CHANGE 5 10	(look for and change something in lines 5 through 10.)

ADD will prompt you with a "?" to insert the new text. SEARCH will prompt you for a word or string of characters. SEARCH will then display the first line in the range that contains the word you are looking for. CHANGE acts like SEARCH, but it also asks for a replacement word or string. When it finds the word you're looking for, it changes it to the replacement word, and then displays the line.

If you give the SHOW, VIEW, or DELETE commands only one line number, they will work with just that line. (E.g., SHOW 5 just shows you line 5.) If you give the SEARCH or CHANGE commands only one line number, they will start at that line, and look through the rest of your text.

If you enter an editor command without any line numbers, it will use the current line number. For example, suppose you SEARCH 1 10 for "armadillo", and it's found on line 5. Typing DELETE without a line number is the same as typing DELETE 5.

Here is main help screen from Caucus:

HELP is available on all aspects of CAUCUS operation. ANY time Caucus is waiting for you to type something, you can type ? or HELP to find out what your choices are.

To learn how to use Caucus, try typing:

"HELP NOVICE"	if you're using Caucus for the first time
"HELP MENUS"	to learn how to use Caucus in the menu mode
"HELP COMMANDS"	to see what a Caucus command looks like
"HELP VERBS"	to see the list of Caucus command verbs
"HELP OBJECTS"	to see the list of objects Caucus can act on
"HELP INSTANCES"	to learn how to specify instances of objects
"HELP MODIFIERS"	to see the list of command modifiers
"HELP EXAMPLES"	to see examples of commonly used Caucus commands
"HELP QUICK"	to see a quick list of Caucus verbs and objects
"HELP SHORTCUTS"	to see some shortcuts for common tasks
"HELP TOPICS"	to see what other help is available

Caucus has an active third party arena. The following download from the WELL describes some of these activites.

Topic 513: CAUCUS — on the WELL
95: Lisa Carlson (lcarlson) Sun, Aug 6, '89 (23:02) 80 lines

Washington Information Services (WISC)

The Caucus Collaborator - from Washington Information Services Inc.

Here's a summary of the enhancements, which are basically 2 packages:
* Caucus Administration Package

* Caucus File Library Package

These enhancements interweave Caucus capabilities with the robust functionality of Xenix. There are significant changes in the basic Caucus interface, but all Caucus commands and syntax are retained. These enhancements should also work with most UNIX systems.

* Administration Package ------------------------

Combines three aspects of functionality and can be linked to the FileLibrary Package.

1. Menu-driven User Interface

- consolidated Caucus SEARCH under a FIND macro with object menu (messages, items, respones, files)

- consolidated SHOW under a READ macro (with same object menu)

- default "options" menu for each conference (i.e., NEW, ONLINE, SEND, SCAN, ROSTER, EXIT or whatever...)

- consoated DOWNLOAD module (with text, Kermit, Xmodem)

- command string-thru for most menu-sequenced functions, i.e.:

- download messages 23-34
- find file graphics.bin
- find title democracy (item title search)
- read file may.sked
- find conference

2. Conference Manager

- menu-consolidated Caucus CUSTOMIZE functions (greeting, intro, add change, freeze, usage log, download log)

- editable default Options menu (all macros and commands available)

- optional file library activation

- file download log viewing
- viewable usage logs (users, sessions, files)

3. System Manager

- menu-consolidated Xenix account, conference and file management tasks
- Xenix and Caucus account maintenance
- file library administration\
- usage tracking and reports
- system entry and exit message editing
- editable list of public conferences (with FIND CONFERENCE)
- conference start and remove

* Caucus File Library Package----------------------------

This module adds an often requested capability, for direct selection of text and binary files. (Upload module is under construction)

For the User:

- "Files" selectible through FIND, READ, and DOWNLOAD routines

For the Organizer:

- optional library for each conference
- editable directory of file titles
- file download display log

For the System Operator

- start and remove a file library from a conference
- start and stop logging download activity
- display log usage by month/year

(lisa's note: what i think is neat about WISC's stuff is that it lets non-techies do all those things by picking them off a menu rather than by typing junk like /u/cat/ blah/blah/blah

Response not possible. Pass? only 96

Topic 513: CAUCUS — on the WELL
96: Lisa Carlson (lcarlson) Sun, Aug 6, '89 (23:04) 95 lines
PANDORA (mark graham)
==
NetLink — Parallel conferencing by Pandora
==

A Product of Pandora Systems

NetLink is a set of tools that enables Caucus to read and write messages in several standard conference interchange formats including RFC1036. This allows unattended operation of parallel conferences between 2 or more Caucus systems and between Caucus systems and other systems running such software as Usenet or the APC software (EcoNet, PeaceNet, GreenNet, Web etc). Other systems will be added. Various import and export facilities are available, in particular Bitnet mailing lists. A key element of the Netlink package are the consultancy services of Pandora, we have several years experience of supporting parallel systems and doing data import and export and are available to customise this package to your own particular needs.

[note: NetLink is currently being used to link several Caucus systems]

===================================
Foxplus online developers toolkit
===================================

A Product of Pandora Systems

=> menu driver — Central to the Foxplus developers toolkit is the menu driver engine. This module is used to easily build and maintain menus for a wide variety of system tools including database searches, access to Caucus, system administration tools, and virtually anything that is needed to navigate and maintain an online system. The menus in Dictionary 42 and other of Pandora's enhancements have a common look and feel and integration between them makes for a virtually

seamless online environment.
=> system use tracking, accounting and reporting — The Pandora enhancements includes a user and service tracking system that records each user's use of the various services and sub-services on a given host system. The start, stop and total times (in seconds) are recorded for services including individual conferences in Caucus. By using the accompanying accounting and reporting tools host and service providers can produce reports about, and bill users for, online sessions based on a schedule of service fees.specific for each application.

=> order entry — Users can be registered on the system and billing information recorded for use by various subsystems such as online ordering of products and services. Users are given the opportunity of confirming their billing method and their orders can be processed without requiring them to re-enter their credit card number or other billing information.

=> automatic menu creation for text files — Using a simple coding scheme text files are processed through a tool that creates custom tree structures and menus based on information contained in the files. This function can be especially useful for applications requiring frequent updates of text information or other times when one wishes to avoid tedious menu development.

=> integration with Caucus — Foxplus, TERM, Script and other application development environments are smoothly integrated with Caucus. Menus, prompts, system responses and other interactions, as well as some functional styles, are consistent with the Dictionary 42 enhancement of Caucus. by using the auto-fire macro of Caucus we are able, for the first time, to bring users directly into an easy to use and understandable Caucus menu environment — directly from other applications — and back again — without the user ever knowing they are moving into and out of Caucus.

=> TERM subsystem — using the TERM software package from Century Software custom gateways (synchronous or asynchronous) can be built to many other systems. By using TERM's built-in command language complex off-site interactions can be easily created to meet the most challenging communications needs. Together with the data capture additions to NetLink (Pandora's Parallel Conferencing tools) this can provide a way to integrate information resources into either Caucus or Foxplus.

============================
SmoothTalk — a chat system
============================

A Product of Pandora Systems

=> SmoothTalk — this subsystem, written entirely in shell scripts, is a full-featured real-time chat system capable of supporting an unlimited number of simultaneous users in a unlimited number of individual rooms. SmoothTalk sports a session tracking capability, aliases, multi-line uninterrupted input and paragraph formatting as well as a menu front-end consistent with other Dictionary 42 tools systems and tools. SmoothTalk is easily accessed from within Caucus.

Mail

Mail is the UNIX mail.

Support

A Caucus license includes full online and telephonic technical support for your system managers for a period of ninety days, renewable in twelve-month increments. This support package includes copies of new releases of Caucus announced for your configuration during the supported period. It also entitles your organization to three memberships in the international Caucus Online Support and Development Network — which "meets" in the "Caucus caucus" conference on Metasystems Design Group's host, the Meta Network.

This network is an active online community of current Caucus licensees, plus the Caucus development and technical support staffs of Camber-Roth, Metasystems Design Group, X-On Software in London, and MDG Japan.

Users

Caucus has become a very popular conferencing package within the last few years as the more powerful PCs have come to market to allow cheaper hardware for multiprocessing and multiple access. Here is a list of some of the systems that are using Caucus. Some of these systems are reviewed in chapter 4.

Blackboard	(New York, New York)
Capital Online	(Washington, DC)
CIGnet	(Seattle, Washington)
Echo	(New York, New York)
Metanet	(Arlington, Virginia)
PEN	(Santa Monica, California)

Bibliography

Mace, Scott. "Menuing Added to Caucus Conferencing Program." *InfoWorld:* 32; January 8, 1990.

3.2.2 COM and Portacom

Jacob Palme
QZ
Stockholm University Computer Center
Box 27322, S-102 54
Stockholm, Sweden

Brief Description

COM was first written by Torgny Tholerus in 1977 for the Swedish National Research Institute. Portacom was written in 1984 to provide portability to the software. Current development is associated with Jacob Palme at Stockholm University.

List of Some Users

COM and Portacom are used widely in Europe. In Europe there are over 200 installations; at Stockholm University the application is called QZCOM.

Hardware Requirements

Portacom is available for VMS, VM/CMS, and UNIX among others.

Description of Software

"This is a sophisticated conferencing system, including messages, 'open' and 'closed' (or public and private) conferences, search and retrieval capabilities, text editing, an voting facilities." (Hiltz) The main version of COM is in Swedish, but there is also an English language version available.

Mail

There is a mail system built into the software; it is menu-driven and easy to use.

Cost

The cost is unknown at this time.

Bibliography

Hiltz, Starr Roxanne, Elaine B. Kerr, and Kenneth Johnson. *Determinants of Acceptance of Computer-Mediated Communication Systems: A Longitudinal Study of Four Systems.* New Jersey Institute of Technology. Computerized Conferencing and Communications Center. Research Report #22. Newark, N.J.: New Jersey Institute of Technology; August 1985.

3.2.3 Confer

Advertel Communication Systems, Inc
2067 Ascot
Ann Arbor, MI 48103
(313) 665-2612

Computing Services Center
Wayne State University
5925 Woodward Ave,
Detroit, MI 48202
(313) 577-4642

Professional Development Office
University of Michigan
610 East University
Ann Arbor, MI 48109
(313) 763-9497

Background

Confer was written in the 1975 by Bob Parnes to run on the MTS (Michigan Terminal Systems) operating system. It was revised in 1980 as Confer II, and is now being rewritten again for a wider range of platforms including UNIX and VAX.

Most users of Confer use it on a university system such as: Wayne State, Univerity of Michigan, or University of Alberta. One company, Hewlett-Packard, has licensed Confer for inhouse use. Confer is available to any organization through Wayne State's and the University of Michigan's computer center. There are many companies and groups using it at one or another of the sites. Advertel will set a conference up and handle the details with the schools for you.

Hardware Requirements

Confer was written for the MTS operating system that runs at the University of Michigan and some of the other schools in the vicinity. The hardware is IBM S/370 or compatible. There is a VAX version as well.

Access

In addition to direct dial to a computer site and Sprintnet access, Wayne State and the University of Mighigan are available on MERIT and Internet. The Internet address for Wayne State is hermes.merit.edu. At the prompt type "wu" to go to Wayne State's system. You have to have an account to get onto the computer at that point, of course.

Costs

Costs depend on which site you are using and they are broken down by cpu charges and kilocharacter transmission for three different periods of the day. I have data that averages $20/hr. during peak hours including Sprintnet communication costs and $15/hr. during nonprime times. I understand that the

Sprintnet costs are at least $10/hr. of those costs. Thus the cost of conferencing via the Internet, where there are no communicaiton charges, is considerably reduced and the online charges are probably in the range of $5 to $10/hr.

Description of Software

Confer has a "book" structure. Basically that means there is no branching off of item responses as with EIES or Participate, but each new train of thought is put into a new item. This tends to keep the discussion on track and it makes it somewhat easier for the user to follow the discussion. The software is command-driven with occasional menus at places. Options at the prompts can be obtained with a question mark.

Each conference has "items" and each "item" has "responses." Messages are mail documents. Confer has "notes" that can be reminders to the owner of the note. "Bulletins" are posted for the whole conference audience. They can be posted for a certain time to be shown and once shown do not reappear. "Files" are separate documents available to users who can control who else can access them. They do not generate "responses." There is a synchronous "meeting" facility and Confer has interesting built in capability for polling users and voting.

Audit trails are extensive, although the reports available without modification are just the basic ones of overall use, numbers of items, number of participants, cumulative number of uses, cumulative number of minutes of use, number of messages sent, items displayed, responses made, and responses seen. It is possible to request and arrange to get statistics on each participant.

Commands

Command	*Abbrev.*	*Modifiers*	*Function*
Bulletin	B	all, new, reverse	view or post bulletins
Change	C	allow, archive, audit, author, buffer, bulletin, category, delete, directory format, header, help, hint, intro, keep, key, next, phone, prime, related, remove, response, text, x	change text of various things
Check	CHEC		see new activity in conferences
Descriptor	D	all, etc, first, focal, headers, last, new,	display descriptors of items

		next, pause, this, unseen, *	
Destroy	DESTR		erase a file
Edit	ED		edit a file or buffer
Empty	EM		erase buffer or file
Enter	E	anonymous, crypt	enter an item
Files	F		get info on files
Find	FIND		searches for expression
Forget	FO	this, *, -*	makes items invisable
Help	H		Provides tutorials
Index	IN	all, *category name*, headers, all author, *item list*	view categories of items
Item	I	all, date, etc, first, focal, *item list*, last, new, next, pass, pause, previous, respond, reverse, text, this, unseen, *, *dummy*	displays items
Join	J	*conference name*	go to a conference
Keep	K		saves text in buffer
Load	L		puts text into buffer
Meeting	MEET		starts a meeting
Message	M	delete, headers, ignore, last, *number*, new, next, reply, skip, this,	displays mail
MTS	MTS		returns you to MTS
Myindex	MY		personal item categories
Mysummary	MYSU		personal item summaries
New	NEW		displays new items and mail
Note	N	all, <mm-dd-yy,>,=	enter and display personal notes

Participant	P	all, count, *name*	displays info on participants
Permit	PE		
Query	Q	conference, name, seen, unseen	displays usage statistics
Quit	QUIT		logoff, leaves the system
Response	R		display responses
Review	REVI		displays the text of a meeting
Stop	STOP		leaves Confer, but stays in MTS
Summary	SU		displays item summaries
Talk	TALK		enters text into meeting
Transmit	T		sends mail
View	V		displays buffer
x(...)			
$			prefix for an MTS command in Confer
*			displays the items with a *
?			displays help message

Users

Confer is particularly of interest to librarians because there are library related conferences on the system, a project of ALA at this time, and it is used regularly by the Library staff at University of Michigan. In addition, because it is available via the Internet and the costs are otherwise quite low, it may well be the best positioned conferencing service on the market today for those instances where an academic group with Internet access is willing to develop conferencing off site.

Support

Support is provided by the conferencing organizer and each conference can ask Bob Parnes and his group to join their conference to provide further back up.

Examples

Here is a sample logon at Wayne State via Sprintnet.

@c 313 202 (telenet access)

313 202 CONNECTED

%Merit:X.25 (DT12:TX01:CRT)

Which Host?wu (to get Wayne State's computer)
%TD01:DT12-DT13:WU11
MTS: Wayne State (Host=WU Task=236 Dev=DT11)
#Telenet network surcharges in effect:
Connect time $3.50/hour
#signon xylk (my signon id.)
#Enter password.
?
#TeleNet,Deferred,Ext
#Last signon was at 23:32:37, Tue Sep 02/86
#User XYLK signed on at 00:15:02, Tue Sep 09/86
#$RUN *NEWS for details on: New WSUnet SCP (722-1500), Services During
#Strike, SCBS Hours, Specialty Consulting, 800 BPI Tapes, WCSC:CENSUS

Confer II (08/85) — designed by Robert Parnes (system set to run Confer automatically). © Copyright and Trademark: Advertel Communication Systems

CONFERence for ENCC:EnergyNet

DO NEXT? i 79

Item 79 23:37 Sep02/86 5 lines 1 response
Brian Williams
Sample item

This is an example of a sample item. This was prepared offline with the text editor in the communications program, then uploaded after the : * command to Confer.

1 response
Sep02/86 23:42
79:1) Brian Williams: Your response can be typed in at the keyboard or also uploaded as any text can be. Just remember that carriage return. Two carriage returns in a row will be the signal that you are finished. If you want to have a blank line anywhere just put a space on that line before the carriage return.

and it will look like a blank line.

RESPOND, FORGET, OR PASS: r

```
 GIVE YOUR RESPONSE
>At any time you display an item and its responses, you will have a
>chance to add another response.
>
 EDIT, VIEW, CANCEL, MORE, OR DONE:  d
 This is response 79:2

 DO NEXT? t
 ENTER YOUR MESSAGE
>Bill,
>Planning to come to the Energy Net conference? If so, could you
>bring a Mac and do some training for me, if the need arises? Looks
>like I will be staying with Mary, et al. Plans?
>
 EDIT, VIEW, CANCEL, MORE, OR DONE:  d
 ENTER RECIPIENT:  bill W
 OK TO SEND TO BILL WILSON?  y
 Message sent at 00:18 Sep09/86
 ENTER ANOTHER RECIPIENT (or press RETURN):
 DO NEXT?  quit
#XYLK 00:15:02 to 00:20:40, Tue Sep 09/86
#  $1.13
#  $34.35
%TD01:DT12-DT13:WU11  Connection  closed
313 202 DISCONNECTED 00 40 00:00:05:57 122 34
```

Bibliography

Quarterman, John S. *The Matrix: Computer Networks and Conferencing Systems Worldwide.* 12 Crosby Drive, Bedford, MA 01730: Digital Press; 1990.

Parnes, Robert and Maya Bernstein. *The Beginners Guide to Confer II.* Ann Arbor, MI: Advertel Communication Systems; 1986.

3.2.4 CoSy

Softwords
4252 Commerce Circle
Victoria, British Columbia
Canada V8Z 4M2
(604) 727-6522 (voice)
(604) 727-6418 (fax)

CoSy was developed at the University of Guelph in Ontario, Canada. CoSy supports electronic mail and the other normal public communications with the nice added touch of allowing the user to follow discussions by reference to each other. The distribution and development rights were purchased by Softwords in Victoria, British Columbia not long ago.

Probably the best known installation of CoSy is BIX, *Byte* magazine's online information resource. CoSy has been very popular with academic institutions and many have had it installed. TRIE at Cal State University is an example.

Hardware Requirements

Most applications of CoSy are running on UNIX, but there are some running on the VM version.

Cost

The basic price for the UNIX version to an educational institution is $3,895. The Xenix version for a microcomputer is $1,995 and the VM version is $12,000.

Description of Software

The following was downloaded from TRIE, a CoSy application run by the California State University system.

** Welcome to CoSy (Conference System) **

The beginning user should only need to know the four basic commands:

"show" will list all conferences of which you are a member

"join" will connect you to a conference; if no conference-name is given, the first conference with unseen text will be joined

"mail" allows you to converse privately with another CoSy user

"bye" terminates your CoSy session

Conferencing Main Menu

[1] Electronic Mail
[2] Conference Subsystem
[3] User Information
[4] Quick Download
[5] Individual Options
[6] Command Mode (to return to menus enter "opt menu on")

[q] Quit conferencing

:help commands

Command Subcommands
------- --

bye
converse ... new, read, delete
edit ... resume, scratchpad, profile, workfile
file ... <CoSy command>
help ... <item to get help on>
join ... <conference name>
mail ... to, read, status
moderate add <participant>, add <topic>, new <conf name>, terminate, ...
noecho
print .. <CoSy command>
read ... all, backward, comment, first, forward, header, last,
    quit, reference, say, skip, <number> to <number>, resign
show ... all, new, participant, resume <name>, who <name>, <conf name>
terse
time
verbose

See also 'help hfiles'

:help hfiles

Help can be obtained on the following commands or options:

add	edit	moderate	reference	status
all	extmail	new	remove	terminate
author	file	noecho	reply	terse
backward	first	order	resign	time
bye	forward	participants	resume	to
commands	header	password	say	topic
comment	help	print	search	undoc
converse	hfiles	profile	send	verbose
create	join	quit	show	who
date	last	rates	skip	withdraw
delete	mark2	read		
-- new for 3.0 --				
mark3	newadd	newread	newsend	option

Use the command 'help <name>' where <name> is one of the above. In addition, certain subsystems (read, converse, etc) may have further help files available.
:help show

The "show" command is used to list information on various things: conferences, mail, participants, etc.

Please do a "show ?" for a complete list of things that can be 'show'n.

:show ?

show

<no option>...........list your conferences
All...................list all conferences
All <string>..........list titles with string
<conf>................list conference details
<conf> <topic>........list topic details
MAil..................list mail headers
New...................conferences with activity
Participants..........members of a joined conference
Participants All......list members of the system
Participants <conf>...members of specified conference
Resume <participant>..resume of a member
Status................status of conference members
Who <string>..........list names with string

Mail

Cosy has its own mail and does not use UNIX mail although you can escape to the UNIX shell if that is desirable.

New Versions

Softwords is working on a microcomputer based front end for CoSy and a distributed version of the software so that conferences could be ported automatically. There is a HyperCard front end for CoSy system called HyperCosy available from MediaGap Communications.

3.2.5 EIES

Computerized Conferencing and Communications Center
New Jersey Institute of Technology
Newark, NJ 07102
(201) 596-3437 (voice)

Background

The Electronic Information Exchange System, EIES I, first available in 1975, is one of the oldest of the software running at this time and has served as a training ground for many of the conferencing crowd around today. Its features are extensive, but hard to learn, and confusing to use until you become accustomed to its structure, even though it is menu-driven. Many EIES I users are enthusiastic members of the conferencing community and EIES I has served as the experimental ground for many of the basic studies on teleconferencing. The Computerized Conferencing and Communications Center (CCCC), which runs EIES, has done the most extensive research on various aspects of conferencing covering a period of fifteen years. Starr Roxanne Hiltz and Murray Turoff, faculty members at New Jersey Institute of Technology and on staff at the CCCC, are two pioneers in the field. They authored the main monograph of the subject in 1978, *The Network Nation: Human Communication via Computer.* One of the main thrusts of exploration today at the CCCC is the virtual classroom—online education.

Hardware Requirements

EIES I was written for the operating system of the Perkin-Elmer computers. EIES I is still available, but the software has been rewritten for UNIX and VM/CMS systems, and completely revised. In its new incarnation the UNIX version is called EIES II and the VM version is TEIES.

Description of Software

EIES I

EIES I and EIES II are completely different from the vantage point of the new user. Both of them are available and being used at this time, although EIES II is the more marketable product for several reasons. I will cover a few of the details of each of the versions.

EIES has conferences made up of a series of 'comments.' The comments are arranged in chronological order and can refer to the previous comment or another comment before that. These comments are thus not all related closely to each other necessarily. When you add a comment to a conference, you tell the system to which comment yours is related. EIES also has 'notebooks,' which are documents that all the conference users can also see; they can be private, which do not have comments, but 'pages.' 'Messages' are mail documents. Conferences, conference comments, and notebooks are given and refered to by their id numbers.

EIES I presents the user with a three tiered level of menus that could be bypassed at any point by substituting commands for the menu choices. Each menu has eight to ten choices. The main menu is:

```
Access to:
        messages        (1)
        conferences     (2)
        notebooks       (3)
        bulletins       (4)
        directory       (5)
        explanations    (6)
        reviews         (7)
        composition     (8)
        monitoring      (9)
Initial Choice?
```

Then if option number 1 was choosen the next menu would be:

```
get items             (1)
  display titles      (2)
  search/ find        (3)
  send/compose/submit (4)
  edit/delete         (5)
  organize items      (6)
  vote/form           (7)
  set options         (8)
  ..................choice?
```

Then if option number 3 were choosen the next menu would be:

```
Search by:
        numbers/names          (1)
        status/type            (2)
        combinations           (3)
        from-to-dates          (4)
        words/phrases          (5)
        associations           (6)
        sequences              (7)
Display structures of:
        keys                   (8)
        associations           (9)
        sequences              (10)
Search Choice?
```

There is a chart of all the menus and their connections in the back of *The Impact of a Computerized Conferencing System on Scientific Research Communities*, among others.

In addition to the menu structure, the user can elect to give commands at any prompt. A few of the main command components are:

Verbs		*Objects*	
A	add	A	associations
C	compose	D	directory
CA	copy and add	C	conference
CY	copy	CC	conference comment
D	display	G	group
E	explain	K	keys
EX	exchange	M	message
F	find/search	MG	member/group
G	get	N	notebook
L	let	NC	new comment
O	organize	NM	new message

P	print	NP	notebook page
R	review	RM	reminder
S	set/send	SA	storage area
SN	set negative	SP	scratchpad
+G	display an item	SS	system status
+D	display the heading of an Item	T	time and date

These can be combined to form commands such as these:

+EDIT	edit an item
+CY	copy an item into the editor
+C	compose text item
+CM	compose a message
+CCC	compose conference comment
+CNP	compose notebook page
+DC	displays titles of all conferences
+DN	displays titles of notebooks
+FC	searches conference titles for a substring
+GWNP	get waiting notebook pages

These command examples are taken from the *Users' Manual for the Electronic Information Exchange System.*

EIES II

Here is a sample logon to the EIES 2 system at NJIT.

ATDT1,201,5962927
DIAL TONE
1,201,5962927
CONNECT 1200

DECserver 200 Terminal Server V3.0 (BL33) - LAT V5.1
NJIT 1200/2400 bps dialup

Please type HELP if you need assistance
Local> c eies2 (Tell it that you want EIES2.)
Local -010- Session 1 to EIES2 established

CCCC @ NJIT EIES2 LAT Services...
Attached to line ttyp1

login: 152 (Give your login id.)
Enter the type of your terminal or 'none' for a dumb terminal.
For DEC compatible terminals or vt100 emulators on PCs, just hit return.
Terminal [vt100] >none (The default gives you screen oriented displays which have the disadvantage that your communications software will not probably be able to record past screens in your buffer. Line oriented display is better if you will want to go back over the activity. Screen oriented looks good and might be-

```
more friendly for some people.)
Sunday August 19, 1990 4:04 PM        08/19/90
There is now 1 user on eies.
EIES2 Release 1.8.7
copying  files.......
running EIES2 ...... please wait while tables are built.
Line Mode
              New Jersey Institute of Technology

            Electronic Information Exchange System 2

Password >

 8/19/90   4:05:09  PM

Greetings  Brian William (BW,152)          Last Session:
                                        8/19/90   3:51:10  PM

 GENERAL INSTRUCTIONS FOR EIES 2:

 Enter a Carriage Return <CR> (also called ENTER or RETURN on some key-
boards) after each line or command you type.

 To make a selection from the horizontal menu at the bottom of the screen, type
the number or the CAPITALIZED letter of the choice, or enter <CR> to select the
highlighted menu choice.

 For general help, enter a "?" .  For help on a specific topic enter a ? and the
choice number or the choice name for which you want help.


WELCOME TO EIES 2, VERSION 1.8.5 (10)
 -1- Continue    (2) set    (3) oveRview    (4) Learn      / use EIES 2    User of
EIES 2  about user   (?) help options  controls   (-) esc
ACTION CHOICE>
```

Here is an abbreviated list of the conferences on the EIES 2 system at NJIT at this time. One of its main functions is as a demo system, as EIES 2 is the product, not this particular system. EIES 1, on the other hand, was primarily a system for public and private use, but that software is now being replaced with the EIES 2 software.

```
CONFERENCE SELECTION  (301)
 -1- Next  (2) Back (3) Enter (4) View (5) Compose (o) Other->
 page     page     conference conference   comment  (?) help   description   (-) esc
ACTION CHOICE> 4

Enter conference numbers (#,#,#) (<CR> for all) >
```

Item 1 out of 31

Number: C 1 (Public)
Name: Welcome Conference
Moderator: System Monitor (EIES,100)

This is the Welcome Conference for EIES 2

Item 2 out of 31
Number: C 1.1 (Public)
Name: EIES 2 Inquiries
Moderator: Eileen Michie (I,1240)

This conference is for questions regarding EIES 2 policies, costs, etc.

Item 3 out of 31
Number: C 100 (Public)
Name: Bugs
Moderator: Eileen Michie (I,1240)

This conference is open to all EIES 2 members who wish to report bugs and/or problems they find on the system.

Item 4 out of 31
Number: C 1000 (Public)
Name: Practice
Moderator: Accounts Manager (Bob A.,102)

This conference is guarenteed to be boring. It is for experimeting with the EIES2 conferencing features.

Item 5 out of 31
Number: C 1002 (Public)
Name: Learning EIES 2
Moderator: James Whitescarver (Jim,982)

Enter this conference to learn how to make the most of your use of EIES2.

Item 6 out of 31
Number: C 1003 (Public)
Name: Student Center
Moderator: Walter Kulyk (PcGuruMan,3128)

The place to hang out between classes.

Item 7 out of 31
Number: C 1005 (Public)
Name: Graffiti
Moderator: Accounts Manager (Bob A.,102)
Enter your pearls of wisdom and other humorous morsels here. Please keep it clean.

Item 8 out of 31
Number: C 1009 (Public)
Name: Opportunities
Moderator: Accounts Manager (Bob A.,102)

This is the place for non-commertial advertising for just about anything.

Item 9 out of 31
Number: C 1080 (Public)
Name: Advertisement
Moderator: Accounts Manager (Bob A.,102)

Even EIES2 has commertials! Enter here for exiting opportunities offered by other members.

Item 10 out of 31
Number: C 110 (Private)
Name: Help Review
Moderator: System Monitor (EIES,100)

This Conference is used to provide help for users

Item 23 out of 31
Number: C 333.1 (Public)
Name: Time For Graphics
Moderator: Dave Hughes (Dave,333)

Discussion, hopefully more development, of the NAPLPS public graphics standard, for truely interactive online text + graphics dialogue. All we need is more low-end drawing/terminal software.

Costs

EIES 1

While prices may change, at the time of this printing, an individual account costs $60/month. An organizational account is $150/month. (There is a 50 percent discount to educational institutions on site licences.)

EIES 2, TEIES, Personal TEIES Site Licences

One machine or 500 users	$10,000
Each additional machine or 500 users	$5,000
Annual maintenance	$10 percent/year
Annual update of new features	$10 percent/year
Account on NJIT's EIES2 system	$600 a year/person

Personal TEIES $70

Costs for accessing the system at NJIT also include Telenet charges of $12/hr. primetime and $4/hr. nonprimetime, unless you dial direct. There are about 2,000 users at this time.

Bibliography

Kerr, Elaine B., Murray Turoff, and Peter and Trudy Johnson Lenz. *Users' Manual for the Electronic Information Exchange System* . Computer Conferencing and Communications Center. Research Report # 17. Newark, NJ: New Jersey Institute of Technology; (no date).

Hiltz, Starr Roxanne. *The Impact of a Computerized Conferencing System on Scientific Research Communities.* Computer Conferencing and Communications Center. Research Report # 15. Newark, NJ: New Jersey Institute of Technology; June 1981.

Hiltz, Starr Roxanne and Murray Turoff. *The Network Nation: Human Communication via Computer.* Reading, MA: Addison-Wesley; 1978.

3.2.6 Notepad

InfoMedia Corporation
(No address available)

Brief Description

Since 1978, the InfoMedia Corporation has offered a conferencing system called Notepad, which runs on an in-house DEC System 20 and is time-shared out at the rate of $60/hour.

Notepad is marketed to the corporate user. The system can be customized for a particular application with extensive training on the use of the system should the user require it. An extensive description of Notepad has been published. (Vallee)

Many businesses and government agencies use Notepad, but there are is no public access and no public systems.

Hardware Requirements

Notepad was written to run on DEC 20 machines and is not portable to other operating systems.

Description of Software

"A Notepad account consists of a number of discussion topics or files called 'activities.' A typical menu of activities that a user might see upon entering the system is shown in the list below.

1. general discussion
2. engineering
3. construction
4. administration
5. suppliers
6. subcontractors
7. planning and scheduling
8. procurement
9. coordination

When a user signs onto Notepad, the above list of activities is displayed. The user selects an activity and reviews any messages or discussions that have taken place since the last access. The user then enters any response pertaining to that activity. These remarks are immediately transmitted to all members of the project team participating in that activity." (Vallee, p.73)

Notepad keeps an audit trail of all user activity, has special features of voting, and can be linked to running programs as part of the session. It has a simple user interface enhanced by the use of a function key strip on some (DEC) terminals. It can support NAPLPS.

The structure of the conferencing is similar to EIES I in that it is chronologically ordered and does not branch. The software is written in assembly and so is very fast. Files are encrypted and several levels of passwording are available.

Bibliography

Vallee, Jacques. *Computer Message Systems.* New York, NY.: McGraw-Hill; 1984.

3.2.7 PARTICIPATE

PARTICIPATE
Participation Systems Inc.
43 Myrtle Terrace
Winchester, MA 01890
(617) 729-1976
Ed Yarrish (215) 821-7777
George Reinhart (215) 770-0650

List of Some Users

PARTICIPATE is now used on CompuServe, Unison, and NWI among others.

Hardware Requirements

It requires UNIX System V, VMS, Primos, VM - CMS, MS-DOS LAN (under development).

Description of Software

PARTICIPATE, often refered to as PARTI, is one of the grandfathers of conferencing software, dating back to development done in the late 1970s. It was first used on the now defunct Source. It is probably now best known for being on CompuServe, but it has been widely used throughout the United States and Japan, on TWIXS. It has a branching structure that allows a user to start a new topic series from any point in an exisiting chain of responses.

What follows is a highly edited version of the PARTICIPATE manual available on Unison.

Messaging

The basic unit of communication in PARTICIPATE are notes. They are usually sent to individual users, although they can be sent to a group. They are designed for short-term communication. You can specify that they are urgent, or request an acknowledgement, as you can with many electronic mail systems. You write your notes in an area known as the scratchpad, then send them to the appropriate addressees. Notes appear in the recipient's Inbox, which is the equivalent of a mail box. Any personal messages will appear in your Inbox for you to read and act upon. Whenever you enter PARTICIPATE, you are told how many Inbox notes are waiting for you.

Meeting

This is the central area of activity in PARTICIPATE. In these electronic meetings, you communicate through notes that develop around a certain topic. A topic is a collection of notes on a certain topic. As meetings develop, it often becomes apparent that certain topics have several important subtopics. In this case, a branching topic can be created to explore related topics more fully. Only those interested join the branching topic.

Notes

A note consists of a header created by PARTICIPATE and text composed by a user. The header contains information about the following:

- the name of the topic or the message number

- the author of the topic or message
- the date and time (including the time zone) the note was sent
- the subject of the note (optional)
- the number of characters the note contains
- the total number of notes in the topic

For example:

==

"MARKETING" by ANNA, Feb. 20, 1984 at 10:30 ET about TO DISCUSS OUR STRATEGY (92 characters & 4 notes)

==

A note can be one of three types:

- a topic entry
- a topic opener
- a message

Notes can be sent to a group of users who have joined a topic, or to individual users.

Topic Entry

A topic entry is a note that is received automatically by all users who have joined that topic. The total number of entries in a topic is indicated in the topic opener. This gives you an idea of how actively a topic is being discussed. Topic entries are seen by all users joined to that topic.

Topic Opener

To start a new topic, you create a topic opener briefly describing the purpose of the topic and inviting a group of addressees to join. If you send an opener to an existing topic, you create a branching topic.This is equivalent to sending the opener to each member of the existing topic (known as the parent topic). A topic opener is note 0, and subsequent entries in the topic are numbered sequentially starting with 1. The note numbers may not be an unbroken sequence, as notes can be deleted by their initiators.

Topics

A topic is a collection of notes. You specify topics by enclosing their names in quotation marks. A topic is initiated when a user sends an opening note (called an opener) to a group of addressees, inviting them to join in the discussion. Subsequent notes in the discussion are usually entries.

Introduction

Your Inbox contains your unread notes. These notes are either messages sent to you personally, or entries in a topic you have joined. Each time you enter PARTICIPATE, the system checks your Inbox, tells youhow many notes there are, and prompts you to take action on those notes. If you don't have any Inbox notes, you will be moved directly to the ACTION==> prompt.

To deal with your Inbox notes, you have several options:

- see an overview of your Inbox (using PROFILE)
- process your notes (using READ, SCAN, or sometimes DELETE)
- ignore your notes until later (using other commands)

Each of these options is explained below.

Joining and Leaving Topics

Joining topics is the way to become actively engaged in PARTICIPATE. When you are a member of a topic, all new notes sent to that topic appear inyour Inbox. To join a topic that interests you, use the command JOIN followed by the-topic name in quotes, as in

JOIN "MARKETING"

You receive a response from PARTICIPATE, informing you that you are now a member of that topic. To stop receiving Inbox notes on a topic that no longer interests you, type LEAVE followed by the topic name in quotes, as in

LEAVE "MARKETING"

After you leave a topic, you can still read the topic notes, or rejoin if you wish.
Command Summary

This is a summary of the commands for Version 4.1 of PARTICIPATE. Before using this command summary, here are a few points to note:

A "note" is written text, sent to a user or a topic. It can be a message, an entry to a topic, or a topic opener.
An "item" is a generic term used to refer to a topic name or message number.
Replacing All the terms in this command summary that must be replaced, terms like note and item, appear in lower case.
COMMANDS Commands themselves appear in upper case.
AbbreviationsMost commands can be abbreviated with their first letter.
Options Options you can use with certain commands appear in square brackets, for example [NONSTOP].
Specifying Topic note(s): topic name in quotations followed by note notes number(s), e.g. "SCHEDULES" 36 Message: message number, e.g. 84.2037
Specifying Use the following format, with a 24-hour clock date and time mm/dd/yy hh:mm e.g. FIND SINCE 5/20/84 13:28

General Commands

? - get a list of available options
H*ELP - get a list of options with a brief explanation for each
?R*EAD - get detailed explanation of specified command or concept
R*EAD - read through notes
[N*ONSTOP] - read notes without pausing
item - read item
item note(s)
- read specified note(s) segment(s)
- read specified segment(s) of your Inbox or Found Notes
FIL*E filename - read specified file
S*CAN [# L*INES] - scan specified number of lines
[N*ONSTOP] - scan notes without pausing
item - scan an item

item note(s) - scan specified note
segment(s) - scan specified segment of your Inbox or Found Notes
FIL*E filename - scan specified file
N*EXT - read or scan your next note
J*OIN "topic" - join a topic to receive future notes
L*EAVE "topic" - stop receiving notes in a topic
W*RITE - enter the scratchpad
P*ROFILE user or item- find out information about users, items, or segments of queue (see separate section)
M*ODIFY characteristics - change characterisitics about yourself or items you created
Q*UIT - exit PARTICIPATE
A*CTION - to return to the ACTION prompt
B*ATCH [S*CAN] - read [or scan] with no pauses for action or for the --more-- prompt
C*ONTINUE - read remainder after scanning part of note
BAC*K - go back to what you were doing before
I*NBOX - get an update of your Inbox notes
FIN*D S*INCE date[time] - find notes sent to you since specified date [and time]
B*ETWEEN date[time] - find notes sent to you between specified
A*ND date[time] dates [and times]
[FR*OM user name] - find notes received from the specified user
[TO user name] - find notes you sent to the specified user
T*IME - find out the current time
FO*RWARD note TO addressee list - forward note to addressee(s), topic(s), or user(s)
K*EEP note - save note in your Inbox for future reference
FIL*E filename item note(s) - store note(s) in a file
D*ELETE item - delete specified item
item note(s) - delete specified note
F*ILE filename - delete specified file
segment# - remove specified segment from your Inbox or Found Notes
V*OTE "poll name" - vote on the questions in a poll
QQ*UIT - exit PARTICIPATE quickly without checking Inbox notes
BYE - exit PARTICIPATE and log out

Scratchpad Commands for writing and sending notes

? - get a list of available scratchpad commands
.H*ELP - see explanation of commands used in the scratchpad
?.command - get detailed explanation of specified scratchpad command
.S*END - send a note to a topic or user
.O*PEN - start a new topic
.A*CKNOWLEDGE - obtain indication that note has been received
.U*RGENT - mark note to appear in special Inbox segment
.DELI*VER date [time] - delay delivery until specified date [and time]
.Q*UIT - leave the scratchpad without sending a note

Editing Notes

.CL*EAR - erase scratchpad contents

.D*ISPLAY - display scratchpad contents
.C*ENTER - center text
.M*ODIFY characteristics - change characteristics about yourself or items you created

Obtaining and Storing Notes

.R*EAD note - see contents of specified note
.PR*OFILE user or item - find out information about users or items
.CO*PY note - insert text from specified note into scratchpad
.CO*PY FIL*E filename - insert text from specified file into scratchpad
.F*ILE filename - store scratchpad contents in a file
.+filename - execute contents of a file

Polling

.PO*LL - begin constructing a poll
.N*EXT - enter a new poll question

Profile Commands for seeing descriptive information

P*ROFILE user or item - find out information about users, items, and segments of queue
MY*SELF - find out information about terminal settings, accounting data, topics, messages, and files
U*SER user name - see the personal profile of specified user item - find out information about items
M*EMBERS - see list of members of specified topic
AD*DRESSEES - see list of addressees of specified item
R*ETENTION - see retention periods associated with specified item
B*RANCHES - see list of all branches of specified topic
[# depth] - see specified number of branching levels
[# start note] - see specified number of branching levels starting with note indicated
ACC*ESS - see what access rights you have to an item
ACK*NOWLEDGEMENTS - see list of users who have read your notes marked for acknowledgment
V*OTES - see voting results of a poll

Modify Commands for changing information and controlling access
M*ODIFY characteristics - change characteristics about yourself or items you created
PR*OFILE - enter or change your self-descriptive information
PA*SSWORD - change your current password
L*INEPAUSE - change number of lines preceding the --more-- prompt
S*CANLINES - change your scan line setting
B*ACKSPACE - turn option to backspace over default on or off
M*ENU - turn menu option on or off
item - change characteristics of specified item
AD*D addressee list - send item to additional addressee(s)
REM*OVE addressee list - remove addressee(s) from an item's distribution list

U*NJOIN member - cause member(s) to leave a topic
RET*ENTION - change retention periods you have specified for an item
AC*CESS - change access rights associated with an item
OR*GANIZER - take control over an item as if you had initiated it
OP*ENER - change text of message or topic opener
S*UBJECT - change the subject line of an item
P*OLL - change certain aspects of a poll

Cost

Up to 1,000 users the cost of the software is $10 per user with a $1,000 minimum. 1,000 users and above is $10,000.

Other Developments

The PC-based front end is Bizlink done by Larry Allen.

3.2.8 PicoSpan

PicoSpan
Network Technologies International, Inc.
Arbor Atrium Building
315 West Huron
Ann Arbor, MI 48103
(313) 994-5255

List of Some Users

The most accessible PicoSpan sites today are the WELL, Arbornet and M-Net.

Hardware Requirements

PicoSpan runs on any UNIX platform.

Description of Software

PicoSpan is basically a simplification of the major ideas of CONFER. Also, where possible, the resident features of UNIX have been used.

PicoSpan, like Confer, has conferences with items and each item has responses. On some systems the items are called topics. Responses are supposed to be on one subject and a new subject is started with a new item in the conference. PicoSpan keeps a participation file for each participant in the users UNIX home directory.

Each item and response are time stamped and also include the author's name. The read command is how items are looked at; if the "NEW" modifier is given, only the items that have changed (since the last update field in the participant file) are presented. After each item is printed, PicoSpan gives you a chance to add more to that item at the "respond, forget, or pass" prompt. At this point, you may add a new response to the item if you choose to do so.

This is the way PicoSpan is intended to be used; it is expected that most sessions will consist of the "R NEW" to read new responses, with the user "passing" on most discussions, but perhaps responding on a few.

Mail

"Mail" accesses the UNIX mail command. PicoSpan will also alert you to the presence of mail each time you check in.

What follows is a highly editied version of a series of the PicoSpan help screens.

PicoSpan Commands:

Read - read items
Enter - create new items
Browse - scan headers
Find - look for "string"
Forget - forget items
Remember - remember forgotten items
Kill - kill (remove permamently) items
Retire - retire an item from general circulation
Unretire - retire an item from general circulation
Print - type items in convenient form for printer
Join - join a new conference
Leave - leave current conference but not PicoSpan
Next - join the next new conference
Check - check status of a list of conferences
Cluster - join another cluster
Sync - make a party item
Async - turn party item back into a normal item
Quit - exit PicoSpan: also stop, exit
Bye - leave the system entirely: also goodbye, bye, off, logoff
Help - get help on topics
Fixseen - pretend we've seen everything
Freeze - stop responses on an item
Thaw - allow responses again on an item
Respond - enter a response to an item directly from OK:
!<UNIX command> - execute one UNIX command underneath PicoSpan.
(Lines starting with '!' are passed through to UNIX, except for text entry mode where ':!cmd' may instead work.)

Miscellaneous commands:

Display - displays various parameters
Participants - displays participants
Change - change them... (same as SET)
Define - defines variables or abreviations
Undef - undefine one or more variables
Who - who is on the system
Chat - with other users
Mail - send or receive mail
Send - just send mail
Help - get help on topics
source — source PicoSpan commands from a file
Echo,echoe,echon,echoen — type short messages out
amsuperuser - abort macros and scripts if not a f-w
Cdate - convert dates to hex
Cd, pwd, cat, files, direct, umask, ed — file operations
Shell - get a UNIX subshell
UNIX - exit to UNIX, or execute a UNIX command
abort - get out quick from PicoSpan
Quit - exit PicoSpan: also stop, exit
Bye - leave the system entirely: also goodbye, bye, off,logoff debug, test, date - test commands

Abort To leave PicoSpan without writing out Participation file or anything else. This means next time you invoke PicoSpan items that were new this session will most likely still be new, and items you've forgotten won't be forgotten any more.

Browse allows you to read items headers
format: browse <items>
Try "browse all," "browse 2," "browse short all," etc.

Browse will print just the header to items — the item #, date entered, author and header. Use the "READ" command to look at a rest of a particular item. [SCAN is equivalent to BROWSE *unless* your local system has redefined this.] Bulletins — this is a file that is typed out on people's screens if they haven't seen the latest copy of its contents.
DISPLAY BULLETIN will redisplay its contents at any time.
The latest contents of the bulletin will of course also be shown automatically to people as they join after a "CHANGE BULLETIN" is done.

bye — logoff the system; also logoff, logout, out, goodbye

Set and change are actually different names for the same command. This command allows you to change a variety of things, including:

name,user allows you to change your name in the current conference password,passwd changes your UNIX password

date, nodate asks that PicoSpan display (or not) dates on response this session
uid, nouid do (don't) display uids on responses
strip, nostripallow (don't) allow funny control characters in responses. Note that "cursor" dances generally are "cute" the 1st time, so-so the 2nd time, and boring the 3rd!
numbered, nonumbered, unnumbered -number, don't number text in responses
chat, nochat, write, nowrite -allow other people to chat with me this session

strip, nostrip PicoSpan will (won't) strip control characters out of text typed in
mailtext, nomailtext let the send mail program collect text instead of us
edalways, noedalways goes directly to the editor upon text entry (respond, enter, mail)?
dot, nodot otherwise, will '.' end text mode, or just ^D only
stay, nostay should RFP stay on current item after a response is made
meto, nometo will I see my responses as "new" after someone else responses
newresponses, reload reload participation file, forgetting what I've seen in this conference since the last session
resign zap my participation file and leave me an observer
join, register-if observer, become member
sane -undefine perconference defines
supersane-undefine perconference and system-wide defines
forget, noforget-turn "forget" range flag on/off. If "noforget" is in effect, some additional responses and items may be displayed. This only works while in the middle of a read command, the next item range specified will reset this flag.
ignoreeof, noignoreeof if "ignoreeof" is in effect (not default), then ^D will not exit PicoSpan from the "OK:" prompt
list -change the .cflist file (see "HELP LIST")
source, nosourc-do (default) or don't source RC files, such as ".cfonce," ".cfrc" and the per-conference "rc" file. The -n flag on the run line for PicoSpan will also suppress this, as well as "/usr/bbs/rc."
nodefault, defaultdon't, do (default) join the "default" conference when starting up. Only useful in a ".cfonce" file. Same as -l on run line.

Chat - talk with another user
form: chat
chat <user>

This will allow you to talk with another person who is logged onto the system at the same time you are.

Responding to Chat

When someone wants to chat with you, you will see a message similar to: Message from person ttyx... show up on your terminal. "Person" is that person's loginid; ttyx is the terminal the user is on. You can respond to this chat by saying "chat person" (at most PicoSpan prompts) and the two of you will be ready to chat.

"O" Convention

After you've issued the chat command, all it does is copy your output, a line at a time, to whomever is on the other terminal. Since the "chat" command is so stupid, a convention has evolved to allow the two of you to converse with a minimum of confusion. When one person is entering lines, the other person waits for the first person to type a 'o' (for "over") on a line by itself. Then it's the second person's turn.

Leaving Chat

To leave chat, just type in ctrl-D or your current interrupt character (either DELETE or ctrl-C). The other person will see a final line of the form "EOF" show up and you will be returned to wherever you initiated the chat command.

Initiating Chat

Turning Chat Off

If you don't want to chat with other people, you can instead type "SET NOCHAT" and other people will then get the message "permission denied" when they try.

Check [conferences]

Check for activity in a list of conferences. CHECK will report the number of "newresponse" and "brandnew" items in each conference specified. A '>' is used to mark the current conference if it is found in the list of conferences.
If no conferences are specified, CHECK will use the same list NEXT uses, from .cflist. See HELP LIST and HELP NEXT for more details. In this case, the pointer is also indicated with a '—.'

Display command:
 display [options] where options is one or more of:
  forgotten, retired, frozen, new list those items
  conference information on this conference
  user, name my name in this conf
  time, date the current time (also date)
  who who is on the system. (same as "who" cmd)
  fws, fairwitnesses fairwitnesses to current conference
  list display current ".cflist" list
  participants participants
  definitions definitions
  strip, dot, meto, stay, chat(&write), default, mailtext, ignoreeof, numbered
  say whether the flags are on (see also "help change")
  seen seen item status
  size, superuser, fds - assorted random debugging info

list .cflist
version version of PicoSpan in use (also in startup herald)
files [-switches] [file-spec]
report on the files given with file-spec.

Note this command just collects its arguments and invokes the UNIX command "ls," it does all the hard work.

find <items> "string"

Find will look through all the matching items and print out the lines that match string. Note that find currently only looks through response text, it ignores headers, authors and anything else not text.

fixseen or "seen" <items>
(defaults to ALL) — pretend we've seen all the responses in all the matching items. Probably most useful if you've somehow trashed your participation file...

forget <item-range>
-forget all the specified items.
(including "PASS" will supress "Forgetting item" messages)
freeze <items> - stop responses on the indicated items. (f-w or author of item only)
An item-range can be:
all - all items (same as first-last) (also '*')
first - first item, usually 1 (also '^')
last - last item in conference. (also "$" [currently, use $])
this - current item (also '.', "current")
next - next item after current item
previous - get item before this item
reverse - reverse item-range when through
- (number) that item
#-# - read a range of numbers
or range, range -commas can be used to combine multiple requests
can include search patterns:
since DATE -match only items with responses entered since this date
"string" -match only items with this string (except FIND uses this string to match the against text instead of the header).
and can include flags:
(affecting choice of items:)
new -only gets "new" items for all and #-#
brandnew - only items entered and not seen at all yet
newresponse - only "old" items with new responses by other people
noforget - process even forgotten items in all and #-#
forgotten - only "forgotten" items
unseen - "old" items we haven't seen yet
(affecting what we do with the items)
noresponse - READ, don't print any responses out before RFP prompt
forceresponse - READ, go directly to RESPOND code
pass - READ, won't stop at RFP prompt. Useful to print out items...
nopass - turn off pass

reverse - display items in reverse order
date, nodate - timestamp (or don't) each response
uid, nouid - print (or don't) uid of creator of each response
numbered, unnumbered, nonumbered - READ: number(or don't) lines typed out
ff, formfeed - (for PRINT), emit trailing form feeds in default
configuration — triggers %(T %) item conditional--only used in zsep with default macros
forceresponse, forcerespond, respond
with read command, immediately enter "response" mode
short - BROWSE, display short 1-line header instead of default numbered, date, Uid; can be turned on with SET command

join — join a different conference
form: join <conference-name>
or join

The first form will switch to that conference; a conference name can consist of either a UNIX path name to a valid conference or a name from a system-wide dictionary of abreviations. Without a parameter, PicoSpan will tell you which conference you're in.

"Help conferences" will print out a list of all the current public conferences

If you join a new conference that you don't belong to, you'll be asked if you want to join "join, observe, or quit."

join: become a member, which in most cases is the correct thing to do
observe: If you don't want your name associated with the conference and don't want PicoSpan to keep track of which items you've seen; select "observe"
quit: if you aren't interested after all, select "quit"

Special keys:
ctrl-Q/ctrl-S to start/stop output
DELETE (rubout) to interrupt whatever's happening
ctrl-H to erase one character of input
ctrl-X to kill an entire line
ctrl-D to send an EOF (end of file)

If a file .cflist is present in your home directory when you run PicoSpan, PicoSpan will read in that file as a list of conferences, one per line. PicoSpan will then start off in the first conference in that list (rather than the system default).

The "NEXT" command will advance through the rest of list until a conference with new items in it is found, leave the current conference, and join the new one. The "CHECK" command will print a brief summary of the activity found on the list. "DISPLAY LIST" will just print the list.

".cflist" is intended to contain a list of common conferences, (starting with the one you wish to enter first, and followed by those you wish to check into on a daily basis.) "CHANGE LIST" (or "edit .cflist") can be used to create and edit this list. If the list has changed in the middle of a session, it is read in again and the list pointer is reset to the start of the list.

mail - send private messages to other users
form: mail to retrieve your mail
mail <login-id> to mail to another user

You will be told if you have any mail each time you join a conference, or if new mail arrives while you are on. <login-id> must be a login-id as provided by the system; the PARTICIPANT command can be used to retrieve this.

This command is legal at both the "OK:" and the "respond or forget" prompts.

next — skip to next new conference
form: next

Skip to the next "new" conference in the list from your ..cflist file, and join it. See "HELP LIST" for details on that.

participants - get a list of participants
form: participants
or participants <list of login-ids>

This command will print out a list of users for this conference including their login-id, the date they were last on the current conference, and their name in this conference. The second form of the command selects a list of login-ids for examination.

Stop - quit PicoSpan
form: stop
or quit
exit

The logoff message for the conference is printed out and the participant file is updated before you leave. The <eof> character, usually ^D, will also do this at the OK prompt.

Read - allows you to read items
form: read <items>
If you've just joined a new conference; you'll want to try "BROWSE ALL" first to get a list of interesting items, after which you'll want to try "READ x" for each item x from your list.

If you're just checking in a conference you already belong to, "READ ALL NEW" (or just R will do) will present you with each item which someone else has responded to. (and Browse All will give you a "preview")

After each item, you will get a "respond or pass?" prompt. At this point, you can type "R" to respond, just <return> to pass, or "Help" for a list of more options.

Remember - allows you to read items.
form: remember <items>
Items forgotten at the "respond, forget, or pass" prompt are remembered again.

Resign -- resign from current conference.
form: resign
Leaves you an observer of the conference. "resign" is the same as "change resign." "change join" (or "change register") will make you a member again.

Respond — add responses onto items
form: respond <items>
adds responses directly to items from the "OK: " prompt

send [<loginid>]
Send mail to the indicated person. If no loginid is specified PicoSpan will ask you for one.

Shell — run a subshell
form: shell

Run a command shell (via the shell variable) as a subprogram, and returns to PicoSpan when the shell exits. ^D can be used to leave most shells. Will normally run the Bourne shell ('/bin/sh') unless the SHELL environment variable or the "shell" PicoSpan variable was set to something else. Warning: running PicoSpan again from the subshell can be confusing.

If your home shell is a 4.2BSD C-shell, then it is faster and more efficient to suspend PicoSpan with a ^Z (and resume it later via '%bbs') than it is to say "shell."

source — source a file.
form: source <filename>

Read PicoSpan commands from <filename> and process them until the end of the file.

PicoSpan will also source a file ".cfrc" in your home directory before the OK: prompt in the first conference, as well as a per-conference "rc" file if it exists, and a global "/usr/bbs/rc" file before the first conference "rc" file.
The STTY program can be used to change these and other functions if needed: it can be invoked by !stty [options] from anywhere inside of PicoSpan.

If !stty is given, it prints the current settings, else it will change them:
!stty kill ^? intr ^E eof ^C will change the line delete, attention and eof characters.

For 1200-baud Apples, teletypes, TI silentwriters, and other terminals that need carriage return/line feed delays, they can be turned on via:

!stty -nl1 | line feed delay

support programs: (define variable program)

var default purpose
editor ed -the editor that :, ed, etc., invoke
pager (none) -output filter for most output (often "more")
shell /bin/sh the shell used to invoke the pager, UNIX, and '!' commands. The usual choice is '/bin/sh.' '/bin/csh' does not perform as well here as '/bin/sh.' PicoSpan (/usr/bin/bbs or whatever) is a very bad choice here, and PicoSpan trys hard to avoid this
readmail mail read (browse) mail
sendmail mail send (transmit) outgoing mail
type file
type the contents of file on on the terminal

umask [nnn]
Set the UNIX "umask" value to the octal value nnn, or report on the current setting if no value is given. Controls the permissions other people have with future files you create. See a good UNIX book for more details.

UNIX — exit to UNIX
form: UNIX
or system
or UNIX string
or UNIX command args [...]

A simpler way to do this from the keyboard in PicoSpan is !UNIX-cmd, with no leading spaces before the !. This is a common UNIX convention in many other programs, including most editor and mail program. From the '>' mode, it is necessary to say ":!" instead. Sorry, '!' does not work in macros.

From UNIX, a variety of other features are usually available, including file up/download, C and other languages, text processors, etc. You will probably want to have a good book on UNIX to make effective use of it — there are probably no menus or help. You can exit UNIX with a ctrl-D or "logout"; this will log off for you.

Warning: saying "UNIX", then "bbs", then "UNIX" is strange — at this point you have two shells running, and ^D would put you back in the first shell. Say "quit" instead of the 2nd "UNIX." Unretire <items> — mark the indicated items as not retired; undo the effects of an inadvertant "RETIRE."

Who — who is on the system
Form: who
display who
displays the people who are currently logged on the system

4. Survey of Conferencing Systems

4.1 INDIVIDUAL SYSTEMS

4.1.1 Arbornet

Arbornet
c/o Spencer and Marae PriceNash
1325 Rosewood Street
Ann Arbor, MI 48104
(voice) (313) 663-3276
(data) (313) 996-4644
(Internet address) anet.ann-arbor.mi.us

The hardware system runs on Altos 68000 and System III UNIX. The number of incoming ports and bauds is three at 300/1200 and one at 2400. The software system used is PicoSpan. The number of users is forty to fifty. The costs of access are $20/month unlimited access with reduced rates for students and additional family members; negotiable for low-income. Arbornet does not currently provide private conferences. Additional information for nonprofit, tax-exempt, user-financed, autodidactic organization is available.

Sample logon:

```
ATDT1,313,9964644
DIAL TONE
1,313,9964644
CONNECT 1200

  >>> You have reached Arbornet <<<

Newusers type help at the login prompt.
If you have problems, log in as gripe.

anet login: bwill
Password:
>> Welcome back to the Arbornet Computer Conferencing System <<
Copyright (c) 1990 by Arbornet, Inc.

bwill logged on: Mon Sep  3 18:08:00 on tty03
last login:     Thu Aug 30 02:55:52 on tty02
You have mail.

%      (This system leaves you at the UNIX shell. Type bbs to execute  picospan.)
```

List of Conferences

**** CONFERENCES ****

You can Join one of the following Arbornet Conferences:

Name:	Join:	What it is:
Administration	(admin)	Discussion of the administration of Arbornet
Altos/System	(altos)	On the operation of this Altos minicomputer
Amiga group	(amiga)	Those interested in the Amiga PCs discussion
Ann Arbor	(aa)	Anything to do with Ann Arbor, Michigan
Atrium	(atrium)	>> The catch-all, or "other" conference <<
Classics	(classic)	The Memorabilia/Hall of Fame Item conf.
Education	(ed)	Topics concerning education - NOT teachers only
Entertainment	(enter)	Reviews and comparisons of entertainment forms
Epistemology	(epist)	Philosophy, religion, knowlege, and more.
Helper	(help)	>> The place to go if having trouble
Lifestyles	(life)	Fun, R and R, life, and talk about how we live it.
Computers	(computers)	Any topics concerning computers
Music	(music)	Music, well-known and obscure. For everyone.
Netwits	(net)	Not describable in one line, besides "weird"
Politics	(poly)	Political debate and information
Practice	(prac)	This is where to practice with conferencing
Programming	(prog)	Programming projects being worked on
Science	(sci)	Science, technology, the world and you.
SciFi/Fantasy	(sf)	SciFi/Fantasy books, stories, movies, etc.
Unclassifieds	(class)	Advertizing entered by Arbornet users
UNIX	(UNIX)	Help UNIX - the operating system used on A'net

Topics in the Help Conference

OK: browse

item nresp header

1 40 Welcome to the Help conference

2 30 Omnibus Item on Login Files: .login, .cfonce, .cflist, Et Cetera

3 22 UNIX commands summary

4 11 Falsie detector

5 17 Printing Out Manuals

6 4 Question

7 22 TCOM means VT100 mean vi?

8 10 Noisy lines.

9 3 Introducing myself to all perns.

10 3 zlat needs help <><>LARENEG NI<><>

11 10 Useful computer task.

12 4 Mail does not get through.

13 4 OG tries out totalitarianism, for a change...

14 15 Why and how do I fix it?

15 9 kill questions.

16 12 Compiler question..

17 2 Does anybody really know what time it is.

18 19 Mail vs mail and what are the commands?

19 12 — more — is less on my terminal...

20 10 Real, Serious, Life-Saving Help needed..

21 20 SET PAGER MORE

22 1 Gripe program installed

23 5 Emulation on the][e

24 13 Interrupt Keys for various machines

25 16 Why doesn't 'Mail' mail ???

26 1 Watch is not a plaid.

27 6 What went wrong? (core)

28 4 Stuck In BBS

29 6 navigating within conference items

30 4 Does a calendar file work here?

31 3 Entering good looking text---HOW?

32 14 msg for scribe in administration

33 3 Restoring Trashed I.D.s

34 10 Advanced Documentation for PicoSpan?

35 1 no

36 2 Stuck with %

37 14 Old stuff for "read new"

38 4 Chat? (panic!)

39 10 Tcom and pager page

40 17 Help for "display forgotten"?

41 25 Certified, return receipt requested.

43 33 Changing a password.

44 19 Need help with chmod and uucp.

45 4 It does not work right.

46 6 Cursor Dancing.

47 8 PicoSlang

48 10 Custom PicoSpan? Editor use? Invoking PicoSpan from %

49 13 hazeltine hassle (capitalization confusion)

50 18 A new word-wrapping input program

51 3 Adding or Changing a Plan

52 17 ':'

53 3 HELP at the Art Fair!

54 23 games people play with calendars

55 12 I forgot armed robbery was illegal

56 23 CAT on a hot tin roof

57 11 Help needed against 1200 baud noise induced lockups

58 26 sjustanothertest

59 6 help with vi

60 2 !Mailer default?

61 6 How do you change login shells?

62 9 Help an Altos 486

63 6 Shell escapes and aliases

64 5 How do you !party alone?

65 6 How can I set up for always paging, Mail?

66 4 a curiosity

67 3 Can WINDOW be used with anet (No, not WINDOWS)? How?

68 11 uucp ?

69 3 assistance

70 23 Trouble with uucp and mail...

71 18 .tar.Z files

72 2 Changing times.

73 9 Oh no, he's got another weird terminal.

74 2 Dust

75 6 UUCP/Internet Mail tutor--send mail to a user on another system

76 48 UNIX for the stupid

77 9 Life dredger. And where is acctcom?

78 3 Canon T70 Camera...FOR SALE...

79 0 Prince Spectrum Comp Tennis Racket...FOR SALE...

80 3 Tamiya SuperShot RC Car...FOR SALE...

81 2 Why can't i Go and Chat with some1?to help me?????????help????????

82 7 Binary transfers through MERIT

83 22 Phone number confusion. We are pissing someone off.

84 27 New Chapter in Arbornet: Net News

85 6 What is .news_time?

86 5 anybody got a letter opener?

87 5 Binary files via email?

88 5 Deni needs help ;)

89 5 changing names in a conf

90 12 Easy way to set up rn

4.1.2 BITNET

A general description of BITNET as a network is in the BITNET section of Chaper 5. This section is an introduction to the BITNET phenomena of listserv communication.

BITNET Listservice

The users of BITNET have evolved a communication system that resembles conferencing in some ways, somewhat like Usenet on the Internet. Discussion groups distribute documents and replies via mailing lists on BITNET. These mailings go to every BITNET site in the world where a subscriber has subscribed to the topic being discussed.

"Some 900 discusion groups active on BITNET cover virtually any topic of academic interest and may have from five to several thousand participants."

(BITNET Network Information Center, *BITNET OVERVIEW)*

A list of all these discussion groups can be obtained by sending the command LIST GLOBAL as the text of a mail message addressed to LISTSERV@BITNIC.BITNET.

The following is a copy of a topic in the telecon conference on the WELL that explains the use of the LISTSERV. It is reprinted with the permission of the writer.

Topic 48: BITNET/Arpanet Listservs
1: Elliott Parker (eparker) Wed, Aug 16, '89 (09:28) 41 lines

bitover(7572 bytes) is a short overview of BITNET. This can be obtained by sending mail to "listserv@bitnic.BITNET" with "sendme BITNET overview" as the only line in the body of the mail. Leave "subject" line blank--do a carriage return.

bithelp(41038 bytes) should familiarize you with the basic concepts of BITNET and how to use it. For a copy, send mail to "listserv@bitnic.BITNET" with "sendme BITNET userhelp" in the body.

bitserv(43160 bytes) is a list of network servers and services. For a copy, send mail to "listserv@bitnic.BITNET" with "sendme BITNET servers" in the body.

listgrps(48340 bytes) describes some BITNET discussion groups/lists and includes a list of ARPAnet Sigs that have BITNET sublists in operation. For a copy, send mail to "listserv@bitnic.BITNET" with "sendme list global" in the body.

listglbl(109066 bytes) is a list of one-line IDs,addresses, and titles of all listserv lists. For the newest copy send mail to "listserv@ndsuvm1.BITNET" with "sendme listserv lists" in the body. There are probably over a 1000 different lists (many are peered, so get them from the nearest listserv). They may not all be available. Some may be inoperative, closed/locked, or just unavailable for some reason.

In addition to the BITNET lists, ARPAnet has lists/sigs. The entire listing runs about 300K. To find out how to get a copy, send mail to "service@sri-nic.arpa" and in the SUBJECT

line, not the body, type "help" to get a copy of what is "srihelp" (1679 bytes) in my directory here. "sriindex" (8685 bytes) is an index to other documents from sri-nic. For the newest copy, send mail to "service@sri-nic.arpa" with "netinfo index" in the SUBJECT line.

Topic 48: BITNET/Arpanet Listservs
2: Elliott Parker (eparker) Wed, Aug 16, '89 (09:31) 66 lines

One of the more confusing things with using LISTSERV (note that it does not have a final "E") on BITNET, is just exactly what it does.

LISTSERV is a VM/CMS-based mailing lists manager by Eric Thomas that enables individuals to add or delete their names from open lists. Most lists will give three addresses:

- one will let you subscribe, search archives, etc
- one will let you send messages to everybody on the list
- and one address may be for the moderator of the list

The important thing is that these LISTSERVs do only specified jobs. You cannot delete your name from the list by using the LISTSERV address that will get you to all the people on the list (everybody will just smile--or worse--when they see your "signoff" request appear).

Using the Wordperfect list as an example: To subscribe to the list, send a mail message to LISTSERV@UBVM.BITNET. The body of the mail would be "sub wp50-l <yourname>" If I was to subscribe, the message would be "sub wp50-l elliott parker" To signoff, I would send another message to LISTSERV@UBVM.BITNET with "signoff wp50-l" in the body.

However, if you have a question, answer, or comment you want to send to the entire readership of the WP50-L list, send it to WP50-L@UBVM.BITNET (the "list-id"). All readers of this list would then see your entry.

To contact a real person, the maintainer of the list, another, different address is required. In this case, it would be "gerland@ubvms.BITNET", the address of Jim Gerland.

When you send a msg. to subscribe, an acknowledgement will be returned that will first tell you HOW TO GET OFF the list and then some other commands that can be used to use the database functions or find out other subscribers (unless they have issued the "conceal" command).

Knowing the structure, the next thing to realize is that not all commands work the same on all LISTSERVs as people try to program the better mousetrap. Some commands are synonymous, for instance, either "signoff" or "unsub" seems to work across the network.

All listservs have a moderator or maintainer who oversees the list and filters out at least some of the dreck, and messages sent to the list that should go to an individual. Almost all the BITNET lists are run from universities so the traffic is low or nonexistent in the summer. If you subscribe now, it may be weeks before you see any messages, although your acknowledgement may return in a day or two depending on where you had to send it. ARPAnet lists are usually maintained by government or commercial entities, so they are not so deserted in the summer.

For a comprehensive description and usage notes on LISTSERV, send mail to LISTSERV@BITNIC.BITNET with SENDME LISTPRES MEMO and/or SENDME LISTSERV MEMO in the body. I think both cmds can be in the same body as long as they are on different lines by themselves.

If you want a brief description of the discussion topic, send REVIEW to the hosting listserv. Using the WP example again, sending mail to LISTSERVE@UBVM.BITNET with "REVIEW WP50-L" in the body would get a short description and list of subscribers.

Topic 48: BITNET/Arpanet Listservs
3: Elliott Parker (eparker) Wed, Aug 16,'89 (09:32) 4 lines

To keep up on new discussion lists, send mail to "listserv@ndsuvm1.BITNET" with "sub new-list <yourname>" in the body. When a new list is started, you will get a short notice and description. It does not automatically put you on the list.

Topic 48: BITNET/Arpanet Listservs
5: Elliott Parker (eparker) Wed, Aug 16, '89 (09:35) 12 lines

JBH Online is "a digest of English-language news and information from outside the USA monitored by shortwave radio" in addition to an eclectic synopsis of a few domestic (US) newspapers. Depending on the news, the compiler, John B. Harland will monitor the VOA, BBC, Radio Nederland, Radio Beijing, et al. It is strictly his hobby, although it does carry an ISSN (0896-8241). Because it is a hobby, it can become occasional. Right now, it is inactive, because he is moving, but it is an excellent way to keep up on how news is playing outside the U. S.

To subscribe, send mail to "listserv@irishvm.BITNET" with "subscribe online-l <your name>" in the body.

Topic 48: BITNET/Arpanet Listservs
6: Elliott Parker (eparker) Wed, Aug 16, '89 (09:37) 6 lines

For continuing information on BITNET, subscribe to *NetMonth — The Independent Guide to BITNET.* To subscribe, send mail to listserv@marist.BITNET with a text line "subscribe netmonth <yourname>. This is published at Yale and like much of BITNET, it is a voluntary effort which means it usually, but not always a monthly.

If you are on the Internet, you would usually send mail to another Internet person with an address like, bwilliam@polyslo.calpoly.edu. To send mail to a BITNET address you would use an address like du389@calpoly.BITNET. From the Internet, .BITNET on the end of the address routes the mail to a BITNET/Internet gateway and it is forwarded from there to the BITNET address.

There are several newsletters that are of interest to librarians, as the following little section of the *PACS* newsletter shows.

From LIBPACS@UHUPVM1.BITNET Thu Aug 2 12:49:58 1990

To: BWILLIAM@COSMOS.ACS.CALPOLY.EDU

(PLEASE SAVE THIS MESSAGE)

Welcome to the University of Houston Libraries'
Public-Access Computer Systems Forum

Overview

The Public-Access Computer Systems Forum is an international computer conference that deals with all computer systems that libraries make available to their patrons. Utilizing the PACS Forum, users discuss topics such as CD-ROM databases, computer-assisted instruction software, expert systems, hypertext programs, locally mounted databases, online catalogs, and remoteend-user search systems. The conference is does not deal with the automation of library staff functions (e.g., acquisitions, cataloging, circulation, and serials control). While many users are librarians, the PACS Forum also serves computer specialists, faculty members, and other types of users. The conference was founded in June 1989. Currently, there are over 1,500 users in twenty-three countries. The Information Technology Division of the University of Houston provides technical support for the conference.

Messages sent to the PACS Forum are reviewed by the conference moderator, who distributes messages on appropriate topics to conference participants. Normally, PACS Forum users receive five to ten messages per day.

The University of Houston Libraries provides the PACS Forum as a public service. It does not verify the accuracy of submitted messages nor does it endorse the opinions expressed by message authors. Authors of PACS Forum messages are solely responsible for content of their messages.

All messages to the conference are automatically archived. PACS Forum users can retrieve the monthly archive files as needed.

Users also can search the entire message database for specific information using complex Boolean queries. The most reliable method of searching the database is to submit batch search jobs of the list server via e-mail messages. Search features include nested Boolean expressions, search limitation by date and time, and SOUNDEX searches.

An electronic journal, called the *Public-Access Computer Systems Review*, was established in January 1990. Articles are stored as individual files on the list server, and an annotated table of contents for each issue is sent out as an e-mail message to all PACS Forum users. After looking over the table of contents, users can retrieve article files of interest. Libraries are authorized to add the *Public-Access Computer Systems Review* to their collections. The journal is cataloged on OCLC.

An electronic newsletter, called the ***Public-Access Computer Systems News***, was established in March 1990. Issues are sent out as messages on the PACS Forum. This newsletter is cataloged on OCLC.

Selected Commands

To join the PACS Forum, send the following e-mail message to LISTSERV@UHUPVM1: SUBSCRIBE PACS-L First_Name Last_Name.

To sign off the PACS Forum, send the following e-mail message to LISTSERV@UHUPVM1: UNSUBSCRIBE PACS-L.

To send a message to the PACS Forum, send your e-mail message to PACS-L@UHUPVM1.

To receive documentation about searching the message database, send the following e-mail message to LISTSERV@UHUPVM1: INFO DATABASE.

To see what files are available, send the following e-mail message to LISTSERV@UHUPVM1: INDEX PACS-L.

To retrieve a file, send the following e-mail message to LISTSERV@UHUPVM1: GET File_Name File_Type. To retrieve the contents file for the first issue of the PACS Review, send the message: GET CONTENTS PRV1N1. To get the contents file for the second issue, send the message: GET CONTENTS PRV1N2.

To obtain a list of PACS Forum users, send the following e-mail message to LISTSERV@UHUPVM1: REVIEW PACS-L.

To get information about accessing library systems via
Internet, send the following message to LISTSERV@UNMVM (do not
send this message to LISTSERV@UHUPVM1): GET INTERNET LIBRARY

For More Information:

```
+----------------------------------------------------------------+
| Charles W. Bailey, Jr.              Voice: (713) 749-4241 |
| Assistant Director For Systems       FAX:   (713) 749-3867 |
| (and Public-Access Computer         BITNET: LIB3@UHUPVM1  |
| Systems Forum Moderator)                                   |
|                                                            |
| University Libraries                <<<<<<<<<<C>>>>>>>>>> |
| University of Houston               >>>>>>>>>>W<<<<<<<<<< |
| Houston, TX 77204-2091              <<<<<<<<<<B>>>>>>>>>> |
+----------------------------------------------------------------+
```

Here are a couple of Pacs_l messages.

From PACS-L@UHUPVM1.BITNET Mon Aug 6 08:12:25 1990
Reply-To: Public-Access Computer Systems Forum <PACS-L%UHUPVM1.BITNET@pucc.PRIN>

Sender: Public-Access Computer Systems Forum <PACS-L%UHUPVM1.BITNET@pucc.PRINCE>
Subject: Library Automation Comments and Questions
To: Multiple recipients of list PACS-L <PACS-L@UHUPVM1>

3 Messages, 60 Lines

Please respond directly to the authors of these messages, not to PACS-L. --Charles

-----

FROM: LIBSSD@EMUVM1

Our library system has recently finished bar coding our collection using code 39 bar codes. We're now looking at getting bar code reader/scanners, and some vendors have recommended that we purchase guns instead of wands because code 39 is difficult to read.

Responding to Stacey Kimmel's query, Emory's experience with Code 39 is that this is *NOT* a difficult code to scan, quite the opposite. Code 39 is tolerant of very sloppy printing (for example, an 8-pin dot matrix printer wilh Intermec and Mini-Bar readers. The Intermec units have superior documentation and are easier to set up, while the MiniBars are very compact and have a wand with a nice "feel". It's hard to over-emphasize the importance of the last point, which can be an important factor in how quickly staff learn to scan successfully.

We experimented with handheld laser guns, but found them to be both bulky and fragile — both were dropped and broken within the first 10 days of service. We currently have 1 laser gun in service; it is wrapped in foam rubber and is used exclusively for checking in materials. A fixed laser scanner might be a different matter — if it fits into your work environment. At almost a 8/1 price differential, I can't see the value of a gun at a circ. desk, where space is usually at a premium, and there is lots of activity. My vote is for something small, holdable, rugged, and cheap.

From: (Stuart Spore) <SPORE@ACF7.NYU.EDU>
Subject: Fire protection

Having just had a bad experience with a burst sprinkler in Technical Services, I am interested whether anyone on PACS-L has any suggestions about alternatives to sprinklers or halon fire suppression in computer rooms?

From: Page Cotton <PCOTTON@CLARKU>
Subject: software for offline recon cleanup

We have been using OCLC's Microcon software for the bulk of our retrospective conversion. Now we are trying to figure out how we can best put the items in our collection that didn't have a match in OCLC into machine readable form. Ultimately we want these records loaded into the OPAC and OCLC.

We have considered entering them directly into OCLC and then uploading them to the OPAC. What have other libraries done about retrospective conversion of items not in OCLC? Has anybody found and successfully used software that will create a bibliographic file offline that is in a format acceptible to OCLC for tape loading?

Page Cotton
Goddard Library
Clark University
Worcester, MA 01610
BITNET: PCOTTON@CLARKU

& dt
Message 17:
From PACS-L@UHUPVM1.BITNET Mon Aug 6 08:59:55 1990
Reply-To: Public-Access Computer Systems Forum <PACS-L%UHUPVM1.BITNET@pucc.PRIN>
Sender: Public-Access Computer Systems Forum <PACS-L%UHUPVM1.BITNET@pucc.PRINCE>
Subject: Local Area Network for CD-ROM
To: Multiple recipients of list PACS-L <PACS-L@UHUPVM1>

An important consideration in CD-ROM server access is CD-ROM vendor/ producer license restrictions. Just because you can technically attach a CD-ROM server to a campus-wide LAN doesn't mean you can legally put any CD-ROM database you want on it. See Tom Wilson's article in the last PACS Review (send the message GET WILSON PRV1N2 to LISTSERV@UHUPVM1).
If anyone has negotiated a CD-ROM license that allows campus-wide access, I would be very interested in hearing about it.

--Charles
----------------------Original message----------------------
II wonder whether network readers can give me the benefit of their experience in establishing a CD-ROM server: whether it is better to place a server on an existing campus network (perhaps remotely) or to establish a LAN within the library accessible to the campus network users; whether a turnkey tower system (which, if it should go down, takes everything with it) is better than a CD-ROM server with several interface cards with drives daisy-chained from each card (and whose components can be easily replaced). I need to know ramifications, pitfalls, cost considerations, environmental and physical limitations (how controlled an environment is required, how secure must the drives and server be). If you have been through all of this, I would appreciate hearing your war stories. My e-mail addresses are listed below.

```
* * * * * * * * * * * * * * * * * * * * * * * * * * * * * *
*   Roy Bruce Baker, Library Systems Analyst               *
*   University Libraries                                   *
*  University of Arkansas   Fayetteville, Arkansas 72701  *
*   PHONE: (501) 575-5418            FAX:  (501) 575-6656  *
*INTERNET:bb24014@uafsysb.uark.eduBITNET:bb24014@uafsysb*
* * * * * * * * * * * * * * * * * * * * * * * * * * * * *
```

To subscribe to the *PACS* newsletter you just send the following e-mail message to "LISTSERV@UHUPVM1: SUBSCRIBE PACS-L First_Name Last_Name." In other words, from an Internet site, you e-mail a message to: LISTSERV@UHUPVM1.BITNET. In the body of the message you say "SUBSCRIBE PACS-L First_Name Last_Name," and nothing more. Anything else in the message will derail it. It figures out who you are and what your address is by your pathname in the message, so send the message from the place you want to be receiving the newsletters. Obviously, you have to be on a system that has a connection to Internet or BITNET, but a great many of the resources in this book have connections to UUCP one way or another.

Another list of interest to librarians:

From PACS-L@UHUPVM1.BITNET Wed Aug 15 08:07:45 1990
Reply-To: Public-Access Computer Systems Forum <PACS-L%UHUPVM1.BITNET@pucc.PRIN>
Sender: Public-Access Computer Systems Forum <PACS-L%UHUPVM1.BITNET@pucc.PRINCE>
Subject: New list: Recruiting rare books catalogers
To: Multiple recipients of list PACS-L <PACS-L@UHUPVM1>

---------------------Original message-------------------------
I bring you greetings from another world - NOTRBCAT, the forum for rare books catalogers.

One of my little genies in New England has suggested that since catalogers, and especially rare books catalogers, are not wont to spend much time on communications terminals, it might be a nice idea to try to spread the word about our new forum among those who are more into communicating - specifically PACS-L. In other words, if there is BITNET access available to the rare books catalogers in your establishments, I would like to ask that you make them aware of this forum, NOTRBCAT@INDYCMS.

NOTRBCAT was founded as a discussion group for rare books catalogers working in the NOTIS system and of course having access to BITNET. Majority opinion in the early days of the forum, however, favored expanding its scope to encompass all rare books catalogers. (Interestingly, we had one non-NOTIS site represented anyway among the early members, and that is where my genie lives.) Now we are up to approximately 37 members, from Brown University in the East to Stanford in the West. Not all members are currently working rare books catalogers. We may need more people who fall into the category of real rare books catalogers to make the discussion group viable.

Please advise your rare books catalogers to send their subscriptions to LISTSERV AT INDYCMS, or LISTSERV@INDYCMS, depending upon your system. Should anyone experience difficulties in subscribing, please ask that person to get in touch with me personally via mail message: LIBKAT@INDST.

As they say in networkdom,

Virtually,

Kathryn Wright
cataloger for rare books and special collections
Cunningham Memorial Library
Indiana State University
Terre Haute, Indiana 47809
phone: (812) 237-3373

Another new list announcement:

LibRef@KENTVM "Discussion of Library Reference Issues"

This list is a discussion of the changing environment of library reference services and activities. Topics include traditional reference services, patron expectations, staff training, as well the impact of CD-ROM and online searching on reference service.

This forum will serve as a professional networking and information source. We will share ideas, solutions and experiences.

Owners =

Diane Kovacs	dkovacs@kentvm
Laura Bartolo	lbartolo@kentvm
Gladys Bell	gbell@kentvm
Mary DuMont	mdumont@kentvm
Julie McDaniel	jmcdanie@kentvm
Carolyn Radcliff	cradclif@kentvm
Kara Robinson	krobinso@kentvm
Barbara Schloman	bschloma@kentvm

This list is run from the LISTSERV at Kent State University and moderated by the Reference Librarians at Kent State University Libraries. The Internet address of the LISTSERV is LISTSERV@library.kent.edu.

You may subscribe to this list by sending a subscribe command by interactive message or by e-mail. To subscribe by interactive message, send the command:

"SUB LIBREF yourfirstname yourlastname"

to LISTSERV@KENTVM. For example:

IBM VM CMS users would enter

tell listserv at kentvm "sub libref A. Librarian"

VAX VMS users would enter

send listserv@kentvm "sub libref A. Librarian"

You may also subscribe by send mail to LISTSERV@KENTVM.BITNET with the command "SUB LIBREF-L your name" in the body of the mail item.

Please do NOT send these commands to the list address LIBREF@KENTVM. Doing so will cause your request to be broadcast to all subscribers and will not cause your name to be added to the list.

Here is a list of several library-oriented BITNET resources.

From PACS-L@UHUPVM1.BITNET Tue Nov 6 20:30:46 1990
Date: Tue, 6 Nov 90 19:56:45 CST
To: Multiple recipients of list PACS-L <PACS-L@UHUPVM1>

LIBRARY-ORIENTED COMPUTER CONFERENCES and ELECTRONIC SERIALS
Date: 11/6/90

A. Computer Conferences

1. Standard BITNET Lists

ARLIS-L@UKCC	Art Libraries Association of North America
ATLAS-L@TCUBVM	Data Research ATLAS Users
AUTOCAT@UVMVM	Library Cataloging and Authorities Discussion Group
BI-L@BINGVMB	Bibliographic Instruction
BRS-L@USCVM	BRS/Search Users
BUSLIB-L@IDBSU	Business Librarians
CWIS-L@WUVMD	Campus-Wide Information Systems
ELLASBIB@GREARN	Library Automation in Greece
GOVDOC-L@PSUVM	Government Documents
INNOPAC@MAINE	Innovative Interfaces Users
LIBPLN-L@QUCDN	Library Planning
MLA-L@IUBVM	Music Library Association
NOTIS-L@TCSVM	NOTIS Users
NOTMUS-L@UBVM	Notis Music Library List
NOTRBCAT@INDYCMS	Notis and Other Rare Book Catalogers
PACS-L@UHUPVM1	Public-Access Computer Systems Forum
SERIALST@UVMVM	Serials Users Discussion Group
SPILIB-L@SUVM	SPIRES Users

To subscribe, send the e-mail message:

SUBSCRIBE List First Name Last Name

to LISTSERV@NODE, where node is the part of the address after the "@."

For example, Jane Doe sends the following e-mail message to to LIST-SERV@UHUPVM1 to subscribe to PACS-L:

SUBSCRIBE PACS-L Jane Doe

2. Other BITNET or Internet Conferences with Special Procedures

Conservation DistList (Conservation of Archive, Library, and Museum Materials)
Send a subscription request to Walter Henry: WHENRY@LINDY.STANFORD.EDU

EXLIBRIS@ZODIAC.RUTGERS.EDU (Rare Book, Manuscript, and Special Collections) Send a subscription request to:
EXLIBRIS-REQUEST@ZODIAC.RUTGERS.EDU
Include your name and e-mail address in the body of the message. Contact Peter Graham for questions:
GRAHAM@ZODIAC.RUTGERS.EDU

LAW-LIB@UCDAVIS.EDU (Law Librarians)
Send subscription requests to: LAW-REQ@UCDAVIS.EDU
Contact Elizabeth St. Goar for technical questions:
ESTGOAR@UCDAVIS.EDU

NOTIS Acquisitions Discussion Group
Send subscription requests to Joyce G. McDonough, JGMCDO01@ULKYVM

SIGLAN@BRYNMAWR (ASIS Library Automation and Networking SIG)
Send the following message to MAILSERV@BRYNMAWR:
SUBSCRIBE SIGLAN
B. Electronic Serials

IRLIST Digest (Information Retrieval)
Send the following message to LISTSERV@UCCVMA:
SUBSCRIBE IR-L First Name Last Name

Newsletter on Serials Pricing Issues
Send the following message to LISTSERV@UNCVX1:
SUBSCRIBE PRICES-L First Name Last Name

Public-Access Computer Systems News
Sent automatically to PACS-L subscribers. See above.
The Public-Access Computer Systems Review
Sent automatically to PACS-L subscribers. See above.

```
+----------------------------------------------------------------+
| Charles W. Bailey, Jr.           Voice: (713) 749-4241         |
| Assistant Director For Systems    FAX:   (713) 749-3867        |
| University Libraries             BITNET: LIB3@UHUPVM1          |
| University of Houston                                          |
| Houston, TX 77204-2091                                         |
|----------------------------------------------------------------|
| PACS-L Moderator (PACS-L@UHUPVM1);                             |
| Editor-in-Chief, The Public-Access Computer Systems Review     |
+----------------------------------------------------------------+
```

4.1.3 BIX

BYTE Information Exchange
One Phoenix Mill Lane
Peterborough, NH 03458
(603) 924-9281
(800) 227-2983 (voice)

Brief Description

BIX is an online adjunct to *Byte* magazine. Most, if not all of *Byte* is online there, but most of the conferencing is not about the magazine but all aspects of computers and other general subjects as the list of conferences below show. The information on computers and related matters is very good and so it is a good place for microcomputer problem solving. *Byte* reproduces parts of BIX within each issue. It is a large system with many users and much activity.

Software

The conferencing is CoSy-based.

Access

DIAL TONE
1,5490770
CONNECT 1200
xxxx`xxxxx~xx`xxxx`xxx~x
please type your terminal identifier
-4255:01-003-
please log in: d2bixx3 (This is an example of a special logon code for flat rates.)
BIX: call connected
Welcome to BIX — ttyx38, 7524
= = BYTE/CoSy - BIX 3.10 = =

Welcome to BIX, the BYTE Information Exchange

McGraw-Hill Information Services Co.
Copyright (c) 1990 by McGraw-Hill Inc.

CoSy Conferencing System, Copyright (c) 1984 University of Guelph

Need BIX voice help...
In the U.S. and Canada call 800-227-2983, in NH and elsewhere call 603-924-7681 8:30 a.m. to 11:00 p.m. EDT (-4 GMT) weekdays
Name? bwilliams
Password:
Last on: Fri Aug 17 21:22:48 1990
You have 0 mail messages in your in-basket.

You are a member of 6 conferences.
============================
system.news/**BULLETIN** #1816, from sysmgr, 618 chars, Mon Aug 20 00:54:00 1990

BIX Highlights

Discuss US options for protecting Saudi Arabia. Join technology/defense

Systems programmers can share code in 'data.center/listings'.
Join data.center

Discuss LAN-based client<->server applications. Join alc/client.server

Monday Specials
East Coast Chat 7 - 10 pm (edt) General CBix
Nexus Inn. 9 - 12 pm (edt) Join d.horizons/cbix
Boldseekers. 9:30 - 11:30 pm (edt) Join the.realms/cbix
IBM CBix. 10 pm (edt) Join ibm.exchange/cbix
Trivia. 10 - 12 pm (edt) Join fun.n.games/cbix
.More..
Lab Lounge. 12 - 3 am (edt) General CBix
No inbasket messages.
No outbasket messages.

Conf/Topic	New Messages
conferencing/applications	1
ask.bix/hints	8
ask.bix/blinks	1
bbs/digest	25
bbs/issues	25
bbs/recommended	1
packet.nets/telenet	2

:

BIX Subscription Fees

BIX is a subscription-based service. An individual BIX subscription costs $39 per quarter, or $156 a year. There are no registration fees, no monthly minimum fees, no account fees, and no extra charges for just using the system.

Only one area of BIX carries additional charges: DasNet Mail. DasNet lets you send and receive mail from users of other electronic services.

BIX subscribers who access BIX via Tymnet will be charged the following hourly rates:

Location	Peak	Off Peak
Lower 48	$6	$3

Canada	$11	$6
Alaska Hawaii	$20	$10

Peak hours are 6 A.M. to 7 P.M., Monday through Friday, evenings, weekends, and announced holidays are off peak. There is no penalty for 2400-baud access.

BIX offers subscribers in the lower forty-eight states an unlimited off-peak Tymnet account. This account provides unlimited use of Tymnet during off peak-hours for a cost of $20 per month. There are no additional fees for 2400-baud access with this account. Contact " bixbilling" via BIXmail to switch to unlimited, off-peak Tymnet.

A limited number of 9600-baud lines are available. The modems are US Robotics dual-standard Courier HSTs. The number to call is (617) 861-9780. There is no extra fee for this service.

List of Conferences

Read:show all

o a.t.and.t	The AT&T computers conference
o absoft	Absoft Corporation
o ada	The Ada language conference
o ai.architects	A.I. Architects Inc.
o alc	Accelerated Learning Center
o ai.theory	The conference on artificial intelligence theory
o algorithms	Using algorithms to solve problems
o amiga	The conference on the Commodore Amiga computer
o amiga.arts	Artistry using the Amiga — programs, tools, examples
o amiga.dev	Amiga's developers-support conference
o amiga.hw	The Amiga and associated hardware design, use, and hookup
o amiga.int	Developing the international Amiga
o amiga.special	Special guests and events for Amiga computer users
o amiga.sw	Programming the Amiga; special regard for developer issues
c amiga.update	Software updates for certified developers
o amiga.user	Amiga users exchange ideas, solve problems, compare notes
c ampra_amrrc	American Medical Review Research Center
o anakin	Anakin Research Inc.
o animation	Animation techniques and forms
o apl	The APL conference
o apple	The Apple II family conference
o apple.tech.pub	Apple Computer Developer Products Publications
o arizona	Computing in the Sun Belt

o asdg	ASDG's customer-support conference
o ask.bix	Questions and answers about microcomputing
o assembler	The assembly language conference
o astronomy	A star party for amateur astronomers
o atari.st	The Atari.ST machines
o ataricorp	Atari's customer-support conference
o atex	Atex user-group conference
o autos	For automobile fans
o aviation	Plane talk about computers in general aviation
o avocet	Avocet Systems Inc.
o basic	The BASIC language conference
o bbs	Dial-up bulletin board systems: what's hot, what's not
c bbx.news	The Bulletin Board Exchange, a premium service for sysops
o bcs	The Boston Computer Society conference
c bcs.activist	A special BCS conference
o beckemeyer	Beckemeyer Development Tools
o best.of.bix	Extended excerpts from BIX conferences
o bix.business	Business information about BIX
s bix.survey	BIX user poll
o boating	The BIX Yacht Club
o borland	The Borland International conference
o bridge	For Bridge players
o brief	The support conference for BRIEF
o britain	Life and computing in the British Isles
o byte.88	Full texts of BYTE, August through December 1988
o byte.89	Full texts of BYTE from January 1989
o byte.90	Full texts of BYTE from January 1990
o byte.bmarks	BYTE's new suite of benchmarks: FOR COMMENT
o byte.covers	Talk about past and future covers with Robert Tinney
o byte.reviews	BYTE Reviews Up to February 1988
o byte.reviews90	BYTE hardware and software reviews for 1990
o byte.reviews89	BYTE hardware and software reviews for 1989
o c.langua	The C programming language conference
o c.plus.plus	Discuss the C++ programming language here
o cad	Computer-aided design
o cats	Cats and computers
s cbix	The CBix Citizen's Band Simulator
s cbwho	See Who's in CBix
o cd.rom	Optical storage for micros
o chaos.manor	Jerry Pournelle's column
o chatter	CB chat area
o cheetah	Cheetah International
o chess	A conference about the game of chess
o chicago	For Chicago-area BIX members
o chips	The conference on semiconductor technology
o cineman	Cineman Syndicate: book, video, music, movie reiews; trivia
o circuit.cellar	Advance looks and support for Circuit Cellar projects
o clarion	Clarion Software International

o clipper	The conference on Nantucket's Clipper
o cobol	The COBOL language conference
o commodore	The Commodore computer conference
o comp.chron	Computer Chronicles
o compaq	The conference about Compaq computers
o compupro	The CompuPro customer-support conference
o computer.innov	The Computer Innovations conference
o conferencing	Computerized conferencing today and tomorrow
o consultants	On the art and business of being a consultant
o contact	Science fiction meets science
o cpm	Discussions of CP/M, dr.dos, CDos, and other DRI products
o cpus	The microprocessor chip conference
o cubicomp	Cubicomp's PictureMaker
o current.events	Discussing the news of the day
o d.horizons	Interactive role=playing games not related to fantasy
o dasnet.info	Information on connecting to other e-mail systems
c dasnet.users	For DASnet subscribers only
o data.center	Data Center managers and supervisors
c datapro	Datapro Planning Conference
o datem	Datem Ltd.
o dbms	The database management program conference
o designtech	Designtech Business Systems Inc.
o desktop.pub	Using micros for publishing
o desqview	Quarterdeck Office Systems
o digital	The DEC computers conference
o digital.gaming	Computer gaming
o digitalk	The Digitalk Inc. conference
o disasters	Natural and man-made disasters
o disktechnician	Prime Solutions Inc.
o dlugosz	Dlugosz Software
o dogs	For a dog's best friend
o dsi.32bit	The Definicon Conference
o ecsd	Everex Computer Systems Division
o education	Computers in America
o elfquest	Find out about things elven with Richard Pini
o engineering	The conference on engineering programs
o ergo.computing	Ergo Computing Inc.
o estec	ESTec Systems Corporation
o financial	Financial news and advice
o flageng	Flagstaff Engineering
o focus	Information Builders
o forth	The Forth programming language conference
o fortran	The Fortran language conference
o fst	Fitted Software Tools
o fun.n.games	Fun, games, group activities
o games	How to program computer games
o gamma	Gamma Productions
o garden	Knowledge Garden Inc.
o gazebo	On-line social life

o gem	The GEM interface
o generic	Generic Software
o golddisk	Gold Disk
o graffiti	Open discussions
o graphic.disp	The conference on graphics displays
o graphic.exch	Graphic exchange (NAPLPS, Videotex)
o graphic.pgms	The conference on programming and graphics
o grief	The public-domain programmers' editor
o gss	Graphic Software Systems
o ham.radio	Computing, digital electronics and amateur radio
o hamilton	Hamilton Laboratories
o handicapped	Adaptive technologies for the handicapped
o hilgraeve	The Hilgraeve vendor-support conference
o hp	The Hewlett-Packard computers conference
c hubb	Hagen Graphics Arts Users Group
o hyperaccess	Hilgraeve Inc. vendor conference
o hypertext	Hypertext publishing
o ibm.at	The IBM AT conference
o ibm.dos	The MS/PC DOS conference
o ibm.exchange	IBM Exchange Clearinghouse
o ibm.listings	Index to all Listings files in the IBM Exchange
o ibm.new.prods	New products for IBM computers
o ibm.os.386	Systems software for the 80386
o ibm.os2	A conference about OS/2, the IBM/ Microsoft operating system
o ibm.other	Applications, printers, modems, etc.
o ibm.pc	The IBM PC/XT conference
o ibm.ps	IBM's new line of computers, the Personal Systems
o ibm.repairshop	Garage and tune-up Shop
o ibm.utils	The utilities conference
o igx.exchange	What's new in the IGX
s index	Searchable keyword index of BIX
o inovatronics	Inovatronics, Inc.
o international	Using computers around the world
o intersoft	International software protection
o interstel	Interstel's customer-support conference
o j.and.l	J. And L. Consulting
o jameco	Jameco's customer-support conference
o janus.ada	The Janus Ada conference
o jlblink	Support for JLBlink
o journalism	For journalists
c journalism.pro	Interaction for working press only
o js.online	Jefferson Software
o komputerwerk	Komputerwerk Incorporated
o ksc	Knowledge Systems Corporation
o lahey	Lahey Computer Systems Inc.
o lans	The conference on local-area networks (LANs)
o laptops	Small, battery-powered portable computers
o lattice	The Lattice Inc. conference
c lattice.beta	Lattice Software Testing Forum

o law	Computers and the law
o learn	A tutorial on using BIX
o leland	Leland Enterprises
o lexicon	About words
o lisp	The Lisp language conference
s listings	Programs from BYTE and from the public domain.
o lmi	The Laboratory Microsystems conference
o logitech	The Logitech conference
o los.angeles	LA county computing
o lworld	Ledinworld
o m2s	M2S
c m2s.beta	For M2S beta testers
o mac.apple	The word from Cupertino
o mac.business	Macs in the office
o mac.desktop	Publishing with a Mac
o mac.external	Information from all over
o mac.hack	Technical information about all aspects of the Mac
o mac.macappda	The Macintosh Developer's Association
o mac.news	Up-to-the-minute information
o mac.novice	For beginners
o mac.products	Listings of new hardware and software
o mac.sandbox	For off-hours fun
o magma	Magma Systems
o mansfield	Mansfield Software Group
o manx.aztec	The Manx Software Systems/Aztec C conference
o marketing	Promotions, sales, public relations and high tech
o mathematics	Talk about high-level mathematics
o media.cyber	Media Cybernetics
o medicine	Computers in the medical and health services fields
o meridian	Meridian Software's customer-support conference
o metamorphose	Metamorphose Engineering computer graphic/imaging products
o microbotics	Microbotics Inc.
o microbytes	Daily news briefs about technology and computing
o microbytes.hw	New hardware products
o microbytes.sw	New software products
o microcode	Microcode Consulting
o microexpert	The MicroExpert conference
o microillusions	Microillusions
o microsmiths	Microsmiths Software
o microsoft	Products from Microsoft
o microway	Microway Inc.
o mks	Mortice Kern Systems
c moderators	The conference for conference moderators
o modula.2	The Modula 2 language conference
o music	Computers and music
o mwc	The Mark Williams Co. customer-support conference
o netware.tech	Netware Technical Journal
o networks	The conference on information networks
o neural.nets	The conference on neural networks

c new.bench	A place to discuss the new benchmark project.
o new.england	On and about New England
o new.writers	Getting started in the writing business
o newtek	NewTek Inc.
o next	The NeXT computer conference
o number.nine	Number Nine Computer Corporation
o oakland.group	The Oakland Group
o oberon	Dr. Wirth's new experimental language
o old.house	Owners and lovers of old houses: repairs, tips, etc.
o ood	The object-oriented development conference
o os.9	The OS-9 conference
o osbornemgh	Osborne McGraw-Hill
o other	Topics not covered elsewhere
o other.brands	The conference for other brands of computers
o other.dos	The conference for other disk operating systems
o other.lang	The conference on other languages
o other.times	Land for fun, relaxing, gameing. Come set a spell
o packet.nets	The conference on packet-switching networks
o paradigm	Paradigm Systems Inc.
o pascal	The Pascal language conference
o pc.write	Quicksoft's customer-support conference
o pce	The Personal Computer Engineers customer-support conference
o periscope	The Periscope Company, Inc.
o philosophy	For philosophers
o phoenix	Phoenix Computer Products' conference
o photo	Conference for photographers
o pmi	PMI
o poetry.prose	Writing both types of English
o postscript	The Postscript conference
o print.queue	Hugh Kenner's Print Queue column
o proapp	ProAPP Inc.'s customer-support conference
o prolog	The Prolog language conference
o prospero	Prospero Software Inc.
o protocols	The conference on small-computer communications protocols
o radical.eye	Radical Eye Software
o raima	The Raima conference
o rational.ic	Rational Systems
o realia	The Realia conference
o reviews.hw	BYTE Hardware Reviews, March 1988 — September 89
o reviews.sw	BYTE Software Reviews, March 1988 — September 1989
o revolution.sw	Revolution Software's conference
o rix	Rix Softworks
o robotics	The robotics conference
o roundhill	Roundhill Computer's customer-support conference
o rwars	The Great Operating System Debate
o ryan.mcfarland	Ryan McFarland

o sas.c	SAS C Compiler
o sca	Society for Creative Anachronisms
o sciences	The conference on scientific programs
o sdnet_works	SDN Project
o seattle	For BIXen and friends in the Pacific Northwest
o security	Security issues and computing
o sf	Science fiction, Star Trek, and fantasy fans
o short.takes	Hands-on looks at new products
o slr.sys	SLR Systems
o smalltalk	The Smalltalk language conference
o soft.eng	Efficient and reliable software design
o softbottling	Software Bottling Company
o softklone	SoftKlone Distributing Corporation
o softworks	Softworks
o solid	Solid Software's customer-support conference
o space	Space exploration and development
o space.sail	The Columbus 500 Space Sail Project
o spi	The Software Products International conference
o sports.leisure	Sports and leisure activities
o spreadsheets	Discussions on spreadsheets
c summit	Summit Computer Systems, Inc.
o sun	The conference on Sun workstations
o supermicros	The supermicro computers conference
o supra.corp	Supra Corporation
s survey.demo	Test the survey code
c svctech	Software Ventures' technical support conference
o sw.author	The business of programming
o switzerland	For Swiss BIXen and friends
c sysops	For BBS sysops only
o system.news	News of changes and improvements on BIX
o tandy	Discussions about Tandy desktop computers
o tech.hardware	The latest in computer hardware discussed
o tech.news	Discuss Microbytes news, product reports, and items
o tech.notes	Collect and discuss useful programming code
o tech.support	Prompt help for programming problems/questions
o technology	New technologies and their impact
o telecomm.pgms	The telecommunications program conference
o telecomm.tech	New telecommunications technology
o telegames	Software Terminal
o television	The technology and uses of TV
o the.realms	Fantasy role-playing games
o ti	The Texas Instruments computers conference
o ti.graphics	The TI graphics chip conference
c tng.script	A collaborative script workshop
o to.wayne	Getting down to business with Wayne Rash
o tojerry	Messages for Jerry Pournelle
o topdown	TopDown Development
o tops	Sitka (formerly TOPS), A Sun Microsystems Company
o travsoft	The Traveling Software conference
o unclassifieds	Buy, sell, and swap on BIX

o UNIX	The UNIX conference
o UNIX.bin	David Fiedler's UNIX/bin Column from BYTE
o user.manual	Help beyond the learn conference level
o users.386	Users discuss their experiences with 80386-based computers
o val	Video Associates Labs
o vcs.windows	Vermont Creative Software
o ven.tel	Ventel's customer-support conference
o w.and.a	The Workman and Associates conference
o washington.dc	For BIX members in Washington, DC
o whats.ahead	Coming events in BYTE
o women	Women's issues
o word.processor	The word-processing program conference
o write.fiction	On writing fiction
o writers	For writers, published or yet to be published
c writers.pros	For professional writers
o writers.talk	Insights from and conversations with professional writers
o xlisp	The XLISP support conference
o zenith	The Zenith computer conference
o zortech	Zortech Inc.

The following are command examples downloaded from the online manual.

APPENDIX A: GUIDE TO BIX COMMANDS

Main System Prompt Commands

COOkie	Displays pithy saying
DOWnload	Receive (i.e., download) data stored in your scratchpad
JOIn CBix	Enter the main CBix area
OPT PAD Q	Display your PAD settings
OPTion	Enter Option subsystem
SHOW OPTS	Displays Option settings
STAtus	Display statistics on mail, conferences, and amount of time online
TIMe	Current time on east coast of U.S.
UPLoad	Send (i.e., upload) data from your computer up to your scratchpad
WHO	Show who is online
WHO [conference]	List names on line in a conference CBix area
WHO ALL	List names in all CBix areas
WHO LISt	List names of CBix users on-line in any conference that you belong to

Conference Commands

null line/return	See next message
number	See message number
number TO number	See messages in that range
AGAin	Redisplay last message

ALL	See all new messages
BACkward	Read in reverse direction; disengage reference
BACkward number TOnumber	See messages in that range in reverse order
BYE	Log off (works immediately)
CLEar	Empty scratchpad
COMment	Make a comment on the message you have just read
CURrent TO LASt	Read first unread message to end of topic
DATe [date] TO DATe [date]	Read messages added on day(s) specified Format: date 24jun85
DOWnload	Receive (i.e., download) data stored in your scratchpad
FILe [option]	Write result to scratchpad
FIRst	Read first message in topic
FIRst TO LASt	Read every message in a topic
FORward	Read forward direction (default); disengage reference
HEAder message number	See message header and first line only
HEAder number TO number	See message headers for specified range
HELp	Display help message
JOIn conf topic	Leave current conference, join another
LASt	Read last message; also use " skip to last."
MAIL	Leave conference, enter Mail subsystem
NEXt	Jump to the next topic on your conference list
OPTion	Enter Option subsystem
ORIGinal	See message to which current one is a comment
QUIt	Return to main level; no more of current message
REFerence	Read by reference
ROOt	See the message that started a thread
SAY	To enter an original note
SEArch `word'	List all occurrences of search word in topic
SEArch number TO number `word'	List all occurrences of search word between message numbers in topic
SHOw [option]	Any show option (e.g., all, participants, who, profile, conference name, scratchpad)
SKIp [option]	Skips messages forward or backward and by date
TOPic	When followed by a topic name, you jump to that topic. Entered alone, it produces a list of topics in that conference. Note: This command cannot be used to move to another conference.
UPLoad	Send (i.e., upload) data from your computer up to your scratchpad
WHO	Show who is online
WHO [conference]	List names online in a conference CBix area
WHO ALL	List names in all CBix areas
WHO LISt	List names of CBix users online in any conference that you belong to
WIThdraw message number	Retract your comment number

Add/Action: Commands

After typing in the text of your message, you have the following options:

ADD	Add the text as a message or comment, and clear the scratchpad
CLEar	Clear the scratchpad, do not add message to conference, return to Read: prompt
EDIt	Invoke the text editor
HELp	Display this message
LISt	Show the message in the scratchpad
QUIt	Leave scratchpad intact, do not add message to conference, return to Read: prompt

Mail: Commands

TO [username]	New message to person(s)
null line/Return	Read first unread message
number	Read message number
BYE	Log off
DELete number	Delete message number
DOWnload	Receive (i.e., download) data stored in your scratchpad or a binary mail attachment
FILe [option]	Write result of option to your scratchpad
INBASKET	Displays your inbasket
JOIn [conference]	Leave Mail and join the conference specified
OPTion	Enter Option subsystem
OUTBASKET	Displays your outbasket
QUIt	Return to main level
REAd	Enter conferencing area
SHOw [options]	Use any show option
STAtus	Lists both of your mail baskets
UPLoad	Send (i.e., upload) data from your computer up to your scratchpad
UNRead	Display only the unread messages in your inbasket
WIThdraw message number	Retract message number

Send/Action: Prompt Commands

ATTach	Upload a binary mail attachment
CC [names]	Send copies to names
CLEar	Empty scratchpad
EDIt	Edit the text of the message
HELp	Display this message
LISt	Show the message in your scratchpad
QUIt	Leave scratchpad intact and return to Mail without sending the message
SENd	Send the message; clear scratchpad

SHOw [options]	Use any show option
SUBject	Re-enter the text to appear on the " Subject:" line
TO	Reenter or add new name(s) to the TO: field

Read/Action: Prompt Commands

AGAin	Redisplay last mail message
DELete	Remove the message
FORward [name]	Forward the message to name
HELp	Display this message
REPly	Start a new message to the sender of the message you have just read

ORIGinalIf you have just read a reply to a message, this displays the original message

LEAve	Leave the message in the inbasket, return to Mail
QUIt	Same as Leave

Option Subsystem Commands

BLInk Yes	Make BIX send full packets with Show Scratchpad
BLInk No	Disengage Blink Yes
DOWnload [protocol]	Set download protocol
EDIt [editor]	Set your editor to the one specified
FILTer No	Pass control characters through without change
FILTer Yes	Make control characters printable
HELp	Display this message
MAILcall [yes/no]	Set Mailcall on or off
NAPlps [yes/no]	Turn NAPLPS on or off
QUIt	Exit the Option subsystem

RECent maximum numberSet the maximum number of messages to see when you first join a conference

RECent minimum numberSet the minimum number of messages to see when you first join a conference

RECent days numberSet the number of days' worth of messages to see when you first join a conference

SYNonym	Make synonym for a command
TERse	Use the abbreviated form for prompts and message headers
TERM pagelength n	Send n lines between .More.. prompts
TERM ANSI	ANSI terminal emulation
TERM TTY	TTY terminal emulation
TERM VT52	VT52 terminal emulation
TERM VT100	VT100 terminal emulation
TERM Width n	Send n characters per line
UPLoad [protocol]	Set upload protocol
VERbose	Use the long form for prompts and message headers

Publications

They publish the *BIX User Manual* and the quarterly *BIX Newsletter.*

4.1.4 Capital Online

Capital Online
Washington Information Services Corp.
1250 24th St., NW, Suite 600
Washington, DC 20037
(202) 466-0522 (voice)
(202) 833-1591 (data)

Brief Description

Capital Online is oriented to the metropolitan Washington, DC area. It uses Caucus, but the standard Caucus interface has been modified so that the system looks quite different at first brush. It is a fairly new system, just getting started in 1990.

Access

To visit Capital Online, and register, call (202) 833-1591 with your modem set to 8-N-1 (3/12/2400-baud). At the connection, hit the spacebar once or twice. At the prompt, type "preview." That will get you into the registration area, then you can look around the system. Costs are a flat $6.50 per month.

Here is a sample logon, as a registered user:

```
ATDT1,202,8331591
DIAL TONE
1,202,8331591
CONNECT1200
bb"CfEgt     (Type a space here after getting this garbage.)

WELCOME!login:capital   (Don't type your user id here. Type
capital.)

   +
  + +
 + + +
 + + +
 + + +
 + + +
 + + +
 + + +
 + + +
 + + +          Welcome to
 + + +
 + + +
```

```
 + + +   C A P I T A L   O N L I N E
 + + +
 + + +
 + + +   Produced by:
 + + +   Washington Information Services Corp.
 + + +   202-466-0522
 + + +
 + + +
+ + + + + + + + + + + + + + + + + + + + + + + + + + + + + + + +
```

Please enter your Capital Online ID: a10085 (Now you type your user id.)
Password: (Then password.)

Welcome, Brian Williams
Here's the status of new activity:
=== Private electronic mail:
You have 0 new email message(s).

=== Conferences you have joined (new activity):

New Items	Items with new responses	Total new responses	Conference
1	0	0	alexandria
2	0	0	amazin
8	9	112	ellipse
11	0	0	newsbytes
19	0	0	telecom

Press RETURN for menu:

```
+
+ +
+ + +
+ + + +   E L L I P S E
+ + +     ______________________
+ +
+   Technology news along Boston's Route 128 now
+   available from the Middlesex News. Join the
+   COMPUTING conference, Item 16.
+
==================================================================
 Assistance: 202-466-0522 * Mon-Fri 8:30 am - 6:00 pm, EST
==================================================================
```

To interrupt text display, press Control-C
Items you have not yet seen are number(s) 18-25
Unseen item number(s) 1
New responses under item(s) 3 5 7 8 9 10 12 13 15

```
TOP menu

You're now in the conference 'ellipse'
You can return to this menu by entering the word: TOP

Here are the Online Centers in Capital Online
------------------------------------------------------------
1 ELLIPSE - The center of Capital Online
2 Communities - Issues and events in your neighborhood
3 COMPUTING - Discussions, user groups, news, services
4 Home - Education, finance, upkeep
5 Work - Professions, business, home office
------------------------------------------------------------
90 Help Menu, including command guide
91 Join a conference if you know its name
99 Exit system and disconnect

Enter an item number or RETURN to stay in 'ellipse': j telecom

Here is a list of the conferences on Capital at this time (8/90).

Conference ......... Description
----------------------------------------------------------------------
airwaves .......   Wireless communications: from DC to daylight
alexandria .........   Issues and events in Alexandria, Virginia
arlington ..........   Issues and events in Arlington County
arundel ............   Issues and events in Anne Arundel County
calvert ............   Issues and events in Calvert County
computing ..........   Events, discussions, references, and services
district ...........   Issues and events in Washington, DC
earth ..............   Local Earth Day '90 projects; ecology issues
education ..........   Linking classrooms and teachers
ellipse ............   Capital Online's public meeting area
fairfax ............   Issues and events in Fairfax County
laptops ............   Products and ideas for the micro on the go
loudoun ............   Issues and events in Loudoun County
montgomery.......   Issues and events in Montgomery County
newsbytes ........   Bi-weekly computer industry news, worldwide
parenting ........   Bringing up baby...and oneself along the way
pg .................   Issues and events in Prince Georges County
sports .............   O's, Skins, Caps, Pros, amateurs, dreams, agents
technology .......   Multimedia, AI, Expert Systems, Neural Nets etc
telecom ...........   Telecommunications - online and voices
trade ..............   International trade issues and opportunities
tv .................   Viewer discussions right here
unisphere90 ......   International trade conference - Wash,DC Apr 1990
venture ............   New business development: events, groups, people
writing ............   Readings, events, assignments, issues, stories
space ..............   The small steps, from Canaveral to the Crab Nebulae
cars ..............   gas, oil, or ideas? Check in here. Fill'er up.
```

Here is list of the topics in the Ellipse conference.

All discussion items in this conference

Item 1 (10) Intro to Ellipse, inquiries and general comments
Item 2 (1) COMMAND LIST READ ITEM 2 to get it
Item 3 (41) Who Will Become the District's Mayor in 1990?
Item 4 (2) Governor Wilder
Item 5 (23) Events, conferences, confabs, meetings of interest
Item 7 (4) COMPUTING: Discussions, user groups, news, services
Item 8 (12) AIRWAVES: Broadcasting, mobile, satellite: technolgy, policy,
Item 9 (4) At Work: Professions, local biz, home office, industries
Item 10 (17) Personal Intros: Add them here
Item 11 (1) COMMUNITIES: Conferences on DC and the surrounding counties
Item 12 (10) Searching Through The Wastebaskets
Item 13 (5) Washington Reporter: New daily paper for DC
Item 14 (1) VENTURE: New business development: sources, activities, news
Item 15 (1) EDUCATION: A focal point for educational issues and ideas
Item 16 (2) EARTH: Global network of schools to study eco problems
Item 17 (0) TELECOM: The amoeba-like industry; it's costs, it's features
Item 18 (0) UNISPHERE 1990: A Common Market for small global firms: 4/20-2
Item 19 (2) The Trial of Marion Barry, June 1990 - _____
Item 20 (1) SPACE: Small steps for man, and how we make them
Item 21 (2) SPORTS: From sandlot to World Cup: players, contests, broadcas
Item 22 (32) Electronic Citizenship presentation ideas/resources needed
Item 23 (1) TV: The Tube, its attractions, productions, assumptions: and u
Item 24 (2) CARS: Our service bay for troubles, myths, ideas on the Auto
Item 25 (1) New Comer's Board

Command Examples

Many of the commands of the standard Caucus software work on Capital, but to illustrate the customization, here is the Capital command set.

= = = Capital Online Brief Command Summary = = = = = = = = =
Conference Specific Commands

NEWShows new e-mail messages, new responses added to discussion items you're following and any brand new discussion items.

INdexList the titles and numbers of available discussion Items in the conference

OPtions Display a list of basic commands for the conference

ROster List the names of the people participating in the conference

Add Response Add a comment to an existing Item: a r 56

Add ItemBegin a new topic discussion; you'll be asked for a title after you've entered the introductory text: a i

DELete Delete the text of a response you've added to an Item, or the text of a new Item.

REAd Begins sequence to read anything available to you: old or new messages, responses in any Item, files from the library.

Examples:

REAd Item Read discussion items and responses
REAd Response Read responses that are part of an item
REAd Message Read your private messages
REAd Message 12 Read e-mail message number 12
REAd File Read files from the file library
REAd File rally Read the file " rally" from the file library

STatusShows how many messages, items, responses have yet to be seen, date and time, how long you've been connected.

DOwnload*Upload a new message, response for an item, text for a new Item or a text or binary file. Examples:

DOwnload Message Download a private email message
DOwnload Item Download text of all responses in an item
DOwnload Response Download a response in an existing item
DOwnload File Download a file
DOwnload File daily Download the file " daily" (for example)
Upload* Upload a new message, response for an item, text for a new Item or a text or binary file. Examples:

Upload Message Upload text of a private email message
Upload Item Upload text to start a new item
Upload Response Upload a response to an existing item
Upload File Upload a file
Upload File daily Upload the file " daily" (for example)

* - Not all conferences have file libraries available. Those that do may have some restriction on user uploads; check with the moderator.

Conference-independent commands

FINd PERsonWith the person's name, or a distinct part of it, displays that person's introduction and phone number, *if* the person has added that information.

Examples:
fin p william connors
fin p will

CHEckShows the names of the conferences you are following and the number of new responses and Items you have not yet seen

Join Leave the conference you are in and move to another one;
dd the name: j ellipse

FINd COnference - Locate a conference by name or by using a word in its description or; - locate discussions about a certain topic that might be available in more than one conference; for instance: fin co development

RECent Show the names of members most recently and/or currently online

People Shows suggested commands for locating, reading about and getting in touch with other members.

SENd Begins the sequence for sending a private message (you are asked for a subject and addressees after writing)

Mail

Mail is the standard Caucus mail. There are at present no gateways to other systems, but they are hopeful of making those available.

Publications

Online rePorter

4.1.5 CIGnet

CIGNET
Chautauqua Communication
P. O. Box 47409
Seattle, WA 98146
(206) 937-0515 (voice)
(206) 938-8398 (data)

Brief Description

CIGnet is a service of Chautauqua Communications. It runs on a platform of the Caucus software for conferencing and Personal Librarian for database management on 386 hardware.

They have one local line and an 800 number for long distance access. The use of the 800 number has to be authorized. There is no packet network access directly to CIGnet. They do have e-mail connectivity to other systems via Dasnet.

They offer a wide range of services including private conferences on this system.

Access

Here is a sample logon:

ATDT1,206,9388398
DIAL TONE
1,206,9388398
CONNECT 1200
s""fEgt (Type a space here)
CIGnet!login: guest (This is their guest account)
Password: (The guest password is tincup)

Welcome to

CIGnet
The online network and groupware toolkit of
Chautauqua Information Group sponsored by

Chautauqua Communication
P. O. Box 47409
Seattle, WA 98146
(206) 937-0515

Guests log directly into the HELPER conference.
If you prefer a menu interface type MENU.
To see a list of available conferences type PUBLIC.
To receive CIGnet membership information type ENROLL.

Please enjoy your visit and feel free to wander around.

Caucus (TM) version 2.2/SX. Copyright (C) 1988 Camber-Roth.

Here is a list of CIGnet conferences.

CIGnet NOW? (ME for menus, ? for help) j list

You are now leaving 'HELPER*'.

book_club*	bps	chinook	core
demonstration*	earth_spirit	ed_issues*	ena*
forum*	hekinanshi	helper*	itc
local_planning	manifestation	network_world*	oceans
plan91	pr*	psec	telecommuting*

The following is a list of the items in the Forum conference.

CIGnet NOW? (ME for menus, ? for help) set screensize 0

CIGnet NOW? (ME for menus, ? for help) list i all brief
Item 1 (2) WELCOME to CIGnet FORUM
Item 2 (7) Where we got the name CHAUTAUQUA
Item 3 (10) Bill visits Japan
Item 5 (1) Cold Fusion Apparently IS Real! Most Important Science of the
Item 6 (1) A Quick Tour of the Real West (Big Sky Telegraph, Colrado and Da
Item 7 (1) Provocations of Dr. Walter Orr Roberts
Item 8 (0) A Business Leader Speaks Out On Nuclear War - Provocation Numb
Item 9 (0) Huge Solar Outbreak - Provocation 254A
Item 10 (1) Science Advisory Mechanism for President Bush - Provocation #
Item 11 (0) The Next Steps in Space Exploration - Provocation #256
Item 16 (1) Privacy and ethics and electronic dissemination of personal in
Item 18 (0) EGAGIF.DOC
Item 19 (5) What is GIF?
Item 20 (1) GIF Standard
Item 21 (1) the world according to ibm
Item 22 (0) new computer languages
Item 23 (9) computer trivia and folklore
Item 24 (14) Exploring on-line relationships
Item 26 (10) Seattle Vignettes
Item 27 (9) earthquake thoughts
Item 28 (8) Illiteracy and Technology
Item 29 (4) Catching up on Japan Talk
Item 30 (27) Military action in Panama...What's happening? What are its co
Item 31 (19) New Year's Resolutions!
Item 32 (5) FCC at it again to add surcharges for modem users
Item 33 (0) looking for laptops
Item 34 (10) MORE - software for taking meeting notes
Item 35 (10) Computerized sales calls
Item 36 (3) First Amendment Rights and BBS
Item 37 (13) PR FOR CHAUTAUQUA IN INFOWORLD MAGAZINE
Item 38 (12) SNOWBALL FIGHT!!!!!
Item 39 (2) UNLOCKING HUMAN POTENTIAL..A Report by Peter and Trudy Johnson-L
Item 40 (2) AIDS - First-Hand story ported from the METANetwork
Item 41 (18) Sysop unavailable by phone for a few days
Item 42 (2) SURVIVING AND THRIVING IN THE INFORMATION AGE
Item 43 (5) DEATH AND TAXES
Item 44 (11) Boston Computer Society on CIGnet
Item 45 (0) Japan_TalkUW archived
Item 46 (12) Earth Week Statistics
Item 47 (12) Front-End software for CIGnet.
Item 48 (8) ARE YOU A LURKER?
Item 49 (11) back in the USSR
Item 50 (0) problems
Item 51 (0) PR for the 1990 ENA conference - join ENA for more detail

Item 52 (1) News (sporadic) from the Soviet Union
Item 53 (7) Santa Monica PEN makes a difference
Item 54 (3) Food for the spirit - a Mozart concert - maybe a CIGnet get-to
Item 55 (24) Alternative, Affordable Housing, CoHousing
Item 56 (11) 1991 ENA CONFERENCE IN SEATTLE - CALL FOR PEOPLE TO HELP MAKE
Item 57 (3) PR FOR CHAUTAUQUA IN WORKING WOMAN MAGAZINE
Item 58 (15) party at kitty's.... July 17th...
Item 59 (2) Just where did these words come from?!
Item 60 (5) "Into the Whirlwind" - Goodwill Games Art Festival Production
Item 61 (3) Invitation to a CHinook Net potluck
Item 62 (2) Yoneda's Diary
Item 63 (0) cheap fares

Mail

Mail is the standard Caucus mail.

Special Features

Team Writing

In June 1989, a group-authoring facility was incorporated into CIGnet. This application makes it possible for an editorial team to enjoy a real-time personalized view of a document as it is developing. Members of the team use their favorite word processing software to access the document and suggest updates. Comments and changes added to a new draft are immediately available for all participants to view and review.

CIGnet is one of the few conferencing systems that encorporate database management into the conferencing environment. In the Forum conference there is reference to the following list of documents online. (This is not the full list.)

CIGnet NOW? (ME for menus, ? for help) toc
TYPE THE <SPACE> BAR TO SCROLL THROUGH THE LIST OF TITLES IN THIS DATABASE.

There are 90 documents in this database. If you wish to look at a particular document, enter the database and type "dbkey" with no quote marks. You may then read the document by typing "D #" without quotes, where # is the number of the document in the list.

1) header: ENA NETWEAVER Volume 4, Number 6, Article 4 (June 1988)
DEVELOPMENT OF A COMPUTER CONFERENCING MODERATOR EDITORIAL TEAM
3) header: 2/13/88 Len Hockley

Addictive Organizations
4) header: 12-JUL-88 Joichi Ito
Perestroika - Ported from TWIC
6) header: 5/20/88 Donald L. (Skip) Conover
The LAN Wo/Man Cometh
7) header: 20-OCT-88 Gordon Cook
The Great Malaise of the Election of 1988: Ported from parti on Nwi
8) header: 23-NOV-88 Frank Burns
Caucus is a development platform.
9) header: The following is a glossary of hypermedia terminology. This information comes from a variety of sources.
11) header: 3/16/88 Lisa Carlson
Paul Strassmann on Productivity and Connectivity
12) header: 20-MAY-88 Gordon Cook
Some Things to Think about BEFORE Buying CC Software
13) header: 25-AUG-88 Taylor Walsh
Electronic Dissemination of Supreme Court Opinions
14) header: 08-OCT-88 Lisa Carlson
More on CSCW by Harry Stevens
16) header: 1/07/88 Skip Conover & Debbi McGlauflin
A "Discovery Model" for the Information Age
18) header: 4/17/88 Donald L. (Skip) Conover
Agency Saves $70,000 Using Computer Conferencing
20) header: 9/08/87 Lisa Carlson
Netweaver 3,8 - Electronic Seminars Part I by Lowell Roberts
21) header: 02-SEP-88 Lisa Carlson
Netweaver August '88 - Computer Conferencing by Stefanie Kott
25) header: 9/08/87 Lisa Carlson
Netweaver 3,8 - CC for Expert Networks by Harry Stevens
27) header: 5/15/88 Lisa Carlson
Mike Greenly's Speech to ENA - It's 20K and worth every byte!
28) header: 07-NOV-88 Lisa Carlson
Groupware
29) header: 01-JUL-88 Scott Burns
The Meta Network -- Technical History and Current Condition
31) header: 16-JAN-89 Norman B. Solomon
The INTERNATIONAL BUSINESS ISSUES NETWORK
35) header: 3/24/88 Donald L. (Skip) Conover
Business Applications of Computer Conferencing
42) header: 8/19/87 Dave Hughes
You Got Graphic Gab!
55) header: 24-OCT-88 Frank Burns
Toward A General Taxonomy of Online Networking Applications
57) header: 3/17/88 Scott Burns
IMPORTANT Using Packet Switch Networks? READ THIS!!
62) header: Carbon Dioxide Measurements from Mauna Loa Observator
Provocation No. 227
63) header: Ecological Crisis at the Aral Sea
Provocation No. 228
65) header: The Sverdlovsk Anthrax Outbreak of 1979

Provocation No. 230
66) header: Yellowstone's Fires a Research Opportunity
Provocation No. 231
71) header: Have We Detected the Greenhouse Warming Already?
Provocation No. 236
72) header: Evidence Mounts for Asteroids as the Dinosaur Kill
Provocation No. 237
75) header: New Measurements of Greenhouse Gases
Provocation No. 240
76) header: A New Finding about the Gaia Hypothesis
Provocation No. 241
77) header: Insurance Against the Greenhouse Heat Trap
Provocation No. 242
80) header: Trees and the Greenhouse Warming
Provocation No. 245
81) header: Provocation No. 246
Greenhouse Effect Invisible over USA

4.1.6 Echo

Echo
Echo Communications Group, Inc.
97 Perry Street, Suite 13
New York, NY 10014
(212) 255-3839 (voice)
(212) 989-8411 (data)

Brief Description

Echo was begun in 1990 by Stacy Horn and friends as an attempt to create an online community in New York City.

Hardware

ECHO requires a 80386 DTK motherboard running at 33Mhz with a 64K memory cache and 613MB Seagate SCSI hard drive ST4702, plus ten phone lines.

Software

ECHO uses Caucus Conferencing software.

Number of Users

The number of users is 250.

Cost of Access

The cost of access is $18.95 for unlimited usage; for private conferences the price is negotiable.

Access

They have one phone number for local access and no provision at this time for access outside for that local line. Here is a sample dialup:

```
ATDT1,212,9898411
DIAL TONE
1,212,989-8411
CONNECT 1200

Echo!login: brianw
Password:
TERM = (vt100-nam)

Terminal type is vt100-nam

 Welcome!  This is  E c h o. (sm)

Material posted on Echo is the sole property of its author. Reproduction in any medium without the express permission of the individual author is strictly prohibited. Echo disclaims all responsibility for the material posted publicly or privately on the system.

Copyright (c) 1990  Echo Communications Group, Inc.

Last login at 18:50:30 on 08/19/90

Caucus (TM) version 2.2/SX.  Copyright (C) 1988 Camber-Roth.

E C H O E C H O
E C H O E C H
E C H O E C
E C H O E
E C H O          Welcome to the Central Conference of Echo!
E C H O   This is where we discuss items of interest to everyone on Echo.
E C H O E
E C H O E C         Your conference Host is Stacy Horn.
E C H O E C H
E C H O E C H O

If you need to talk to us on the phone call : (212) 255-3839.
Someone will be available to talk you between: 9AM - 8PM.

Unseen items are:
```

1 5-6 13-14 19 33 39 43 50
59 61 67 69 72-73 80-81 84 86-87
89 91-92 96 98-100 102 104-105

New responses on items:
12

*** New Messages are 1-2

AND NOW? (ME for menus, ? for help) show n m

List of Conferences

JOIN which conference? list

books	business	central	classified
computer	conferences	culture	dontpanic
elsewhere	feedback	humor	jewish
law	love	media	money
netweaver	newyork	novel	parenting
plain_wrapper	politics	psych	science
sf	telecommunications	virtual	writing

JOIN which conference? dontpanic

From *The Restaurant at the End of the Universe* by Douglas Adams:

"There is a theory which states that if ever anyone discovers
exactly what the Universe is for and why it is here, it will
instantly disappear and be replaced by something even more
bizarre and inexplicable.

There is another which states that this has already happened."

Mail

Mail is Caucus mail.

Gateways

In October 1990 we will have a gateway to Usenet. ECHO is working on distributed conferencing between other Caucus systems and The WELL in California for 1991.

Special Features

ECHO is installing a File Library System. ECHO plans to have text search but it is researching more sophisticated systems. It also is investigating several database programs.

Help Available

If you're online and having trouble, you can now get help from another person online. Type " support" at the AND NOW? prompt and if someone is online to help you they will send you a YO!

If it happens that no one is online to help you, you will get a message saying so and a telephone number to call for help over the phone.

Bibliography

Hall, Trish. "Coming to the East Coast: An Electric Salon." *New York Times: Lifestyle* 39; January 28, 1990.

Additional Information

ECHO has a private online Group Therapy Conference run by a state licensed Ph.d psychologist. It also provides free conferencing and support to groups whose activities will benefit the community — that's community in the larger sense, the world 'out there.' The most popular conferences on ECHO are PSYCH, Love, Writing and Culture.

4.1.7 Institute for Global Communications

Institute for Global Communications
3228 Sacramento St.
San Francisco, CA 94115
(415) 923-0900 (voice)

IGC, the Institute for Global Communications began in 1984 as Peacenet, one of the Apple Community Affairs grantees. The Apple groups used Tymnet's Ontyme as a basis for conferencing, but IGC quickly evolved beyond that. They received a grant from the San Francisco Tides Foundation, bought bigger equipment and began developing conferencing based on a package from PLATO called 'Notesfile.' In 1987, they expanded and bought out the existing Econet, another Apple Community affairs group coordinated by the Farralones Institute. IGC brought Econet in as one arm of the organization and kept Peacenet as the other. They changed their name from Peacenet to International Global Communications and the rest is history.

Both the environmental and the peace themes have stimulated growth on the network and they established a network connection to the GreenNet in Britain in 1987. At that point they established the Association for Progressive Communications, which is an umberella for many similarly oriented conferencing systems in several different countries. Most of these systems are using the same software and connections are made with some of them to copy conference activity every hour.

The system runs on a 80486-based microcomputer with 32MB of RAM and a gigabyte of disk storage. The operating system is ATT UNIX system 5 v.3.2. There are six incoming lines with modems, one 9600-baud, and an x.25 connection. They are available from the Telenet packet switching network. Their telenet address is c 408 346. They can support about fifty users online at one time now. They are in the process of developing database untilities for the system. When those are in place you should be able to switch to information retrieval in addition to the communications available at this time.

Their Online Introduction

The Association for Progressive Communications (APC) is a collection of affiliated computer networks cooperating to provide international services. They currently include:

** Alternex in Brazil;
** FredsNaetet in Sweden;
** GreenNet in the United Kingdom and Europe;
** The IGC Networks: PeaceNet, EcoNet, HomeoNet, and ConflictNet; in the U.S.A;
** Nicarao in Nicaragua;
** Pegasus Networks/EarthNet in Australia; and
** Web in Canada.

All affiliated networks share most of the same network services.
There are electronic conferences that are common to some or all networks, and you may send electronic mail to any member of any affiliated network.

Questions about how to use the Network can be sent via electronic mail to " support," or can be posted in the conference called " help."

General — PeaceNet, EcoNet, HomeoNet, and ConflictNet are services of the Institute for Global Communications (IGC), a division of the Tides Foundation, a San Francisco-based public charity exempt under sections 501 (c) (3) and 509 (a) (1) of the Internal Revenue Code. These networks are to be used to help educate users and the general public in efforts to achieve world peace, justice, environmental quality, and health.

Copyright Information — All information on the Network, except where otherwise noted, is in the public domain. It is our intent to distribute information to as broad a spectrum of people as possible; however, it is up to the users of the system to abide by local, state, and federal copyright laws. Therefore, all material posted should contain appropriate source references where applicable.

Telex and Fax Link

You can send and receive telex messages and send faxes via the Network. You cannot receive faxes on the Network. Telex and fax are particularly useful for communicating to colleagues who do not have computers and rely on telex or fax machines for their electronic communications.

Gateways to Other Systems

Email messages can be sent between most other electronic mail services, both commercial (AT&T Mail, MCI Mail, Dialcom, etc.) and academic (Internet, Usenet, etc.) and in particular the other APC; networks (GreenNet; in the United Kingdom, Web; in Canada, Alternex; in Brazil, Nicarao; in Nicaragua, Pegasus; in Australia, etc.). Up-to-date details of the networks we connect to, and how to communicate with users on them, are in the " gateways" conference. Their internet address is igc.org.

IGC Network's Rates and Discount Policies

** Sign-up charge: There is a one-time $15 sign-up charge to join the IGC Networks.

** Monthly subscription fee and off-peak discount: The basic subscription to the IGC Networks costs $10 per month. This includes one hour of free, off-peak connect time (off peak time is 6 p.m. - 7 a.m. weekdays and all hours on weekends) per month. Any free time left over at the end of the month is not applicable to subsequent months.

** New user off-peak discount: All new subscribers receive an additional free hour of off-peak connect time during their first 30 days of use.

** System access and connect rates: Additional off-peak connect time costs $5 per hour. Prime connect time (7 a.m. - 6 p.m. weekdays) costs $10 per hour. The free monthly hour of off-peak time does not apply to prime connect time.

Note: If an IGC Network session is begun during peak time (for example, 5:59 p.m. on a weekday), the entire session is billed as peak time. Similarly, a session begun during off-peak time carrying over into peak time is billed as off-peak time. Off-peak rates are also in effect on New Year's Day, Independence Day, Labor Day, Thanksgiving Day, and Christmas Day.

** Storage charges: All IGC Network users are given 100 kilobytes (50 pages) of free storage space. The charge for additional storage space is $0.005 per kilobyte (one cent per page) per month. You will be notified on the Network if you are exceeding the free storage limit.

** Credit for referring new users: If you refer a new user to the Network, you will receive two free hours of off-peak time, or the equivalent credit in additional storage space. This credit can be used over any number of months.

** Group discounts: A person or organization bringing a group of 10 or more new users to the IGC Networks will receive a discount of $1 per user per month. For example, if you brought on a group of 14 new users, you would receive a discount of $14 per month. (In addition, you would be credited 28 hours of off-peak connect time, or the equivalent in storage space, for referring 14 new users.)

** Payment: Users paying with Visa, Mastercard or American Express will have their credit card accounts billed at the beginning of every month for the previous month's Network usage. No deposit is required.

Users paying by check must open their Network account with a $50 deposit. You will receive a monthly billing statement of your Network charges, payable within 30 days. If you decide to end your IGC Network subscription, your deposit will be returned to you.

Here are some excerpts from the IGC online manual.
Network commands: (c)onf (h)elp (m)ail (s)etup (u)sers bye

This tells you that there are new entries in some of your regular conferences. Also, you are informed that there is new mail waiting for you. Additional messages, referred to as " Tips and Teasers" may also appear. These are generated by Network staff to draw your attention to important events or changes on the system.

At this point, you have six " top-level" choices for proceeding:

(c)onf takes you into conferences;
(h)elp enters the online tutorial that looks much like this manual;
(m)ail enables you to send and receive electronic mail;
(s)etup enables you to modify your password, terminal type, or delete key;
(u)sers allows you to get a complete or partial list of other users on the system; and
bye logs you off the system.

There are three levels within conferences: the conferences themselves, topics within conferences, and responses to each topic.

A conference consists of a series of messages called Topics. Each Topic deals with a major aspect of the overall Conference subject. For example, within the " carnet.nicanews" conference, you can find such topics as " Nicaraguan Agricultural Policy" and " Crime and the Contras - A Report." After each topic, you can enter responses; - or, responses to other responses.
The Network keeps track of which topics and responses have been read by each account.
Conferences are entered from the main command menu: OK: (c)onf (h)elp (m)ail (s)etup (u)user bye ? **c** <RETURN>Conf?

Usually, when you go to a conference and ask to see the (i)ndex (type i and hit <RETURN>), only the last, most recent page of the index appears. If you want to skip around, you need to use the following commands:

b BACK a page.
f FORWARD a page.
< Show FIRST index page.
> Show LAST index page.

Conf? < <RETURN>

When you first sign up to the Network, you are given a " regular" list of conferences that we feel might be of interest to the general Network subscriber. To (m)aintain your regular list of conferences, you go into maintenance mode from the " Conf?" prompt.
Conf? m <RETURN>
Regular conferences: (a)dd (d)elete (l)ist (r)eorder (? for help) l <RETURN>
Your regular conferences are: 1.netnews 2.help 3.ideas 4[others]

When you type the (v)isit command, the system starts the check of your regular conference list, looking at each conference in turn to see if there are any unread messages in that conference.If there are no new messages in a conference on your list, then the visit command goes on to the next conference. To read the first unread message, use the (u)nread command.

Downloading Conferences

You have three options for downloading while in a conference:
** downloading one topic or response at a time;
** downloading one topic and all of its responses (if any); or
** downloading all unread topics and/or responses.
All of them begin with the (c)apture command.

If you want to (d)elete a message right after you have written it, you can do so as follows:Conf? d <RETURN>Really delete? (y)es (n): y <RETURN>

Using (m)ail From Within Conferencing
In addition to sending copies of conference entries to an individual through mail, you can also send someone a new mail message while still in conference mode.

Leaving Conferences

To (q)uit out of conferencing, type q <RETURN> in response to the " Conf?" prompt. You will be returned to the main command line.

Stringing commands together

Command letters can be strung together if you precede them with a comma (","). For example:
,wrc (w)rite a (r)eply in this (c)onference
,xp e(x)it this conference and (p)retend you read everything
,xpvi -e(x)it this conference and (p)retend you read everything then (v)isit the next conference and show its (i)ndex.
,wnm - (w)rite a (n)ew message in (m)ail
,r 13.7 (r)ead response 7 of topic 13
,wf auser (w)rite (f)orward a copy of topic or response to "auser"

Basic Commands

b/f (b)ackward/(f)orward one page of the index
u show next (u)nread message
v (v)isit next regular conference
q (q)uit from conf
i show (i)ndex page
n/p show (n)ext/(p)revious message
t show next unread (t)opic
g (g)o to a conference
h provide more (h)elp
w (w)rite a topic/response or mail message
Advanced and Director Commands

< show first page of index (except when terminal type isset to capture)
l (l)ist conferences
d (d)elete a message
m conference list (m)aintenance
P backup to last seen message
! enter director mode
> show last page of index (except when terminal type is set to capture)
x e(x)it conference
(f)orget you read any entries
(p)retend you read all entries
e (e)dit a message
r (r)ead the current message
delete any message
^ toggle director mode of message

Here is a list of the conferences as of 8/90.

— Conference Directory —
Network: (a)ll, (o)ther, or <RETURN> for EcoNet (? for help): a
Enter name, keyword, or <RETURN> for all (? for help):
Do you want: a (s)hort, (m)edium or (l)ong listing (? for help): m

Conferences marked with a `*' are privately listed to your group `enmisc'.

*** IGC Nets - System Wide Resources ***:
help — Questions and answers on using IGC Networks
netnews — News and Information about IGC Networks
facilitators — Support for and discussion with conference facilitators
gateways — Gateways with Other/Remote Networks
ideas — Explorations of Applications for the IGC Family of Networks
intlaccess — Information for accessing IGC Networks from outside the USA
micro — Discussion of microcomputer issues
micro.hardware — Using equipment discussion: printers, IBM PC, Apple, Mac
micro.software — Computer programs, public domain word processing, database
techhistory — Technical History the IGC Network system

conferences — Names and descriptions of all conferences on IGC Networks
test — Conference to be used for practice and experimentation
welcome — Well, I'm on IGC Networks, now what?

*** Northern California Council of Mediators ***:
cn.nccm — Public conference for the Northern California Council of Mediators

*** ConflictNet Sytem Wide Resource ***:
cn.guide — Consumer Guide and Directory for choosing 3rd party neutrals
cn.classifieds — Classified directory for the field of conflict resolution
cn.calendar — A national calendar of events and activities
cn.education — A directory of colleges and university programs
cn.training — Training programs and materials
cn.dialogue — Open forum for dialogue about issues concerning the field
cn.resources — Resources and materials for the conflict resolution field
cn.feedback — An open forum for feedback and dialogue about ConflictNet
cn.general — ConflictNet's online newsletter — articles, announcements, legislative changes

*** EcoNet - Network Wide Resources ***:
en.agriculture — Agriculture, nutrition, world hunger, chemicals
en.alerts — Short and time-urgent alerts for the EcoNet community
en.announcements — News and Events of interest to the environmental community
en.cleanair — Acid rain, pollution, precipitation
en.climate — Climate Change: Causes, Consequences and Responses
en.jobs — Public conference listing jobs in environmental fields
en.disasterinfo — Disaster Assistance - discussion, articles, news, requests
en.energy — Energy - discussion, articles, news, requests
en.europe — European Environmental Issues
en.ussr — Soviet Eco-Systems and Global Environmental Sustainability
en.enveducation — Environmental Education - discussion, articles, news, etc
en.forestplan —National Forests - discussion, articles, news, requests Maui Epicenter, and David Fisher Business Consultant:
en.hawaii — Workspace for all interested in Hawaii's environment

Earthcare Interfaith Network:
en.globescope — U.S. Citizens' Response to " Our Common Future"

*** EcoNet - Network Wide Resources ***:
en.health — Medicine and Science - discussion, articles, news, requests
en.marine — oceans seas water pollution
en.microenvirons — Micro Environments - discussion, articles, news, requests
en.parks — State Parks Admin - discussion, articles, news, requests
en.pesticides — agriculture poison wildlife
en.recycle — Industrial Recycling - discussion, articles, news, requests
en.ruraldev — Rural development solutions through telecommunications
en.toxics — Toxic Materials - discussion, articles, news, requests
en.toxics.cleanup — Cleanup of contaminated sites and methods for detoxification

Right-To-Know Network:

en.toxics.right-to-know—Right-to-know about toxic materials, contamination and hazardous wastes

*** EcoNet - Network Wide Resources ***:

en.waste — Waste management, recycling, energy, pollution control
en.wildlife — Wildlife Species - discussion, articles, news, requests
en.calendar — Interactive Calendar of Environmental Events

*** PeaceNet - Network Wide Resources ***:

pn.alerts — Short and Time Urgent Announcements
pn.announcements — Community-Wide Announcements
pn.classifieds — Goods and Services available from and sought by PeaceNet users
pn.jobs — Job Openings
pn.calendar — Calendar of events of interest to Peace Movement

*** HomeoNet - Network Wide Resources ***:

hn.alerts — Short notes on important events
hn.announce — Miscellaneous announcements
hn.conferences — Listing and Descriptions of HomeoNet's Public Conferences
hn.consults — Users post difficult cases for help of other practitioners
hn.hello — The perfect place to introduce yourself
hn.reviews — Reviews of conferences and books
hn.studygrps — Information exchange between study groups; #s, activities
hn.tidbits — Miscellaneous news, rumors and tidbits from the community
hn.topics — Articles, questions and discussion re homeopathic prescribing
hn.cal — An international calendar of homeopathic events

*** Web - Public Conferences ***:

web.alerts — General News Items
web.cafeteria — A free for all, multipurpose discussion area
web.cal — General Calendar
web.canpeace — Canadian peace issues, NORAD, NATO alliance, Cruise testing
web.cengen — Canadian Environment general topics
web.energy — Canadian Environment energy
web.envcan — Discussion area for Environment Canada Minister's Office
web.forest — Forestry Caucus area
web.fortrade — General trading, barter, sales and other member exchanges
web.francophone — French and francophone related issues
web.freetrade — Canada/US cross-border trade agreement; assessing impact
web.jobs — Volunteer/employment opportunities
web.native — North American aboriginal peoples
web.ontenergy — Ontario energy - Ontario Hydro, nuclear vs alternatives
web.ontenv — Ontario environment - Provincial environmental issues
web.parks — Canadian Parks and Wildlife Preserves
web.politics — General political, government policy discussion
web.poverty — social/political/economic issues affecting poor eg housing
web.toronto — Local Metro Toronto activities

*** Regional Conferences ***:
aia.news — Africa Information Afrique—News of Southern Africa
reg.africa — African news bulletins
reg.carib — Caribbean: Trinidad,Bermuda,Haiti,Grenada,Barbados,Jamaica
reg.china — See also the Centasia conference
reg.eeurope — Eastern European Affairs: Bulgaria, Rumania, Hungary etc
reg.mideast — Israel, Arab states, Iran and Iraq
reg.namerica — North American regional issues
reg.safrica — S. Africa: S. Africa,Botswana,Mozambique,Zimbabwe,Namibia
reg.samerica — South America: Brazil, Bolivia, Argentina, Colombia, Peru, Chile
reg.sasia — South Asia: India, Goa, Sri Lanka
reg.seasia — South Eastern Asia: Indonesia,Thailand, Malaysia,Japan, etc
reg.ussr — North Asia: USSR, Mongolia etc
reg.weurope — Countries around the Mediterranean, Baltic and North Seas
*** Public Conference ***:
accessnet — A distributed conference taking place on progressive Fido networks

African Political Change:
africa.glasnost — News and views on African political change

AIDS Coalition to Network, Organize and Win:
actnow.aidsinfo — AIDS Research, Issues and Communication for Activists

Amnesty International:
ai.uan — Amnesty International Urgent Action Network
The American Peace Test:
apt.alerts — Information about nuclear weapons tests
apt.general — Information about the American Peace Test

Action Southern Africa:
asafrica.forum — Open Forum on Southern Africa Peace and Justice

American Wind Energy Association:
awea.windnews — Summarizes environmental articles from news media

British American Security Information Council:
basic.nato — Information about NATO

Beyond Containment Project of the Coalition for a New Foreign Policy:
bc.beyondcontain— Beyond Containment — Toward a new U.S. foreign policy

Beyond War Foundation:
bw.directory — Directory of BW contacts in US
bw.grapevine — A vehicle for the sharing of ideas between local BW areas
bw.introduction — Basic info on the Beyond War Foundation and its activities
bw.quotes — Quotes for a sustainable world

Campaign Against U.S. Bases in the Philippines:
cab.philippines — General discussion of Philippine political and other issues

Central America Resource Center:
carcmn.ens — Monthly summaries of news articles on Central America
Central America Resource Network (CARNet):
carnet.alerts — Central America human rights alerts, urgent action requests
carnet.congress — Congressional news re Central America issues
carnet.contadora — Contadora Process
carnet.cubanews — News and information about Cuba
carnet.elsalnews — News items about events in El Salvador and related US policy
carnet.general — General topics and discussions of Central America issues
carnet.guatenews — Guatemala News
carnet.help — CARNet help
carnet.hondnews — News items about events in Honduras and related US policy
carnet.ideas — Forum for discussion on use of CARNet
carnet.irancontra — News of the Iran-Contra scandal and all investigations of it
carnet.ladb — Twice-weekly Central America Update, Latin America DataBase
carnet.nicanews — News items about events in Nicaragua and related US policy
carnet.panama — News and analysis on Panama

Casa de Proyecto Libertad:
carnet.refugees — Refugee and U.S. border news, issues, and interaction

Instituto Latinoamericano de Estudios Transnacionales:
carnet.southpaz — South American peace from militarism to democratic security

Children in Crisis Network:
cc.childnews — News of children in war zones, poverty, and other crises

Center for Conservation Biology:
ccb.update — Newsletter from Stanford's Center for Conservation Biology

Citizen Diplomacy, Inc:
cdi.sovsis — A conference for US-Soviet matched city efforts

Community Data Processing:
cdp.general — CdP general discussion

Center for Economic Conversion:
cec.dialogue — Open forum for interchange of ideas on economic conversion
cec.update — Info sharing on current economic conversion activities

*** Public Conferences ***:
ced.community — Local economic development, barter, politics
ced.coops — Worker, member co-operatives and co-op living, co-op housing
The Christic Institute:
chr.contragate — Firsthand Contragate Information and Christic Institute News

Center for Innovative Diplomacy:
cid.citdip — The people and groups in US-USSR citizen diplomacy

California Institute of Integral Studies:
ciis.gaianet — Gaia Consciousness: Spirituality and Ecology

Council for A Livable World:
clw.hotline — CLW Nuclear Arms Control Hotline w/ Update and Action Request

Coordinadora Regional de Investigaciones Economicas y Sociales:
cries.actualidad — Analysis and Documents on Cent. Am. Peace Process, Span and Eng
cries.regionews — Bi-Weekly News and Analysis on C.America-C'bean: from Managua

*** Public Conferences ***:
dev.humansettle — cities, towns, and villages
dev.international — International development

*** Web - Public Conferences ***:
dev.inttrade — International trade - commodities, futures, technology
eao.general — A new environment network for Ontario

Electronics and Computing for Peace:
ecp.news — Electronics and Computing for Peace: news, events, discussion

Earth Day 1990:
ed.general — Earth Day 1990 Information
ed.campusearth — College Environmental Networking
ed.earthdayintl — An international forum to disseminate information about Earthday 1990
ed.newengland — Earth Day planning in New England

Earth First!:
ef!.general — Topics of interest and discussion for Earth First! movement

Environmental Grantmaker Association:
en.consdigest
ega.directory — Environmental Funding Organizations
ega.grants — Grants Given by EGA Members

General EcoNet:
en.bioanaerobic — Extraction of marsh and landfill gas; biogasification
en.bioconversion — Use of woody plants and bioconversion of biomass for energy
at.general — Discussion and networking on appropriate technology issues
at.library — Database of documents related to appropriate technology

United Nations:
en.unced — Info about 1992 UN Conference being held in Brazil
en.unced.update — current information regarding the UNCED 1992 conference

Education:
aee.noticies -Postings of current AEE events; background on the AEE organization, on AEE network centers; information on joining AEE and/or becoming a network center
aee.news -Current Alliance newsletters: broken down out by departments and major articles
aee.calendar — Alliance calendar of events for the U.S.
aee.workshops — Listings and information on upcoming AEE workshops
aee.directory — Up-to-date directory of the AEE Network Center system
aee.funding — Alliance-provided information on funding
aee.curriculum Reports on trends and practices found in current environmental education curricula
aee.biblio Teaching aids, classroom experimenting and exploring kits, books on environmental education methods and topics to cover, etc.
aee.questions — Questions to the Alliance

Northcoast Environmental Center:
en.coastal — Coastal Issues: California and Beyond

Internews:
en.earthtv — Earthscan TV series script conference

Friends of the Earth:
en.urban — Cities for People - A Project of Friends of the Earth

Friends of the Earth\World Rainforest Movement:
wrm.rainforests — Rainforests, Forest Peoples, TFAP, Sustainable Management

Energy Network:
enet.currevents — Current Energy Related News and Events

*** Public Conferences ***:
epa — Canadian Environmental Protection Act

National Execution Alert Network:
execution.alerts-provides an alert update for pressing execution dates across the USA

Friends Committee on National Legislation:
fcnl.updates — Updates of taped FCNL legislative information

Green Alternative Information for Action:
gaia.planning — GAIA Network Planning and Development

General, non-organizational:
gen.art — Critical cultures, music and art
gen.bigbro — State security activities, surveillance, tapping, controls
gen.diffable — For the differently able
gen.gaylesbian — Gay and lesbian issues
gen.maleness — Maleness — and the redefinition thereof

gen.media — Mass media issues
gen.nativeam — General Information about Native American Issues
gen.newsletter — Articles for Newsletters, All Topics
gen.newtools — Using the new communications technology
gen.philos — Philosophy, Metaphysics, etc

Palo Alto Friends Peace and Social Action Committee, Quaker Electronic Project:
gen.quaker — Quaker Electronic Project

General, non-organizational:
gen.racism
gen.radio — Community radio, shortwave, packet radio, tv, satellite,
gen.references — For pointers to sources of good information
gen.right — Conservative political activities, republicans
gen.techeffects — The negative impacts of using new technology. Vdts
gen.women — Women's issues, abortion, exploitation, oppression

Geonet Bulletine Board:
geo2.antenna — 3rd-World/NGO Telecommunications/labor/labour
geo2.coops — Worker Cooperatives\labor\labour

gn.labor — Discussion of labor movement

Survival International:
gn.tribalsurvive — Issues concerning the survival of indigenous peoples

Greenpeace:
gp.natlnews — Greenpeace's Weekly National Newsletter
gp.press — Greenpeace's Press Releases Greens:
green.general — To further enhance Green organizing and Networking
green.genetech — To discuss and organize opposition to ice-minus/frost-ban
green.library — A library of documents pertaining to the U.S. Green Movement

Grassroots Online:
gri.philippines — Philippines. A Grassroots International Project

Global Walk for a Livable World:
gw.general — Global Walk for a Livable World: Information and Discussion

Homeopathic Academy of Naturopathic Medicine:
hanp.board — A private conference for internal discussions of HANP board

Homeopathic Academy of Naturopathic Physicians:
hanp.cert — Private conference for the creation of the HANP exam

General Homeonet, non-organizational:
hngen.fringe — The fringe of homeopathic treatment and thought
hngen.vet — Homeopathic Veterinary conference
Hahnemann Pharmacy:
hp.newrem — News about newly produced Quinn potencies

Northern Rockies Conservation Cooperative, Jackson, Wyoming:
hw.water — National and International Water Resource Info and Resources
Institute of Cultural Affairs:
ica.associates — Accelerating the dissemination of ICA participatory methods
ica.dialogue — Meeting place for supporters of ICA work around the globe
ica.mexcon — Facilitate electronic communications between ICA offices and members
ica.ocf — A new story waiting to be written, Oaxtepec Mexico nov88
ica.training -Conference on initiating a training and certification program for people interested in leading ICA courses/workshops
ica.earthwise — Curriculum development for planetary living in the 90s
Institute for Global Communications:
igc.db — IGC / CdP Database Development Issues
igc.history — History of System Development
igc.intlcomm — International Communications Development
igc.management — Private - IGC Management Discussions
igc.operations — Discussion of Day-to-Day IGC Operations

Institute for Peace and International Security:
ipis.highschool — Strategy for recruiting high-school students to the P.M.

Institute for Security and Cooperation in Outer Space:
iscos.bulletin — ISCOS weekly bulletins on space related issues

Kent Homeopathic:
ka.macrepertory — News, updates and feedback about MacRepertory

Japan Congress Against A- and H-Bombs (Gensuikin):
kin.nonukejapan — Movement against Nuclear Weaponry and Energy in Japan

labor.writings — Published and unpublished articles on labor and related

Moscow Aviation Institute:
mai.newtimes — Prospects for Co-operation of Peaceful Space Exploration

Meiklejohn Civil Liberties Institute:
mcli.peacelaw — Summaries of Facts and Law in 135 Cases

Center for Innovative Diplomacy:
mfp.data — News on municipal foreign policy initiatives
mfp.talk — Discussion among municipal foreign policy activists

Materia Medica Project:
mm.newinfo — Unpublished proving/cured symptoms or complete remedy image
mm.quizzes — Materia medica quizzes

msn.news — Newsletters relevant to news and events from Mozambique

National Center for Homeopathy:
nch.news — The latest news within the homeopathic community

National Campaign on Strategic Homeporting:
ncosh.homeporting — Navy plan to build 13 new ports for nuclear-armed ships

National Coalition to Stop Food Irradiation:
ncsfi.foodirrad — Food Irradiation News

New Directions:
nd.autoworkers — Autoworkers' union democracy movement

Nicaraguan Entrepreneur Project:
nep.nicabiz — Nicaraguan Business
Regional Coordinator for Economic and Social Investigations:
ni.centam-elect — Information about electoral processes in Central America
ni.elec-centroam — Informacion sobre los procesos electorales en Centroamerica

Nicaragua Network:
nicanet.brigades — Nicaragua Network Construction Brigades Info. exchange

Networking For Democracy:
nfd.gen — Conference supporting progressive media workers
nfd.ifeatures — Insight Features; Progressive news service

National Lawyers Guild:
nlg.interact — National Lawyers Guild, Legal Support for the Movement
National Peace Institute Foundation:
npif.usip — News from United States Institute of Peace

Native Peoples Support Group of Newfoundland and Labrador:
npsg.milflight — Health and environmental impacts of military flight training

New Society Publisher:
nsp.resources — New Society Publishers' resources for activists

Nuclear Times Magazine:
nt.altsecdialog — A dialog on current trends in alternative security

Options 2000 Nuclear Sovereignty Project:
nusp.freezone — Global nuclear free zone issues, focus on Pacific and Palau

New World Agriculture Group:
nwag.news — Progressive Agriculture Research and Development

Nuclear Weapons Freeze Campaign:
nwfc.lobby — Current info on Freeze legislation; updated every Tues.
nwfc.local — Local groups sharing information about their work
nwfc.media — Sample press releases/statements to be adapted locally
nwfc.strategy — Current working draft of 1987-88 strategy paper

*** Pegasus - Public Conferences ***:
oz.projects — To invite input, expertise or backing for Real-Time projects

Planetary Commission, Western North Carolina Chapter:
pc.innerpeace — Prayer Requests; Peace Meditations; World Healing Events

General PeaceNet, non-organizational:
pn.ca — Sharing new, events, want ads, etc. for state of California

DC-Online:
pn.dc — Events and contacts in the Washington, DC metro area

General PeaceNet, non-organizational:
pn.ia — Statewide forum for Iowa's PeaceNet users—visitors welcome
pn.nycnews — News and events for New York City and vicinity activists

Peace Studies Consortium of Ohio Colleges and Universities:
pn.oh — Ohio peace studies and peace action communities

Prescott Peace Network:
ppn.food+hunger — World hunger and food issues
ppn.nukematerial — Nuclear mining, milling, processing, fabrication, waste

Physicians for Social Responsibility:
psr.bulletins — PSR News
psr.clearinghouse — An ongoing conference designed for dialogue between PSR chapters

Rainforest Action Network:
ran.ragforum — Discussion of info and events for Rainforest Action Groups
ran.tropictimber — Info for working on the Tropical Timber Hardwoods campaign

Coordinadora Regional de Investigaciones Economicas y Sociales:
redcr.esquipulas — News and analysis on Central American peace process

News on Citizen Computing:
reset.nl — Reset: News on Citizen Computing; public newsletter editing

sc.icne — News and views of New England Sierra Club International Comm

Sierra Club:
sc.natlnews — A summary of news concerning the nation's environment

Green Committees of Correspondence:
spaka.community — US Greens' policy on issues of community
spaka.ecology — US Greens' policy on environmental issues
spaka.economics — US Greens' policy on economics issues
spaka.general — US Greens' stategy and policy development: general info
spaka.humanneeds — US Greens' policy on issues of human needs
spaka.organizing — US Greens' policy on issues of strategy
spaka.peace — US Greens' policy on issues of peace and nonviolence
spaka.personal — US Greens' policy on issues of personal values

spaka.politics — US Greens' policy on issues of government and politics
spaka.socialjust — US Greens' policy on issues of social justice
spaka.strategy — US Greens' policy on issues of organizing

New York On-Line/SouthScan:
sscan.news — Southscan, a weekly bulletin on events in southern Africa

*** Web - Public Conferences ***:
sweap.general — Metropolitan Toronto Solid Waste Environmental Plan

Theosophic Action Network:
tan.beginning — Cooperation as the Essence of Theosophy

*** Web - Public Conferences ***:
tech.web — Detailed/ Advanced WEB help

Tides Foundation:
tf.internal — Private conference for Tides F. Board and staff

Third World Resources:
twr.nl — Current issue / Third World Resources Quarterly Newsletter
Union for Democratic Communications:
udc.gen — UDC coordination of on-line activities
udc.media — The Media: theory, critique, use, access, democratization

United Nations Association:
un.ssd3 — Special Session on Disarmament - Discussion and Updates

University for Peace:
up.declaration — Drafting a Universal Declaration of Human Responsibilities
up.general — Information and discussion related to University for Peace

Political, social and economic change in Eastern Europe:
usagdr.glasnost — Council on USA-GDR Relations

Unitarian Universalist Association:
uua.board — UUA Board of Trustees
uua.general -Discussion of social justice, education, organizational process, computer use, and so on.

World Congress of Organizations for a Peaceful Earth:
worldcope.forum — A Global Forum of Civic Organizations on World Affairs

World Association for World Federation:
worldfed.comsec — UN reports, other articles, w/focus on strengthening UN
worldfed.ssdiii — UN SSDIII reports w/focus on proposals to strengthen the UN

Institute for Global Communications:
whatsnext — A conference on movement strategies from IGC conferences

Windstar Foundation:
ws.cal — Windstar Foundation and Connections calendars of events
ws.connections — Windstar International Connections Program
ws.gen — Windstar General Forum
ws.localact — Local/regional Windstar Connection-sponsored projects
ws.media — Windstar communications forum
ws.networking — Windstar Networking Forum
ws.resed — Windstar Foundation/Connection research and education projects

United Nations:
undp.rla.enviroment — UNDP activities and environmental projects in Latin America
undp.rla.ideas — brainstorming on possible new UNDP projects in Latin America

The Technical Education Research Centers, Inc.:
terc.gl.general — TERC Global Laboratory general info and material
terc.gl.data — Data collected by students in the TERC Global Lab project

California ReLeaf:
releaf.calendar — CA ReLeaf tree plantings and events calendars
releaf.treenews — CA Releaf urban forestry news and problem-solving

*** PeaceNet - Network Wide Resources ***:
pn.publiceye — Defending civil liberties in an age of repression and spying

Servas International:
servas.travel — a worldwide peace movement that facilitates face-to-face communication and homestays

United Nations Non-Governmental Liaison Service:
ngls.news — Newsletter

Media Transcripton Service:
mts.script — Media Transcripts from United Kingdom

Global Action Network:
gan.actionalerts — Alerts of immediate and specific actions you can take
gan.actionguide -A step-by-step guide to assist in starting an action group, or to empower and strengthen existing groups, organizations or chapters
gan.agencies -Addresses and phone numbers of key U.S. Government Offices and Agencies engaged in environmental matters
gan.congressbystate — Complete list by state of all Senators and Representatives in Congress
gan.eesi -"Status of Major Legislation" excerpted from EESI's WEEKLY BULLETIN developed for members of Congress
gan.globalwarming — Comprehensive information and what you can do about global warming
gan.housecommittees-Key House Committees and Subcommittees engaged in environmental matters
gan.membership — Action Group information and enrollment form

gan.pesticides — Comprehensive information and what you can do about pesticides
gan.population — Comprehensive information and what you can do about population
gan.recycling — Comprehensive information and what you can do about recycling
gan.senatecommittees-Key Senate Committees and Subcommittees engaged in environmental matters
gan.tropicalforests— Comprehensive information and what you can do about tropical forests
gan.wetlands — Comprehensive information and what you can do about wetlands
gan.wilderness — Comprehensive information and what you can do to about wilderness

Dolphin Net:
en.stranding — Records of marine mammal stranding incidents

institute for technology and development—tecnica:
tecnica — volunteer jobs and project updates in Nicaragua and Africa

Usenet - Academic/Industrial Conferencing Network: (All newgroups are representated.)

IGC makes Usenet newsgroups available as regular conferences. You do not have to run either the rn or the postnews programs to use the newsgroups.

Sample session follows:

ATDT1,3278146
DIAL TONE
1,3278146
CONNECT 1200

TELENET
805 17B

TERMINAL=d1
@c 408346 **"(This is IGC's telenet address)"***

408 346 CONNECTED

login: (? for help): bwilliams
Password: (? for help): xxxxxxx
Terminal = generic (hit <RETURN> or enter new terminal type):

Welcome to EcoNet II. For help, type " ?"
You have new conf entries in help netnews ideas ...

You have new mail messages

```
EcoNet commands: (c)onf  (h)elp  (m)ail  (s)etup  (u)sers (bye)
? c

Type '?' for list of commands, 'h' for help.
Conf? g en.alerts

visiting en.alerts...16 unread topics, 1 unread response
'u' to see next unread item, '?' for command summary, 'h' for more help
Conf? i
en.alerts

 2/26/90  1*Game Plan for Mount Graham    econet
 6/07/90  2*ATTACK: pub. hearing partic.: 5/7  econet
 6/17/90  3*Melbourne RAG - Timbersales    econet
 6/19/90  4*Burn Pits Closure MEETING    econet
 6/21/90  5*EF!Support Rally, 6/22, Oakland    econet
 7/01/90  6*Geothermal Plan and Hawaii's Rainfor  econet
 7/11/90  7*Call For EF! Bombing Investigation  1 econet
     8*MARINE MAMMAL PROTECTION ACT  econet
     9*ef!.general - Calendar and Events  econet
 7/24/90  10*Multinat'l Mining in N. Wisconsin  econet
 7/26/90  11*Sea Turtle Conservationists Attacke  econet
     12*From the Creators of Napalm    econet
 7/31/90  13*Hiroshima Day Calendar- Bay Area  econet
     14*Greek Activists Seek Int'l Support  econet
 8/02/90  15*Call for Support      econet
     16*Berkeley and Nuclear Waste Dereg.  econet

     **** End of Topics ****
Conf? 15
Topic 15    Call for Support
econet  en.alerts    1:12 pm  Aug  2, 1990

Subject: Call for Support

Anthony Whitworth, one of our very active Alaskan users,
has entered some text in explanation of the Senate Bill 1224
and is asking for general support.

Please see the item in the conference 'en.energy' named
 " Call for Support of S. Bill 1224"

Conf? q
EcoNet commands: (c)onf  (h)elp  (m)ail  (s)etup  (u)sers (bye)
? mail support
Subject: manual and CC

Hit <RETURN> to enter/edit a message, or 'u' to (u)pload a file:
Start entering text; hit <Return>.<Return> for help or when done:
Hi Support,
```

Could you send me the 2.4 manual please? And I would also like to have the doc, Creative Conferencing.

Thank you
Brian Williams

Hit <RETURN> to save/send text, 'e' to edit:

Cc:
Message sent.
Mail? **q**

EcoNet commands: (c)onf (h)elp (m)ail (s)etup (u)sers (bye)
? **bye**

49 pages worth of free mail storage left; see (h)elp command.
Goodbye! elapsed time DayHrsMinSec snd rcv
408 346 DISCONNECTED 00 00 00:00:35:58 1200 170

Help

There is online help available. It is menu driven and the screens are similar to the online manual.

Facilitation

The administration of the conferences is somewhat tedious. Anyone can enter a new topic, but new conferences have to be set up by the system adminstrators of the whole system based on data that conference coordinators supply.

Publications

IGC publishes a monthly newsletter for its users called *Netnews.*They have a manual that is well organized and easy to use.

Bibliography

Newton, James W. and Rohwedder, W.J. "Environmental Computer Networks." *E: The Environmental Magazine* 1(2):45-47; March/April 1990.

Phinney, David. "Econet: Environmental Bulletin Board." *Computerland Magazine* 5(3):21-22; March/April 1990

4.1.8 Metanet

Metasystems Design Group, Inc.
2000 North 15th Street, Suite 103
Arlington, VA 22201
(703) 243-6622

Brief Description

The Meta Network is the online support system for Caucus, among other things. Much of the command summary given in the Caucus section is taken from the Metanet system. They also sponsor and run the distance education conferencing system IRIS, a part of Metanet.

Hardware

Compaq Deskpro 386/20 with 5MB of 32 bit Memory Miniscribe 676MB ESDI Hard Disk w/Adaptec ESDI Controller Backup is on an Irwin 150MB QIC tape drive I/O is done with two Digiboard Com/8 serial cards for sixteen serial ports. Eight connected to dialup modems, three to terminals, five unused. One RB14 X.25 PAD w/NetCom II network management software provides two links to an X.25 network with thirty-two virtual circuits each. One link is currently accessed via the telenet PDN.

Software

Operating System is SCO Xenix System V/386 Release 2.3.1
Application Programs are Caucus Computer Conferencing Software for Conferencing and SCO Foxbase Plus for Database Management.

Communications Connections

UUCP and off system Mail handling via UUNET. Distributed Conferencing between Metanet and Pandora Systems' host in San Francisco. It also connected with distributed conferencing to the London Caucus in England, and TESS in Tokyo.

Conferencing Applications

The Meta Network is an online community for people interested in organizational change.

The Caucus Support and Development Network is for online support of Caucus licensees and product feedback from those licensees and interested parties.

Iris is a network for educators.

Private Conferences for groups and organizations are available.

Users

Metanet has about 1,000 user ids.

Costs

Conference:
Initial private conference setup fee $ 100
Monthly private conference maintenance fee $35

Individuals in your conference:
Initial registration fee for each individual $15
Monthly membership fee per individual $35

Access Charges

Local access is free, via CPN the cost is $6/hr.

Sample Logon

```
ATDT1,703,2439696
DIAL TONE
1,703,2439696
CONNECT 1200
u

tmn!login: bkwill
Password:

Last login on -=*> Sun Aug 12 00:23:42 1990 EST
Caucus (TM) version 2.3/SX. Copyright (C) 1988 Camber-Roth.

     ****************************
      ***     Welcome to     ***
     ***   THE META NETWORK   ***
     ****************************

Owned and Operated by:
   Metasystems Design Group, Inc.
   2000 North 15th Street, Suite 103
   Arlington, VA 22201
   703-243-6622
```

If you need assistance, type HELP and press <RETURN>.

JOIN WHICH CONFERENCE? (enter conference name or LIST) list

It should be noted that the following lists of conferences and conference topics are as of August 1990. They are meant to be suggestive of the kinds of things going on only, not an exact list of current conferences and topics.

amshelp	amsnet	demonstration	demos
dg	ena	ena89	guide
hermes_beta	hive	member_profiles	oldsalon
potomac	pr	salon	sci_med_aids
telelaw	test_links	test_twicstmn	user work

JOIN WHICH CONFERENCE? (enter conference name or LIST) oldsalon

SALON is the "FREEPORT" conference of The Meta Network. Everybody is allowed here, and we encourage everybody to join!
Do you wish to join this conference? y

(some text deleted)

AND NOW? (enter MENU, a command, or ? for help) l i all brief
Item 1 (997) Welcome to our SALON!
Item 2 (414) Please Introduce Yourself!
Item 3 (178) Electronic Democracy (continues ....)
Item 4 (369) The Public Electronic Network in Santa Monica
Item 5 (109) Further Packet Radio Adventures of Dave Hughes <and Anyone else
Item 6 (15) ENA f-t-f in May '89 - Call for Input for Nonprofit Networking
Item 7 (9) A Map of the Territory - Public Conferences Here
Item 8 (55) Internet Virus Running Amok!
Item 9 (2) English Journal Interview with Lisa Carlson - Global Networkin
Item 10 (301) Housekeeping - A Proposal for a New Way to Organize This Network
Item 11 (61) Sato Goes to Boston
Item 12 (65) What Would Nietzsche Say?
Item 13 (26) Networking Forum '89 - Japan - April 27-29, 1989
Item 14 (38) Ballot Initiatives - the other votes
Item 15 (6) Computer Professionals for Social Responsibility - Meeting Nov
Item 16 (87) How We Decide - Next Time ....
Item 17 (31) World Lenders Facing Pressure from Ecologists
Item 18 (82) John Kenneth Gailbraith on Leveraged Buyouts From Stupidity
Item 19 (129) Links to the Middle Kingdom?
Item 20 (55) Contrasts in a Capital
Item 21 (5) The Role of Sports in National Culture
Item 22 (218) YES Computer Learning Center Needs YOU!
Item 23 (66) Does the number 23 really *mean* anything?
Item 26 (44) John Draper in Russia - crossloaded from usenet
Item 27 (7) financial services networks
Item 28 (59) kickoff of Chautauqua Communications

Item 32 (11) Ultra-Light Lap Portable Computers
Item 33 (17) computer purchase
Item 34 (118) An Enlightened Military As a Key to No More Vietnams????
Item 35 (14) Executive - Savant Relationships
Item 36 (29) Computer-Integrated Agriculture
Item 38 (24) Byte Magazine Reviews Caucus & Other Groupware Products.
Item 39 (6) Research Analyst position, fulltime temporary, AIDS surveying
Item 40 (47) An Enlightened Public as a Key to No More Vietnams????
Item 41 (16) Electronic image scanning
Item 42 (18) Around the White House . . . .
Item 43 (21) education project at OTA
Item 45 (94) leadership is..... some thoughts....
Item 46 (25) Interactive National Talk Radio & Computer Communications
Item 47 (5) job hunt
Item 48 (33) Gorby's U.N. Speech
Item 49 (8) Dear Santa
Item 50 (79) help me figure this out. re aidsnet (aidsnyet?)
Item 51 (22) MDG in the Business Media
Item 52 (10) Finding a Fresh Christmas Tree
Item 53 (50) Was that two hundred... to four hundred... quarts?
Item 54 (15) The Dragons Tale - an update
Item 55 (21) communications connection problem
Item 56 (86) Helping Big Sky Telegraph Become an Economic Development Link
Item 57 (20) World watch state of the world 1989
Item 58 (3) consultant, desktop publishing, wanted
Item 59 (9) Running down Tamalpias
Item 60 (5) very tired questions
Item 61 (12) A Long Proposal from Harry Stevens on Interactive Telecom with
Item 62 (4) A Christmas Carol
Item 63 (21) Shumpei Kumon is coming to Meta Net
Item 65 (15) Montana Winter Wonderland
Item 66 (45) NHK • New Years • Japan
Item 67 (5) The Universal Message of Muppets
Item 68 (7) Electronic Glasnost
Item 69 (95) Van Gyi
Item 70 (38) DC's Mayor
Item 71 (3) For BB
Item 72 (35) The end of Showa era seems to coming, what do you think ...
Item 74 (89) OTA distance learning project
Item 75 (7) Four Days in Washington
Item 76 (125) IBIN • The International Business Issues Network • KPBS
Item 77 (29) Pacific Views - by Ray Alden
Item 78 (34) PET PEEVES
Item 79 (32) Message to a new president
Item 81 (67) EUROPE IN THE MAKING .... changes and opportunities.
Item 82 (7) The Business of Business is Learning
Item 83 (14) New Software: WP Menu & Watson
Item 84 (40) Poem on Mandelbrot, Fractals, Chaos, & Discovery by a Future
Item 85 (12) Zen conferencing
Item 86 (30) AHP Conferences
Item 87 (17) MacWEEK article on Susan Valdez and Technology Transfer

Item 89 (25) 5th Annual Space Symposium
Item 90 (14) NEW NAME NEWS
Item 91 (126) What is COMMUNITY? How and when is it important ONLINE?
Item 92 (20) Student Pugwash - Putting Values into Science and Technology
Item 93 (108) Electronic Educational Exchanges via BitNet
Item 95 (20) Happy Valentine's Day (belated)
Item 98 (1) CITIZEN ACTION
Item 99 (137) Satanic Verses
Item 100 (74) The Online Hotline
Item 101 (132) life 101 the adventure continues-an interactive journal
Item 102 (95) Santa Monica Gets Wired - From the *Front Page* of the LA TIME
Item 103 (2) UNIX seems to be catching on. . .
Item 104 (43) Bioethics - Body parts for sale?
Item 105 (397) Japan Talk (This item is now frozen and continued in item #323
Item 106 (33) The National Congress of Am. Indians letter on Investigation
Item 107 (25) An invitation to try CIGnet
Item 108 (22) caucus in mexico
Item 109 (56) Want to know how many calls have been made to The Meta Network
Item 110 (12) old salon?
Item 111 (10) Coach Thompson's Message to DC Youth on the Computer Learning
Item 112 (2) In search of a used car . . .
Item 113 (72) DC Computer Learning Centers Need You!!!
Item 114 (39) Name This Magazine! Name This Line of Books! A Contest....
Item 115 (122) Burma
Item 116 (1) Comments, please
Item 117 (55) Tower story
Item 118 (43) Demming and quality
Item 119 (45) USA-UK LINKS
Item 120 (32) ON LINE CONSULTING —TOTAL QUALITY MANAGEMENT
Item 121 (25) A Day on the Electronic Road in Colorado
Item 122 (4) UUCP Email Map of Japan (Intsructions on how to Get 97k long F
Item 123 (33) Thoughts against Khomeini
Item 124 (8) Gender-differentiated editions of novel — curiousity
Item 127 (66) conflict
Item 128 (40) Networking Forum '89 - The Online Symposium
Item 129 (84) Networking Forum '89 - Global Reports
Item 130 (28) TELECOMMUTING
Item 131 (72) Student Bloopers - A Mid-Week Pick Me Up!
Item 132 (15) Celebration in Colorado
Item 133 (11) Cyber Punk * Science Fiction * Jack In!
Item 134 (44) What If An Online Community Was A Living System?
Item 135 (6) TED2 Technology Entertainment Design Conference
Item 136 (67) Queries about the Caucus environment
Item 137 (8) a
Item 138 (16) a
Item 139 (26) Dry Bones
Item 140 (10) Visitors from Beyond the Fringe: NPR Meets MDG!
Item 141 (9) PROF BOB SHAYON'S SPEECH IN MONTANA TO BIG SKY'S INFOTECH CONF
Item 142 (20) Some Bumps in the Road to Paradise on Big Sky Telegraph

Item 143 (16) Colorado Musings with Uncle Dave...and a Ghost Town "High"
Item 144 (4) china connection
Item 145 (13) Prince William Sound Day - April 23, 1989
Item 146 (11) Groundwork - Grassroots community organizing across America
Item 148 (14) Takeshita/Recruit Scandal - How do the Japanese feel?
Item 149 (9) confort in a stressed out environment - or how do you slow dow
Item 150 (15) Cold Fusion: March 31, 1989 — Most Important Discovery of Our
Item 151 (95) Pro Choice March - Continuation of a thread begun in item #1
Item 152 (18) Is This Life in the Future?
Item 153 (1) David's Item
Item 154 (1) help on computer networking for training in the US
Item 155 (45) Training for school administrators in restructuring
Item 156 (19) Dave Hughes Story Revealed for the First Time: Read It and Aspire
Item 157 (15) Information Anxiety
Item 158 (15) News FLASH: Control Data Corp Exits the Supercomputer Business
Item 159 (3) Laos and networking
Item 160 (11) electronic networking: Israel & Istanbul?
Item 162 (19) Deleting and Resurrecting an item.. should the reader be told
Item 163 (10) OPEN FORUM on Petition Rights
Item 164 (3) Introducing the Next Mayor of DC - Sharon Pratt Dixon!
Item 165 (21) Waiting for North
Item 167 (14) Endings and New Beginnings
Item 169 (27) Some Observations about Japan
Item 170 (7) USA GO May Article and Kickoff Letter Coincide
Item 171 (3) Latest in Supercom't Graphics: 3D Tour Through the Living Brai
Item 173 (20) HELLO FROM OHSU
Item 174 (159) Rogue Bureaucracy Revisited
Item 175 (6) QUESTIONS
Item 176 (3) CC Technology Transfer Investment Fund: Whacko Idea Goes Spla
Item 177 (19) War of 1812 Marker in Takoma Park
Item 179 (12) YOUR CHANCE TO INFLUENCE CONGRESS RE: COMPUTER CRIME
Item 180 (27) PeaceNet/EcoNet
Item 181 (27) War and Rememberance — Brutal TV — Should We Be Allowed to F
Item 182 (5) A View of Network Society by Shumpei Kumon (full text = 30K)
Item 183 (5) Helpful Caucus Hints
Item 184 (14) Total Isolation?
Item 185 (179) DIRECT FROM CHINA
Item 187 (17) A Territory Day
Item 188 (163) June 21st Russian American Space Bridge (please Port FREELY)
Item 189 (7) Of Hands and Hormones
Item 193 (9) International Community Economic Dev'l - A little help for a f
Item 194 (86) Summer trip of Aizu Family to U.S.
Item 196 (14) Participate in a Global Workshop: Now through June 21st
Item 197 (8) ANTERIOR NETWORK (input to item #10)
Item 198 (6) Help! BITNET Access.
Item 199 (14) WHOLE EARTH REVIEW on Caucus...
Item 200 (14) GLOBAL COMMUNCIATION?
Item 201 (9) ANY JOB OPPORTUNITIES FOR ME OUT THERE?
Item 202 (3) New Jersey and You: Imperfect, Not Together

Item 204 (17) HELLO!!
Item 206 (22) JoJo tests the trees
Item 208 (29) Plan for a Voice-to-Text Transcription Service
Item 209 (1) A Washington Post Indian Advocate Dies - and Lives
Item 211 (25) LONESOME NO MORE! - Taking Vonnegut Seriously
Item 212 (1) PC-LINK
Item 213 (30) Welcome to Soviet and American Youth Ambassadors - Global Work
Item 214 (4) MAJOR JOB FAIR - 50 FEDERAL AGENCIES - DIRECT HIRE
Item 215 (12) Links to Russia: Russian Response and Wither Do we Go from Here
Item 222 (2) Awakening Technology's Summer Program
Item 223 (82) A plea for information on the USA College system
Item 224 (55) Compuserve Buys Out and Will Close Down the Source
Item 225 (7) Has Artificial Intelligence (AI) been around for (at least) 40
Item 226 (33) Nanotechnology: Is anyone else interested in the subject?
Item 227 (0) HOME AND GARDEN TO SHARE
Item 228 (41) HOW FAR HAS CONFERENCING COME IN THE LAST TEN YEARS?
Item 229 (0) The Micro Trach, New Treatment for Lung Diseases
Item 230 (12) San Francisco Moscow Teleport Online
Item 232 (29) AFTER THE STORM - IN CHINA
Item 233 (34) OPPORTUNITY - World Future Society General Assembly
Item 234 (14) Computer Conferencing and "Oral History"
Item 235 (6) WFS Report - Biosphere opening session
Item 236 (8) WFS Report - (Biosphere) - Lifestyles and Energy Consumption
Item 237 (67) Family Conferencing
Item 238 (62) "Virtual Relationships" vs the Old Kind
Item 239 (12) Switzerland is ready for CC. Can you help?
Item 240 (23) "Houston, this is Tranquility Base. The Eagle has landed."
Item 241 (0) WFS Report: Strategic Planning (Futurists) and Congress
Item 242 (5) *** PARENTS NEED HELP URGENTLY - PLEASE PORT ***
Item 243 (15) First World Electronic Media Symposium & Exhibition in Geneva
Item 244 (21) Request for Speaker Suggestions: Council on Foundations Annua
Item 245 (49) Announcing CompuServe Access CHANGES
Item 246 (8) MURPHY'S LAWS OF COMBAT
Item 247 (19) Computer Conferencing: Socialization Toy or Business Tool?
Item 248 (39) Whither BBS/CC Connections in the 90s?
Item 249 (12) AT&T now freed by Judge Green to get into Information Business
Item 252 (2) Computer Conferencing and Oral History
Item 253 (4) Computer Conferencing/Networking for Small Groups
Item 254 (60) Seth's Report on the World Future Society Assembly
Item 255 (14) Computer Conferencing and Linguistic Revival
Item 256 (19) CC Demonstrations at f-t-f meetings
Item 257 (11) Computer Conferencing and Linguistic Revival
Item 258 (4) ELEGY FOR AN ELECTRONIC PASSING
Item 259 (5) Mickey Leland
Item 260 (23) Houston, this is Tranquility Base. The Eagle has landed.
Item 261 (10) Watching the Lunar Eclipse — and Thinking about it.
Item 262 (7) Independent Book Publishing
Item 263 (12) Caucus to Support European Business and Languages Learning Pro
Item 264 (6) Flexa-place bill for federal employees

Item 265 (10) The Bad/Good Face of Computer Communications
Item 267 (39) Cadets Online
Item 268 (84) "How I Spent My Summer Vacation in China" !!
Item 269 (87) Military intervention in Columbia? A "drug-free world-place!"
Item 270 (7) Say "No" to Negativity
Item 271 (52) What are the causes of drug abuse in America?
Item 272 (31) The Television Debate
Item 273 (16) Henri's
Item 274 (13) The Dolphin Network and what should we do about tuna fishing
Item 275 (6) Legalize Drugs?
Item 276 (5) looking for mr goodbar -err- Dr. Waggoner
Item 277 (8) ALCNet - deciding on a host system...
Item 279 (119) The Great Distance Learning Experiment
Item 281 (10) Learning about Learning Communities
Item 282 (12) Weather * Lessons from Mother Nature
Item 283 (33) Takehito Imai Coming to the U.S.
Item 284 (4) Call for help on learning abut CN
Item 285 (23) Clifford Stoll's The Cuckoo's Egg. Shocking New Book on Comp.
Item 286 (28) ABC's Coverage of the Education Summit
Item 287 (19) IRIS - an Online Network for Teachers and Schools
Item 288 (54) Computers in Education - is it time for the revolution?
Item 289 (7) request for informatin about China demonstration in DC
Item 290 (3) Personal Computing's 4th Annual Computing in America Issue
Item 291 (11) Recycling
Item 292 (11) Wanted: Telecom Literate, New Jersey, High School Math curriculum
Item 293 (22) Capital Online: New Caucus-based Online Service for DC
Item 294 (5) Oat Bran with Fish Oil?
Item 295 (41) welcome back meta
Item 296 (25) Pacific Bell cancels its videotex gateway trial
Item 297 (8) Clifford Stoll's The Cuckoo's Egg. Shocking New Book on Comp.
Item 298 (18) NY Tel Strike GOING STRONG!
Item 299 (12) Reflections on "The Great Distance Learning Experiment"
Item 300 (9) PROHIBITION TWO
Item 301 (42) A Turtle, Orizuru, and the Wedding Ring
Item 302 (26) Is the von Neumann Supercomputer Center Dead? Long live the Ne
Item 303 (78) The Great San Francisco Earth Quake of 1989.
Item 304 (46) Brain Toy
Item 305 (3) online publications
Item 309 (8) Anyone for Golf? (formerly Item 306)
Item 310 (3) Big Sky News Bulletin
Item 311 (17) Grassroots Activist Network
Item 312 (29) New business opportunity in U.S. Need your help.
Item 313 (62) Great Distance Learning Experiment (part 2) Worth Every kilobyte
Item 314 (71) Shortest Rogue Bureaucracy (six lines)
Item 316 (54) Opportunity To Participate in Global Networking "Vision" Proje
Item 318 (12) Full Text of Rogue Bureaucracy, 11/14/89
Item 319 (7) SAVE IKEGO!! The forest is still alive but in danger...
Item 320 (18) Where Have All the People Gone?
Item 321 (6) The Next 'Great Crime?'
Item 322 (26) Puzzles and imagination

Item 323 (107) Current Japan Talk
Item 324 (34) Big Grant for Big Sky
Item 325 (2) Congressional Study
Item 326 (0) New Decade/Millenium Celebrations!!
Item 328 (4) Three things MDG has been up to
Item 329 (22) Dream about a Great Telecom Service...
Item 330 (6) The Last Word
Item 331 (5) New Info
Item 332 (13) Juanita Stiles needs to sell Bob's computer equipment

The conferencing, editing, and mail commands are those of the Caucus section.

4.1.9 LITA: MicroUsers

Tom Wilson
Library
University of Houston
Houston, TX 77204.
(713) 749-4300

Brief Description

LITA: MicroUsers is a conference sponsored by LITA (Library and Technology Association) a subgroup of the American Library Association (ALA). It uses Confer at the University of Michigan. Users must be a member of LITA. You can register for the conference by sending a request to Tom Wilson at the Library of the University of Houston, Houston, Texas 77204, phone (713) 749-4300. Payment for the use of the conference is done in advance directly to the University of Michigan's Computer Center (Information Technology Division, Resource Administration). The user is responsible for monitoring the remaining balance in the user account.

Access

LITA: MicroUsers can be reached either by Sprintnet, via the Internet, or any of the paths to reach the Merit Network. The conference is on the system by reaching the hermes.merit.edu internet address. To reach the conference via Sprintnet (telenet), the address is C 31362.

Costs

Costs are billed against your account at rates that depend on the time of day and type of service. In general it varies from $5/hr at nonprime time to about $15/hr primetime.

Sample Session

```
SLONET >connect hermes.merit.edu
 Connecting ...
 Trying Address 35.1.48.149 (35.1.48.149 0.23) Success.

%Merit:Hermes (CCB04E:TN07:VT100:EDIT=MTS)

Which Host?um
%TN07:CCB04E-AY44:UM19

  MTS Ann Arbor          (Host=UM Task=525 Dev=AY19)
#sig sxte
#Enter password.
?
#Charging Rate: Terminal,Low,Non-Univ,UM,IBM 3090-600E
#Last signon was at 19:08:33, Wed May 15/91
#User SXTE signed on at 19:54:05, Wed May 15/91
#REMINDER:  You should change your password to something
# other than that set by the Computing Center or your
# project manager.
#
#To change your password enter $SET PW and follow the instructions.

#Information on system problems: $Copy NEWS:SYS.DOWN (Updated 4:00pm
14May)
#so lita:microusers
#$Run CNFR:Confer t=5 par=LITA:MicroUsers
#Execution begins   19:54:38

 Confer II (08/89) - designed by Robert Parnes
 Copyright & Trademark: Advertel Communication Systems

  Free Confer II Lecture/Demo in Auditorium 3 of MLB.
  Mon. May 20 6:30-8-00 pm.


                         LITA:MicroUsers

               An Online Computer Conference for the
             Library and Information Technology Association
             Microcomputer Users Interest Group Organizers

             Elizabeth Lane, Jane Sessa, & Thomas C. Wilson
                         LITA:MICROUSERS

 Type MENU for help
 DO NEXT?  q
 On May15/91 LITA:MicroUsers has
      34 items, and
```

```
     17 participants.
Since Oct28/88 there have been
    672 uses which have lasted
   2351 minutes total.
There have been
     88 messages sent,
    550 items displayed,
    145 responses made,
    630 sets of responses seen, and
   2393 DO NEXT? commands issued.

LITA:MICROUSERS
Type MENU for help
DO NEXT?  quit
You are leaving LITA:MicroUsers.  Thank you for visiting with us!

                Come back again soon.

#SXTE 19:54:05 to 19:55:16 Wed May 15/91
#     $.22
#   $71.77
#     $.04
%TN07:CCB04E-AY44:UM19 SXTE Connection closed
```

A List of all the Items on the Conference-

```
Item 8    22:17 Mar27/89    4 lines    7 responses
Thomas C. Wilson
Micro Maintenance

Item 10   16:10 Jun20/89    6 lines   20 responses
Steve Cisler
Internet access to resources

Item 11   10:58 Jun26/89    3 lines   11 responses
Thomas C. Wilson
Public Access Micro Management

Item 12   17:32 Jul06/89    3 lines    1 response
Thomas C. Wilson
Standard Interfaces

Item 13   23:01 Jul09/89   10 lines    2 responses
Steve Cisler
Elec. Networking Assn. conference

Item 14   12:32 Jul11/89    4 lines    6 responses
Thomas C. Wilson           Prime=9
Dallas Review
```

Item 15 11:52 Jul26/89 64 lines 5 responses
Steve Cisler
The Matrix (book review)

Item 16 21:31 Aug08/89 6 lines 14 responses
Elizabeth Lane
CD-ROM Feedback

Item 17 22:11 Nov26/89 12 lines 5 responses
Thomas C. Wilson
Computer Searching Managers

Item 19 14:38 Apr02/90 11 lines No responses
Frank Freeman
Microcomputer-based integrated library systems

Item 21 08:36 Jun06/90 5 lines No responses
Thomas C. Wilson
CD-ROM Networking Info

Item 22 07:22 Jun13/90 3 lines No responses
Thomas C. Wilson
Management Info

Item 23 07:24 Jun13/90 5 lines 4 responses
Thomas C. Wilson
Searching Stats

Item 24 07:30 Jun13/90 2 lines No responses
Thomas C. Wilson
Token Ring Diagnostics

Item 25 07:34 Jun13/90 8 lines No responses
Thomas C. Wilson
External Info Need

Item 26 07:38 Jun13/90 5 lines 2 responses
Thomas C. Wilson
E-Mail Use

Item 27 07:45 Jun13/90 2 lines No responses
Thomas C. Wilson
Chaos Theory

Item 28 11:15 Jun15/90 10 lines 2 responses
Thomas Dowling
PC Repair/Maintenace/Purchase Policies

Item 29 11:41 Jun21/90 8 lines 1 response
Thomas Dowling Prime=17
Ready Reference Online Searches vs. $$$

Item 30 15:48 Jul19/90 9 lines No responses
Thomas Dowling
Amiga?

Item 31 20:24 Sep16/90 115 lines No responses
Thomas C. Wilson
Microcomputer Users Interest Group Official Annual Meeting Minutes

Item 32 20:27 Sep16/90 4 lines 2 responses
Thomas C. Wilson
Account Troubles

Item 33 10:52 Dec21/90 2 lines 4 responses
Thomas C. Wilson
Suggestions for MUIG Midwinter

Item 34 12:35 Feb15/91 7 lines No responses
Thomas Dowling
UNIX Hypermedia?

Sample Conference Item -

Item 11 10:58 Jun26/89 3 lines 11 responses
Thomas C. Wilson
Public Access Micro Management

I am interested in discussing issues dealing with management of public access micros particularing CD-ROM workstations. We have had a great demand for these resources. How are others dealing with this challenge?

11 responses
Jun29/89 17:14
11:1) Steve Cisler: At Apple Library we just have one station for Books in Print. We used to order books for the whole company, and now we are turning that over to individual departments. We don't know if they will want to buy their own copies of BIP, call us for info <not our goal>, or go online for the latest info. We hope to add other drives for certain titles and have empty drives to try archive discs. We are archiving both internally produced titles and commercial ones. Interest is growing in the medium, but we don't have a lot of room in our building.

In addition, we will be mounting certain discs on the Ethertalk network.
Steve
- - - - -
Aug01/89 17:07
11:2) Thomas Dowling: IIT is in the process of going from no CD-ROM products to three (Science Citation Index, ABI/Inform, and a census product from GPO), with plans to add Compendex this fall. Trouble is, we've only got one CD-ROM drive, and that's a loaner. To what extent have others been successful in dividing the time of one workstation among several databases?
- - - - -

Aug02/89 17:56
11:3) Thomas C. Wilson: We have three products dedicated and eight running on "pool" machines. This has been working reasonably well for a year. We created packets that hold the discs and the locally developed documentation for each of the "pool" products. I wrote a program that recognizes what discs is in the CD drive and loads the appropriate software and manages a statistical count of the product use. I think that this arrangement is a cost effective alternative to networking. While we are limited to one user at a time, at least we are able to offer multiple products without one per machine.

- - - - -

Aug08/89 17:26
11:4) Thomas Dowling: Sounds like a good system, Tom. Any chance you could send me a copy of that program? I know that some systems, SCI particularly crash when the wrong disk is in the drive.

- - - - -

Aug08/89 21:29
11:5) Elizabeth Lane: I'm impressed. You ought to consider distributing that little program as shareware. (I'd suggest commercial, but that seems so callous.) There's a very good library bbs here in DC which I'm sure would *love* to have it. What was it written in? Details, please!

- - - - -

Aug18/89 09:34
11:6) Thomas Dowling: Liz, what's the number of that BBS?

- - - - -

Sep06/89 08:32
11:7) Thomas C. Wilson: Turn on party line—I'm not sure how our university handles distribution of home-grown software; I do know that some has been marketed through other concerns. I will find out in a timely fashion and notify y'all. —Turn off party line. :) The program, CD-Manager, has passed a rather rigorous 6 months of use in our library...it seems to have held its own. It is written in Quick Basic, a compiled Basic, primarily because the language was available and I wrote an early version of the program in it. My plans have included porting it over to Pascal, but other projects have taken priority. I would like to make some modifications so that it would be more useful to other libraries. More to come...!

- - - - -

Sep10/89 19:20
11:8) Elizabeth Lane: Thomas D. — that BBS is ALIX, the Automated Library Information eXchange, and it's run by Fedlink at the Library of Congress. Although the focus is Federal libraries and librarians, the information there is excellent and spans a broad range of non-Federal concerns. The number is (202) 707-9656.

- - - - -

Oct20/89 16:10
11:9) Linda Benedict: I have some *beginner* questions? Are all CD-ROM databases compatible with all drives? e.g. Can BIP+ or LePac be read by any drive? Does anyone know a source for a MS-DOS micrc with 4 internal CD-ROM drives (for public access)? Are there problems accessing several discs from one micro? No networking being considered here.

- - - - -

Oct21/89 00:53
11:10) Craig Summerhill: There are alot of questions there...

No, not all CD-ROMS can be read by all drives. Although most CD manufacturers have settled on the High Sierra standard, there are still alot of products out there that have their own interface. The proprietary interface tends to enhance the software product's sales.

It is possible to access more than one disc from a single PC, however it does present some problems. One solution is daisy chaining the CD-ROM drives, but this tends to slow response time (and generally only works for a single product on multiple discs).

Don't feel too left out. You're asking the same questions alot of us are, and I'm not sure any of us are getting good answers.

Nov26/89 22:00
11:11) Thomas C. Wilson: Another issue to consider is what the particular vendor software you have supports...some do allow daisey chaining or networking, but not all. That is really a design issue and most vendors are willing to say whether or not their products run in a particular fashion.

}iI second Craig's comment about not all products working on all drives. Although this is becoming less of a problem than it was in the past, it still warrants our concern. What I have noticed lately is that some vendors want us to use a newer drive (we use Hitachi 1503s) because performance has improved, but the tradeoff is that not as many products have been tested on the newer drives. That will continue to be an issue, I'm sure. The two standards I'm most concerned about are the High Sierra (ISO 9660) Craig mentioned and the Microsoft CD-ROM extensions that allow DOS to address CD-ROM drives.

On the issue of how many drives you may physically put into a micro... that depends on the bay size of the PC you are using. In a standard desktop unit there are usually two to four bays. If you have one floppy drive and one hard drive, that limits your space. However, if you have a hard drive on a card, that would free up a bay. Or if you have an AT style case, there are more bays. I have seen configurations that have four internal CD-ROM drives in the case.

RESPOND, FORGET, OR PASS: p

Special Features

There are other conferences on the University of Michigan system that can be accessed once you have an account to logon to LITA: MicroUsers. The sample logon below shows a list of the other conferences available.

LITA:MICROUSERS
Type MENU for help
DO NEXT? view cnfr:conferences
This file contains a list with a brief description of many of the computer conferences using CONFER that are open to general participation. To join one of them enter the MTS command $SOURCE followed by the name of the conference. E.g.,
$SOURCE CRLT:ORGANIZER
There are many other computer conferences using CONFER that are restricted in their membership.

For more information call Bob Parnes, (313) 665-2612

USER:OpenForum - John Dorsey, organizer
A general-purpose conference in which the participants kick around broad-ranging topics such as music, books, war, religion, death; even computers if it's interesting. Think of it as a cocktail party, only with more intelligent discourse and no drunks.

-

CRLT:MICROS - Karl Zinn and Gordon Leacock, organizers
For a statewide discussion of the role of microprocessor based computer systems in education. To link up various people interested in the future of microcomputers.

-

WORD:Processing - Michael Lougee and Mark Weishan, organizers
WORD:Processing serves as an on-line users group for U-M users of the text processors FinalWord II and Microsoft Word. In addition, it discusses more general text processing issues such as other word processors, typesetting, telecommunication of text, etc. It is open to anyone interested in text processing in the academic environment.

-

TEX:FORUM - Co-organizers Kari Gluski and Hal Varian.
TEX:FORUM is a conference for the users of TeX, a complex and powerful text-processing and typesetting language. The conference is intended to present news about TeX, help users solve problems, and guide further development of TeX at U-M.

-

C:FORUM - Dave Snyder, organizer.
The primary topic of discussion of this conference will be the C programming language and library support. In particular there will be discussion of planned improvements to MTS and Computing Center programs such as *CBELL which will make it easier to transport C programs from UNIX environments to the MTS environment and which will create a good C development system on MTS.

-

PC2:!CONF - Dave Koziol and Mike Kuniavsky, organizers
PC2:!CONF is a conference devoted to public domain and user-supported ("Freeware") software for the Macintosh series computers. Most of the items relate to the software packages available for downloading from the PC2 ccid.

-

PC:KERMIT.CONF - Richard Conto, organizer.
To provide help, share experiences, and provide a documentation place for us-

ing the various Kermit file transfer programs on Mainframes (MTS and others), Minis, and Microcomputers. The Kermit programs allow transfer of files (text and data) from one computer to another, over Telenet or the telephone. All are welcome, novices and experienced alike, since answering questions of novices in a public place is a good method for documenting a service.

-

PC1:!CONF - Allan Bjorklund and Sarah Gray, Organizers.
This conference is dedicated to the discussion of public domain and user supported (Shareware/Freeware) software for the IBM PC and its compatibles. The software being discussed is available for copying
from PC1 and/or Terminator. The conference is cloned on UB, so that more information-exchanging will take place.

-

OSAS:Info — Cliff Allo, organizer.
OSAS:Info is sponsored by the Office of Substance Abuse Services in the Michigan Department of Public Health. OSAS is responsible for alcohol and other drug treatment and prevention services in Michigan. The conference will list grant opportunities of which OSAS is aware, provide opportunities to seek and to provide technical assistance, and provide a forum to discuss issues arising out of alcohol and other drug use, abuse, treatment, and prevention. While intended for professionals in the field, other scholars, and interested persons are more than welcome. In keeping with the strong tradition of confidentiality in alcohol and other drug abuse
treatment, pseudonymous responses are permitted.

-

REMC:FORUM - Tom Switzer, Jack Keck, David Frankel, and Mike Waggoner organizers
REMC:FORUM is a public computer CONFERence dedicated to discussion of issues and problems in education and to the general exchange of information among educators. It has been organized specifically for Michigan, but anyone who feels that they may benefit from participation is welcome to join. All topics are encouraged: from early childhood through K-12 to higher education and adult and continuing education. This venture is a collaborative effort of the University of Michigan, School of Education and the Michigan Regional Education Media Centers.

-

DBMS:DBMS - Larry Kostecke, organizer.
Participants discuss all kinds of DBMSs: relational,
hierarchical, network, flat, numeric, bibliographic, textual, graphical. Also personal-filers, meta-machines, query
interfaces, natural-language queries, and data-entry interfaces. Participants discuss experiences with specific products and try to understand where they are especially useful and where they are not. The hardware they use includes micros, minis, and maxis. Participants are database users, designers, managers, and researchers.

-

CRLT:EDMICROS - Bob Kozma, organizer.
EdMicros was started to give those interested in the educational application of computers a dedicated forum for discussing their concerns and interests.

-

STAT:FORUM - Daniel Fox, organizer.
Will focus on statistical problems of general interest, including data analysis and statistical computing. Possible topics include general statistical problems (e.g., multiple comparisons), statistical software, techniques of data manipulation, and statistical computation.

-

MICH:GIFTED Nancy Mincemoyer and Scott Satterlund, organizers
This conference is designed to facilitate communications between any individuals (educators, parents, students or others) interested in the education of gifted and talented students. Topics include: updates, meeting dates, mentornet for students, job opportunities, program inquiries and others.

-

USER:NETWORKS — Ron Loveless and Andy Palms, organizers
This is a forum for anyone interested in computer networks. The scope of the conference is broad and is intended to cover all aspects of networking from local area networks with
microcomputers to wide area or packet switching networks. The
conference is intended to teach novices about the basics as well as allowing the "experts" a place to share ideas and new
technologies. If you have questions about networks, this may be the best forum for answers.

-

WING:SPAN — Sarah Gray and Joyce French, organizers
WING:SPAN is a continuing dialogue among women and men,
people of all colors and sexual orientations on issues and ideas of importance to women. Please join us and let us hear your voice too! WING:Span is a clone of the UB conference and is funded by the Affirmative Action Office and ITD.

-

CRLT:MAC.Notes - Mike Gallatin and David Allan, organizers.
All aspects of the Apple Macintosh computer, ranging from very technical matters to questions raised by first-time users. There's a clone conference on UB with the same name.

Mail

Confer has a mail facility built-in along with the conferencing. Users also have use of the mail system that is provided by University of Michigan with their LITA: MicroUsers account. The University of Michigan mail system gives users access to Internet listservs and such.

Publications

Parnes, Robert and Berstein, Maya A. *The Beginner's Guide to Confer II.* Ann Arbor, Mich; Advertel Communication Systems: 1988.

4.1.10 PEN

Ken Phillips
City of Santa Monica
Director, Information Systems Department
1685 Main Street
Santa Monica, CA 90401
(213) 458-8381 (voice)
(213) 394-2962 (fax)
tmn!philips (Internet address)

The City of Santa Monica, California, launched the Public Electronic Network (PEN) in February 1989 by distributing free user accounts to residents who register with the city. These accounts can be used from one's home or work terminal or any one of the dozens of public terminals in libraries, schools, and city buildings. PEN's services include electronic bulletin boards of city information, electronic mail for sending messages to and from city hall, or other residents, and computer conferences. The city's computer network also provides dial-up access to the library's card catalog. The key objectives are:

1. To provide easy electronic access to public information for use by city residents.

2. To provide an alternative means of communication for residents to convey their needs, preferences, and intentions to their local government and to other residents.

3. To enhance delivery and awareness of public services available to residents, and to facilitate the public serives inquiry process.

4. To provide an electronic forum for participation in discussions of issues and concerns of residents in order to promote an enhanced sense of community.

5. To extend to all members of the community the opportunity to understand computer technology, and to provide access to the hardware and software needed to learn to communicate via an electronic network.

Citizens can participate in three ways:
1) read-only boards posting city information
2) private e-mail between citizens or between citizens and city hall
3) public postings in any of six teleconferences

Topics addressed in these public conferences span a wide range of issues. Popular conferences include the following:

Crimewatch run by the police department

PENhelp online hints on how to use the system
Planning a forum about land use, zoning, and development
Environment incorporating discussions of air quality, water pollution, and recycling
Santa Monica including rent control, neighborhood organizing, community events, and news of boards and commissions

Social issues are discussed in several additional conferences. Topics include: nuclear weapons, drinking and driving, the media, abortion (currently the most popular item), gun control, foreign policy, health, intergroup relations, Jewish culture, AIDS, human rights, sexism, and racism.

In the first year PEN signed on over 2,000 residents and was accessed over 52,000 times.

Hardware

It requires a Hewlett-Packard host computer, series 9000 model 840, 52MBs of CPU memory, and1,200MBs of disk memory

Number of incoming ports and baud rates are thirty-two modems (for public dial-ins) at 3/12/2400-baud and fifteen publicly accessible terminals.

Software

PEN uses Caucus for conferencing and e-mail, HP's Allbase for large, searchable files, and a menu system written in-house.

Costs

Access is free to Santa Monica residents. Residents dial in from home and terminals are located throughout the city, in the library, etc.

Number of users is currently around 2,600.

Mail

Mail is Caucus mail.

4.1.11 Portal

Portal Communications Company
10385 Cherry Tree Lane
Cupertino, CA 95014

(408) 973-9111 (voice)
(408) 725-0561 (data) or C PORTAL (SprintNet/Telenet)
(408) 725-1580 (fax)
CS@cup.portal.com (Internet address)

Hardware

A network of various SUN 4s or SUN OS 4.1 are required.

Number of incoming ports and bauds:

32 x 300/1200/2400
2 x 9600/19200
This does not include network access.

Software

Proprietary

Service began in 1987
The number of users is undisclosed.

Costs

Account startup (usual) $19.95
Monthly use $10 (Flat fee)
Storage (disk) charge $0.04/k/month *

Telenet access charges as of October 1988

Type	Peak	Off-Peak
A-type	$5.50/hour	$2.50/hour
B-type	$10.00/hour	$2.50/hour
C-type	$15.50/hour	$2.50/hour

*You are not charged for the first 100K of storage. This is based on an average daily balance.

Private Conferences

Private conferences are available, starting at $100 per month

Gateways

Internet, Bitnet/CREN, UUCP, FIDO, and more

Sample Logon

TELENET
805 17A

TERMINAL=d1

@c portal

PORTAL CONNECTED
Portal on-line. One moment, please.
Communications charges will be billed to your Portal account.

Welcome to the PORTAL* Online Communications Service, Version 11.21
Copyright (c) 1986 - 1989 by Portal Communications Company
All rights reserved. Use: 8 bits, No parity, 1 stop bit

* PORTAL is a service mark of Portal Communications Company.

Enter name, NEW, INFO, or HELP: brian k williams
Enter password:

*** New hardware installed - type "Go HARDWARE" for details ***

INFO - System Info, Special Interest Group Announcements and Schedules.
"Go GLANCE" for Portal Activities at a Glance.

RADIO - GO
*PIRATES*PIRATES*PIRATES*PIRATES*PIRATES*PIRATES*PIRATES

WAR - For hourly UPI updates on the Kuwait invasion subscribe to Clarinet.
Type "go war" for details.

** Tuesday's Activities **

- 10 PM ET - PANDEMONIUM In The Hot Tub With Jeepster And Susie In Meetings!

—— ——

Remember, this is an open system where you are responsible for what you say and how you use it. Please report problems to "Customer Service."
Portal Communications 10385 Cherry Tree Lane Cupertino CA 95014 408/973-9111
Press <RETURN> to continue
Main menu mail
/
1.5
——-

0 - Home [directory]
1 - Using Portal [directory]
2 - Portal Activities at a Glance [directory]
3 - Organizations [directory]
4 - Computer Groups [directory]
5 - Gateways [directory]
6 - Meetings [directory]
7 - Services [directory]
8 - Special Interest Groups (SIGs) [directory]
———

List of Conferences

Over 1,200 topics on the international Usenet, plus exclusive Portal SIGs covering science, radio, arts, lifestyles, computers, and more.

Command Examples

Help/Beginner
Lines 1 to 87 of 87 (100%)
———
0 - Places to 1 - Examples
———

Beginner's Information

Welcome to Portal! This help file will give you the basic information you need to use Portal. There are also several additional topics that give you more detailed information about specific parts of the system.

If you don't know how to use the help system, please type 'help help' for details.

Forms

All of your interactions with Portal are through forms. Forms are the standard screen display that we use to display information, read data, and execute commands. The help information you are now reading is displayed on a form.

Forms are divided into three parts. The top, or headers, display information about where you are. The middle is where we display and read information. It can contain a menu of choices, fill in the blank fields to be completed, or text. The bottom, or command area, contains a list of the commands that you can use and a place to enter them. Individual forms will vary, but they all share this basic structure.

Commands

Commands are entered at the "Command:" prompt. The commands that you can use are listed at the bottom of your screen. Some commands are used throughout the system, while others are only used in some areas.

Portal will only recognize your commands if you enter them at the "Command:" prompt. To move the cursor there, type <CONTROL-C>.

Getting Someplace

Portal is a multilevel, menu based system. The highest level is called the "top" and contains about ten different items. These ten items are the second level. Second level items can contain third level items, and so on. The levels are organized around topics, so you move from general high level items to specific low level ones.

At each level, you are shown a menu of your choices. This is a numbered list of places to go. Going someplace is easy — just enter its number from the menu at the "Command:" prompt. To move back to where you were, enter 'done.' If you get lost and want to return to the top of the system, just type 'top.' These three commands will let you navigate throughout most of the Portal system.

Entering Information

In some parts of the system, you will have to enter information. For example, to send a letter, you have to enter the name of the addressee, the subject of the letter, and the text. This information is entered into fields, which appear in the middle of your form.

All fields work the same way. You type your information, then press <RETURN> to move to the next field. When you have completed the last field, the <RETURN> will move you to the "Command:" prompt. As explained above, <CONTROL-C> will move you to the command prompt at any time.

After you have completed the fields, there are three basic commands that you should know. The first, 'ok,' means that you correctly entered the information and wish to proceed to the next step. The second, 'try_again,' means that you made a mistake and want another chance to enter your information. The third, 'quit,' means that you want to quit without doing anything. These three commands work anyplace where you are entering information.

Special Commands and Characters

There are a few additional commands that will make using Portal easier. Also, we use some special characters to do useful things.

The 'page forward' command (abbreviated 'p f') will display the next page of information. Note that in most cases, <RETURN> will do the same things.

The 'page back' command (abbreviated 'p b') will display the previous page of information.

The 'logout' command logs you off, no matter where you are in the system. If you are in the middle of doing something, it stops whatever you were doing.

The <BACKSPACE> character erases the character to the left of the cursor.

The <CONTROL-L> character redraws the screen. This is useful if your screen has been garbled by a communication error.

Here is the partial list of "go" comand locations:

pals	new user orientation
usenet	all usenet groups
upi	UPI news feed
apple	Apple II SIG
tandy	Tandy/Radio Shack SIG
ibmsig	IBM SIG
writers	Writers' Forum
getters	Entrepreneurs' SIG
chat	real-time meetings
games	general games area
pirates	clandestine radio broadcasting
cryonics	Alcor Cryonics SIG
uucp	information on the Portal UUCP Connection

Mail

Unlimited connections to most public and corporate mail networks, including Internet, Bitnet/CREN, UUCP, MCIMail, Compuserve, etc.

Special Features

Large Usenet archives, online meetings, large computer SIG file libraries, Clarinet (UPI, Newsbytes, etc), UUCP connections. The UUCP connection allows another UNIX site to exchange mail and files with Portal and thus, with the Internet and other networks that Portal is connected to.

Help Available

Help available for every location and command.

Publications

"Portal's Guide to Using the Usenet."

Bibliography

Lytel, David. "Portal: Silicon Valley's Best and Brightest." *Link-UP*: 23; Sept./ Oct. 1987.

Swartz, Joh. "Portal's global strategy for on-line market." *MacWEEK*:13; Oct. 27, 1987.

4.1.12 TRIE

Technology Resources In Education Electronic Information Service
California Technology Project (CTP)
P.O. Box 3842
Seal Beach, CA 90740-7842
(800) 272-TRIE (voice)
(213) 985-9446 (voice)
atl.calstate.edu (Internet)
130.150.102.33(Internet)

Brief Description

The Technology Resources In Education (TRIE) Electronic Information Service is sponsored by the California Technology Project, the California State Department of Education, and the California State University.

This service is of four types: an electronic bulletin board, computer conferencing, electronic mail, and online databases.

The CTP, in cooperation with the California State University's Telecommunications and Networking Resources group, operates the Technology Resources In Education (TRIE) electronic information service. California educators can access this service free of charge to communicate with other educators across the state and to learn more about various educational technology programs. Mr. Steven Pinney, editor of the *CTP Quarterly*, and Yvonne Andres, a teacher from Oceanside, have been piloting the use of TRIE to exchange student materials between northern and southern California classrooms. The service was begun in 1988. They can provide private conferences for their users.

Hardware

AT&T 3B2/600, 12MB RAM, .5 Gigabytes storage, twenty-four 1200–9600-baud ports

Software

Operating System: UNIX System V Release 3.1.1 AT&T 3B2
Application: CoSy 3.2 Conferencing software

Access

Access is via CSUNET, a computer network of the California State University System. There are local phone numbers set up in each local dialing area around one of the eleven Cal State Campuses for accessing TRIE. Call the TRIE office for the latest information on phone numbers.

Costs

TRIE is free to qualified educators in California.

The number of users is 1,500.

Sample Login

```
SLONET.TCP >connect csunet
 Connecting ... (129.65.25.191 1.23) 168679A1 Success.

  NET/X.25 slo03, port 7

Pad> c .swrl/33          (.swrl/33 is theTRIE address on CSUNET.)

com
login: ctp      (Login as ctp; no password.)
UNIX System V Release 3.1.1 AT&T 3B2
atl
Copyright (c) 1984, 1986, 1987 AT&T
All Rights Reserved

TERMINAL TYPE (default is ibmpc) = vt100   (Put your terminal type here, in
UNIX language.)

Will you be using the (d)elete key or (b)ackspace key to erase characters? (de-
fault is backspace)

   Welcome to The California State University

      California Technology Project

      TECHNOLOGY RESOURCES
      IN EDUCATION  (TRIE)
      Electronic Information Service

      This Service is Made Possible, in Part,
      by the Following Organizations:

      AT&T
      The California State University
      The CSU Advanced Technology Laboratory
      The California State Department of Education

       02:50:02 PM Monday, July 23, 1990

      [Press <RETURN> to continue]

      CSU California Technology Project (CTP)
      TECHNOLOGY RESOURCES IN EDUCATION (TRIE)
```

Information Service

MAIN MENU

[a] Overview of the California Technology Project
[b] Request an Account
[c] Change Your Password
[d] Access CTP Electronic Services
[e] CTP Acknowledgements
[f] News

[q] Quit this TRIE Session and Log-Out

TRIE uses the CoSy software developed at University of Guelph in Ontario, Canada. They chose it because it was UNIX-based, inexpensive, and easy to modify. A more extensive description of CoSy is given in the earlier section covering conferencing software.

Here is the list of conferences on TRIE at 8/90.

:show all

o ab1470.grants	Educators' Information Exchange About AB1470 Grants
o acnotes	ACInfo
o advice	Questions and Answers on Computer Caused Problems
o api	Academic Program Improvement Conference
o api3	Internationalizing Curriculum
o associate	INFORMATION UPDATES
o astute	Assoc. of State Tech-Using Teacher Educators (ASTUTE)
o bestnet	BINATIONAL ENGLISH AND SPANISH TELECOMMUNICATION NETWORK
o biologycouncil	Biology Council for ITL (Teaching and Learning Issues)
o california	CALIFORNIA BIOMES NETWORK
c cap.math.team	CAP math writing team K-12
c carver	Student teacher lessons
o cecc	CALIFORNIA EDUCATIONAL COMPUTING CONSORTIUM
c clp.direct	California Literature Project Directors/Leaders
o communications	Data Communications Withing the CSU
o compchem	Computational Chemistry Conference
o computer	campus computer center managers
o cooplearning	CoopLearning
o csulb.lib.tech	Forum/Conf. for Library/Media Educators
c ctp.coord	CTP Corrdinators Conference
c ctp.endorse	Planning Conf for CTP Coordinators for TRIE Screening

o ctp.fredmail	CTP/FrEdMail Idea Exchange
c ctp.grants	CTP AB1470 Adaption/Adoption Grants Admin Planning
o ctp.lounge	CTP Lounge—A place to Meet Other Educators
c ctp.rtf	Cal Tech Project RFT File Sharing
o ctp.tech.coord	Statewide technology coordinators meeting place.
c ctp.telecom	CTP Telecommunications Planning
o dem.statue	Democracy Statue for China Project
o dis	disabled students
o distance.learn	Distance Learning in California
c ebcue	Planning Conf For Round Two of EBCUE Telecom Grants
o facilities	Facilities Planning For Technology
c faculty	OUR NEW COMPUTER SYSTEM
c florence	Nursing Conference AC
o gis	Geographic Information Systems
o housesales	house listings
o hypermedia	Hypermedia (K-12) for Apple II, Mac & MSDOS
o intercultural	Graduate Seminar in Intercultural Communication
c itc.tla	Plan Inland Tech Consortium's Tech Leadership Academy
o jokes	clean jokes for all seasons
o k-1.classroom	K-1 Teachers Sharing Ideas
o kimba	Student teachers
o learn	Learn CoSy
c learn.arc	Learn Conference Archive
o lounge	A Lounging Place For All
o modtech	So. Calif. Regional CTP Consortium
o mothers	Jean Casey Conference
c nafsa.xii	NAFSA Region XII Leadership Team
o scscience	Santa Clara Science Association
c sheilas	Creative Units
o sirc	Science Inservice for Rural California
c sjusd.tech.group	Technology Support Group for San Jose Unified
o spr	workshops
o sungrant	Sun Grant Phase 1 and 2 Issues
c testconf	Test conference to try things
o tla.ctp	Technology Leadership Academies
c uc.telecom	UC Berkeley Extension-Telecom Projects in Education
c videodisc	Interactive Videodisc in the CSU
o wecc	WECC training conference
o word.exchange	Welcome
o workgroup	Conference for Systemwide Committees and Workgroups
o leadership	leadership and motivation in organizations
c fake	dummy model
o kids2kids	kids2kids

(o=open, c=closed)

Mail

Mail is CoSy mail.

Gateways

Trie is on the Internet, its address is atl.calstate.edu.

4.1.13 Usenet

Usenet is a set of electronic newsletters, or newsgroups, a network of computers, and a distribution system. At this time there are over 1,200 newsgroups and 5,000 sites and an estimated one million readers. It is available to all UNIX sites that meet certain minimal conditions, so it can be expected to grow with the increased use of that operating system for the forseeable future. It can be run on any size machine with enough disk storage for the newsgroups that the site receives.

Originally, in 1979, the distribution software was written as shell scripts, or UNIX operating system macros, for the distribution of files between Duke University and University of North Carolina by Tom Truscott and James Ellis. These were rewritten in C in 1980 by Tom Truscott and Steve Daniel as Netnews Release A. When this became more popular, the B version was released by Mark Horton and Matt Glickman of UC Berkeley in 1982. The Usenet software is a package of several utilities: software to manage the distribution and updating of files, software to facilitate reading the newsletters and software to post followup messages to the newsletters.

Distribution uses the UUCP software that is available on most UNIX platforms and handles communication between two UNIX machines. They can be connected via modems and phone lines, have an ethernet connection, or any other type of physical connection. The 'news feeds' are distributed from 'backbone' sites to other backbone sites and to sites that are called leaf nodes that do not in turn pass the feeds on to other UNIX systems. The major backbone sites push new news on until it has been distributed to all the nodes. Not every site receives all news. Local material may not be fed back up into the net, and each node can specify which newsgroups it wishes to receive.
This distribution system is very different than the structure of the normal conferencing system where all the information is centrally located, as a rule. The good points are that there is built in redundancy of information, so it is very hard to distroy any sizeable percentage of the usenet data and that it is reachable via a local site, making its access rating very good. As networks continue to grow and to become more available, however, it will be found that local access is less and less valuable. At that point, maybe there will be a tendency for some centralization of the Usenet material, as the storage required to keep very much Usenet material on site can be considerable, on the order of 10

megabytes a day. Every site is duplicating that required storage, so it is very inefficient of storage overall. On the other hand storage costs are decreasing. One of the disadvantages of the storage problem is that the material cannot always be kept for very long.

Even though Usenet began on academic UNIX systems, and they still dominate the list of nodes, it is increasingly available on publically available systems. The WELL, a public conferencing system in San Francisco, carries many newsgroups for its users, and Portal in Cupertino, California, is predominantly a Usenet access business for the public at low rates. Portal is an example of a UUCP service from which you can download the newsfeed and exchange Internet mail to your UNIX system for a reasonable fee. You would normally find such a resource in your geographical region to keep phone costs of connection to a minimum.

A few newsgroups are listed here with subjects to show their diversity. A more complete list, taken from the WELL in San Francisco is included in section 7.6 below. The longer list reflects the local character of the material. A similar list from another part of the country would have other local newsgroups representing interests of that area.

aus.acsnet Discussions of ACSnet (incl bug reports) [Australian]
aus.jobs Jobs available and wanted [Australian]
aus.jokes Jokes, humour, and boring trivia [Australian]
aus.jokes.d Discussions of why that joke was no good [Australian]
ca.earthquakes What's shakin' in California
ca.environment Environmental concerns in California
ca.general Of general interest to readers in Calfornia only
bit.listserv.ozone Save Nature list
bit.listserv.pacs-l Library systems — CDROM, CAI, AI etc.
comp.arch Computer architecture
comp.archives Descriptions of public access archives (Moderated)
comp.binaries.amiga Encoded public domain programs in binary (Moderated)
comp.binaries.apple2 Binary-only postings for the Apple II computer
comp.binaries.ibm.pc Binary-only postings for IBM PC/MS-DOS (Moderated)
comp.infosystems Any discussion about information systems
comp.ivideodisc Interactive videodiscs — uses, potential, etc.
misc.headlines.unitex International news from the UN and related (Moderated)
misc.invest Investments and the handling of money
misc.jobs.misc Discussion about employment, workplaces, careers
news.announce.newgroups Calls for newgroups and announcements of same (Moderated)
news.announce.newusers Explanatory postings for new users (Moderated)
news.groups Discussions and lists of newsgroups
rec.arts.comics Comic books and strips, graphic novels, sequential art
rec.arts.drwho Discussion about "Dr. Who"
rec.food.cooking Food, cooking, cookbooks, and recipes
rec.food.drink Wines and spirits
rec.food.recipes (Moderated)

sci.edu	Science education
sci.energy	Discussions about energy, science, and technology
sci.environment	Discussions about the environment and ecology
bionet.agroforestry	Discussion of Agroforestry
bionet.general	General BIONET announcements

This is a very brief sample. See section 7.6 for a longer list. Notice that some of the BITNET LISTSERV lists are included here as Usenet newsgroups. New users are recommended to subscribe to the news.announce newsgroups above.

To read the newsgroups, there are at least four user interfaces that have been developed. The oldest is readnews and its use is simple and straightforward. To make an increased number of options available, in the spirit of UNIX, rn was developed by Larry Wall. Its basic use is also not hard to learn, but its advanced features probably remain obscure for most rn users. There is also vnews and nn, but readnews and rn are the most common interfaces.

A few sample rn commands are given below. An edited version of the manual pages for rn is included in the appendix. The .newsrc file referred to below in the documentation is a file in your UNIX home directory that lists the newsgroups you want to read and what of each newsgroup you have already read.

At the newsgroup level you can give the following commands at the appropriate prompt:

y	Do this newsgroup now
=	Do this newsgroup now, but list subjects before displaying articles
n	Go to the next newsgroup with unread news
p	Go to the previous newsgroup with unread news; if there is none, stay at the current newsgroup.
-	Go to the previously displayed newsgroup (regardless of whether it is before or after the current one in the list).
$	Go to the end of the newsgroups list
g newsgroup	Go to newsgroup. If it is not currently subscribed to, you will be asked if you want to subscribe.
/pattern	Scan forward for a newsgroup matching pattern. Patterns do globbing like filenames, i.e., use ? to match a single character, * to match any sequence of characters, and [] to specify a list of characters to match.
u	Unsubscribe from current newsgroup
l string	List newsgroups not subscribed to which contain the string specified
L	Lists the current state of the .newsrc
m name	Move the named newsgroup somewhere else in the .newsrc

c	Catch up-mark all unread articles in this newsgroup as read.
q	Quit
x	Quit, restoring .newsrc to its state at startup of rn

At the article level you can give these commands after reading each article:

n	Scan forward for next unread article
^N	Scan forward for the next article with the same subject, and make ^N default (subject search mode)
p	Scan backward for previous unread article. If there is none, stay at the current article
^P	Scan backward for the previous article with the same subject, and make ^N default (subject search mode)
^R	Restart the current article
^L	Refresh the screen
b	Back up one page
q	Quit this newsgroup and go back to the newsgroup selection level
$	Go to the last article (actually, one past the last article)
number	Go to the numbered article
j	Junk the current article-mark it as read
m	Mark the current article as still unread
/pattern	Scan forward for article containing pattern in the subject
/pattern/h	Scan forward for article containing pattern in the header
/pattern/a	Scan forward for article containing pattern anywhere in article
k	Mark as read all articles with the same subject as the current article
r	Reply through net mail
f	Submit a followup article
C	Cancel the current article, but only if you are the contributor or superuser
c	Catch up in this newsgroup; i.e., mark all articles as read
u	Unsubscribe to this newsgroup
s	destination Save to a filename or pipe using sh
=	List subjects of unread articles
#	Print last article number

To reply to an article, you either mail the author or post a followup. Both of these actions are from the rn commands at the article level. To post an entirely new article, postnews is used. Postnews prompts you for the subject, keywords, appropriate newsgroup, and distribution extent. Your favorite UNIX editor is invoked and after the text is written and editor quit, postnews asks if you want to proceed. As long as you are familar with the UNIX editors, and you can specify which one you would want to use, posting material in Usenet is very straightforward. Until it is sent on, anything you post can be deleted. As postnews leaves, it checks your directory for a .signiture file that it will use to put a few lines of your id at the bottom of your article. That usually just has your various addresses and phone numbers.

There is some controversy about whether Usenet can be considered a conferenceing system. Certainly as a conferencing system it is rudimentary and lacks many of the management tools, controls, and communication features that many conferencing systems have and that are desirable. The communication that takes place on Usenet is much more of the bulletin board type than the conferencing style. It seems to be used as an informal communications system and it would be interesting to see if it could be tailored to provide more seriously a meeting place for a group or organization. The reason Usenet is included here is that, even though the communication tools are weak in meeting facility and related communication resources, it is very strong in availability and very low-cost, and good in general interest information. Additionally, it is possible to run the Newsnet software without the news, so it could be used as a wholly internal system of discussion groups very cheaply. Thus it can be considered as public domain conferencing software for UNIX platforms.

Bulletin board Usenet sites are listed in a document that can be FTP'd. The most current list is included in the appendix (Nixpub sites). Here are a few selections from that list with the ftp addresses.

(Format is: Phone Name Location Baud Hours)

02/90 408-423-9995 cruzio Santa Cruz , CA 12/24 24
Tandy 4000, Xenix 2.3.*, Caucus 3.*; focus on Santa Cruz activity (ie directory of community and goverment organizations, events, ...); USENET Support; Multiple lines; no shell; fee: $15/quarter. Contact: ...!uunet!cruzio!chris

08/89 313-996-4644 anet Ann Arbor , MI 3/12 24
Altos 68000 - Sys III, no limits, 1st month free, fees range up to $20/month (negotiable), accepts equipment/software in lieu of fees, Picospan conferencing, 120M, non-profit, user-supported, community-based, ideal autodidact educational system. Tax-deductible donations okay.

07/89 415-753-5265 wet San Francisco CA 3/12/24 24
386 SYS V.3. Wetware Diversions. $15 registration, $0.01/minute. Public Access UNIX System: uucp, PicoSpan bbs, full Usenet News, multiple lines, shell access. Newusers get initial credit! contact:{ucsfcca | claris | hoptoad}!wet!cc (Christopher Cilley)

01/90 617-739-9753 world Brookline, MA 3/12/24/96 24
Sun 4/280, SunOS 4.03; Shell, USENET, E-Mail, UUCP and home of the Open Book Initiative (text project); fees: $5/mo + $3/hr (8a-8p) and $2/hr (8p-8a); Multiple lines: 2400 MNP used on listed number,
Telebits used on others; login as "new"; Contact: geb@world.std.com

07/88 619-444-7006 pnet01 El Cajon, CA 3/12/24 24
BSD UNIX, 3 lines, login::pnet id: new, some USENET, email, conferencing Home of P-Net software, mail to crash!bblue or pnet01!bblue for info. Contributions requested UNIX accounts available for regulars, PC Pursuit access 2/88.

12/89 719-632-4111 oldcolo Colo Spgs , CO 12/24/96 24
386 - SCO-XENIX frontend, 2 CT Miniframes backend, e-mail conferencing, databases, Naplps Graphics, USENET news. 7 lines 8N1, 2400 on 2906, USR Dual 9600 on 2658. Self registering for limited free access (political, policy, marketplace) Subscriptions $10, 15, 18 mo for full use. Dave Hughes SYSOP.

12/89 212-420-0527 magpie NYC NY 3/12/24/96 24
? - UNIX SYSV - 2, Magpie BBS, no fee, Authors: Magpie/UNIX,/MSDOS two lines plus anonymous uucp: 212-677-9487 (9600 bps Telebit modem) NOTE: 9487 reserved for registered Magpie sysops & anon uucp Contact: Steve Manes, {rutgers | cmcl2 | uunet}!hombre!magpie!manes

This list is maintained by Phil Eschallier on lgnp1. Any additions, deletions, or corrections should be sent to one of the addresses below. The nixpub listings are kept as current as possible. However, you use this data at your own risk and cost — all standard disclaimers apply!!!

Lists available from lgnp1 via anonomous uucp.
+1 215 348 9727 [Telebit access]
login: nuucp NO PWD [no rmail permitted]
this list: /usr/spool/uucppublic/nixpub
short list: /usr/spool/uucppublic/nixpub.short
or from news groups pubnet.nixpub, comp.misc or alt.bbs.

A short classic introduction to Usenet is included in the appendix, *A Primer on How to Work With the Usenet Community* by Chuq Von Rospach. This is one of the 'must read' documents of the Usenet beginner.

Bibliography

Anderson, Bart, Bryan Costales, and Harry Henderson. *UNIX Communications.* Indianapolis, Indiana: Howard W. Sams; 1987.

Todino, Grace and Dale Dougherty. *Using UUCP and Usenet.* Sebastopol, CA: O'Reilly and Associates, Inc.; 1989.

4.1.14 WELL

WELL
27 Gate Five Road
Sausalito, CA 94965
(415) 332-4335 (voice)
(415) 332-6106 (data)

The WELL is in the San Francisco Bay area, but with access via nationwide packet switching network in addition to local lines. The conferencing uses PicoSpan T3.3 on a Sequent Balance with the Dynix (UNIX) operating system. They are located in Sausalito, California, and are affiliated with the *Whole Earth Review*. *Whole Earth Review* #67, Summer 1990, had a short article on the WELL with its history and description.

Access

The WELL has forty-eight incomming phone lines. At least one of those is from the CompuServe Packet Switching Network and the others are local phone lines. Their CPN name is 'well.'

```
OK:!cat /etc/ttys.doc
# ttys.doc
# updated 6 July 1990 KAH
#

# Sausalito lines
# line      port
332-6106    ttyh0  # base of 1200 baud modems
332-6258    ttyh1       332-6292    ttyh2
332-7395    ttyh3
332-7398    ttyh4  # base of 2400 baud modems
332-7190    ttyh        5332-7217   ttyh6
332-7230    ttyh7       332-7241    ttyh8
332-7358    ttyh9       332-7404    ttyha
332-0928    ttyhb       332-1396    ttyhc
332-1475    ttyhd       332-1476    ttyi4
332-1477    ttyie       332-3970    ttyi6
332-3973    ttyi5       332-3974    ttyia
332-3975    ttyic       332-3976    ttyi8
332-3977    ttyib       332-3978    ttyid
332-3979    ttyi3
CPN         ttyx*  # CPN lines

# NOTICE: The numbers given, their relationship to the ports, and the order of
#       the numbers in the hunt may change without notice.
```

Sample Logon via CPN

ATDT1,5498605
DIAL TONE
1,5498605
CONNECT 1200

07SLO

Host Name: **WELL**

Connected to 10WELL

This is the WELL

DYNIX(R) V3.0.14 (well)
Type your user name or "newuser" to register
login: **bkwill**
Password:
Last login: Fri Aug 3 20:51:23 on ttyx9
DYNIX(R) V3.0.14 NFS #2 0: Fri Jun 8 12:09:09 PDT 1990
Copyright 1984 Sequent Computer Systems, Inc.

You have reached the WELL (Whole Earth Lectronic Link). Material posted on the WELL is the sole property of its author. Reproduction in any medium without the express permission of the individual author is strictly prohibited. Opinions of conference hosts do not necessarily reflect those of WELL management or ownership.

For voice phone support, call +1 415 332 4335, Monday through Friday, between the hours of 09:00 and 17:00 (5:00 PM) Pacific Time

—> For personal online help, type support

—> For information on long-distance packet access to the WELL, type cpn at a prompt.

PicoSpan T3.3; designed by Marcus Watts copyright 1984 NETI; licensed by Unicon Inc.

Mail is received and file transfered via UUCP; thus users can mail out to the Internet, BITNET, and other sites and as well as being reached from other sites. Costs are $10 a month and $2 per hour for WELL time. CPN costs are $4.50 per hour. There are no extra costs for higher speed access. Up to 500K disk space is free, above that is $20 per megabyte per month.

The WELL has approxiamately 4,000 users.

The WELL has about 150 public conferences at this time plus private ones. The following is a list of conferences.

OK:?conf
**** CONFERENCES ****

CONFERENCES ON the WELL

WELL "ScreenZine" Digest (g zine)

Best of the WELL (g best)

Business - Education

Apple Library Users Group	(g alug)	Agriculture	(g agri)
Brainstorming	(g brain)	Classifieds	(g cla)
Consultants	(g consult)	Consumers	(g cons)
Design	(g design)	Desktop Publishing	(g desk)
Education	(g ed)	Entrepreneurs	(g entre)
Homeowners	(g home)	Legal	(g legal)
Newsletter	(g per)	One Person Business	(g one)
Periodical	(g per)	Stock Market	(g stock)
Telecomm Law	(g tcl)	The Future	(g fut)
Translators	(g trans)	Travel	(g tra)
Work	(g work)		

Social - Political - Humanities

Aging	(g gray)	AIDS	(g aids)
Archives	(g arc)	Berkeley	(g berk)
Buddhist	(g wonderland)	East Coast	(g east)
Emotional Health*	(g private)	Environment	(g env)
Christian	(g cross)	Couples	(g couples)
Current Events	(g curr)	Dreams	(g dream)
Drugs	(g dru)	Firearms	(g firearms)
First Amendment	(g first)	Fringes of Reason	(g fringes)
Gay	(g gay)	Geography	(g geo)
German	(g german)	Hawaii	(g aloha)
Health	(g heal)	History	(g hist)
Interview	(g inter)	Jewish	(g jew)
Liberty	(g liberty)	Mind	(g mind)
Miscellaneous	(g unclear)	Men on the WELL*	(g mow)
Nonprofits	(g non)	North Bay	(g north)
Northwest	(g nw)	Parenting	(g par)
Peace	(g pea)	Penninsula	(g pen)
Poetry	(g poetry)	Philosophy	(g phi)
Politics	(g pol)	Psychology	(g psy)
San Francisco	(g sanfran)	Sexuality	(g sex)

Singles	(g singles)	Southern	(g south)
Spirituality	(g spirit)	Transportation	(g transport)
True Confessions	(g tru)	WELL Writer's Workshop* (g www)	
Whole Earth	(g we)	Women on the WELL*	(g wow)
Words	(g words)	Writers	(g wri)

Arts - Recreation - Entertainment

ArtCom Electronic Net (g acen)		Audio-Videophilia (g aud)	
Boating	(g wet)	Books	(g books)
CDs	(g cd)	Comics	(g comics)
Cooking	(g cook)	Flying	(g flying)
Fun	(g fun)	Games	(g games)
Gardening	(g gard)	Jokes	(g jokes)
MIDI	(g midi)	Movies	(g movies)
Motorcycling	(g ride)	Music	(g mus)
On Stage	(g onstage)	Pets	(g pets)
Radio	(g rad)	Restaurant	(g rest)
Science Fiction	(g sf)	Sports	(g spo)
Television	(g tv)	Weird	(g weird)

Grateful Dead

Grateful Dead	(g gd)	Deadplan*	(g dp)
Deadlit	(g deadlit)	Feedback	(g feedback)
GD Hour	(g gdh)	Tapes	(g tapes)
Tickets	(g tix)	Tours	(g tours)

Computers

AI/Forth	(g ai)	Amiga	(g amiga)
Apple	(g app)	Atari	(g ata)
Computer Books	(g cbook)	Art & Graphics	(g gra)
Hacking	(g hack)	HyperCard	(g hype)
IBM PC	(g ibm)	LANs	(g lan)
Laptop	(g lap)	Macintosh	(g mac)
Mactech	(g mactech)	Microtimes	(g microx)
OS/2	(g os2)	Printers	(g print)
Programmer's Net	(g net)	Software Design (g sdc)*	
Software/Programming (software)		UNIX	(g UNIX)
Word Processing	(g word)		

Technical - Communications

Bioinfo	(g bioinfo)	Info	(g boing)
Media	(g media)	Netweaver	(g netweaver)
Packet Radio	(g packet)	Photography	(g pho)
Radio	(g rad)	Science	(g science)
Technical Writers	(g tec)	Telecommunications	(g tele)
Usenet	(g usenet)	Video	(g vid)

Virtual Reality	(g vr)		

the WELL Itself

Deeper	(g deeper)	Entry	(g ent)
General	(g gentech)	Help	(g help)
Hosts	(g hosts)	Policy	(g policy)
System News	(g news)	Test	(g test)

* Private Conferences

Each conference is subdivided into topics. For instance, the current list of topics for *Entry* conference is:

Topic - Number of responses - Header

1 4 Announcements
2 2 The Online Manual
<topic is frozen>
3 19 Questions About the Manual
4 69 Online Assistance
5 173 Introductions
6 114 General Questions
7 38 Where To Find It
8 4 Some Things To Try
9 0 Logging Off or Leaving the WELL
<topic is frozen>
10 3 Usenet
<topic is frozen>
18 8 WELL Policies
<topic is frozen>
<linked topic>
20 20 Finding Information About Other WELL Users
31 1 Changing Your Conference List (the fun and Easy way)!
32 21 Suggestion Box
35 6 the WELL User's Manual: Suggestions and Feedback
36 12 WELL buzzwords
37 15 Those Weird Symbols
38 1 What Are the WELL's Modem Phone Numbers?
<topic is frozen>

The first number listed is the number of the topic and the second number listed is the number of responses for that topic. A frozen topic cannot be added to with new responses. Within each topic there is a first Topic entry and then numbered topic responses.
Here is an example of a conference, topics, and responses from the Apple Libraries User Group conference.

OK:g alug

*.**.

Welcome to the Online Apple Library User's Group!
People talking about libraries and Apple Computers of all kinds!

The coordinator is Jean Armour Polly (polly).
==

Anyone posting messages here agrees that their words may be compiled and moved to any other form without additional permission. For example, discussions here may find their way to the ALUG newsletter or other journals.
==

Type a B to browse all topics, B N to see new ones.

First topic 1, last 18
No new items matched.

OK:b

Topic - Number of responses - Header

1 21 Introduce yourself here
3 14 Libraries and Internet
4 0 A place to ask WELL questions
5 20 Hypermedia
6 11 True Tales From Chicago ALA
7 5 The Dreaded Virus Attack!
8 1 Information about ALUG
9 6 For a good time try topic #
10 9 Apple Telecom programs
11 11 Accessing AppleShare from remote sites
12 5 New technology in libraries
13 16 What online catalogs do you use or have created?
14 9 Keeping up with technology
15 5 Help Build ALUG ONLINE to YOUR Specs
16 7 Librarianship in the 90s and BEYOND
17 40 Apple Library Users Group Newsletter 7/90
<topic is frozen>
18 4 ALUG Newsletter comments and questions

OK:s 14

Topic 14: Keeping up with technology
By: Steve Cisler (sac) on Sat, Jul 14, '90
9 responses so far

In topic 13, response 9, David Lerner talked about keeping our eyes open to see the big picture.

How do alug readers keep up with technology? What publications to you follow? What electronic sources of info are important to you, and which are the best conferences to attend, both national and local? That will help us to provide more useful information here in this conference.

9 responses total

Topic 14: Keeping up with technology
1: Eric Lease Morgan (emorgan) Sun, Jul 15, '90 (16:10) 8 lines

I read as much as I can get my hands on. When I worked with DOS machines I read _PC Magazine_. Now I read _Mac User_. I read _Mac World_ once in a while. I log onto ISAAC, a computer conference sponsored by the University of Washington and IBM. I also log onto ETNET every once in a while to see whats happening in the world of health science CAI.

The copyright to material is expressly retained by the person who makes the contribution. While this sounds egalitarian, it makes porting communication and reprinting it a nightmare. I believe that it is better to consider all matetial posted in conferences to be in the public domain unless otherwise claimed, as is the case with Usenet material, for instance. Some conferences specifically state outright that material posted in that conference is available for copying. The basic WELL commands are:

? conf List conferences
g <name>Go to a conference <name>, g by itself shows what conference you are in at present
b List the Topics of a conference
s See topics (can be s # for the number of the topic, or an number of other options.)
r Respond to a topic entry, add an entry to the responses
e Add a new topic
quit logout of the WELL
mail *user* To send mail to user
Control c Stops scrolling or processing of a command

Commands can be listed from the help menus online. For instance:

OK:help commands
**** COMMANDS ****
After you have mastered the basic WELL commands, there are lots of other features you may wish to try. Help screens are available for some of these features by typing at the "OK" prompt, help keyword where "keyword" is one of the words listed below.
find look for "string"
forget forget topics
remember remember "forgotten" items
next go to next conf on .cflist containing new text
check check status of .cflist
addresses local and net mail addresses and formats
netmail sending mail to other nets
usenet where to find out about usenet
filetransfer basic file transfer info

```
xmodem      basic info on xmodem file transfers
 hosts      basic info on hosting a conf
 editor     basic editing info
 etiquette  a short tip about good manners on the WELL
 set        change variables
 display    display various parameters
 change     change variables
 define     define variables or abreviations
 UNIX       exit to UNIX, or execute a UNIX command
 fixseen    mark all topics in conf as having been seen to    date
 abort      get out quick from PicoSpan
```

OK:help join
**** JOIN ****
To go to any conference on the WELL, type g name at the "OK (? for help):" prompt, where "name" is the abbreviated name of the conference you want to join. For example, to go to the Parenting conference, you would type g par .

You can find out the names and abbreviations of available public conferences by typing ?conf at the "OK" prompt.

To be able to read and respond in a conference, type a j at the "join, quit or help?" prompt when you arrive at a conference for the first time.

Typically the WELL user has selected a set of conferences that he or she wants to keep up with. This set of conferences is a list in the users home directory, .cflist. When PicoSpan starts up for that user, it looks at that file to see where they will want to go and a simple n will take them to the next conference that has unread activity.

Any conference or topic can be marked as forgotten, which will take it off of the to read list. Also all topics can be marked as seen, if the user simply wants to skip all the new material. You can search through a conference material for a string with the find command. Here is an example of it from the ALUG conference:

```
OK:find "CDROM"
Topic 1 response 3:
   15: have IBMS running CDROMS or Follett CAT PLUS programs.
Topic 12 response 5:
   1: On a more usual theme, CDROM:
   2: Saw a good demo of CDROM for Apple IIe/c/gs at the July    30 meeting
   10: As usual, we got debating the merits of CDROM on IIs and    MACs and
   14: of data and graphics on CDROMs and laserdiscs, to be    picked up by
Topic 13 response 16:
   2: Gaylord SuperCAT CDROM. Message posted on Eastern Oregon    Network:
```

A user may never need more commands than just those basic ones above. But there is a more advanced level of use where some of the conference activity can be automated. For instance, when you see conference topics typically, by default, you will be shown one page of twenty or so lines at a time and the system will stop at the end of each topic with a question about whether you wish to responds or not. This can get to be irritating and it can be turned off. In your home directory are several files, or you can create several files, that can be used to control these actions.

These files can be edited with the UNIX editor you feel most comfortable with or they can be downloaded to your editor on your microcomputer, edited, and saved as a text file, and then uploaded into your home directory. Here is an example of the files in a home directory:

```
OK:ls -a
.  .deeper.cf  .netweaver.cf  .rnlast     News
..  .entry90.cf  .news89.cf  .rnsoft      mbox
.alug.cf  .gentech.cf  .newsrc      .tcom87.cf  news89.bak
.cflist  .help87.cf  .oldnewsrc  .UNIX.cf
.cfonce  .hosts.cf  .ota.cf      .usenet.cf
.cfrc  .login      .plan       .we.cf
```

The files that start with .rn are files that are created by the rn utility that reads Usenet material (newsletters). The files with .cf after then are keeping track of which items have been read in each topic in that conference as the following shows. (Cat filename displays the file on the screen.)

```
OK:cat .alug.cf
!<pr03>
Brian Williams
1 22 26bb2e13
3 15 26bb2e16
4 1 268afa7b
5 21 26bb2e1a
6 12 269c1a7d
7 6 26a2af2b

etc
```

This is how PicoSpan knows which topics and responses you have seen and what your name is on the conference. The .cflist file is a list of your currently active files. That is the file that PicoSpan looks in to see which conference to go to next when you give the n command. You visit those conferences in the order that they are listed in these files.

```
OK:cat .cflist
usenet
deeper
netweaver
newsletter
```

```
alug
```

The other two files that can be used to automate your conference activity somewhat are the .cfrc and the .cfonce files. You don't have to have either of these two files, so don't make them up until you have become comfortable with the basic operation of PicoSpan.

```
OK:cat .cfrc
s new pas
n
```

In the .cfrc file you should put all the commands that you want to execute each time you go to a new conference. This file is looked at each time a new conference is entered. "s new pas" is the command to see the new material and say pass at the respond prompt of each topic. If I want to respond, I will go back to that topic and give resonse, but in most cases I do not want to respond, so this saves time online. The n just goes to the next conference in my .cfrc list after all the responses have been seen in all the topics in the current conference.

```
OK:cat .cfonce
define editor "/usr/ucb/vi"
define prompt "\n\nOK:"
nopager
check
```

The .cfonce file has commands that are executed once when you first logon to the WELL. This file has a line that defines the UNIX vi editor as my default editor, so that is the editor I get when I make a response or use mail, and a line that changes my prompt from the standard default OK(? for help): to just an OK:. You can change your prompt to be anything you want it to be. "Nopager" says that I don't want material to be displayed a page at a time, I want it to scroll by. The reason for that is that I can always go back with my communications program to look at material that I could not read as it passed. Or I can just let that go to the buffer or a file and read it offline. Again, it saves a little time, but is not necessary. "Check" looks and reports the new material, so with that in the .cfonce file I get a little report when I log in about new material. .cfonce files can get very complicated. This is a simple one.

Mail

The electronic mail available is UNIX mail, but they also have a slightly easier front end called elm. Users familiar with UNIX mail will feel right at home, and those who are not familiar with UNIX mail will not find it hard to learn. There are many users available who are sympathetic helpers of any of these available features. Briefly, to invoke mail, you type "mail" with the username of the person you want to send mail to. Their username is not their real name, but the name they have been given by the system. After "mail username," you will be prompted for a subject, then the body of the letter. After you have typed in a letter, a period on a line by itself ends the letter and it is sent. UNIX mail has many features that you can learn from the available manuals. Here is an example of a mail to an address on the Internet sent late afternoon.

OK:mail brian@library.calpoly.edu
Subject: test message via Internet
This is a test of mailing a letter from the WELL to the library at Cal Poly.
Although this will not arrive as soon as it would from another Internet
site, it should get to the Library before Land mail would!

Mail sent

And it arrived at my site later:

Message 2:
From well!bkwill@apple.com Mon Aug 6 08:05:04 1990
Date: Sat, 4 Aug 90 18:36:19 pdt
From: well!bkwill@apple.com (Brian Williams)
To: brian@library.calpoly.edu
Subject: test message via Internet

This is a test of mailing a letter from the WELL to the library at Cal Poly.
etc

Help

Online support is available by typing help support or mailing a note to the system administrators. In addtion there is an extensive set of help screens available. There is also a full set of UNIX manual pages for more information on the UNIX commands. The WELL manual is extensive and well written and they supply a WELL Commands and WELL map quick reference quide. Here is an example of a help screen:

OK:**help**
Help screens are available at the "OK (? for help):" prompt,
the "(r)espond, (p)ass, or ? for help:" prompt, and at the "join, quit, or help?"
prompt.

To get help on a specific topic, type help <word> where <word>
is one of the following keywords:
join ....going to a conference
browse ....seeing the topic list in a conference
read ....reading topics
respond ....responding in topics
enter ....creating a new topic
mail ....sending and receiving email
send ....sending an immediate message to another user
reply ....responding to a send

huh ....reviewing messages you have been "sent"
billing ....finding out about your account
who ....finding out info on users
stop,
quit, bye ....ways to exit the WELL

For example, to see the help screen on billing when you are the "OK" prompt, type:
OK (? for help): help billing

More advanced help screens are available for keywords listed on the help commands screen.

Other Features

The user has access to many of the basic UNIX commands and can create and store files in their directory. A basic knowledge of the UNIX operating system is not required, but helpful while using the WELL. There is much discussion of UNIX commands on the WELL and it is a good place to learn some UNIX. They have all the popular editors available, and make the C compilers available as well. Dynix is a BSD compatible UNIX.

Both a text and binary file transfer is available. Some of the conferences have binary files in them for downloading. They support x,y, and z modem protocols.

The WELL gets a Usenet feed from Apple. They have both the rn and the nn readnews utilities that are executed in the Usenet conference. Since there are a great many people just starting out to become familiar with Usenet and Bitnet Listservs, the WELL is a great place to practice using these communication media.

Summary

The user community is very literate in all subjects and especially computers. The UNIX conference is active and instructive, but there are equally interesting and impressive exchanges going on in the fields of art, literature and current events. For general discussion, this system is certainly the most interesting and active today.

Bibliography

Brand, Stewart. "Gate Five Road." *Whole Earth Review* # 47:103-104; July 1985.

Coate, John. "The WELL Turns Five." *Whole Earth Review* # 67: 126-129; Summer 1990.

Ojala, Marydee. "Entrepreneurs Find a WELL of Experience." *Link-Up* 7(2):14-15; March/April 1990.

5. Survey of Networks

5.1 INTRODUCTION

The public packet-switching networks we use to access the resources covered in the book and the traditional computer resources such as, DIALOG and BRS, are networks of leased phone lines and computer communications equipment owned by private companies or government sponsored networks.

For instance, Tymnet has communication equipment in 850 cities and towns around the United States attached to phone lines that can be reached by phoning those phone numbers. Once connected to the modems on those phone lines, you are connected to regional computer facilities owned by the service that routes your call to the desired resource by the resource name that you supply when you connect to the network. The resource, on its end, has an agreement with the network to provide access that may stipulate how many lines can come into that resource and how much they must pay each month, per minute and per packet of characters depending on what time of day the connection is made. In most cases, these resources pass these network costs on to the user as directly as possible. In all cases, the resource must average out their network costs, however, as the flat monthly charges cannot be distributed any other way conveniently. Most resources derive a use charge based on minutes of use to cover all of these charges.

The principle networks in use today in the United States are Tymnet, Telenet, and CompuServe Packet Network, not to be confused with its sister product CompuServe Information Systems. The main differences between the networks is their cost, the number of nodes they have, and access to high-speed nodes. The table below summarizes some of this data.

Network Characteristics

Network	Cities	Nodes	9.6kbps?
CPN	418	750	331
Tymnet	850	13,540	70

Most of the networks have some access to nodes in other countries. In most cases, such foreign access requires an agreement between the user and the packet network, or phone company, in the foreign country before those network nodes can be used.

As baud rates at higher and higher speeds have become common, it is easier to find local numbers with 1200- and 2400-baud access. On the upswing at this time is the use of the MNP protocol, which allows speeds up to 9.6kbs, or 9600-baud. A user must have a modem that supports the MNP protocol at their end to match the MNP modem at the network number. If they don't have an MNP modem, the network modem will match the highest speed that the user's modem supports. Most conferencing is speed dependent and access at the higher speeds will be cost effective. This is true also for computer literature searching.

Some of the network services have developed 'outdial' services. An example of this is Telenet's (Sprint's) PC Pursuit. These services are usually priced lower and are primarily aimed at the enthusiast market who can make use of the off-peak low-rate more easily. With these services, you don't dial directly to a network customer at the other end, but to a phone switching equipment at the other end that can in turn connect you to any phone line and thus to any incoming modem at some site you want to reach. That means that the resource you want to connect to does not have to have contracted with the network to provide access, which makes the smaller system more likely to be available. Due to the lower rates that the network's charge for this access, your connect charges are not going to be higher than they would be if your resource had a contract with the network. The drawbacks are: there are far fewer outdial lines than network nodes and thus the likelihood of one being where you need it is not high unless you are calling from one large city to another, the fewer lines means that they are more apt to be busy, the savings are primarily for off-peak use, and the connection is not as high grade as it would be direct so you are more likely to get some line noise. In many cases, these disadvantages are more than offset by the reduced costs.

If there is no network node in your local calling area, then it would be best to get a list of the closest ones and analyze with telephone company pricing information to see which ones are going to be the least expensive to use. As a rule it is dependent on milage, but not in all cases. In addition, it may prove less expensive to use a higher speed connection even if it is a little further away than a low-speed node.

5.2 NETWORKS

5.2.1 BITNET

"Bitnet is an electronic communication network linking institutional and departmental computers at the 500 participating US CREN members, which include universities, colleges, and collaborating research centers. With its Cooperating Networks in other countries, BITNET is part of a single logical network connecting 1,300 sites in thirty-eight countries for the electronic exchange of noncommercial information among the faculty, students, and staff of its subscribers. In addition, gateways allow the exchange of electronic mail between this network and the Internet, CSNET, USENET, and many other networks worldwide, which use other communication protocols.

BITNET users share information via electronic mail to individuals and shared-interest groups; transfer of documents, programs, and data; access to BITNET server machines and associated data services; and brief, nearly-interactive messages. Some 900 discussion groups active on BITNET cover virtually any topic of academic interest and may have five to several thousand participants. To facilitate use of BITNET, its members incorporate BITNET access into their local computer mail systems.

BITNET user support and information services are provided by the BITNET Network Information Center (BITNIC) and by individuals throughout the network. The BITNIC services include two electronically distributed newsletters, *BITNEWS* and *TECHNEWS*; online and telephone assistance for campus support staff; and online file servers that send documentation, node and subscriber information, and archival files upon receipt of appropriate commands over the network.

BITNET is a store and forward network; information originating at a given BITNET-connected computer is received by intermediate nodes and forwarded to its destination. Computers in BITNET are interconnected by leased lines. BITNET functions with both IBM and non-IBM computers can communicate using IBM's RSCS/NJE protocols. Most software required to interface mainframe and minicomputer systems to BITNET is readily available.

BITNET is operated by the Corporation for Research and Educational Networking (CREN), a nonprofit membership corporation that also operates CSNET. Day-to-day operations and support are provided by the BITNET Network Information Center located at EDUCOM and funded through membership fees. The cost of CREN membership and BITNET services is based on the budget of the member institution; it is independent of the number of computers connected to BITNET and the amount of network use by those computers and the member's staff and students."

(BITNET Network Information Center, *BITNET OVERVIEW*)

Bitnet started in 1981 as a small group of computers at the City University of New York. The name stands for 'Because It's Time Network,' or 'Because It's There Network.' In 1989, BITNET became CREN (pronounced kren).

BITNET Connectivity

500 members	1,700 nodes United States
650 sites	800 nodes Europe (EARN)
65 members	180 nodes Canada (NETNORTH)
20 sites	30 nodes Latin America
65 sites	100 nodes ASIA

Commonly, BITNET sites are linked via 9.6Kbps lines. In 1986, the TCP/IP protocol was added to some sites and at this time about 30 percent of BITNET traffic is over the Internet at higher than 9.6Kbps speeds.

Lists of BITNET members and sites are available from BITNET@BITNIC or EDUCOM, (202) 872-4200. There is also a very helpful list in *The User's Directory of Computer Networks.*

Between two BITNET sites running the JNET protocol package, which is the basis for BITNET communication, users can send "messages" preceding with the 'tell' or 'send' command, depending on whether they are using a VM or a VMS machine. Internet to BITNET users cannot use these comands. On the other hand, the mail system on both networks are tied together at gateways, so that mail can be sent from one of the networks to the other easily.

BITNET sites can have 'servers' running on them. Servers are programs that respond to mail or messages from other sites that contain commands such as 'help' or 'sendme' or 'subscribe.' The server will respond to that command and send you mail about it to the address from which you mailed. A server that is used to control a mailing list is called a list server. When you want to receive mailings from a list server you send mail or a message to the listserv for that mailing list. For example, say it is called say Pacs-L, you do not send the mail to the Pacs-L address, but to the listserv for Pacs-L When you send comments to the mailing list, you do send those to the Pacs-L address. For more information on listservs, see the BITNET chapter in the systems section.

Bibliography

BITNET Overview from Listserv@bitnic.bitnet

Britten, William A. "BITNET and the Internet: Scholarly Networks for Librarians." *College and Research Libraries News.* Feb. 1990: 103-107.

Condon, Christopher. BITNET Userhelp (from listserv@bitnic.bitnet)

5.2.2 CompuServe Packet Network

CompuServe Packet-Switched Data Network
500 Arlington Centre Blvd.
Columbus, OH 43220
(800) 848-8980 (voice)
(800) 848-4480 (data)
This is not to be confused with the CompuServe that is the CompuServe Information Service, a sister product of the company. They also have begun to provide network services, although small in comparison to Tymnet and Telenet at this point, they do offer some advantages.

They have service to about 418 cities in the United States, with a total of 750 lines, 331 of those support MNP.

A typical dialup looks like this:

ATDT1,5498605 Communications program dials the phone number for the node.
DIAL TONE
1,5498605
CONNECT 1200 Give a couple of enters here.

09SLO

Host Name: HELP Here you would normally type in the host name, but there is some help.

If you are attempting to access
the CompuServe system, please
enter a ^C (ASCII ETX) in the
future. If you are unable to
issue a ^C, enter either CPS or
CIS at the 'Host Name: ' prompt
to access the CompuServe Commercial system or the CompuServe
Information Service, respectively.

If you are attempting to access
a CNS host, please enter the
appropriate host name.

Host Name: Here you would type in the host name.

Host names are usually regular characters. The WELL is well, for instance.

You can get node numbers by dialing a 800 number, (800)848-4480, at the Host name: prompt, type NETWRK.

5.2.3 Internet

The Internet is a network of over 400 networks running the TCP/IP (Transmission Control Protocol/Internet Protocol) protocols. It is connected by gateways that share names and addresses. The Internet can be broken down into subnetworks, begining with Arpanet, the first part of the Internet established in 1969. In 1983, Arpanet split into Arpanet and MILNET, creating the Internet. It is now a combination of many such subnetworks, with NSFNET being one of the largest. Arpanet can be broken down into its constituent parts. Some of the other participating networks are: BARRNet, in the San Francisco Bay area; CERFnet; Merit; NYSERNet; CSNet (partly); and links to overseas networks. Estimates of Internet's size range to 500,000 hosts and to over a million users. Speeds range from 9.6Kbs to T1, or 1.45Mbs. Internet has plans to increase speeds to T2 and T3 (44.736 Mbps) for most of the backbone of the network in the mid-1990s. The addressing of machines and sites is administered centrally. Every site on the Internet has its own Domain and IP (Internet Protocol) address.

The Domain address looks like library.calpoly.edu. The numerical equivalent of that, or the IP address, is 129.65.25.20 The address is an expression of a tree node representing that site. Under the root or top layer, there are nodes of:

MIL U.S. Military
GOV U.S. Government
EDU Educational
COM Commercial
NET Network Centers
ORG Nonprofits

At the root level there are geographical nodes for the United States, other countries, etc. Below that level are many nodes for each campus, business, state, or whetever. Below that level there are nodes for individual sites on campus, cities, and so on. The nodes are read from the bottom up, leaving out the root node. In the example given, the library has an address under the campus, Calpoly, which is under the educational branch of the tree, or edu. The administration of the nodes at the bottom levels is done locally in conjunction with the Domain Name System (DNS). Notice that the numerical equivalents are not so hierarchically constructed, but that they still have some structure built into them.

One of the factors in the exponential growth of the Internet is the availablility of the tools for using the network that were built into the Berkeley versions of the the UNIX operating system, BSD 4.2 and 4.3, which have been so widely used on academic campuses. All sites support telnet, ftp, and SMTP mail utilities to effect communcation and file transfer between sites. In distinction to BITNET, this is not a store and forward system, all traffic is real-time. A mail message sent now from a California Internet site to an East coast site will reach its intended receiver as soon as it leaves the California site, or so it will seem. In addition to electronic mail, TCP/IP allows a user at one host to log onto another connected host using the telnet utility that comes with most UNIX systems. This greatly increases the access to resources. The Internet is a giant step toward bringing the information and the user together, regardless of the geographical distance between them.

Telnet is a utility that allows a user to remotely log-on to another site as if they were in the building. To execute it you simply give the command telnet IPADDRESS or domain name, where the ipaddress is. For example, say you want to access the Internet address for the University of California's Melvyl catalog, or melvyl.ucop.edu or 31.1.0.11(sometimes). Here is a telnet session to Melvyl:

Telnet>>open melvyl.ucop.edu
Telnet to ... (31.1.0.11 0.23) Success.

DLA LINE 188 (TELNET) 23:58:06 08/06/90 (MELVYL.UCOP.EDU)

Please Enter Your Terminal Type Code or Type HELP for a List of Codes.

TERMINAL? help
Please enter the Terminal Type Code for your terminal.

Supported Terminal Types and their character codes are:

TERMINAL CODE	TERMINAL	TERMINAL CODE	TERMINAL
TTY33	Teletype 33 (TTY)	BANTAM	Perkin Elmer Bantam
ESPRIT	Hazeltine Esprit	ADM3A	ADM 3a
PE1100	Perkin Elmer 1100	HAZ1500	Hazeltine 1500
HARDCOPY	Decwriter/Gencom	HAZ2000	Hazeltine 2000
IBMPC	IBM Personal Computer	HEATH	Heathkit H19
KERMIT	KERMIT Emulation	VT100	Dec VT100
ACT5A	Microterm Act5a	ADDS	ADDS/NCR
HP2621	Hewlett Packard HP2621	BITGRAPH	BBN Bitgraph
TI700	TI Silent 700	TTY40	Teletype 40(TTY)
TELE920	Televideo 910, 912, 920	DISPLAY	IBM Displaywriter
OTHER	All Others		

Please Enter Your Terminal Type Code or Type HELP for a List of Codes.
TERMINAL? vt100
Press RETURN for the MELVYL Catalog ->

Welcome to the University of California's

MELVYL* LIBRARY SYSTEM

```
———————————— =>> SYSTEM NEWS <<=————————————

(c) 1984. *Registered trademark of The Regents of the University of California.
==========================================================================
 OPTIONS:   Choose an option or type any command.

   HELP    - For help in getting started.

   [return]   - Press RETURN to choose a database for searching.

   START <db>   - Type START <database name> to begin searching in a database.
->
```

etc.

In a similar way you can log onto any resource connected to the Internet as long as that resource permits it. There is a growing list of libraries that are making their catalogs available this way. CARL provides an extensive range of information services via the Internet, although some of them, like Uncover, a periodical database, require special access arrangements. A list of those libraries accessable over the Internet is included in the appendix. Researchers from any location on the globe with Internet access can search several library catalogs for desirable information without having to visit those libraries. Many of the information services used by libraries, such as DIALOG, are planning to make themselves available via Internet. RLIN is on the Internet. As there is no charge to the end-user for Internet use, this availability should lower information access costs for libraries and patrons.

Ftp is a utility that allows file transfer between sites both running TCP/IP. If you know the name of a file that you would like to receive on some system on the Internet, then you can do what is called an anonymous ftp and have that file sent to your directory or wherever you are ftping from. Ftp is the command the user gives to the system to access the utility that asks for the name of the site to which you want to connect. It then logs you into the remote site (as anonymous, for instance), and waits for you to give a command like get. After file transfer has been completed and the file is put into your home directory with the same name it had, overwriting anything in your home directory with the same name, then you will exit ftp to return to your system's normal prompt.

Here is a sample anonymous ftp session from my library computer to one called polyslo.

```
% ftp polyslo
Connected to polyslo.calpoly.edu.
220 polyslo FTP server (Version 5.52 Sun Apr 1 18:17:32 PDT 1990) ready.
Name (polyslo.calpoly.edu:brian): anonymous       (Type this is in as name.)
Password (polyslo.calpoly.edu:anonymous):    (Type your name as password.)
```

```
331 Guest login ok, send ident as password.
230 Guest login ok, access restrictions apply.
ftp> ?            (You can also type help.)

Commands may be abbreviated. Commands are:

!       debug    mdelete   sendport   send
append    dir      mdir      put      status
ascii     form     mget      pwd      struct
bell     get      mkdir     quit     tenex
binary    glob     mls       quote     trace
bye      hash     mode      recv      type
cd      help      mput     remotehelp   user
close     lcd      open      rename     verbose
delete     ls      prompt     rmdir      ?
ftp> ls     (List files.)
200 PORT command successful.
150 Opening ASCII mode data connection for file list.
bin
etc
pub
tmp
226 Transfer complete.
16 bytes received in 0.01 seconds (1.6 Kbytes/s)

ftp> cd pub      (Change directory to pub.)
250 CWD command successful.

ftp> ls -l      (List files in long format.)
200 PORT command successful.
150 Opening ASCII mode data connection for /bin/ls.
total 1304
-r—r—r— 1 root   227151 Oct 4 1989 Internet.E-Mail.list.Z
-r—r—r— 1 root    878 Nov 14 15:36 README
drwxrwxr-x 2 root   2048 Feb 6 1989 TR
-r—r—r— 1 root   95233 Apr 12 1990 byteUNIX.tar.Z
-r—r—r— 1 root   33697 Aug 2 1989 conqdoc4.3.sh.Z
-r—r—r— 1 root   37502 Aug 2 1989 conqdoc4.3.tar.Z
-r—r—r— 1 root   26496 May 27 1990 distribute.shar
-r—r—r— 1 root   379708 Sep 30 15:32 fsuu11r5.zip
dr-xr-xr-x 2 root   2048 Aug 17 1989 hgi
-r—r—r— 1 root   275599 Aug 4 1989 hosts
drwxr-xr-x 2 root   2048 Sep 20 14:41 rfc
-r—r—r— 1 root   6403 Aug 7 1989 short_usenix_files.Z
-r—r—r— 1 root   13228 Nov 14 15:36 spaceout.tar.Z
-r—r—r— 1 root   24881 Jul 19 11:12 spider.tar.Z
-r—r—r— 1 root   32257 Mar 7 1990 sxi-1.0.tar.Z
-r—r—r— 1 root   42444 Nov 14 15:36 top2.0.tar.Z
-r—r—r— 1 root   53955 Aug 2 1989 usenix_tape_files.Z
226 Transfer complete.
1014 bytes received in 0.51 seconds (1.9 Kbytes/s)
```

```
ftp> cd hgi   (Change directory to Hitchhikers Guide to Internet.)
250 CWD command successful.

ftp> ls    (List files. There are three versions of the text, all compressed.)
200 PORT command successful.
150 Opening ASCII mode data connection for file list.
hgi.me.Z
hgi.ps.Z      (This is a postscript version in compressed form (Z).)
hgi.txt.Z
226 Transfer complete.
28 bytes received in 0.01 seconds (2.7 Kbytes/s)

ftp> binary      (Do file transfers in binary mode, as a rule.)
200 Type set to I.

ftp> get hgi.ps.Z      (Transfers file to where I came from.)
200 PORT command successful.
150 Opening BINARY mode data connection for hgi.ps.Z (49136 bytes).
226 Transfer complete.
49136 bytes received in 0.39 seconds (1.2e+02 Kbytes/s)

ftp> close      (Leave remote site.)
221 Goodbye.


ftp> quit         (Quit the ftp program.)

% uncompress hgi.ps.Z   (Uncompress the file.)

% ls -l hgi.ps    (File is now uncompressed.)
-rw———— 1 brian   127882 Dec 10 09:27 hgi.ps
```

Frequently, the files are not only compressed but also 'tared.' A tared file has been converted with the program tar to a tape archive format. It needs to be untared once you have it. You do that with the tar -x command.

Files available for ftp vary from documentation of system and network use to public domain software for all platforms. This is a natural way for libraries to make electronic documents available to their patrons, for instance. A list of ftp sites on the Internet with a suggestion of the type of material at the sites is located in the appendix.

Electronic mail between most Internet sites is just as easy as it is within your own building as long as your .sendmail.cf files on your UNIX system are set up correctly.

The Internet does not have the 'servers' of BITNET, but a very similar information distribution system has evolved called Usenet or Netnews. This is described in section 4.1.13. Internet UNIX sites can be tied together using the

UNIX utility UUCP. Even machines that are not Internet sites can connect with machines that are on the Internet and exchange files and mail with them.
As transmission speeds increase and it becomes easier to transmit several megabytes of text, the transmission of electronically stored text will be more common. Thus document delivery will follow electronic remote access to library catalogs. Major problems with this are being addressed now as resolution of graphic transmission standards are developed and standards evolve for library catalogs.

Both Quarterman's and LaQuey's books include good descriptions of the Internet. LaQuey has extensive lists of host addresses for each subnet in domain and also in IP address order so that you can translate many of the IP addresses that you may see into their domain form. Usually the whois command can be used to translate a domain name into an IP address and vice versa.

Bibliography

LaQuey, Tracy L., ed. *The User's Directory of Computer Networks.* Bedford, MA: Digital Press; 1990.

Quarterman, John S. *The Matrix: Computer Networks and Conferencing Systems Worldwide.* Bedford, MA: Digital Press; 1990.

5.2.4 SprintNet

SprintNet
12490 Sunrise Valley Drive
Reston, VA 22096
(800) 835-3638 (voice)
(703) 689-5177 (fax)

Telenet, along with Tymnet, is a common network in place today for data communications between your microcomputer or terminal and the host computer running the software you want to use, like a conferencing package. Telenet is owned by US Sprint and is now called SprintNet.

ATDT1,3278146 The Microcomputer communications program calls the number.
DIAL TONE
1,3278146
CONNECT 1200 After the connect, type a couple of enters.

TELENET
805 17D
TERMINAL= Here you type a terminal id or enter.

@ Here you type in the host id.

The host ids are usually given as 'c xxxx' where xxxx is some host id number or series of characters.

An online list of node numbers can be accessed at the @ prompt either from a SprintNet node you know the number for or from their 800 number, (800) 546-2000. If you use the 800 number, type "mail" at the @ prompt, and phones at both the user name and the password prompts, as below.

TELENET
805 17C
TERMINAL=

@mail (Type mail at the @ prompt.)

User name? phones (Type phones as user name.)
Password? (Type phones again as password.)

AUGUST 1990

```
**************************************************
**                        **
**    !!! ATTENTION !!!            **
**                        **
** NEW INTERNATIONAL SPRINTNET ACCESS CENTERS NOW AVAILABLE **
**                        **
** Select 2 on the main menu for local access telephone        **
**  numbers in international locations.        **
**                        **
**                        **
**    !!! ALSO AVAILABLE !!!           **
**                        **
**  DOMESTIC ASYNCHRONOUS V.32 9600 BPS SITES        **
**    IN SELECT LOCATIONS        **
**                        **
**  Select 1 on the main menu for a complete listing.        **
**                        **
**************************************************
```

Welcome to US Sprint's online directory of SprintNet local access telephone numbers.

SprintNet's Dial Access Services provide you access to the SprintNet data network 24 hours a day for reliable data transmission across town and worldwide. You can access the network with a local phone call from thousands of cities and towns or by using SprintNet In-WATS service. The network is also accessible from nearly 100 international locations.
Depend on SprintNet's Dial Access Services for:

* dial-up flexibility with access on demand
* error protected network transmission and
* 24-hour customer service and network management

For customer service, call toll-free 1-800/336-0437. From overseas locations with non-WATS access, call 703/689-6400.

US SPRINT'S ONLINE
LOCAL ACCESS TELEPHONE NUMBERS DIRECTORY

1. Domestic Asynchronous Dial Service
2. International Asynchronous Dial Service
3. Domestic X.25 Dial Service
4. New Access Centers and Recent Changes
5. Product and Service Information
6. Exit the Phones Directory

Please enter your selection (1-6): 1

DOMESTIC ASYNCHRONOUS DIAL SERVICE

- for asynchronous applications
- at 300, 1200, 2400 and 9600 bps
- with optional local error protection

Asynchronous Dial Service enables you to conveniently access the SprintNet data network with a local telephone call from thousands of U.S. cities and towns. For areas without local access in the U.S., use SprintNet's In-WATS service.

In-WATS Service	Telephone Number
300-2400 bps	1-800/546-1000
9600 bps (V.29)	1-800/546-2000
9600 bps (V.32)	1-800/546-2500

Consult the Data Network Rate Schedule for In-WATS pricing.

Domestic Service Requirements

SPEED:	MODEM TYPE:
300 bps	Bell 103 compatible
1200 bps	Bell 212A compatible
2400 bps	V.22 bis compatible
9600 bps (V.29)	Microcom V.29 compatible
9600 bps (V.32)	CCITT V.32 compatible

Optional Local Error Protection

When using local error protection for speeds of 2400 bps or less, your modem must be MNP compatible, or you can use MNP compatible software in your PC. For V.29 9600 bps service, your modem must be MNP compatible. For V.32 9600 bps service, your modem should be MNP or V.42 compatible.

Note: Dial the 2400 bps access number when using local error
protection at 300, 1200 or 2400 bps.

DOMESTIC ASYNCHRONOUS DIAL SERVICE

1. 300-2400 bps Access Numbers by State
2. All 300-2400 bps Access Numbers
3. All 9600 bps Access Numbers
4. Return to Main Menu

Please enter your selection (1-4): 4

US SPRINT'S ONLINE
LOCAL ACCESS TELEPHONE NUMBERS DIRECTORY

1. Domestic Asynchronous Dial Service
2. International Asynchronous Dial Service
3. Domestic X.25 Dial Service
4. New Access Centers and Recent Changes
5. Product and Service Information
6. Exit the Phones Directory

Please enter your selection (1-6): 6

Thank you for using US Sprint's Online
Local Access Telephone Numbers Directory

This mail session is now complete.

MAIL DISCONNECTED 00 40 00:00:02:30 154 8

One of their services is the popular out-dial service, PC Pursuit. This service provides a flat fee for all calls made from one metropolitan area to another. You pay a one-time signup fee of $30 and then $30 per month for up to thirty hours of off-peak connect-time (6P.M. to 7A.M.). Peak connect hour charges are $10.50, which may or may not be competitive with other services. It can reduce your costs for online connection somewhat, provided that it is available for your area and your traffic is fairly high. This type of service is similar to an 'outdial' network service of Tymnet. It allows you to call a network node in your area, which connects to equipment in the desired city by regular phone lines so that you can 'call' any computer resource's modem from that point as a local call. The fact that the service only really effects costs that are off-peak means that all of your data transfer has to be batched and scheduled for those hours. Support for PC Pursuit is at (800) 336-0437.

5.2.5 Tymnet

Tymnet
2560 North First Street
P.O. Box 49019
San Jose, CA 95161-9019
(800) 336-0149
(800) 872-7654

Tymnet is one of the oldest and most common of the public packetswitching networks. At this time it is a subsidiary of British Telecom, which also owns Dialcom and Dow Jones, among other things. They have 850 access points in the United States (13,540 local ports) and eighty in countries around the world. They can support over 16,480 simultaneous users. Over 11 billion characters are sent daily. Local Tymnet numbers are listed in the phone book under "Tymnet Network access," supposedly, but the easiest way of getting the nearest node to you is to call their support number at (800) 336-0149. Most nodes operate at 300-, 1200-, or 2400-baud. There are a few sites that support lower baud rates and a few that support MNP and 9.6kbps (approx. 9600-baud).

A normal transaction with Tymnet is shown below:

ATDT1,5490770 Microcomputer calling local Tymnet node number
DIAL TONE
1,5490770
CONNECT 1200
xxxx`xxxxx~xx`xxxx`xxx~x Here it is necessary to type a couple of carriage returns
please type your terminal identifier Here type an a, or whatever your terminal id is.
-4255:01-003-
please log in: At this point you would give the host name, like brs.
Tymnet gives you sixteen seconds to enter your terminal identifier after the connect message. Valid terminal identifiers are:

Microcomputer	a
Most terminals	a
Terminet	g
Ascii (150 Bps)	j
Beta (150 Bps)	f
All other 150 Bps	b

Selectric p
All 110 Bps d
Printer types:
Matrix (1200 bps) i
Impact (300) c
Thermal (300) e,i
Belt (300) g

You can also enter a carriage return as a default to a.

If you type "information" at the log-on prompt you are loged onto a Tymnet computer with a variety of useful information, such as node numbers.

please log in: information

TYMNET INFORMATION SERVICE

Welcome to TYMNET's Information Service! TYMNET is the world's largest Public Data Network, with local access in over 750 U.S. and Canadian cities and access to and from over 70 foreign countries.

MAIN MENU

1. Direct Dial & Outdial (R) Access
2. Data Base and Timesharing Services
3. International Access
4. Certified Products
5. Computers Interfaced to TYMNET (R)
6. Sales Office Directory
7. Technical and User Documentation
8. Special offers

If you need assistance, type 'HELP'. When you are finished, type 'QUIT'.

Type the number of the desired menu item at the prompt.

YOUR SELECTION:1

TYMNET DIRECT DIAL & OUTDIAL ACCESS INFORMATION

TYMNET has local dial-up access in over 750 cities in the domestic United States, its territories, and several international locations using a variety of industry standard modem technologies.

1. Access Locations Index
2. Access Numbers for a Specific Location
3. All Access Locations by State, Territory, or Province
4. All Access Locations by Node Number
5. Regional Bell Operating Company (RBOC) Access Numbers
6. 2400 bps Access Numbers Sorted by Location and City
7. Asynchronous Outdial Access Sorted by Location and City
8. Newly Changed Access Numbers and New Cities
9. Modem and Other Network Access Information
10. All TymDial 9.6 (R) Access Numbers
11. All TymDial X.25 (R) Access Numbers

If you need assistance, type 'HELP'. When you are finished, type 'QUIT'.
To return to the main menu, type 'TOP'.

YOUR SELECTION:2

DATA BASE AND TIMESHARING SERVICES AVAILABLE

Many of TYMNET's customers provide data base and timesharing services for applications in almost every area of interest.

1. Company Index
2. Service Classifications Index
3. Companies in a Specific Classification
4. Brief Information on Companies in a Specific Classification
5. Detailed Information About a Specific Company

If you need assistance, type 'HELP.' When you are finished, type 'QUIT'.
To return to the main menu, type 'TOP.'

YOUR SELECTION:4

TYMNET CERTIFIED PRODUCTS

Tymnet has an ongoing program for certification of various types of products intended for use over the TYMNET Network. Tymnet has certified (and re-certified) over 250 products from more than 100 companies.

1. X.25
2. Personal Computer Software
3. Terminals (Async-to-3270 Service)
4. Modems (X.PC)

If you need assistance, type 'HELP'. When you are finished, type 'QUIT'.
To return to the main menu, type 'TOP'.

YOUR SELECTION: quit

In addition to the 850 nodes that Tymnet has, there is also an 'outdial' service that can connect you directly to a phone number in a desired location in the United States. Thus if you wanted to connect to a PC somewhere you could stil use the Tymnet node in your area, just call the 'outdial' number in the city of the resource and then the destination phone number. Outdial service is billed at about $165 per month plus kilocharacter and per hour charges. If there are line costs at the other end, you are billed for those too, of course. There is a third party that resells Tymnet out-dial services more affordably called Starlink.

5.2.6 Starlink

Galaxy Starlink International
2625 Pennsylvania NE
Albuquerque, NM 87110
(505) 881-6988

Starlink is not part of BT Tymnet, but uses Tymnet's out-dial services to provide access more affordably to those who are not within PCPursuit's target areas. For instance, if you have a local Tymnet node in your area, then Starlink may be the best way for you to access a resource that does not have an account with Tymnet and thus cannot be directly contacted via Tymnet. But you can only access it if that resource is located in an area that has an outdial modem, so it is restricted. They have three types of accounts, but regular and unlimited being the main ones. Regular accounts have a cost per kilocharacter of $.01 over 200,000/ hr. Unlimited accounts do not have this cost. There is a $50 registration fee in any case; rates are:

Type	Primetime	Nonprimetime
Regular	$14.00	$1.50
Unlimited	$14.00	$4.00

Galaxy has its own bulletin board, the Galaxy Information Network that has many typical bulletin board resources, i.e., games, downloadable software, electronic mail. Connect-USA is another service of galaxy that is beginning to establish direct lines to resources.

6. Computer Conferencing Resources

6.1 INTRODUCTION

This is a list of names and address of parties involved with computer conferencing. The keywords help identify the services provided by the entries and include subject descriptors listed below and names of software packages and vendors relevant to the entry.

Keyword Definitions

conferencing software: a software package for computer conferencing

conferencing system: an online resource that provides conferencing — either public or private

distributor: a source for conferencing software

information system: an online resource that offers conferencing, but also provides significant services of another type

microcomputer: a resource of particular relevance to microcomputers

network: a data network for transmission of computer communication

online education: Distance Learning; a resource providing services primarily to the educational community

organization: a resource without an online system

6.2 RESOURCE LIST

Advanced Network and Service
100 Clearbrook Rd.
Elmsfird, NY 10523
(914) 789-5380
Keywords: organization, network

Advanced Technology Information Network (ATI Net)
California Agricultural Technology Institute
School of Agricultural Sciences and Technoliogy
California State University, Fresno

Fresno, CA 93740-115
(209) 278-4872 (voice)
(209) 278-4849 (fax)
(209) 278-4615 (data)
Keywords: conferencing system, CoSy

Advertel Communication Systems, Inc
2067 Ascot
Ann Arbor, MI 48103
(313) 665-2612
Keywords: conferencing system, conferencing software, distributor, Confer

ALANET Electronic Information Service
American Library Association
50 East Huron St.
Chicago, Il 60611
(800) 545-2433 x 4392 (voice)
Keywords: information system, Dialcom
(Non-operational as of January 1992)

Alternex
IBASE
Rue Vincente de Souza 29
2251 Rio de Janiero
Brazil
(21) 2860348
Keywords: conferencing system, APC

America Online
Quantum Computer Services,
8619 Westwood Center Dr.
Vienna, VA 22180
(800) 227-6364 (voice)
Keywords: Apple, conferencing system

Arbornet
c/o Spencer and Marae PriceNash
1325 Rosewood Street
Ann Arbor, MI 48104
(313) 663-3276 (voice)
(313) 996-4644 (data)
(Internet address) anet.ann-arbor.mi.us
Keywords: conferencing system, PicoSpan

Awakening Technology
695 Fifth

Lake Oswego, OR 97034
(503) 635-2615
Keyword: online education, conferencing system

B.C. Schools TeleLINK Consortium
Dr. Lucio Teles
Simon Fraser University
Burnaby, B.C. Canada V5A 1S6
(604) 291-3395
Internet: lucio_teles@cc.sfu.ca
Keywords: online education

BITNET
The BITNET Network Information Center
EDUCOM
1112 16th St., NW, Suite 600
Washington, DC 20036
(202) 872-4200
(202) 872-4318 (Fax)
INFO@BITNIC
Keywords: network

BIX
Byte Information Exchange
1 Phoenix Mill Lane
Peterborough, NH 03458
(800) 227-2983
Keywords: conferencing system, CoSy

BT Tymnet
(see Tymnet)

Capital Online
Washington Information Service, Inc.
1250 24th St., NW, Suite 600
Washington, DC 20037
(202) 466-0522 (voice)
(202) 466-3079 (fax)
(202) 833-1591 (data)
Keywords: conferencing system, Caucus

Caucus
(See Metasystems Design Group, Inc.)

CIGNET
Chautauqua Communication

P. O. Box 47409
Seattle, WA 98146
(206) 937-0515 (voice)
(206) 938-8398 (data)
Keywords: conferencing system, Caucus

Cleveland Free-Net Community Computer System
319 Wickenden Building
Case Western Reserve University
Cleveland, OH 44106
(216) 368-2733 (voice)
(216) 368-5436 (fax)
(216) 368-3888 (data)
Internet: cwns5.cwru.edu (129.22.8.47)
Internet: aa001@cleveland.freenet.edu
Keywords: conferencing system

Coalition for Networked Information
1527 New Hampshire Ave., NW
Washington, DC 20036
(202) 232-2466 (voice)
(202) 462-7849 (fax)
Internet: padler@umdc.bitnet
keywords: organization

Coconut Computing Inc.
7946 Ivanhoe Ave., Suite 303
La Jolla, CA 92037
(619) 456-2002 (voice)
(619) 456-0815 (data)
Keywords: microcomputers, IBM, UNIX, conferencing software

COM and Portacom
Jacob Palme
QZ
Stockholm University Computer Center
Box 27322, S-102 54
Stockholm, Sweden
Keywords: conferencing software

CompuServe
P.O. Box 20212
Columbus, OH 43220
(800) 848-8990
Keywords: conferencing system, PARTICIPATE
(see also: CPN)

CONFER II
(see Advertel Communication Systems, Inc.)

Connect Business Information Network 1.08
Connect Inc.
10161 Bubb Rd.
Cupertino, CA 95014
(800) 262-2638, (408) 973-0110
Keywords: information system

Connected Education
92 Van Cortlandt Park South, #6F
Bronx, NY 10463
(212) 549-6509
(212) 601-3403 (fax)
Keywords: organization, online education

CoSy (see Softwords)

CPN
CompuServe Packet-Switched Data Network
500 Arlington Centre Blvd.
Columbus, OH 43220
(800) 848-8980 (voice)
(800) 848-4480 (data)
Keywords: network

CREN (Corporation for Research and Educational Networking)
see Bitnet

Delphi
General Videotex Corp.
377 Putnam Ave.
Cambridge, MA 02139
(617) 491-3393
Keywords: conferencing system

Dialcom
6120 Executive Blvd.
Rockville, MD 20852
(301) 881-9020 (voice)
(800) 881-9016 (voice)
(Info also available from BT Tymnet)
Keywords: information system

ECHO
Echo Communications Group, Inc.
97 Perry Street, Suite 13
New York, N Y 10014
(212) 255-3839 (voice)
(718) 398-4779 (data)
Keywords: conferencing system, Caucus

EIES
Computerized Conferencing and Communications Center
New Jersey Institute of Technology
University Heights
Newark, NJ 07102
(201) 596-3437 (voice)
Keywords: conferencing system, conferencing software, EIES

Electronic Frontier Foundation
One Cambridge Center, Suite 300
Cambridge, MA 02142
(617) 577-1385 (voice)
(617) 225-2347 (fax)
eff@well.sf.ca.us (Internet)
Keywords: organization

Electronic Networking Association (ENA)
2744 Washington Street
Allentown, PA 18104-4225
Keywords: organization, netweaver

EPRINET
Electric Power Research Institute
P.O. Box 10412
Palo Ato, CA 94303
(415) 855-1000
Keywords: information system

Executive Technology Associates
2744 Washington Street
Allentown, PA 18104-4225
(215) 821-7777 (voice)
Keywords: organization, distributor, PARTICIPATE

FredsNaetet (PeaceNet Sweden)
Timmermansgraend 4
S-116 27 Stockholm
Sweden

(8) 720 0001
Keywords: network system, APC

Galaxy Starlink International
2625 Pennsylvania NE
Albuquerque, NM 87110
(505) 881-6988
Keywords: network

GreenNet
26-28 Underwood Street
London N1 7JQ
(01) 490 1510
Keywords: conferencing system, APC

Institute for Global Communications
(Econet, Peacenet, HomeoNet, ConflictNet)
3228 Sacramento St.,
San Francisco, CA 94115
(415) 923-0900
(415) 923-1665 (fax)
Internet: cdp!econet@arisia.xerox.com
UUCP: uunet!pyramid!cdp!econet
Telenet:
Direct Data:
Keywords: conferencing system, APC

Institute for Networking Design
1-5-19-801 Shimomeguro, Meguro
Tokyo 153 Japan
Keywords: conferencing system, conferencing software

IRIS
c/o Metasystems Design Group, Inc.
2000 North 15th Street, Suite 103,
Arlington, VA 22201
(703) 243-6622 (voice)
Keywords: online education, conferencing system

LITA:MicroUsers
c/o Thomas Wilson
University of Houston
Houston, TX
(713) 749-7163
Keywords: organization, conferencing system, Confer

MediaGap
#1102 - 9541 Erikson Dr.
Burnaby, B.C.
Canada V3J 7N8
Keywords: organization, CoSy, HyperCoSy

Metasystems Design Group, Inc.
2000 North 15th Street, Suite 103
Arlington, VA 22201
(703) 243-6622 (voice)
Keywords: conferencing software, conferencing system, distributor, Caucus

Mist+
New Era Technologies, Inc.
2025 Eye St., Northwest
Suite 992
Washington, DC 20006
(202) 234-2117
Keywords: conferencing software, Mist+

National Public Telecomputing Network
Box 1987
Cleveland, OH 44106
(216) 368-2733
(216) 368-5436 (fax)
Internet: aa001@cleveland.freenet.edu
Keywords: organization

Nicarao
Proyecto de Telecommunicacion/Nicarao
CRIES
Apartado 3516
Managua, Nicaragua
(2) 26228
Keywords: conferencing system

NSFNET
Merit Computer Network
1075 Beal Ave.
Ann Arbor, Michigan 48109-2112
(800) 66-merit
(313) 747-3745 (fax)
nsfnet-info@merit.edu (Internet)
Keywords: network, Internet

NWI
Networking and World Information
333 East River Dr.
East Hartford, CT 06108
(800) 624-5916
Keywords: conferencing system, Parti

Online Librarian's Microcomputer User Group
Brian Williams
Kennedy Library
Cal Poly
San Luis Obispo, CA 93407
(805) 756-2190 (voice)
brian@library.calpoly.edu (internet)
Keywords: organization, Confer

Participate
Participation Systems Inc.
43 Myrtle Terrace
Winchester, MA 01890
(617) 729-1976
Keywords: conferencing software, Parti

PC Pursuit
(800) 835-3638
Keywords: network

Pegasus Networks
P.O. Box 424
The Epicentre, Border St.
Byron Bay 2481 NSW
Australia
(8) 56789
Keywords: conferencing system, APC

PEN
City of Santa Monica
Information Systems Dept.
1685 Main Street
P.O. Box 2200
Santa Monica, CA 90406-2200
(213) 458-8383
Keywords: conferencing system, Caucus

PicoSpan
Network Technologies International, Inc.

Arbor Atrium Building
315 West Huron
Ann Arbor, MI 48103
(800) 638-4832
Keywords: conferencing software

Portal Communications Company
10385 Cherry Tree Lane
Cupertino, CA 95014
(408) 973-9111 (voice)
(408) 725-0561 (data) or C PORTAL (SprintNet/Telenet)
(408) 725-1580 (fax)
CS@cup.portal.com (Internet address)
Keywords: conferencing system

Santa Monica
(see PEN)

Softwords
4252 Commerce Circle
Victoria, British Columbia
Canada V8Z 4M2
(604) 727-6522 (voice)
(604) 727-6418 (fax)
Internet: softwords.bc.ca (134.87.11.x)
DataPac (3020 6480463)
Keywords: distributor, conferencing software, CoSy

SprintNet
12490 Sunrise Valley Drive
Reston, VA 22096
(800) 835-3638 (voice)
(703) 689-5177 (fax)
Keywords: network

Starlink
(see Galaxy Starlink International)

Technology Resources in Education (TRIE)
(800) 272-TRIE (voice)
Keywords: CoSy, online education

TECHNET
New York Institute of Technology
Academic Computing Lab
Building 66, Room 205

Central Islip, NY 11722
(800) 462-9041
Keywords: online education, conferencing system

Telenet
(see Sprintnet)

Tymnet
2560 North First Street
P.O. Box 49019
San Jose, CA 95161-9019
(800) 336-0149, (800) 872-7654
Keywords: network

Unibase telecomm, Ltd.
3002 Harding St.
Regina Sask., Canada S4P 0Y4
(306) 789-9007
Keywords: online education

Unicon, Inc
120 Enterprise Drive
Ann Arbor, MI 48103
(313) 996-2663
Keywords: organization, distributor, PicoSpan

UNISON
700 West Pete Rose Way
Cincinnati, OH 45203
(800) 334-6122
Keywords: conferencing system, Parti

UUNET Communications Services
3110 Fairview Park Drive, Suite 570
Falls Church, VA 22042
(703) 876-5050
(703) 876-5059 (fax)
uunet-request@uunet.uu.net
Keywords: organization, Internet

Wayne State University
Computing Services Center
5925 Woodward Ave
Detroit , MI 48202
(313) 577-4642
Keywords: conferencing system, Confer

Web
456 Spadina Ave.
2nd Floor
Toronto, Ontario M5T 2G8
Canada
(416) 929-0634
Keywords: conferencing system, APC

Washington Information Services Inc.
(See Capital Online)

WELL
27 Gate Five Rd.
Suite 65G
Sausalito, CA 94965
(415) 332-4335 (voice)
(415) 332-6106 (data)
Keywords: conferencing system, PicoSpan

Western Montana College Big Sky Telegraph
710 South Atlantic
Dillon, MT 59725
(406) 683-7338
(406) 683-7695 (fax)
(406) 683-76809 (data)
Keywords: online education

7. Appendices

7.1 INTERNET-ACCESSIBLE LIBRARY CATALOGS AND DATABASES

Introduction

Internet-Accessible Library Catalogs and Databases is a list coauthored by Dr. Art St. George of the University of New Mexico and Dr. Ron Larsen of the University of Maryland, and is widely available through a number of Internet nodes. Dr. St. George says this document "began as an effort to provide additional service to the network community locally. However, it became apparent that the library resources were of broader appeal than that."

In its current state the listing contains information on over 100 online library catalogs and databases available within the United States and beyond. It contains listings of U.S. and international library catalogs and databases, dial-up libraries, Campus-Wide Online Information Systems, and bulletin board systems. Each listing gives a brief description of the resource and instructions on how to access it, as well as places to contact for more information. Listings include such material as Columbia University's online library catalog (CLIO), Pennsylvania's State University online card catalog system (PENpages), and the Colorado Alliance of Research Libraries (CARL) and its 25 individual resource listings of libraries and information databases, such as the Metro Denver Facts database.

This catalog is an ongoing project. If you have any suggestions, comments, or additions, please send them to Dr. Art St. George by electronic mail to stgeorge@unmb.bitnet or stgeorge@bootes.unm.edu.

The listing is currently broken down into six sections, with their contents as follows:

Section 1: Catalogs and Databases Accessible Without Charge

ALABAMA
- Auburn University

CALIFORNIA
- California State University, Long Beach
- Cal Poly State University, San Luis Obispo
- The University of California's online catalog
- University of California, Berkeley

COLORADO
- Colorado Alliance of Research Libraries - CARL

DELAWARE
- University of Delaware Libraries DELCAT2

FLORIDA
- State University System

GEORGIA
- Emory University

HAWAII
- University of Hawaii at Manoa Online Catalog

ILLINOIS
- Northwestern University "LUIS"
- University of Illinois, Chicago
- University of Chicago
- University of Chicago/Urbana-Champaign

INDIANA
- Purdue University
- T H O R -THe Online Resource
- The University of Notre Dame Library

KANSAS
- The University of Kansas Library

MAINE
- University of Maine System Library Catalog

MARYLAND
- AIM (Access to Information about Maryland)
- UMCAT (Online Catalog for UM Libraries)

MASSACHUSETTS
- Boston University "TOMUS"
- Harvard University- HOLLIS, Harvard OnLine Library Information System

MICHIGAN
- The University of Michigan
- Michigan State University Libraries
- Wayne State University

MINNESOTA
- The University of Minnesota

MISSOURI
- The University of Missouri

NEW HAMPSHIRE
- Dartmouth College
- Dartmouth College Library Online Catalog

NEW JERSEY
- Princeton University Library

NEW MEXICO
- The University of New Mexico
- University of New Mexico General Library
- University of New Mexico Medical Center Library
- New Mexico State University

NEW YORK
- Cornell University
- New York University
- Rensselaer Polytechnic Institute
- State University of New York at Binghamton

OHIO
- Case Western Reserve University
- Kent State University
- Ohio State University
- University of Toledo

OREGON
- University of Oregon

PENNSYLVANIA
- University of Pittsburgh
- Miscellaneous Online Catalogs and Databases

RHODE ISLAND
- Brown University

TENNESSEE
- University of Tennessee
- University of Tennessee, Memphis
- Health Science Library
- Vanderbilt University

TEXAS
- Texas A&M Library System
- UT Arlington Library System
- UT Austin Library System UTCAT
- University of Texas at Dallas

UTAH
- University of Utah Marriott Library

VIRGINIA
- The Old Dominion University Library
- Virginia Commonwealth University Library System

WISCONSIN
- University of Wisconsin Library Catalogs

Section 2: Catalogs and Databases Accessible For a Charge

CALIFORNIA
- Research Libraries Information Network

Section 3: International Catalogs

AUSTRALIA
- Australian National University's Library
- Deakin University Library

NEW ZEALAND
Victoria University of Wellington
GERMANY
University of Konstanz
MEXICO
The Instituto Tecnologico y Estudios Superiores de Monterrey's Online Catalog
Library of the Universidad de las Americas, Pueblas

Section 4: Dial-Up Libraries and Catalogs

Section 5: Other Online Resources

BULLETIN BOARDS
AGRICULTURE
BUSINESS/ECONOMICS
HEALTH/NUTRITION
LAW
MISCELLANEOUS
NATURAL RESOURCES
NEWSPAPERS
SPACE/SCIENCE
SPORTS AND RECREATION
OTHER FEDERAL GOVERNMENT OR RELATED BBS

Section 6: Campus-Wide Information Systems

Columbia University
Cornell's CUINFO
MIT TechInfo
New Mexico State University NMSU/INFO
NYU
PNN - Princeton News Network
University of New Mexico
University of North Carolina at Chapel Hill INFO

7.1.1 Catalogs and Databases Accessible Without Charge

The following entries are representative of the St. George/Larsen list and should provide an indication of the depth of information provided.

CALIFORNIA

University of California, Berkeley
GLADIS - the UC Berkeley Online Catalog
GopAC.BERKELEY.EDU

Instructions:

Telnet to GopAC.BERKELEY.EDU

VT100 emulation is possible but not explicitly present. Logoff instructions are provided.

GLADIS is public access and it does not require a password for access. The catalog covers the holdings of most UCB libraries, including the main library, the Moffitt Undergraduate Library, the Bancroft Library and some 23 branch libraries. The catalog is complete for monographic holdings from 1977 to the present and incomplete for monographic holdings prior to that date. We are in the process of converting older monographic records, so more of these records appear in the catalog daily. All of the serial titles, both past and present, are re_ected in GLADIS. GLADIS also contains records for maps, manuscripts, audiovisual materials and computer software. Circulation information (whether an item is checked out or not) is available for some library locations (six libraries as of September, 1989).

FOR MORE INFORMATION, CONTACT:
Roy Tennant
Public Service Automated Systems Coordinator
(415) 642-3532
RTENNANT@LIBRARY.BERKELEY.EDU
roy@ucbgarne

COLORADO

Colorado Alliance of Research Libraries - CARL
PAC.CARL.ORG

Colorado Alliance of Research Libraries
777 Grant, Suite 306
Denver CO 80203-3580
(303)861-5319

E-mail: help@carl.org
Instructions:

Telnet to pac.carl.org
VT100 emulation is supported and logoff instructions are provided.

CARL offers access to the following groups of databases:

1. Library Catalogs

2. Current Article Indexes and Access (including UnCover)

3. Information Databases (including Encyclopedia)

4. Other Library Systems

5. Library and System News

Enter the NUMBER of your choice, and press the <RETURN> key >>1

LIBRARY CATALOGS

6. Auraria
7. Colorado School of Mines
8. C.U. at Boulder
9. C.U. Health Sciences Center
10. C.U. Law Library
11. Denver Public Library
12. Denver University
13. Denver University Law School
14. University of Northern Colorado
15. University of Wyoming
16. Regis College
17. Luther College
18. State Department of Education
19. Colorado State Publications
20. Government Publications—DPL and CU
21. CCLINK—Community Colleges
22. Colorado Health Sciences Libraries

CARL Library catalogs now contain over 4 million records.

Enter the NUMBER of your choice, and press the <RETURN> key >>2

CURRENT ARTICLE INDEXES AND ACCESS

ARTICLE INDEXES UNION LISTS

34. UnCover — Article Access
36. Boston Library Consortium

CURRENT RECEIPTS LOCAL ARTICLES

35. New Journal Issues
37. Info Colorado

NATIONAL SERIALS CATALOGING DATABASE

38. Conser
Enter the NUMBER of your choice, and press the <RETURN> key >> 3

INFORMATION DATABASES

39. Encyclopedia

40. Choice Book Reviews

41. Metro Denver Facts

37. Info Colorado

Enter the NUMBER of your choice, and press the <RETURN> key >> 4

OTHER LIBRARY SYSTEMS

42. Boulder Public Library (Boulder)

43. MARMOT Library System (Western Slope)

44. Pikes Peak Library System (Colorado Springs)

Enter the NUMBER of your choice, and press the <RETURN> key >> 5

News is currently available for:

1. Auraria
2. C.U., Boulder
3. Denver Public Library
4. Denver University
5. Denver University Law Library
6. School of Mines
7. U.N.C.
8. Regis College
9. University of Wyoming
10. C.U. Health Sciences Center
11. InfoColorado
12. Government Pub.
13. Luther College
14. CC Link (Community Coll.)
15. GENERAL PAC NEWS
16. Technos : January

DATABASE: UnCover

This database contains records describing journals and their contents. Coverage is rapidly growing as CARL member holdings are processed. UnCover will soon include more than 10,000 titles, and descriptions of over 600,000 articles will be generated each year. Articles can be retrieved individually or displayed as the table of contents for any given journal issue.

Note: UnCover is restricted to use by the patrons of CARL's member Libraries. Others may make special arrangements. Please send e-mail to: uncover@carl.org or contact Rebecca Lenzini at (303) 861-5319 for more information.

DATABASE: Encyclopedia

The Academic American Encyclopedia, published by Grolier Electronic Publishing, Inc. is the equivalent of a 20 volume printed encyclopedia. It contains over 30,000 articles of general interest in the humanities, science and the social sciences, as well as information about sports and contemporary life. Many biographies are included and the information is updated regularly.

Note: The encyclopedia is restricted to use by the patrons of certain of CARL's member libraries.

DATABASE: Choice Book Reviews

CHOICE: Current Reviews for College Libraries.

The file includes reviews from September 1988 forward, supplied by the Association of College and Research Libraries. Data are copyright ACRL, and CARL thanks the Association for allowing us to use its records.

DATABASE: BLC Union List

This database contains the current journal holdings of the Boston Library Consortium, a cooperative association of academic and research libraries in the Greater Boston area.

Boston College
State Library of Massachusetts
Boston Public Library
Tufts University
Boston University
University of Massachusetts/Amherst
Brandeis University
University of Massachusetts/Boston
MIT
University of Massachusetts/Worcest.
Northeastern University
Wellesley College
DATABASE: Conser

The CONSER file is a subset of the authenticated MARC CONSER file. It contains approximately 220,000 bibliographic records for serials that were coded c (current) in byte 6 of the 008 field. Update tapes containing new records and changes are processed monthly. The records are cataloged using the same indexing rules that are applied to the CARL bibliographic files. Libraries may access this file for downloading bibliographic records through CARL Serials Control.

DATABASE: Metro Denver Facts
METRO DENVER FACTS is "a statistical summary of metropolitan Denver's growth and assets as a business location." The data is supplied by the Economic

Development Group of the Greater Denver Chamber of Commerce, and is presented here as a project of the METRO DENVER NETWORK and CARL.
DATABASE: InfoColorado

InfoColorado is a pilot database pertaining to the business and economy of Colorado and its municipalities. It is made up of newspaper abstracts dating from November 1986 as well as from selected issues of area business journals and reports. All call numbers refer to Auraria Library. This project has been developed with financial assistance from the Friends of the Auraria Library and from the Adolph Coors Corporation.

DATABASE: New Journal Issues

Information about journal issues received the previous business day by some of the CARL libraries.

FLORIDA

State University System
NERVM.NERDC.UFL.EDU

TN3270 emulation is required.

LUIS (Library User Information Service) is the online catalog of the State University System (SUS) libraries. LUIS runs on hardware belonging to the NERDC. The software is maintained by the Florida Center for Library Automation (FCLA), a SUS agency.

There are actually nine LUIS catalogs, one for each university. For each library, the percentage of its collection searchable in LUIS is different and is always changing. To find out what a library's LUIS catalog covers, contact that library.

LUIS is available

7:30 a.m. - 1:00 a.m. Monday - Friday
8:00 a.m. - 1:00 a.m. Saturday
10:00 a.m. - 1:00 a.m. Sunday

Logging On to LUIS from the Internet

Use a tn3270 version of telnet to connect to nervm.nerdc.ufl.edu over the Internet. After reaching nervm, press enter to get past the VM logo screen. CP READ will be displayed in the lower right corner. Type DIAL VTAM and press enter. The screen will clear and the message NERDC VTAM IS ACTIVE will be displayed.

From this point, you will need to work your way through several screens to sign on to LUIS. The following steps show the procedure for signing on. For each step, type the text in quotes (without the quotes), then press your enter key.
1. From NERDC VTAM IS ACTIVE, type "nerluis" on the next line and press enter.

NERDC VTAM IS ACTIVE
nerluis

2. You will see the WELCOME TO NERLUIS screen. Type "1" here after ENTER SELECTION HERE and press enter.

3. You will see the NERDC SECURITY MODULE screen. Type "fcl" after GROUP-ID. The cursor will automatically tab to the next line after "fcl" and your operator ID, so do not press enter. For demonstration purposes, type "aaya" for both the operator ID and the password (this will "charge" the session to the University of Florida for statistical purposes). The password will not display as it is typed. Press enter after typing the password. If you receive the message INVALID OPERATOR ID or INVALID PASSWORD, retype the ID or password in the proper space and press enter.

NERDC SECURITY MODULE

PLEASE SIGN ON

GROUP-ID fcl

OPERATOR aaya

PASSWORD aaya (not displayed)

4. You will see the message SIGN-ON COMPLETE. Press the clear key to clear the screen, then type "luis" and press enter to display a menu showing each of the catalogs available in LUIS. Type the number associated with the desired LUIS catalog, and press enter. This places you in that card catalog and gives you the LUIS: LIBRARY USER INFORMATION SERVICE introductory screen. You have successfully signed on to the catalog of your choice. Follow the instructions on the screens for searching LUIS.

5. To change catalogs, type "menu" from the command line of any screen to return to the catalog menu screen.

How to Search in LUIS

LUIS is a "user friendly" computer system. It has self-instructing introductory screens, "help" screens, and prompt messages on each screen that you can consult for guidance. You need only know that a search of the catalog must be made under AUTHOR, TITLE, or SUBJECT by typing one of the following commands into the terminal and pressing the ENTER key.

a = author's name (last name first)

(e.g., a = asimov)

t = title of a book or journal

(e.g., t = robots of dawn)

s = subject heading

(e.g., s = computer)

sm = medical subject heading

(e.g., sm = genetics)

By following other basic card catalog rules (such as ignoring initial articles), you can rapidly gain access to all catalog entries that match the request. Typing in a full author, title, or subject heading is not necessary to get a response.

Exiting LUIS

To exit LUIS, press your clear key once or twice until the screen is clear. If you have problems clearing your screen with the clear key, you can clear the screen by typing #$#$ on the command line and then pressing enter. This gets you out of the catalog you are in, but you are still signed on to LUIS. When the screen is clear, type

logoff

and press enter. When you see the message SIGN-OFF IS COMPLETE, you are logged off and the message NERDC VTAM IS ACTIVE will reappear. You are not logged off if you do not see these messages. To terminate the telnet connection, type UNDIAL and press enter when the NERDC VTAM IS ACTIVE message reappears.

Questions and Problems

If you get the message "APPLID NOT AVAILABLE" when you enter "nerluis," then LUIS is not available and you will have to try later.

Problems accessing LUIS from the Internet should be directed via electronic mail to <postmaster@nervm.nerdc.ufl.edu>.

Questions about individual library catalogs and holdings should be directed to the staff at that library.

ILLINOIS

Northwestern University "LUIS"
PACX.ACNS.NWU.EDU

Connecting

VT100 emulation is supported and logoff instructions are provided.

Northwestern University's "LUIS" online catalog may be accessed from other academic institutions via the Internet, using telnet. The library catalog's telnet address is PACX.ACNS.NWU.EDU. Once connected, press <ENTER> or <RETURN>; you will receive the prompt "enter class". Type 60, then press <ENTER> or

<RETURN> twice. At this point you will be prompted for a terminal type; VT100 is to be preferred, assuming your local communications software will provide VT100 emulation. Pressing <ENTER> or <RETURN> again will provide you the online catalog's introductory screen.

To sign off, please enter a percent sign (%) at any prompt. You can then disconnect your telnet session. PLEASE NOTE that the online catalog AUTOMATICALLY disconnects if there is no keyboard activity within a two-minute period.

Remote users of Northwestern's LUIS catalog who may be familiar with other NOTIS-based online catalogs will note some differences in our implementation. Of particular interest may be NU's provision of cross-references in the online catalog, a feature that is to appear in the commercial release scheduled for the end of 1990. This LUIS version does not provide keyword/Boolean searching, but does offer what we call "research qualification," the ability of a user to limit an author, title, or subject search result by any of several elements present in the coordinated indexes: date, format (e.g., serial, video), other word, or holding library. Use of this feature is explained in a help screen which may be accessed by typing an ampersand (&).

Contact: Brian Nielsen
Northwestern U. Library
b_nielsen@nuacc.acns.nwu.edu
(708) 491-2170

University of Illinois/Urbana-Champaign
SYSTEM: ILLINET Online

VT100 emulation is possible but not explicitly present. Logoff instructions are provided.

Online system for the University of Illinois collection, and statewide system or over 800 academic, public, and special libraries throughout Illinois.

ACCESS: telnet GARCON.CSO.UIUC.EDU

HOURS:
Monday - Saturday: 8:00 a.m. - Midnight
Sunday: Noon - Midnight

If the user's software does not allow specific port addressing, you can telnet to the host or the address and enter LCS at the login prompt.

Database Scope:

Use ILLINET Online to search over 3 million titles in the collection at the Uni versity of Illinois Library. ILLINET Online also provides searching access to the collections of over 800 libraries in the state (over 20 million items.) IL LINET Online consists of two separate but closely linked systems: LCS and FBR.

LCS is a short-record circulation system, with information about a book's check out status, location, and call number. It contains records for nearly everything cataloged at the Univ. of Illinois Library. LCS also includes records for over 30 other academic libraries in Illinois. LCS searching is made easy through the LCSgated interface. Online help and instructions are available by typing HELP when you log on to the system.

FBR contains more in-depth information about subjects, authors, titles, and series for books cataloged since 1975 and most serials cataloged since 1977 (over 1.5 million books) at the University of Illinois Library. Online help for searching FBR is available by typing INFO when you enter the system.

FOR MORE INFORMATION, CONTACT:

Beth Sandore
Automated Systems
Off.: (217) 333-2592
Fax.: (217) 244-0398
SANDORE@UIUCVMD.BITNET

MASSACHUSETTS

Harvard University
HOLLIS - Harvard OnLine Library Information System
128.103.60.31

1. telnet or TN3270 to hollis.harvard.edu (128.103.60.31).

2. If the next screen you see begins "Mitek Server..." press ENTER or RETURN. Default VT100 emulation is provided. (Only terminals connecting as ascii devices see this screen.)

3. The next screen will begin "HARVARD UNIVERSITY / OFFICE FOR INFORMATION TECHNOLOGY". Type "hollis" after the prompt and press ENTER: ==> hollis
"Welcome to HOLLIS" should display.

No password is required to enter HOLLIS. The union catalog of the Harvard libraries (database HU) and the database of older Widener Library materials (database OW) do not have any access restrictions. However, some other databases within HOLLIS may have access restrictions because of vendor requirements.

To exit, use whatever command your local software provides for escaping back to telnet. If (and only if) you came in through the screen that began "Mitek Server...", you can also exit by pressing the Escape key and typing the letter "x" twice: ESC xx. These users can also see their default vt100 keyboard mapping by pressing the Escape key and typing the letter "h":
ESC h.

FOR FURTHER ASSISTANCE, CONTACT: library@harvarda.harvard.edu

UTAH

University of Utah Marriott Library
LIB.UTAH.EDU

To access University of Utah Marriott Library via Internet:

telnet to Utahlib or to Lib.Utah.Edu using TN3270 emulation. You will be greeted by a VM logon screen.

Type <enter> to move to the next screen. Type D UNIS, followed by <enter>. Type <enter> to get the catalog screen.

Perform your searches as with any NOTIS system.

To disconnect, break your telnet connection in your usual way with an interrupt key, typically PF3, PF4, PA1, Ctl-C, Ctl-Z, etc. Any interval longer than two minutes with no keystrokes will also end the session.

FOR MORE INFORMATION, CONTACT:
Kenneth Luker
Assistant Director Systems and Technical Services
Marriott Library
University of Utah Provo, UT 84112
(801) 581-7994
KLUKER@LIB.UTAH.EDU

VIRGINIA

The Old Dominion University Library
GEAC.LIB.ODU.EDU

The Old Dominion University Library holds over 1.6 million items in a variety of formats - microform, recordings, newspaper, periodical and book. The library is a selective depository of U. S. government publications and documents of the State of Virginia.

ACCESS FROM telnet: type - telnet geac.lib.odu.edu and press <Enter>. After a short wait, you should see several messages, among them the following: telnet escape character is Control -] This means that the connection has been established. Make a note of which character serves as your escape character. It differs from system to system. The escape character is useful for getting out of problem situations. Press <Enter> ONCE to get GEAC's attention. The GEAC catalogue then comes online. At the end of the session, type END or QUIT, or for CMS users type F4. While online, type HELP for help. Good luck!

Contact: Albert C. Liu
Assistant Librarian
Technical and Automation Services
Old Dominion University
Norfolk, VA 23529

(804) 683-4141
BITNET: HSW100U@ODUVM

Virginia Polytechnic Institute and State University runs VTLS. The VTLS system is connected to the outside world through the campus IBM ROLM CBX.

Telephone access to the CBX is provided through an inbound modem pool at phone number (703) 231-4000. Speeds up to 2400 baud are accepted. There is no charge at this time for dialing into the CBX.

The CBX can be accessed via the Internet using: telnet 128.173.5.4

Volunteer surveyors were unable to connect to this system.

After connecting to the CBX and getting the informative prompt, issue the command CALL VTLS to connect to the VTLS system running on the Library's HP3000 Series 950 computer.

FOR MORE INFORMATION, CONTACT:
Harry M. Kriz, KRIZ@VTVM1

Virginia Commonwealth University Library System
VCUVM1.VCU.EDU

Virginia Commonwealth University Library System
Richmond, VA 23284-2033

Contact:
Janet Woody
(804/367-0032).
BITNET: jwoody@vcuvax

Accessing the Virginia Commonwealth University Library System:
Telnet: VCUVM1.VCU.EDU Type: telnet vcuvm1.vcu.edu Response: "Trying ..."
At the "VM" screen (which requests USERID, PASSWORD, and COMMAND), the cursor should be at the USERID ===> prompt.

Type: <ENTER>
Response: If your host computer supports full 3270 emulation, the VCU computer will respond "Enter one of the following commands" and will list four commands (LOGON, DIAL, MSG, and LOGOFF). [If DIAL is NOT one of the options provided, see the footnote below.]

Type: DIAL VTAM. Press <ENTER>.
Response: "VM/IS VTAM" [the "VTAM Screen"] is displayed in the upper left corner, and the screen displays a menu.

Type: the letter L (for VCU library catalog). Then press <ENTER>.
Response: Displays the message "Press Enter for access to the VCU library catalog ..."

Type: <ENTER>
Response: Provides on-screen instructions to use the catalog.

To End the Session:

Type: CTRL and Z (1-3 times).
Response: Screen is blank.

Type: LOGOFF.
Response: Return to the VTAM screen.

Type: UNDIAL at the VTAM screen prompt SELECT SYSTEM ===>. Press <ENTER>
Response: RConnection closed by Foreign HostS

FOOTNOTE ON 3270 EMULATION:

1. If your host computer does NOT support full 3270 emulation, the VCU computer will respond "Enter one of the following commands" and will list only TWO commands: MSG and LOGOFF. In this case, type LOGOFF. Start over by substituting the command "tn3270", instead of "telnet", i.e., type:

TN3250 VCUVM1.VCU.EDU OR TN3250 128.172.001.066
If TN3270 is supported by your host, you will get the four choices, including DIAL. Type DIAL VTAM. Follow the instructions above continuing from the section: "Type the Letter L (for VCU Library Catalog)"

2. If both the "telnet" and "tn3270" commands do not work properly, it will not be possible at this time for you to use Internet to connect to the VCU library catalog.

WISCONSIN

University of Wisconsin Library Catalogs
Madison and Milwaukee Campuses Network Library System (NLS)
NLS.ADP.WISC.EDU

Contact: Automation Help Desk
212F Memorial Library
University of Wisconsin
728 State Street Madison, WI 53706
E-mail: glshelp@vms.macc.wisc.edu
Phone: (608) 262-8880

Description:

The Network Library System (NLS) is the online public catalog of the libraries at the University of Wisconsin-Madison and the University of Wisconsin-Milwaukee. NLS supports separate online catalogs for each campus.

The UW-Madison online catalog contains more than 1.7 million titles cataloged since 1976, located in 25 libraries on the campus and at the Center for Research Libraries in Chicago. This represents roughly 50% of the collections. The UW-Milwaukee catalog contains approximately 900,000 titles and represents 85% of the general collection.

Network Access:

If available on your system, please use tn3270 (telnet supporting 3270 emulation) to access blue.adp.wisc.edu. When connected you are presented a menu from which you select NLS1, the library catalog. (If you don't know how your function keys are mapped, TAB to the option you want and press ENTER.)

Telnet access is also available via a gateway machine providing the necessary 3270 emulation. From your local host use telnet to access nls.adp.wisc.edu. You will be prompted to enter a terminal type. VT100 is the default, or you can enter the command list to display a list of supported terminal types. Upon entering a valid terminal type, select NLS1 from the menu displayed to connect to the library catalog.

Upon entering NLS, a screen is displayed at which you either press ENTER to search the Madison catalog or type Mil and press ENTER to search the Milwaukee catalog.

To exit, enter the command exit on any screen to return to the Main Menu. Here you select the option to quit. This returns control to your local host.

Who Can Use The Catalog:

The University of Wisconsin library catalogs for the Madison and Milwaukee campuses are currently available to all interested parties.

Miscellaneous Information:

Xterm users or other windowing software users must set their window size to 80 characters x 25 lines.

For help using NLS or to obtain a free NLS Computer Catalog User's Guide, contact the Memorial Library Information Desk at (608) 262-3193, or Dennis Hill via the Internet: dhill@vms.macc.wisc.edu.

More detailed information on accessing NLS via the Internet is documented in: "TCP/IP Network Access to the NLS Catalog via Tn3270 and telnet". For a copy of this document, or any other information, contact the Automation Help Desk at (608) 262-8880, or via the Internet at: glshelp@vms.macc.wisc.edu.

Note on keyboard mappings:

Because keyboard mappings are de^ned by the tn3270 software on the client's host computer, we are not able to tell you definitively how your keyboard will be mapped. The following chart shows a selection of the tn3270 keyboard mapping used on many UW Madison VAX computers. These definitions are also used when accessing NLS via telnet as they are provided by the 3270 software on the gateway machine.

KeyPurpose	*Keyboard Definition*
Send (called the BLUE key in NLS)	ENTER or RETURN
Erase-to-end-of-field (called the YELLOW key in NLS)	Ctrl-e
Delete character	Ctrl-d
Escape key	PF11 (default mapping)
Insert/Overstrike toggle	Escape space
Function keys PF1 - PF9	Escape 1 - Escape 9
Function key PF10	Escape 0
Function key PF11	Escape -
Function key PF12	Escape =

Section 2: Catalogs and Databases Accessible For a Charge

CALIFORNIA

Research Libraries Information Network
RLG.STANFORD.EDU

RLIN features: on-line union catalog complementary databases _exible searching integrated acquisitions, cataloging and ILL system on-line authority ^les description and management of archival materials support of non-Roman scripts database generated products electronic mail and bulletin board.

Internet access: $119 for 10 hours connect time.

Contact: RLIN Information Service Electronic mail to bl.ric@rlg

Section 3: International Catalogs

AUSTRALIA

Australian National University's Library
ACTS11.ANU.OZ.AU

The Australian National University's Library catalogue is called URUCA.

Telnet to FACTS11.ANU.OZ.AU

URICA requires VT100 emulation.

When access to the network has been obtained, the following will normally appear on your screen:

CONNECT ANU CSC MICOM Classes are: ANUB COOMBS CSC0 CSC1 CSCUNIX

FAC0
FAC1 FAC2 FACUNIX URICA ENTER CLASS

Type in URICA in response to this prompt.

A URICA screen will appear. All URICA enquiries are menu driven.

The URICA software is always logged on except from 5 p.m. on Fridays to 1 p.m. AEST on Saturdays when the system closes for maintenance.

Useful keys to know when searching URICA:

To get a help screen, press the backslash key "\"

To terminate a URICA search (but not to exit from the network), press the full stop key.

Enter "#4" to go back to the main menu.

To disconnect send a break.

The network will automatically disconnect a terminal which has not been used for 15 minutes.

If you need assistance contact:
Tony Barry
Tony_Barry@library.anu.oz.au or TXB750@csc1.anu.oz.auILANET MLN 207550

Voice: (06) 2494632
Fax: (06) 2490734
Telex: 10717252

Deakin University Library
LIBRARY.DEAKIN.OZ.AU (128.184.1.1)

Details follow for Deakin University Library, Victoria,
Australia Region: VICTORIA (AUSTRALIA)

Chief Librarian: Margaret Cameron (mac@deakin.oz.au) Systems Librarian:
Tony Mays (tonym@deakin.oz.au)
Library System: ALICE

ALICE - the Deakin University Library OPAC

Telnet to LIBRARY.DEAKIN.OZ.AU (128.184.1.1)

Internet access to Deakin University Library (ALICE)

Access to the Deakin University Library's online library system can be gained from any terminal which is connected to the INTERNET network.
The Library's online system contains records for all items held in the Library, as

well as items which are on-order. In addition, the on-line system also contains similar information on the holdings at the Gordon Technical College (GTC) Library.

Instructions on the use of ALICE is given in the booklet "Guide to the Public Inquiry Terminals" available from the Library's Information Desk. Ph: +61 52 471351.

NB Access can also be obtained by direct dial-in or by using X.25, details of which are available separately.

To gain access

0 Terminal setup: no specific terminal settings required. Terminals already connected to AARNet should not be altered.
1. telnet to: library.deakin.oz.au.

You may need to have already established a session on a computer at your institution, which is connected to AARNet. Alternatively, you may be able to establish a connection directly from your terminal server. Consult your local Computing Centre for further advice.

2. If the connection is successful, you will receive something similar to:-

    SunOS UNIX (sol.deakin.OZ.AU.)

    login:

3. Type: alice Press: [RETURN]

4. The system will then indicate when ALICE was last used, display any "messages of the day", and then try to determine the type of terminal being used. If it cannot be determined automatically, the system will prompt you for the device type.

    TERM = (unknown)

Type: <the code corresponding to your terminal type>. Some terminal types are:- tatung Tatung VT-4100 vt100 DEC VT-100 vt52 VT-52 v3 TV1-910,920 6310 hazeltine 6310 (other codes on request from the Assistant Systems Librarian - craige@deakin.oz.au)

    Press: [RETURN]

(If you don't know the terminal type, simply press [RETURN] and the system will attempt to provide a reasonable format).

5. The system will try to establish a connection to the Library's computer. If the connection fails the system will respond with "Remote is busy". The system will then break the connection with your terminal, and you will need to restart from Step 1 to establish a new connection.

If the connection is established, the system will respond with:-

a) clearing the screen
b) give instructions for starting and finishing an ALICE session i.e.

Type "Q" to start, <CR>~.<CR> to end.

You can now start ALICE, and any subsequent commands will need to be ALICE commands. Usually, the appropriate ALICE commands are displayed at the bottom of the screen, but a user should consult the above-mentioned Guide before any serious use of the system.

To leave ALICE

1. At any stage of a search within ALICE, you may leave it.

Press: [RETURN]
Type: ~. (i.e. tilde, dot) Press: [RETURN]

2. The system will immediately break the connection to the Library's computer, and then break the connection between your terminal and the system.

PROBLEMS IN USING THE SYSTEM SHOULD BE ADDRESSED TO:

CRAIGE HICKS
DEAKIN UNIVERSITY LIBRARY
DEAKIN UNIVERSITY
VIC 3217
+61 52 471345

AARNet: craige@deakin.OZ.AU

NB Expert users can also gain access to ALICE, by using the *nix command (or equivalent): rlogin library.deakin.oz.au. -l alice

alice.aarnet CMH/LE 15/5/90

Section 4: Dial-Up Libraries and Catalogs

The following is the result of a first survey of libraries with dial-up access. Time did not permit its integration, where possible, into the listing of libraries by state.

Please send corrections or additions to:

Robert W. Bethune 34 Echo Lane Warwick, NY 10990 UUCP: cboard!rwb@oswego.edu
Phonenet: Voice: 914-986-7020 Data : 914-986-0697
The following is a list of 21 systems that offer dial-up access to one or more large library on-line card catalogs. Please send updates, additions, and corrections to the above address.

Boston University TOMUS.
Brandeis University LOUIS.
Massachusetts Institute of Technology BARTON.
Tufts University TULIPS.
Wellesley College INNOPAC.
University of Massachusetts at Boston ULYSIS.
Boston Library Consortium Union List of Serials.
DALNET (Detroit Area Library Network).
MERIT.
Michigan State University MAGIC.
University of Kansas OCAT.
University of Wisconsin NLS Network Library System.
University of Oregon JANUS.
University of Illinois ILLINET.
University of Texas at Austin UTCAT.
University of Michigan MIRLYN.
University of California MELVYL.
Renssalaer Polytechnic Institute INFOTRAX.
Colorado Alliance of Research Libraries (CARL).
Ohio State University Library.
Dartmouth College.

Section 5: Other Online Resources

BULLETIN BOARDS

There have been a large number of requests from Internet users to expand the Internet Library list by adding other online resources. One such resource that has repeatedly been requested is a list of bulletin boards. The following list was compiled by Marty Solomon, Vice President of Computing and Communications at the University of South Carolina and Diane Kovacs, Government Documents Coordinator, Ellen Clarke Bertrand Library, Bucknell University. Please send corrections or additions to them: Marty can be reached at SOLOMON@UNIVSCVM and Diane is at KOVACS@BKNLVMS.

Unless otherwise noted, set your modem for eight data bits, no parity and one stop bit. ANSI or VT100 terminal emulation will work almost anywhere.

AGRICULTURE

301-344-8510 - ALF, Agriculture Library, Berwyn MD. Agricultural information.

314-882-8289 - AgEBB, Columbus MO. Agricultural information.

402-472-6615 - HPRCC, Weather Data, Lincoln NE. Regional agricultural weather.

BUSINESS/ECONOMICS

202-377-3870 or 202-377-0433 - Dept. of Commerce, Office of Business Analysis. Current economic news from DoC Economic Affairs(EA) agencies including press releases, economic indicators, official DoC summaries of economic news, information on how to obtain data tapes, and summaries of reports and studies produced by EA agencies. Also included are press releases issued by the Bureau of Labor Statistics. After connect, enter 1 or 2 returns to start.

202-523-4784 - US Dept of Labor DC. News releases.

202-357-8997 - Fed. Energy Reg. Comm., DC. Daily issuances, press releases.

202-377-2870 - The Economic BBS, DC. Commerce Dept. information (fee).

202-272-1514 - The COE Manpower BBS OPEN board. Army Corps of Engineers, Rich Courtney.

202-697-6109/3632 - Export License Status Advisor, Department of Defense.

202-786-3640 - Budget/Finance Board OPEN board (don't use in mid-day. Immigration and Naturalization Service, Mike Arnold.)

202-537-7475 - Fannie Mae BBS OPEN board. Federal National Mortgage Association, Ken Goosens.

202-477-8500 - World Bank OPEN board, Ashok Daswani.

202-376-2184 - Info Technology Center BBS OPEN board. Veteran's Administration, Jay Anderson.

202-737-7264 - Federal Deposit Insurance Corporation.

202-566-4602 - Export-Import Bank of the US OPEN board, Joel Kahn/Bob Hughes.

800-222-4922 - (Outside DC Metro area) 202-626-9853 (DC calls) OERI Electronic Bulletin Board OPEN board. US Department of Education, Tom Litkowski.

206-924-4102 - Labor Mkt. Econ. Anal., WA. Seattle area economic information.

301-948-5717 - Computer Performance Evaluation Group, National Science Foundation OPEN board. 300 Baud only.

301-948-5718 - Microcomputer Electronic Information Exchange, National Bureau of Standards OPEN board. 300 or 1200 Baud.

301-948-2048 - Data Management Information Exchange, National Bureau of Standards. OPEN board. 300 or 1200 Baud.

301-763-4576 - Census Microcomputer Information Center, Bureau of the Census. Microcomputer news, software and hardware reviews, public domain software, training programs for Census and Commerce personnel. After connect, enter 1 or 2 returns to start.

301-763-1568 - State Data Center, Maryland DC area census bureau statistics.

301-948-5718 - Institute for Computer Sciences and Technology (ICST), The National Bureau of Standards, Department of Commerce. Information on the acquisition, management, and use of small computers. Other files containing sources of information on topics such as: conferences, federal publications and activities, user groups, other bulletin boards, etc. After connect, enter 1 or 2 returns to start. If you do not receive a carrier after two rings, hang up and call again.

301-353-5059 - Megawatts BBS OPEN board. Department of Energy, Bruce Birnbaum.

301-763-5225 - Federal-State Cooperative for Population Estimates, Bureau of the Census. Information and news about population and demographic projections. After connected, enter "RUN" to start.

717-654-7673 - DEVIN, Pennsylvania. Pittston, economic information.

HEALTH/NUTRITION

301-436-6346 - National Center for Health Statistics, Public Health Service. Contains statistical data on NCHS surveys.

301-436-5078 - Nutrient Data Bank, Hyattsville MD. USDA nutrition info.

402-280-3023 - National Drug Info. Omaha NE. Pharmacological info.

404-377-9563 - AIDSQUEST Online, Atlanta GA. AIDS, cancer info.

504-588-5743 - Health Ed. Electronic Forum, New Orleans LA. Health info.

800-624-2723 - NBIAP Biotechnology, VA. Genetic engineering.

LAW

301-738-8895 - NCJRS, MD. Nat. Criminal Justice Reference Service. This is a finicky board I could never make work with ProComm. It wants to see TeamTerm which NCJRS will supply free to any law enforcement agency or other qualified user.

415-556-3075 - 9th Circuit Court, San Francisco CA, and 513-684-2842 - CITE, Cincinnati OH. 6th Circuit Court cases. Both above are pilot projects to provide information on cases before the courts. Not known if past decisions can be searched online.

202-786-3640 - Dept. of Justice, Comptroller of Immigration and Naturalization Service, Budget/Financial Board. Messaging and file transfer service for INS.

718-463-1091 - Immigration Law USA, NY. Immigration law info. Run by an attorney in private practice, specialist in immigration law. Primarily for his own clients but he will answer reporter's questions.

MISCELLANEOUS

202-366-3764 - FEBBS, DC. Federal highway information.

202-426-2961 - Federal Highway Administration BBS.

202-529-0140 - USA-GDR Databank, DC. East European events.

202-775-1237 - IDI Job Board. Job opening in Washington DC area.

202-475-1973 - NANci. U.S. Navy, Naval Aviation News. Reference on naval aviation history. Message access to the magazine. Operates 5pm to 7am.

202-557-3769 - Pesticide Programs BBS. Environmental Protection Agency.

301-725-1072 - Public Access Link Federal Communications Commission.

202-275-1050 - Information Technology Center, General Accounting Office.

202-535-7661 - Information Resources Services, Government Services Administration.

202-453-9008 - Information Technology Center, National Aeronautics and Space Administration.

202-287-9656 - Federal Library Committee BBS, Library of Congress.

216-368-3888 - Cleveland FreeNet. Run by Case Western Reserve University. Thom Boughton (71641,1326 on CIS) is a sysop. No charges of any type. Use the command "GO OUTDOORS" to access the outdoor forum.

301-948-5718 - Micro Electronic Information Exchange. Technical information with emphasis on computer security.

703-243-9696 - NewsUSA, VA. Consumer news (7-E-1).

NATURAL RESOURCES

617-439-5699 - Boston Citinet, NMFS "green sheets."

202-272-1514 - U.S. Army Corps of Engineers. Because this board is also internal information exchange within the Corps, some sections are restricted access.

NEWSPAPERS

213-432-3592 - Electric Newspaper, Long Beach CA. Press-Telegram.

402-593-2000 - Omaha CityNet, Omaha NE. World-Herald (DEMO LINE).

508-872-8461 - Fred the Computer, Framingham MA. Middlesex News. Intended for local readers sending letters to the editor.

516-454-6959 - Newsday Online, New York NY. Newsday.

817-878-9800 - Star Text, Ft Worth TX. Star-Telegram (DEMO LINE).

SPACE/SCIENCE

202-586-8658 - Energy Info Admin, DC. Energy statistics.

202-634-1764 - Science Resources DC. National Science Foundation.

301-763-8071 - Climate Analysis Center, National Weather Service, Department of Commerce. Historical climate information - daily, weekly, and monthly, heating degree days, weekly climate bulletins.

301-454-8700 - National Weather Service, U.S. Department of Commerce. Marine weather and nautical information for coastal waterways. Information includes data for bays and sounds, coastal waters, and offshore waters; tropical storm advisories; tidal information, and important weather, nautical, and ^shing news. Data are primarily about the middle Atlantic region. The bulletin board is open to the public and free of charge. Users must preregister by calling Ross Laporte, National Weather Service, 301-899-3296. Information about similar bulletin boards for other regions available.

314-882-3874 - SCI-FIND, Columbia, MO. Science news reference. Reference and bibliographic service at the University of Missouri's Science Journalism Center.

205-895-0028 - NASA Spacelink, Huntsville, AL. NASA news, info.

303-494-8446 - Space Network, Boulder, CO. Boulder Center for Science and Policy. Space news, research.

713-483-5817 - NASA JSC, Houston, TX. Shuttle schedules.

800-358-2663 - USGS Earthquake QED, Golden, CO. Earthquake epicenter info. Carries info on "felt" earthquakes around the world.

902-566-7390 - Energy Centre, Canada. Govt energy info.

SPORTS AND RECREATION

301-622-2247 - Maryland, Silver Bullet.

301-944-3495 - Maryland, League of American Wheelmen. Evenings/weekends only.

303-972-9023 - Colorado, Chatfield Armory.

304-343-5871 - West Virginia, The Gunslinger.

318-797-8310 - Louisiana, Dawn Patrol.

318-741-3422 - Louisiana, Peacekeeper.

415-537-1777 - California, Combat Arms.

512-441-6300 - Texas, National Firearms Assoc.

614-294-5216 - Ohio, Crossfire.

619-934-9695 - Private Events, Mammoth Lakes, CA area. Has a local weather forum maintained by a resident weatherman and a fishing forum updated by the Eastern Sierra Fly Fishers.

703-971-4491 - Virginia, The Bullet 'N Board.

707-545-0746 - California, Survival Communications Forum.

713-682-6508 - Texas Two Wheelers BBS. BikeNET echo.

714-653-0494 - California. F&W Guns.

901-873-0387 - Tennessee, North End.

904-488-3773 - Florida, FishLINE. Sysop: Scott Hardin, 904-488-4066 (voice).

918-838-1615 - Oklahoma, The Gunner's Mate.

919-781-7047 - North Carolina, Small Time BBS. BikeNET echo.

OTHER FEDERAL GOVERNMENT OR RELATED BBS

ADAIC BBS (ADA Programming) Line 1: 202-694-0215 ADA Information Center Line 2: 301- 459-3865

Automated Library Information Exchange Line 1: 202-707-9656 Fed. Library and Information Ctr. Comm.

Commerce Department Line 1: 202-377-1423 US Department of Commerce.

DC Info Exchange Line 1: 202-433-6639 US Navy.

Education/OERI Line 1: 202-37-6011 US Department of Education.

FDIC Line 1: 202-371-9578 Fed. Depository Ins. Corp.

GSA - IRSC Line 1: 202-501-2014 General Services Office.

JAG Net (Navy-legal) Line 1: 202-325-0748 US Navy Judge Advocate General.
Metro Net Line 1: 202-475-7543 US Army Military Dist. of DC.

Minority Energy Info Clearinghouse Line 1: 202-586-1561 US Dept. of Energy.

NADAP Line 1: 202-693-3831 US Navy.

NARDAC - Laser Line 1: 202-475-7885 US Navy.

Naval Observatory (1200/E/7/1) Line 1: 202-653-1079 US Naval Observatory.

NAVDAC Line 1: 202-433-2118 Naval Data Automation Command.

Census Bureau Personnel Line 1: 301-763-4574 US Bureau of the Census.

MSG-RBBS Line 1: 301-227-1042 David Taylor Naval Research Ctr. Line 2: 301-227-3428.

OPM New Jersey (Federal Job Listings) Line 1: 201-645-3887 Office of Personnel Management.

DASC-ZSA Line 1: 703-274-5863 Defense Logistics Agency.

Ft. Myer O Club Line 1: 703-524-4159 Fort Myer Officers Club.

Geological Survey Line 1: 703-648-4168 US Geological Survey.

Section 6: Campus-Wide Information Systems

A large number of campuses allow access to their campus-wide information systems via the Internet. The information in this list was compiled from submissions to CWIS-L@WUVMD.

Direct additions and corrections to Judy Hallman (hallman@unc.bitnet), Manager of Information Services, Academic Computing Services, CB# 3460 311 Wilson Library, University of North Carolina, Chapel Hill, NC, 27599-3460. Phone (919) 962-9107.

Please note that on-line information systems often have a limited number of ports. Users are asked not to tie them up for long periods.

Columbia University
cal.cc.columbia.edu
Login as calendar
Contact: David Millman <dsm@cunixf.cc.columbia.edu>

Cornell's CUINFO
cuinfo.cornell.edu
Connect to port 300 Different version of telnet or TN3270 have different syntax for defining the port. The following are the common ones... telnet cuinfo.cornell.edu 300 or telnet cuinfo.cornell.edu..300. And some VMS versions want telnet cuinfo.cornell.edu /port=300 Contact: Steve Worona <SLW@CORNELLA>

MIT TechInfo
techinfo.mit.edu

Login as techinfo. Password is techinfo (lowercase only—system is UNIX). Once you're in, you can use upper or lowercase. When you're done, use the QUIT command. Contact: Tim McGovern <tjm@EAGLE.MIT.EDU> TechInfo is an electronic document retrieval system available on MIT.

New Mexico State University NMSU/INFO
info.nmsu.edu
Userid is INFO, and there is no password.
Contact: D. Brian Ormand <bormand@nmsu.edu> or
<bormand@nmsuvm1.bitnet>

NYU
info.nyu.edu
(information.nyu.edu) will connect to the main server.
Contact: Stephen Tihor <TIHOR@NYUACF>

PNN - Princeton News Network
pucc.princeton.edu
When you see the VM 370 logo, clear it, and instead of logging on, enter pnn (case does not matter). Clear the information screen that appears (after reading it carefully, of course) and you'll be in PNN. PNN is a full-screen VM/CMS based system (the public version is slightly restricted). In the near future UNIX and HyperCard version will be available. PNN VM/CMS is available free on an as-is basis.
Contact: Howard Strauss <Howard@PUCC>

University of New Mexico UNM_INFO
bootes.unm.edu
At the login prompt, enter UNM_INFO No password is required.
Contact: Art St. George <STGEORGE@UNMB>

University of North Carolina at Chapel Hill INFO
info.acs.unc.edu or 128.109.157.1
Log on with username INFO.
Contact: Judy Hallman <HALLMAN@UNC.BITNET>

7.2 NIXPUB Long List

April 5, 1990

nixpub long listing
Open Access UNIX (*NIX) Sites [Fee / No Fee] for mapped sites only
[April 5, 1990]

Systems listed (74):
[agora alphacm althea amazing anet bigtex bucket]
[chinet cinnet compnect conexch contact cpro cruzio]
[dasys1 ddsw1 dhw68k disk eklektik esfenn gagme]

[gensis grebyn i-core igloo jack jdyx lgnp1]
[loft386 lunapark m-net m2xenix madnix magpie marob]
[medsys ncoast netcom nstar nuchat nucleus oldcolo]
[ozdaltx pallas pnet01 pnet12 pnet51 point polari]
[portal quack raider rtmvax sactoh sir-alan sixhub]
[stanton stb sugar telly tmsoft tnl turnkey]
[usource uuwest vpnet well wet wolves world]
[wybbs xroads ziebmef zorch]

Last Contact Date	Telephone #	Sys-name	Location	Baud	Hours

08/89 201-846-2460 ^althea New Brunswick, NJ 3/12/24 24
AT&T 3B2/310 - Unix SVR3.1, no fee. USENET, e-mail, C development, games. Single line.
Contact: rjd@althea.UUCP (Robert Diamond)

02/90 206-328-4944 polari Seattle, WA 3/12 24
Equip ???; 8-lines, Trailblazer on 206-328-1468; $30/year (flat rate);
Multi-user games, chat, full USENET.
Contact: uunet!microsoft!happym!polari!bruceki

04/90 209-952-5347 quack Stockton, CA 3/12/24/96 24
Sun 2/170, SunOS 4.0; Aka - The Duck Pond; XBBS at no charge,
Shell - $2/mo ($4/mo expanded quota); Trailblazer access; lo gin: bbs.

12/89 212-420-0527 magpie NY, NY 3/12/24/96 24
? - UNIX SYSV - 2, Magpie BBS, no fee, Authors: Magpie/UNIX,/ MSDOS two lines plus anonymous uucp: 212-677-9487 (9600 bps Telebit modem) NOTE: 9487 reserved for registered Magpie sysops & anon uucp
Contact: Steve Manes, {rutgers | cmcl2 | uunet}!hombre!magpie!manes

03/90 212-447-1522^ dasys1 NY, NY 3/12/24 24
Unistride - SYS V, multiple lines, fee $5/mo AKA Big Electri Cat,USENET, games, multi-user chat, e-mail, login: new, passwd: new
Contact: ...!rutgers!cmcl2!rsweeney or rsweeney@dasys1.UUCP

02/90 212-675-7059 marob NY, NY 3/12/24/96 24
386 SCO-XENIX 2.2, XBBS, no fee, limit 60 min.
Telebit Trailblazer (9600 PEP) only 212-675-8438
Contact: {philabs | rutgers | cmcl2}!{phri | hombre}!marob!clifford

09/89 213-397-3137^ stb Santa Monica, CA 3/12/24 24
AT&T 3b1; BBS and shell access; uucp-anon: login: uucp NO PASSWD 3 line on rotary -3137 2400 baud.

03/88 213-459-5891 amazing Pacific Palisades, CA 3/12/24 24
AMT 286 - Microport David's Amazing BBS Fee $7.50/month; $35 6;$60/year 5

lines on rotary; Unique original software with conferencing, electronic bar, matchmaking, no file up/downloading

07/88 214-247-2367 ozdaltx Dallas, TX 3/12/24 24
INTEC/SCO XENIX 2.2.1, OZ BBS, Membership only adult BBS, fee $40 /year. Multiple lines. Closed system, carries limited USENET newsgroups. Login: guest (no PW). Voice verification on all new users.

01/90 215-348-9727 lgnp1 Doylestown, PA 3/12/24/96 24
'386 mutt w/ SCO-XENIX — Telebit on dial in line. UUCP access only... Public access to the nixpub lists using anon-uucp [see footer of this list]. Fee services include edes/routing for e-mail and USENET News, plus access to *NIX specific PD source code library. Contact: phil@ls.com.

01/90 216-582-2460 ncoast Cleveland, OH 12/24/96 24
80386 Mylex, SCO Xenix; 600 meg. storage; XBBS and Shell; USENET (newsfeeds available), E-Mail; donations requested; login as "bbs" for BBS and "makeuser" for new users.
Telebit used on 216-237-5486.

01/90 217-525-9019 pallas Springfield, IL 3/12/24/96 24
AT&T 6386, 380 meg disk space; 4 lines w/ USRobotics Dual Standard modems; BBS available at no fee (UBBS), shell access for $50/year; "guest" login available.

04/90 219-289-0286 nstar Notre Dame/South Bend, IN 24/96 24
386/25, Unix System V 3.2; 4 high speed lines all locked at 19.2 kbps, Hayes V-Series V.42 lead number listed, Trailblazer on 289-3745, UUR HST 14.4 carrier on 287-9020; full Usenet (600 groups) available via Waffle BBS, downloads, no fees, registration required and verified, free high speed feeds available; contact root@nstar

09/90 312-283-0559 chinet Chicago, IL 3/12/24/96 24
'386, SysVr3.2.1; Multiple lines including Telebit and HST;
Picospan BBS (free), USENET at $50/year (available to guests on weekends).

10/89 312-338-0632 point Chicago, IL 3/12/24/96 24
North Shore / Rogers Park area of Chicago. 386 - ISC 2.0 1(SysV3.2), multiple lines, Telebit PEP on 338-3261, USRobotics HST on 338-1036, AKCS bbs, some usenet conferences available. 200+ MB online storage. Downloads, full usenet & shell access in the works.

03/90 313-623-6309 nucleus Clarkston, MI 12/24 24
AMI 386 - ESIX 5.3.2, no fee. Shell access, full usenet access, online games, AKCS conferencing system, large online sources archive and extensive tape library of public domain source code.
Contact: jeff@nucleus.mi.org

02/88 313-994-6333 m-net Ann Arbor, MI 3/12 24
Altos 68020 - SYS III, limits unstated, fee for extended service Picospan confer-

ence system, multiple lines, 160 meg, packet radio

08/89 313-996-4644 anet Ann Arbor, MI 3/12 24
Altos 68000 - Sys III, no limits, 1st month free, fees range up to $20/month (negotiable), accepts equipment/software in lieu of fees, Picospan conferencing, 120M, non-profit, user-supported, community-based, ideal autodidact educational system. Tax-deductible donations okay.

08/89 314-474-4581 gensis Columbia, MO 3/12/24/48/96 24
Gateway 386 system w/ SCO Xenix V/386, DataFlex, Oracle, CHARM, & VP/ix. No fee. Online gaming, game design, and (oddly enough) database design are the main focus. Modem is Microcom MNP 6.

10/89 404-321-5020 jdyx Atlanta, GA 12/24/96 24
386/ix 2.0.2. XBBS. Usenet (alt, gnu, most comp and a few others) and shell access. Second line (2400 below) (404) 325-1719. 200+ meg current Usenet and GNU sources. Specializing in graphics and ray-tracing under 386/ix (with/with out X11). Yearly fee for shell and/or downloads.
Telebit access. Contact: ...gatech!emory!jdyx!tpf (Tom Friedel)

05/88 407-380-6228 rtmvax Orlando, FL 3/12/24 24
mVAX-I - Ultrix-32 V1.2 USENET & UUCP Email Gateway. XBBS front end for new user subscribing. No Fees. Primary function is Technical exchange.
Contact: { cbosgd!codas, hoptoad!peora }!rtmvax!rob

09/89 408-245-7726 uuwest Sunnyvale, CA 3/12/24 24
SCO-XENIX, Waffle. No fee, USENET news (news.*, music, comics, telecom, etc) The Dark Side of the Moon BBS. This system has been in operation since 1985. Login: new Contact: (UUCP) ames!uuwest!request (Domain) request@darkside.com

02/90 408-249-0290 netcom San Jose, CA 12/24/96 24
UNIXXSsyv r3.2 (486) - USENET (21 days), UUNET Sources, News Feeds, Shell Access (Bourne, Korn, C), UUCP support, E-Mail, Compilers. Fee $10.00/mo +one time Registration of $10.00. Login as guest (no password). Telebit on (408) 249-0576.

02/90 408-423-9995 cruzio Santa Cruz, CA 12/24 24
Tandy 4000, Xenix 2.3.*, Caucus 3.*; focus on Santa Cruz activity (ie directory of community and goverment organizations, events, ...); USENET Support; Multiple lines; no shell; fee: $15/quarter.
Contact: ...!uunet!cruzio!chris

10/89 408-725-0561 portal Cupertino, CA 3/12/24 24
Networked Suns (SunOS), multiple lines, Telenet access, no shell access fees: $10/month + Telenet charges (if used) @ various rates/times conferencing, multi user chats, usenet

02/90 408-996-7358 zorch Cupertino, CA 12/24 24
Wicat 200 - Unix SVR2; 4 lines, 1200 only on 7361, 7378, 7386; $10/month, $100/year, flat rate, no time limit. E-mail, USENET, games, utilities, online man pages,

Bourne, C, Korn shell. 400M online, 80M source archive. Registration required, verified; login as newuser, password public. Contact: scott@zorch.SF-Bay.ORG or (ames | pyramid | vsi1)!zorch!scott

10/89 412-431-8649 eklektik Pittsburgh PA 3/12/24 24
UNIX PC- SYSV - UNaXcess BBS, new system - donation requested for shell, login: bbs for BBS, uucp-mail, limited Usenet news feeds. Gaming SIGS. Contact: ...!gatech!emoryu1!eklektik!anthony

11/89 415-332-6106 well Sausalito, CA 12/24 24
6-processor Sequent Balance (32032); UUCP and USENET access; multiple lines; access via CPN; PICOSPAN BBS; $3/hour. Contact (415) 332-4335

06/88 415-582-7691 cpro Hayward, CA 12/24 24
Microport SYSV 2, UNaXcess bbs, no fee, 60 min limit, shell access

11/89 415-623-8642 jack Fremont, CA 3/12/24 24
3b2/522. 2 BBS's. E-mail, USENET News, and NFS links to 2 3b1's. No fee. 5 lines on rotary. Contact: steve@jack.SNS.COM5 lines on rotary.

07/89 415-753-5265 wet San Francisco, CA 3/12/24 24
386 SYS V.3. Wetware Diversions. $15 registration, $0.01/minute. Public Access UNIX System: uucp, PicoSpan bbs, full Usenet News, multiple lines, shell access. New users get initial credit!
Contact: {ucsfcca | claris | hoptoad}!wet!cc (Christopher Cilley)

05/89 415-783-2543 esfenn Hayward, CA 3/12/24 24
System ????; USENET news; E-mail; No charges; Contact esfenn!william.

11/89 416-438-2855 contact Toronto, ON 3/12/24 24
386 clone - Xenix 2.3.1, fee optional. USENET, e-mail, multi-user chat, games. Contact: eisen@contact.UUCP martin loeffler

11/89 416-452-0926 telly Brampton, ON 12/24/96 24
386 SysVr3.2; proprietary menu-based BBS includes Usenet site searching. News (all groups, incl biz, pubnet, gnu, CanConfMail), mail (including to/from Internet, Bitnet), many archives. Feeds available. $75(Cdn)/year.
Contact: Evan Leibovitch, evan@telly.on.ca, u net!attcan!telly!evan

12/88 416-461-2608 tmsoft Toronto, ON 3/12/24/96 24
NS32016, Sys5r2, shell; news+mail $30/mo, general-timesharing $60/mo, all newsgroups. Willing to setup mail/news connections. Archives:comp.sources.{unix,games,x,misc}
Contact: Dave Mason <mason@tmsoft> / Login: newuser

07/89 416-654-8854 ziebmef Toronto, ON 3/12/24/96 24
AT&T 3B1, Sys V, shell, news, mail, no fee (donations accepted) Carries most newsgroups (willing to add extra ones on request) Telebit access, willing to give mail feeds
Contact: Chris Siebenmann, {utzoo!telly,ncrcan}!ziebmef!cks

01/90 502-968-5401 disk Louisville, KY 3/12 24
386 clone, Interactive System V 3.2, 600 meg. 6 lines 5401 thru 5406. Carrying most USENET groups, Shell access, multi-user games (including Realm) multi-user chat, downloads, and more. Rate info available via a free trial account. Also offering news/mail feeds to the local area. Now reachable via Starlink!

12/88 503-254-0458 bucket Portland, OR 3/12/24 24
Tektronix 6130, UTek 2.3(4.2BSD-derived). Bit Bucket BBS publically available; login as 'bbs'. BBS is message only. Users interested in access to Unix should contact SYSOP via the BBS or send e-mail to ..tektronix!tessi!bucket!rickb. Unix services include USENET News, e-mail, and all tools/games/utility access. Alternate dial-in lines available for Unix users.

12/89 503-297-3211 m2xenix Portland, OR 3/12/24 24
'386/20, Xenix 2.3. Shell accounts available, N OBBS. No fee. E-mail, USENET News, program development.
Contact: ...!uunet!m2xenix!news or on Fido at 297-9145

05/89 503-640-4262^ agora PDX, OR 3/12/24 24
Intel Xenix-286, $2/mo or $20/yr, news, mail, games, programming two lines with trunk-hunt, 4380 supports MNP level 3.
Contact: Alan Batie, tektronix!tessi!agora!batie

01/90 512-346-2339 bigtex Austin, TX 96 24
SysVr3.2 i386, anonymous shell, no fee, anonymous uucp ONLY,
Telebit 9600/PEP; Mail links available. Carries GNU software.
anon uucp login: nuucp NO PASSWD, file list /usr3/index
anon shell login: guest NO PASSWD, chroot'd to /usr3
Contact: james@bigtex.cactus.org

10/89 513-779-8209 cinnet Cincinnati, OH 12/24/96 24
80386, ISC 386/ix 2.02, Telebit access, 1 line; $7.50/Month; shell access, Usenet access; news feeds available;
login: newact password: new user to register for shell access

01/90 517-487-3356 lunapark E. Lansing, MI 12/24 24
Compaq 386/20 SCO-UNIX 3.2, lunabbs bulletin board & conferencing system, no fee, login: bbs password: lunabbs. Primarily UNIX software with focus on TeX and Postscript, also some ATARI-ST and IBM-PC stuff 2400/1200 —> 8 N 1
Contact: ...!{mailrus,uunet}!frith!lunapark!larry

12/88 518-346-8033 sixhub upstate, NY 3/12/24 24
PC Designs GV386. hub machine of the upstate NY UNIX users group (*IX) two line reserved for incoming, bbs no fee, news & e-mail fee $15/year Smorgasboard of BBS systems, UNaXcess and XBBS online, Citadel BBS now in production.
Contact: davidsen@sixhub.uucp.

09/88 602-941-2005 xroads Phoenix, AZ 12/24 24
Motorola VME1121, UNIX 5.2, Crossroads BBS, Fee $30/yr + $.50/.25 (call) prime (evenings)/non-prime, USENET news, multi-chat, online games, movie

reviews, adventure games, dos unix/xenii ifles for dload, multi lines

08/89 605-348-2738 loft386 Rapid City, SD 3/12/24/96 24
80386 SYS V/386 Rel 3.2, Usenet mail/news via UUNET, UUNET archive access. NO BBS! News feeds avaliable. 400 meg hd. Fees: $10/month or $25/quarter. Call (605) 343-8760 and talk to Doug Ingraham to arrange an account or e-mail uunet!loft386!dpi

08/88 608-273-2657 madnix Madison, WI 3/12/24 24
286 SCO-XENIX, shell, no fee, USENET news, mail, login: newuser
Contact: ray@madnix

08/89 612-473-2295 pnet51 Minneapolis, MN 3/12/24 24
Equip ?, Xenix, multi-line, no fee, some Usenet nnws, e-mail, multi-threaded conferencing, login: pnet id: new, PC Pursuitable UUCP: {rosevax, crash}!orbit!pnet51!admin

01/90 615-288-3957 medsys Kingsport, TN 12/24/96 24
386 SCO-UNIX 3.2, XBBS, no fee, limit 90 min.
Telebit PEP, USENET, login: bbs password: bbs
anon uucp —> medsys Any ACU (speed) 16152883957 login: nuucp ssword: \r
Contact: uunet!medsys!laverne (LaVerne E. Olney)

03/90 615-896-8716 raider Murfreesboro, TN 12/24 24
WAFFLE BBS, no charge, shell accounts $40/yr,$25/6,$15/3. News and mail links free of charge; just one hop from uunet. Limited archives. 19.2kb coming soon. Contact: root@raider.MFEE.TN.US (Bob Reineri)

02/90 616-457-1964 wybbs Jenison, MI 3/12/24/96 24
386 - SCO-XENIX 2.3.2, no fees, two lines, shell access, usenet news,150 meg storage, XBBS, Telebit access, interests: ham radio, xenix AKA: Consultants Connection Contact:
danielw%wybbs@sharkey.cc.umich.edu
Alternate phone #: 616-457-9909 (max 2400 baud)

01/90 617-739-9753 world Brookline, MA 3/12/24/96 24
Sun 4/280, SunOS 4.03; Shell, USENET, e-Mail, UUCP and home of the Open Book Initiative (text project); fees: $5/mo + $3/hr (8a-8p) and $2/hr (8p-8a); Multiple lines: 2400 MNP used on listed number, Telebits used on others; login as "new"; Contact: geb@world.std.com

01/90 619-259-7757 pnet12 Del Mar, CA 3/12/24/96 24
Xenix, multi-line, no fee, full Usenet, e-mail, multi-threaded conferencing login: pnet id: new
Contact: ...!uunet!serene!pnet12!rfarris

07/88 619-444-7006 pnet01 El Cajon, CA 3/12/24 24
BSD Unix, 3 lines, login::pnet id: new, some USENET, e-mail, conferencing
Home of P-Net software, mail to crash!bblue or pnet01!bblue for info. Contributions requested
Unix accounts available for regulars, PC Pursuit access 2/88.

12/89 703-281-7997 grebyn Vienna, VA 3/12/24 24
Vax/Ultrix. $25/month. GNU EMACS, USENET, PC/BLUE archives, Telebit used for uucp only, archives, Ada repository, comp.sources.(misc,unix,games) archives, net.sources archives, 3 C compilers, Ada compiler, 1.2GB disk, multiple lines

11/89 708-272-5912 igloo Northbrook, IL 12/24/96 24
3B2-300; accounts by invitation only, no limit/no fee; full usenet; 132megs HD; 2 lines rotary, 9600 telebit on 272-5917
Contact: igloo!postmaster

01/90 708-318-7133 gagme Niles, IL 12/24 24
3B2/300 - System V 3.2. E-mail, netnews, sources. Donation requested but not required.

11/89 708-566-8911 ddsw1 Mundelein, IL 3/12/24/96 24
Televideo 386 -SCO XENIX 386, guest usr 1 hr daily, fee extends use ACKS bbs, fee $30/6 months $50/year, Authors of AKCS bbs multiple lines, 9600 bps available, anonymous uucp, ~/README for info
Contact: Karl Denninger (...!ddsw1!karl) Voice: (708) 566-8910

11/89 708-833-8126 vpnet Villa Park, IL 12/24/96 24
386 Clone - Interactive 386/ix R2.0 (3.2), no fee. Akcs linked bbs including several Usenet conf's. No charge for shells. Trailblazer. Mail lisbon@vpnet.UUCP

07/89 713-438-5018 sugar Houston, TX 3/12/24/96 24
386/AT (2) networked - Bell Technologies V/386, usenet, news, downloads Homegrown BBS software, Trailblazer+ access, currently no charges

10/89 713-668-7176 nuchat Houston, TX 3/12/24/96 24
i386; USENET, Mail, Shell Access; 300M On-line; Trailbazer Used; No fee.

12/88 714-635-2863 dhw68k Anaheim, CA 12/24 24
Unistride 2.1, no fee, also 714-385-1915, Trailblazer on both lines, USENET News, /bin/sh or /bin/csh available

05/89 714-662-7450 turnkey Inglewood, CA 12/24 24
286 - Xenix SYSV, XBBS

01/90 714-821-9671 alphacm Cypress, CA 12/24/96 24
386 - SCO-XENIX, no fee, Home of XBBS, 90 minute per login, 4 lines, Trailblazer pluses in use.
uucp-anon: login: nuucp NO PASSWD

05/89 714-842-5851 conexch Santa Ana, CA 3/12/24 24
386 - SCO Xenix - Free Unix guest login and PC-DOS bbs login, one hour inital time limit, USENET news, shell access granted on request & $25/quarter donation. Anon uucp: login: nuucp NO PASSWD. List of available Unix files resides in /usr3/public/FILES.

08/88 714-894-2246 stanton Irvine, CA 3/12/24 24
286 - SCO Xenix - donation requested, limit 240 min, XBBS, USENET news UNIX access granted on request through BBS, 20$/year, access includes C development system (XENIX/MSDOS), PROCALC 1-2-3 clone, FOXBASE+ anon uucp: login: nuucp, no word, 2400/1200/300 MNP supported

03/90 717-657-4997 compnect Harrisburg, PA 3/12/24 24
Equip ???; The Data Factory BBS; Multiple line, 1200 baud on 675-4992; No fee, restricted access to adult areas, some USENET, no shell;
Contact: ...!uunet!wa3wbu!compnect!dave.

12/89 719-632-4111 oldcolo Colo Spgs, CO 12/24/96 24
386 - SCO-XENIX frontend, 2 CT Miniframes backend, e-mail conferencing, databases, Naplps Graphics, USENET news. 7 lines 8N1, 2400 on 2906, USR Dual 9600 on 2658. Self-registering for limited free access (political, policy, marketplace). Subscriptions $10, $15, $18 mo. for full use. Dave Hughes SYSOP.

01/90 801-269-0670 i-core Salt Lake City, UT 3/12/24/96 24
286 SYS V, Unidel BBS and Newsreader; a.k.a. Bitsko's Bar & Grill BBS, no limit, no fee; UseNet and Citadel feeds available. Home of Unidel room-based newsreader and UNIX Citadel network gateway; Telebit 19200
Contact: ken@i-core.UUCP or uunet!iconsys!caeco!i-core!ken

01/90 802-865-3614 tnl Burlington, VT 3/12/24 24
80386 w/ SCO XENIX. No Fee. 2 hour session limit. XBBS/USENET, shell. Login as 'new' for a shell account, no validation. AKA: Northern Lights.
Contact: norstar@tnl.UUCP or uunet!uvm-gen!tnl!norstar (Daniel Ray)

08/88 813-952-1981 usource Sarasota, FL 12/24 24
386 - SCO-XENIX, fee depends on services provided, no fee for bbs. New users subscribe by logging in as 'help' or 'newuser' (no password). Primary purpose is technical forum. 6pm-8am M-Th, 24 hrs weeekends (6pm Fri-8am Mon)
uucp-anon: 1200/2400 bps —> login: auucp word: gateway
uucp-anon directory: /usr/spool/uucppublic; contact: frank@usource.UUCP

02/90 814-337-0348 sir-alan Meadville, PA 3/12/24/96 24
SCO XENIX 2.3; no fee; XBBS; USR DS on 337-034882/496/12), TB+ on 337-3159(24/19.2/12); archive site for comp.sources.[games,misc,sun,unix,x], some alt.sources, XENIX(68K/286/386), files from UUNET(X11R3,TeX,etc.).
uucp-anon: login: pdsrc NO PASSWD
uucp-anon directory: /u/pdsrc, /u/pubdir, /u/uunet, help in /u/pubdir/HELP
Contact: sir-alan!mikes@uunet.uu.net (814-337-5528 voice)

09/89 916-649-0161 sactoh0 Sacramento, CA 12/24/96 24
3B2/310 SYSV.2, SAC_UNIX; $2/month, limit 90 min, 2 lines, TB on line, 2400/1200 baud on 916-722-6519; USENET, e-mail, Games; login: new
Contact: ..pacbell!sactoh0!sysop

089 919-493-7111 wolves Durham, NC 3/12/24 24
AMS 386/25 - UNIX SysVr3.2, XBBS, no fee for bbs. Rates for UNIX access and USENET are being determined. Developing yet another UNIX bbs (ideas wel-

come!) Single line, telebit coming soon.
Contact: wolves!ggw or wolves!sysop [...duke!dukcds!wolves!...]

===

This list is maintained by Phil Eschallier on lgnp1. Any additions deletions, or corrections should be sent to one of the addresses below. The nixpub listings are kept as current as possible. However, you use this data at your own risk and cost—all standard disclaimers apply!!!

———

Lists available from lgnp1 via anonomous uucp.
+1 215 348 9727 [Telebit access]
login: nuucp NO PWD [no rmail permitted]
this list: /usr/spool/uucppublic/nixpub
short list: /usr/spool/uucppublic/nixpub.short
or from news groups pubnet.nixpub, comp.misc or alt.bbs.

———

E-MAIL ...
uucp: ..!uunet!lgnp1!{ phil | nixpub }
domain: { phil | nixpub }@LS.COM
CIS: 71076,1576

===

COMPAQ, IBM, PC Pursuit, [SCO] XENIX, UNIX, etc. are trademarks of the etc.

7.3 Anonymous FTP Sites

The following is a recent example of a list developed by Jon Granrose of Internet sites accepting anonymous ftp. To access:

user name: anonymous
password: <your mail address> (i.e. "odin@pilot.njin.net")

If you are sending this on to someone or in any other way providing this for someone else, please leave this header intact. Otherwise, I get many questions which this would have answered. Thanks.

This list is posted to comp.misc, and comp.sources.wanted, on Usenet and is distributed via anonymous FTP from pilot.njin.net (128.6.7.38), and is available from several other FTP sites (see list). I am also running a simple mail-server from my account on pilot. For more information, mail odin@pilot.njin.net with a subject of "listserv-request" and a message body of "send help." Rather than requesting the latest list from me by mail, simply send the request to the listserv. If you send it to me, I will send you the help file for the listserv.

I don't have the time to read all these newsgroups so if there is anything you want me to see, please use e-mail. There is also a mailing list which was being used to distribute the list; now I use it more for getting feedback on new ideas. If you wish to be added to the mailing list, mail me at pilot.

Special thanks go to Ed Vielmetti for all the work he does posting new archive information to comp.archives.

If there are any corrections/updates/etc. to be made, please mail me at odin@pilot.njin.net. That applies to descriptions of the archives. I don't have time to personally check each and every site so, if you use a site regularly, and can put together a better description, please tell me so I can update this list. This is especially true for sites described as "unknown" or with vague descriptions. Those sites are ones that I either didn't have enough time to sort through or couldn't tell what was available.

Thanks,

Jon Granrose
March 31, 1990

REMINDER: Anonymous FTP is a privilege, not a right. The site administrators for the sites listed below have made their systems available out of the goodness of their hearts. Please respect their wishes and restrict your FTPing to non-prime hours (1900 - 0600 hours local time for the site). This is especially true for sites in other countries. Please keep that in mind when you are FTPing. None of us want to see sites start to close down because a few are being inconsiderate.

>Jon Granrose | ARPA: odin@ucscb.UCSC.EDU jonthan@sco.com | // Only |
>Cowell College, UCSC | odin@pilot.njin.net 74036.3241@compuserve.com | \X/ Amiga! |
>Santa Cruz, CA 95064 | UUCP:..!ucbvax!ucscc!ucscb!odin Bitnet:odin@ucscb.bitnet |
> Please send any Anonymous FTP information to odin@pilot.njin.net |
Sat Mar 31 22:54:33 EST 1990

Site Name	I.P. Address	Description
a.cs.uiuc.edu	128.174.252.1	TeX, dvi2ps, gif, texx2.7, amiga, GNUmake, GNU
a.cs.uiuc.edu	128.174.252.1	TeX, dvi2ps, gif, texx2.7, amiga, GNUmake, GNU
a.gp.cs.cmu.edu	128.2.242.7	psprep
a.nl.cs.cmu.edu	128.2.250.143	unknown
a.psc.edu	128.182.65.1	GPLOT, GTEX
acad3.fai.alaska.edu	192.31.214.33	unknown
acf4.nyu.edu	128.122.128.14	unknown
acf8.nyu.edu	128.122.129.2	unknown
acfcluster.nyu.edu	128.122.128.16	VMS UUCP, news, DECUS library catalog

acns.nwu.edu	129.105.49.1	virus info/programs, maps
ads.com	128.229.30.16	internet mailing lists, vision-list, info-graphics
aelred-3.ie.org	192.48.115.36	enhanced billing design paper
aeneas.mit.edu	18.71.0.38	GNU emacs, kerberos
ahwahnee.stanford.edu	36.56.0.208	pcip interface specs
ajpo.sei.cmu.edu	128.237.2.253	all the ADA you could ask for
akbar.cac.washington.edu	128.95.112.1	unknown
albanycs.albany.edu	128.204.1.4	best of comp.graphics
allspice.lcs.mit.edu	18.26.0.115	RFCs1056 (PCMAIL) stuff, MIT snmp
alw.nih.gov	128.231.128.251	NIH Image 1.19
amelia.nas.nasa.gov	129.99.23.5	unknown
ames.arc.nasa.gov	128.102.18.3	pcrrn, GNU grep, conf, grep, iso.ps,mmdf, popd, sail, xfer, zmodem, AT&T 6300+ archives, SCUBA, Space archives, 3b2 source and info
andy.bgsu.edu	129.1.1.2	Unix sysadm tools, Unix Vote by mail, Unix etc., College hockey stats, Monty Python scripts
anise.acc.com	129.192.64.22	Berkeley utils ported to A/UX, Motorola DSP 56000 repository
anna.stanford.edu	36.14.0.13	Anna (Annotated Ada) softare and docs
apple.com	130.43.2.2	tech-notes, worm papers
aramis.rutgers.edu	128.6.4.2	idea, RFCs
argus.stanford.edu	36.56.0.151	netinfo
ariel.unm.edu	129.24.8.1	university networking ethics documents
arisia.xerox.com	13.1.100.206	sunfixes, mac, LispUsers, tcp/ip, IDA sendmail kit, Portable Common Runtime
arpa.att.com	192.20.239.129	fio library routines
arsun.utah.edu	128.110.192.93	NSF latex
arthur.cs.purdue.edu	128.10.2.1	RCS, buildtex, deTeX, mac32, Purdue Tech Reports, xspeed
athos.rutgers.edu	128.6.4.4	dvidoc
augean.ua.oz.au	129.127.4.2	unknown
aurora.arc.nasa.gov	128.102.21.1	unknown
b.psc.edu	128.182.65.2	GPLOT, GTEX
b.scs.uiuc.edu	128.174.90.2	LaTex
ba.excelan.com	130.57.8.6	misc. (looking for suggestions)
bach.berkeley.edu	128.32.135.1	amiga (ray-tracing)
bbn.com	128.89.0.122	uumap
bcm.tmc.edu	128.249.2.1	nfs list, Texas UUCP maps
beak.andrew.cmu.edu	128.2.26.21	unknown

bellcore.com	128.96.32.20	mgr, spiff, RFCs, track
bikini.cis.ufl.edu	128.227.224.1	comp.simulation, IBM RT BSD patches
bimbo.tn.cornell.edu	128.84.253.208	tn3270 for DEC 3100
bitsy.mit.edu	18.72.0.3	mit worm paper
blake.acs.washington.edu	128.95.136.2	rim, c version of web
bmc1.bmc.uu.se	130.238.4.81	VMS news, drivers over Decnet, X25 and SLIP for CMU TCP/IP v6.3
bnlux0.bnl.gov	130.199.128.1	looking for suggestions
bobcat.bbn.com	128.89.2.103	unknown
bodega.stanford.edu	36.14.0.200	ham radio, space science, highspeed networking papers
boombox.micro.umn.edu	128.101.95.95	networking stuff (POPmail)
boulder.colorado.edu	128.138.240.1	3b1, sun, Esperanto, ghostscript
brazos.rice.edu	128.42.42.2	pub/X11R3/core.src
brillig.umd.edu	128.8.128.79	unknown
brokaw.lcs.mit.edu	18.30.0.33	pc-omega, bison, scheme utilities
brownvm.brown.edu	128.148.128.40	mac, tn3270
bu.edu	128.197.2.6	RFCs, mail utils, games source, siod, lpd spooler for iris, etc.
buacca.bu.edu	128.197.2.4	math software (/u/mike/netlib-paper)
bugs.cs.wisc.edu	128.105.8.56	nhfsstone
bugs.nosc.mil	128.49.16.1	Minix, ada math
bull.cs.williams.edu	137.165.5.2	unknown
bulldog.cs.yale.edu	128.36.0.3	dict, uucp paths, kafka
burdvax.prc.unisys.com	128.126.10.33	diana
c.scs.uiuc.edu	128.174.90.3	unknown
cac.washington.edu	128.95.112.1	unknown
cad.berkeley.edu	128.32.132.3	apte
cadre.dsl.pittsburgh.edu	128.147.128.1	JOVE, misc.
caf.mit.edu	18.62.0.232	giraphe3
caip.rutgers.edu	128.6.37.16	almost nothing
calpe.psc.edu	128.182.66.148	GPLOT, GTEX
cardinal.lanl.gov	128.165.96.120	cellsim (cellular automata)
cayuga.cs.rochester.edu	192.5.53.209	Xfig, JOVE, NL-KR mail list, ET++
cc.sfu.ca	128.189.32.250	msdos, mac
cc.utah.edu	128.110.8.24	unknown
ccb.ucsf.edu	128.218.1.13	comp.sources, GNU stuff
celray.cs.yale.edu	128.36.0.25	ispell, dictionary
cerl.cecer.army.mil	129.229.1.101	path #7 for Pcomm
cert.sei.cmu.edu	128.237.253.5	virus-l archives
cfdl.larc.nasa.gov	128.155.24.55	vmail
chalmers.se	129.16.1.1	RFCs, sunet information (runs whois server)

chamartin.ai.mit.edu	18.43.0.171	liar, scheme
charon.mit.edu	18.80.0.13	perl+patches, xdvi, world map data
cheddar.cs.wisc.edu	128.105.8.19	Common Lisp stuff, X11 courier fonts
cheops.cis.ohio-state.edu	128.146.8.62	alt.sources, unix-pc
chiris.stevens-tech.edu	192.12.216.114	unknown
chx400.switch.ch	130.59.1.2	news archive, GNU (swiss ftp server)
cica.cica.indiana.edu	129.79.20.22	misc unix, pc, NeXT updates
citi.umich.edu	35.1.128.16	pathalias, CITI macIP, webster
cli.com	192.31.85.1	unknown
clouso.crim.ca	192.26.210.1	RISQnet related documents, mail lists, reports, and announcements, awa: ca domain reg., RFCs, IEFT, etc.
clover.ucdavis.edu	128.120.57.1	eepic, fig2epic, HOL
clvax1.cl.msu.edu	35.8.2.1	MS Windows
clvms.clarkson.edu	128.153.4.4	CMU TCP V6.3 for VMS V5, VMODEM
cmns.think.com	131.239.2.100	Connection machine starlisp simulator
cms.cc.wayne.edu	35.60.4.1	unknown
col.hp.com	15.255.240.16	NOS
columbia.edu	128.59.16.1	NEST network simulation testbed
connemara.math.arizona.edu	128.196.224.5	irisplot
coral.hss.cmu.edu	128.2.229.218	unknown
cqpi.mrc.wisc.edu	128.104.142.12	unknown
crvax.sri.com	128.18.10.1	RISKS Digest archive
cs.arizona.edu	128.196.128.118	Icon, SR, SBprolog, SNOBOL4 languages, xkernel communications kernel
cs.columbia.edu	128.59.16.20	ispell
cs.orst.edu	128.193.32.1	Xlisp, smalltalk, TOPS Terminal, NeXT
cs.toronto.edu	128.100.1.65	AIList, sun-Spots, many other mailing list archives, CA domain reg. forms, RFCs, NETINFO, DOMAIN, IETF, INET-DRAFTS, Current C News, dvix, logging ftpd, Jove, sunOS SLIPet al, S/SL, TeX, UofT BIND, X applications
cs.ubc.ca	128.189.97.5	raster files, MuTeX, ca-domain regs,sun utils, ASCII-Postscript filter
cs.uiuc.edu	128.174.252.1	epoch
cs.uoregon.edu	128.223.4.13	raytracing archive (markv), not much

cs.utah.edu	128.110.4.21	Worm Tour, amiga, forth, utah raster
cs.utexas.edu	128.83.139.9	QSIM, FIG
cs.utk.edu	128.169.201.1	DECnet mail gateway for VAXen and suns
cs.williams.edu	137.165.5.2	unknown
cs.wm.edu	128.239.1.30	texsun, animal-rights, pargen, ALV, raster images
csab.larc.nasa.gov	128.155.26.10	unknown
csd4.csd.uwm.edu	129.89.2.4	high-audio
csd4.milw.wisc.edu	129.89.2.4	high-audio
cse.ogc.edu	129.95.40.2	suntools graphics tools, old Kerberos, old mush, neuro-evolution mailing list archive, speech recognition archive
cse.ogi.edu	129.95.40.2	grtool for suns, old kerberos, recent mush, neuro-evolution mailinglist archive, speech recognition archive, tiny and errata for the book Optimizing Supercompilers for Supercomputers
csli.stanford.edu	36.9.0.46	Gandalf
csri.toronto.edu	128.100.2.30	unknown
csus.edu	130.86.90.1	NeXT, vectrex
csvax.caltech.edu	192.12.18.1	p2c
ctrsci.math.utah.edu	128.110.198.1	TeX fonts, make, Beebe VAX drivers
cu-arpa.cs.cornell.edu	128.84.254.3	Isis, bromley
cunixf.cc.columbia.edu	128.59.40.130	MM mailer, CAP/KIP
curie.cs.unc.edu	128.109.136.151	GIF, graphics programs
cuvmb.cc.columbia.edu	128.59.40.129	mailer, kermit, ibm tcp/ip mods
cyclone.stanford.edu	36.83.0.188	unknown
dagon.acc.stolaf.edu	130.71.128.18	NeXT
dartvax.dartmouth.edu	129.170.16.4	dartmouth stuff (rn, mail, etc.)
dcsprod.byu.edu	128.187.7.3	unknown
decoy.cc.uoregon.edu	128.223.32.19	VAX book
dendrite.stanford.edu	36.83.0.61	mcface
dept.csci.unt.edu	129.120.1.2	Texas Packet Radio Society, MixView, GNUPlot
derby.cs.wisc.edu	128.105.2.162	tinytalk
devvax.tn.cornell.edu	192.35.82.200	tn3270, gated
dftsrv.gsfc.nasa.gov	128.183.10.134	VMS stuff
dg-rtp.dg.com	128.222.1.2	GDB
dinorah.wustl.edu	128.252.118.101	X11R3/core.src, portability issues text
dkuug.dk	129.142.96.41	unknown
doc.cso.uiuc.edu	128.174.49.2	msdos (pcsig), mac
dolphin.mit.edu	18.86.0.5	X11r3 device driver for S, LISA

dopey.cs.unc.edu	128.109.136.82	sunOS 3.5 traceroute, theorem prover
drycas.club.cc.cmu.edu	128.2.232.11	ANU_NEWS, TALK
dsl.cis.upenn.edu	130.91.6.12	GIF, IBM
dsrgsun.ces.cwru.edu	129.22.16.2	Minix, TOS Atari ST, gcc from bammi
durer.cme.nist.gov	129.6.32.48	mm backup (Exabyte), pdes, microemacs 3.10
dustbin.cisco.com	131.108.1.27	Mac telnet w/slip
dxi.nih.gov	128.231.128.11	unknown
ea.ecn.purdue.edu	128.46.129.2	unknown
eddie.mit.edu	18.62.0.6	nothing
ee-switch-1.ee.cornell.edu	128.84.239.201	rstat
ee.ecn.purdue.edu	128.46.129.15	unknown
elbereth.rutgers.edu	128.6.7.26	sci-fic works, startrek guides, etc.
elroy.jpl.nasa.gov	128.149.1.100	ANU_NEWS
emil.csd.uu.se	130.238.4.2	Old GNU, X R10
ems.media.mit.edu	18.85.0.6	unknown
emsworth.andrew.cmu.edu	128.2.30.62	Andrew Toolkit
emunix.emich.edu	35.157.1.2	Ultrix, VMS (soon)
emx.utexas.edu	128.83.1.33	net directory
encore.com	129.91.1.14	mach.doc, nfsstone benchmark
eng.clemson.edu	130.127.8.11	sendmail, pop3, 3c505
enh.nist.gov	129.6.16.1	unknown
eniac.seas.upenn.edu	130.91.6.22	unknown
eru.mt.luth.se	130.240.0.9	gnews 19, gated, plp, gcc (old)
expo.lcs.mit.edu	18.30.0.212	X, portable bitmaps, CLX and CLUE, gwm
f.ms.uky.edu	128.163.128.6	mac, msdos, unix-pc
fcs280s.ncifcrf.gov	129.43.1.11	unknown
fed.expres.cs.cmu.edu	128.2.209.58	Space digest archive
fergvax.unl.edu	129.93.33.1	nothing yet
fiol.uib.no	129.177.10.24	pcip packet driver
fits.cx.nrao.edu	192.33.115.8	FITS (astronomy image transfer system)
fnord.umiacs.umd.edu	128.8.120.3	misc DECstation stuff
foobar.colorado.edu	128.138.243.105	BDF fonts
freebie.engin.umich.edu	35.2.68.23	unknown
freja.diku.dk	129.142.96.1	nn, gnu, x11r4, tex, isode, scheme, sun rpc, rfc, ietf, misc
funet.fi	128.214.1.1	msdos, minix, FUNET/NORDUNET info, isode, pc nfs server, telnet & ftp-resolver binaries, RFCs, amiga (many Fish disks), BSD sources, NeWS software
gaffa.mit.edu	18.62.0.11	unknown

gang-of-four.stanford.edu	36.8.0.118	unknown
gargoyle.uchicago.edu	128.135.20.100	named-kit
gatekeeper.dec.com	16.1.0.2	X11, recipes, cron, map, Larry Wall stuff, STDWIN, lots of source
genbank.bio.net	134.172.1.1	60National Repository for Gene Sequence Data
genvax.psycha.upenn.edu	128.91.22.103	unknown
geom.umn.edu	128.101.25.31	Differential Geometry stuff
geomag.gly.fsu.edu	128.186.10.2	unknown
girch1.hsch.utexas.edu	129.106.4.1	Physiological Research info and programs
giza.cis.ohio-state.edu	128.146.8.61	X11R3, PEX
gmu90x.gmu.edu	129.174.1.4	nothing
gmuvax2.gmu.edu	129.174.1.8	Intel Hypercube library, hp28 software, statistical software
gollum.hcf.jhu.edu	128.220.2.19	some stuff
goober.phri.nyu.edu	128.122.136.10	cnews, nntp, kcl docs, psnup, sequence analysis stuff
grape.ecs.clarkson.edu	128.153.13.196	Opus BBS, msdos, graphics, lots
gregorio.stanford.edu	36.8.0.11	vmtp-ip, ip-multicast
grinch.umiacs.umd.edu	128.8.121.1	unknown
gtss.gatech.edu	128.61.4.1	amiga rexx stuff
gumby.cc.wmich.edu	35.132.1.114	MAINT (VMS)
gumby.dsd.trw.com	129.193.72.50	some RFCs, networking progs
gw.ccie.utoronto.ca	128.100.63.2	alt.sex archive, cold fusion papers (pub/cld.fsn)
gwen.cs.purdue.edu	128.10.2.8	cypress
hamlet.caltech.edu	131.215.139.3	Nanny (VMS)
hanauma.stanford.edu	36.51.0.16	Vplot graphical system, comp.graphics archive
handies.ucar.edu	128.117.64.4	uucp maps, src, feminism archive
harvard.harvard.edu	128.103.1.1	sendmail, rmtlib.shar, lots of VMS
hcfdemo.hcf.jhu.edu	128.220.2.15	unix-pc
helens.stanford.edu	36.2.0.99	kjv, sultrix, secure.tar.Z
hemuli.tik.vtt.fi	130.188.52.2	unknown
hercules.csl.sri.com	192.12.33.51	unknown
herky.cs.uiowa.edu	128.255.28.100	theorem prover
hipl.psych.nyu.edu	128.122.132.2	Jove (v4.9 is latest)
hmcvax.claremont.edu	134.173.4.32	cyrillic fonts
hobbes.cs.umd.edu	128.8.128.41	homebrew C compiler
hobiecat.cs.caltech.edu	131.215.131.167	unknown
hogg.cc.uoregon.edu	128.223.32.9	NorthWestNet site info
hotel.cis.ksu.edu	129.130.10.12	XBBS, msdos, U3G toolkit, unix-pc, pd-modula
hp4nl.nluug.nl	192.16.202.2	GNU, ABC

hplpm.hpl.hp.com	15.255.176.205	Neuron digest archives and software
hpserv1.uit.no	128.39.60.50	HP stuff, X11, unix, etc.
hub.cs.jmu.edu	134.126.20.10	Mic-1 microarchitecture simulator, package to boot minix from hard drive
hub.ucsb.edu	128.111.24.40	UNISEX
hubcap.clemson.edu	130.127.8.1	RFCs
hurratio.tde.lth.se	130.235.32.22	GNU stuff, some local elisp stuff
husc6.harvard.edu	128.103.1.56	pcip, appleII, uumap copy, ucb tahoe
hydra.helsinki.fi	128.214.4.29	misc, TeX, X, comp.sources.misc, comp.sources.sun, comp.sources.unix,comp.bugs.4bsd.ucb -fixes, comp.binaries.ibm.pc
ibm1.cc.lehigh.edu	128.180.2.1	Virus-L programs/archives
icarus.cns.syr.edu	128.230.1.49	misc Syr U. and other net doc
icarus.riacs.edu	134.12.1.1	SLIP, chkpt, macdump, Xpostit
icdc.llnl.gov	128.115.2.1	unknown
ics.uci.edu	128.195.1.1	perfect hash function gen., web-to-c, Protoize/ Unprotoize
ifi.uio.no	129.240.64.2	results of DS5400 vs. DS5810
indri.primate.wisc.edu	128.104.230.11	macintosh TransSkel TransDisplay TransEdit
inria.inria.fr	128.93.8.1	RFCs, /pub (edu dirs)
interviews.stanford.edu	36.22.0.175	InterViews X toolkit
ipac.caltech.edu	131.215.139.35	gated, sendmail, named, kermit, ftp-list
iraun1.ira.uka.de	129.13.10.90	unknown
iris613.gsfc.nasa.gov	128.183.10.147	tn3270 for IRIS and HPUX, other IRIS programs
irisa.irisa.fr	131.254.2.3	NFF, TeX, iPSC2, tcsh, alt.sources, comp.binaries.atari.st, comp.binaries.ibm.pc, comp.binaries.mac, comp.sources.atari.st, comp.sources.games, comp.sources.mac, comp.sources.misc, comp.sources.sun, comp.sources.unix, comp.sources.x
isdres.isd.usgs.gov	130.11.1.2	U.S. Geological Survey public files
isy.liu.se	130.236.1.3	GNU stuff, screen 2.0, world map, ccmd, ftpd, TIFF library,

Cellsim		
iubio.bio.indiana.edu	129.79.1.101	biology archive, molecular bio
iuvax.cs.indiana.edu	129.79.254.192	artificial life, scheme84, SIGPLAN, usenet oracle, webster, whitewater
ix1.cc.utexas.edu	128.83.1.21	amiga
ix2.cc.utexas.edu	128.83.1.29	amiga
j.cc.purdue.edu	128.210.9.2	comp.sources.unix, comp.sources.x, comp.sources.amiga, elm, uupc, NeXT, comp.binaries.amiga, comp.sources.sun
jacobs.cs.orst.edu	128.193.32.13	assorted stuff, mainly games
jade.berkeley.edu	128.32.136.9	NNTP, ping, kermit, gcc
jim.ultra.nyu.edu	128.122.129.21	unknown
jpl-devvax.jpl.nasa.gov	128.149.1.143	perl, patch, warp
jpl-mil.jpl.nasa.gov	128.149.1.101	TeX, mac, GNU, X11R2, X11R3
june.cs.washington.edu	128.95.1.4	TeXhax, dviapollo, SmallTalk, web2c, gated, presto, maitrd
jyu.fi	128.214.7.5	unix, atari, amiga, mac, etherprint, abermud, ularn, conquer, knight, larn, moria, nethack 3.0
kampi.hut.fi	130.233.224.2	DES routines (unrestricted), GNU pascal
kappa.rice.edu	128.42.4.7	X11R3, GNU for Sequent S27, Sun3
kl.sri.com	128.18.10.6	unknown
kolvi.hut.fi	130.233.160.32	kermit stuff, radio amateur stuff (ka9q etc.), memacs 3.10, packet radio
krypton.arc.nasa.gov	128.102.29.20	VMS Vnews, Swing, Profile
kth.se	130.237.72.201	misc, sendmail 5.61 w/ida
kuhub.cc.ukans.edu	129.237.1.10	VMS news
kukulcan.berkeley.edu	128.32.131.190	moria archives
l.cc.purdue.edu	128.210.2.8	nothing
labrea.stanford.edu	36.8.0.47	GNU, X, official TeX sources, lots of other stuff
lamont.ldgo.columbia.edu	129.236.10.30	parse, sunacct, pkunzip, boeing graph
lampwick.berkeley.edu	128.32.131.141	unknown
lancaster.andrew.cmu.edu	128.2.13.21	CMU PCIP, RFC1073 telnetd, RFC1048 bootp
lancelot.avalon.cs.cmu.edu	128.2.242.79	Tinymud docs
larry.cs.washington.edu	128.95.1.7	Poker
larry.mcrcim.mcgill.edu	132.206.4.3	RFCs, X, local nameserver, games, scred (sun bitmap editor)

lcs.mit.edu	18.26.0.36	RFCs, Map, telecom archive
lib.tmc.edu	129.106.5.1	nntp
lilac.berkeley.edu	128.32.136.12	POP3 for BSD/Ultrix/sunOS
linc.cis.upenn.edu	130.91.6.8	psfig for ditroff, TeX, unix-pc
lindy.stanford.edu	36.54.0.11	unknown
lll-crg.llnl.gov	128.115.1.1	X11R4
lll-lcc.llnl.gov	128.115.1.2	Sun Local Users Group arch. (huge!!)
loke.idt.unit.no	129.241.1.103	mh 6.6, news, rrn, nntp, sun-spots, webster server, GCC vms binaries, net directories
louie.udel.edu	128.175.1.3	net.exe, minix, NORD<>LINK, MH, amiga
lth.se	130.235.16.3	NeWS, cnews, bind, nntp, sendmail, Poskanzer rasterxs, X11R4
lurch.stanford.edu	36.22.0.14	InterViews
lut.fi	128.214.25.8	GIF, PD sources modified for hp-ux, PC antivirus, uEmacs 3.10
m2c.m2c.org	128.188.1.2	Archives for cavers mailing list
m9-520-1.mit.edu	18.80.0.45	xim utils
macbeth.stanford.edu	36.21.0.13	nothing
maddog.llnl.gov	128.115.10.1	AWM X tutorial, PCP preprocessor & libraries, Generic MCPI environment, uw for mac, plot library
mandarin.mit.edu	18.82.0.21	unknown
mango.miami.edu	129.171.0.18	unknown
marvin.cs.buffalo.edu	128.205.32.4	RFCs, sun
max.sunysb.edu	129.49.21.100	MGR for unix-pc
maxwell.physics.purdue.edu	128.46.135.3	King James Bible, Commodore Kermit binary files
mazama.stanford.edu	36.51.0.8	unknown
mcnc.mcnc.org	128.109.130.3	layout synthesis benchmarks
mcnc.org	128.109.130.3	ftpd bugfix, intro NIC docs, VLSI CAD tool benchmarks, some RFCs, triangle.jobs archive
mcs.nlm.nih.gov	130.14.1.1	unknown
mcs213k.cs.umr.edu	131.151.6.11	xgif
me10.lbl.gov	128.3.128.110	hp 800 frecover patch
meadow.stanford.edu	36.64.0.20	unknown
media-lab.mit.edu	18.85.0.2	interesting
merit.edu	35.1.1.42	RFCs, ideas
merlin.cs.purdue.edu	128.10.2.3	ConcurrenC, Xinu, mac, GIF
mgm.mit.edu	18.82.0.114	homegrown GNUemacs hacks
mibsrv.mib.eng.ua.edu	130.160.20.80	bitmaps, GIF, games
miki.cs.titech.ac.jp	131.112.16.39	Nemacs
milnetgw.ornl.gov	26.16.0.162	unknown

milton.u.washington.edu	128.95.136.1	star trek info
mims-iris.waterloo.edu	129.97.129.116	laser fonts & utilities
mimsy.umd.edu	128.8.128.8	RCS, declarative languages bib, SLIP, misc
monk.proteon.com	128.185.123.16	cc:mail to smtp gateway
mordor.s1.gov	26.3.0.95	unknown
morris.andrew.cmu.edu	128.2.110.12	unknown
mrcnext.cso.uiuc.edu	128.174.73.105	amiga
mthvax.cs.miami.edu	129.171.32.5	homebrew, constitution, worm, elm, nn
mtsg.ubc.ca	128.189.103.1	msdos, unix, amiga, os2
munnari.oz.au	128.250.1.21	graphics progs (vogle, vopl, vort)
ncnoc.concert.net	128.109.193.1	misc local network info
net1.ucsd.edu	128.54.16.10	mac
network.ucsd.edu	128.54.16.3	anime gifs
newell.arc.nasa.gov	128.102.25.43	unknown
next.com	129.18.1.2	unknown
nic.ddn.mil	10.0.0.51	netinfo, RFCs, IEN, IETF
nic.mr.net	137.192.1.5	Minnesota Regional Net traffic data
nic.near.net	192.52.71.4	unknown
nigel.ee.udel.edu	128.175.2.18	unknown
nis.nsf.net	35.1.1.48	Merit info, NSFnet Link Letter
nisc.jvnc.net	128.121.50.7	unknown
nisc.nyser.net	192.33.4.10	GNU Emacs, others, Nysernet, IETF, GOSIP
nisca.ircc.ohio-state.edu	128.146.1.7	alt.fax
njitgw.njit.edu	128.235.1.2	unknown
nl.cs.cmu.edu	128.2.222.56	Fuzzy Pixmap 0.84
nnsc.nsf.net	192.31.103.6	Network Info, Internet Resource Guide
noc.byu.edu	128.187.7.2	byu-telnet (login:guest, password:anonymous)
nog.calstate.edu	130.150.102.100	unknown
nova.cc.purdue.edu	128.210.7.22	unknown
nyssa.cs.orst.edu		128.193.32.17 GIF, games, misc.
nyu.edu	128.122.128.2	mod.sources, Tihor
oddjob.uchicago.edu	128.135.4.2	NNTP, Sendmail, utils, Ethernet stuff
oddput.efd.lth.se	130.235.48.4	xps (postscript previewer)
omnigate.clarkson.edu	128.153.4.2	PS maps of DNS, Clarkson NCSA telnet
orc.olivetti.com	129.189.192.20	unknown
oregon.uoregon.edu	128.223.20.2	unknown
orion.arc.nasa.gov	128.102.18.10	unknown
orville.nas.nasa.gov	129.99.23.7	hyperchannel network device driver, panel-library (Sil. Graph. workstation graphical interface builder), Kyoto

Common Lisp for Cray2		
osi.ncsl.nist.gov	129.6.48.100	misc OSI info
osi3.ncsl.nist.gov	129.6.48.108	GOSIP
osu-20.ircc.ohio-state.edu	128.146.8.22	unknown
oswego.oswego.edu	129.3.1.1	GNU, mac, kermit
otax.tky.hut.fi	130.233.32.32	Mikkar accounting program
p6xje.ldc.lu.se	130.235.133.7	NCSA telnet 2.2ds, PC networking, etc.
pacific.mps.ohio-state.edu	128.146.37.18	dvi2ps
panarea.usc.edu	128.125.3.54	Archive for "maps"
patience.stanford.edu	36.8.0.154	unknown
paul.rutgers.edu	128.6.5.60	omega
pawl.rpi.edu	128.113.10.2	sun rasters, showtool, raytracer, fluid dynamics model
peace.waikato.ac.nz	130.217.64.62	unknown
pemrac.space.swri.edu	129.162.150.4	convex users group
pescadero.stanford.edu	36.8.0.8	dvi2ps
phoenix.princeton.edu	128.112.128.43	mail stuff
pilot.njin.net	128.6.7.38	Original distribution point of ftp-list
pine.circa.ufl.edu	128.227.128.55	this list, RFCs, Internet Worm reports
pit-manager.mit.edu	18.72.1.58	stories (Alice's PDP-10, Mel and thedrum memory)
pitt.edu	130.49.1.254	local nameserver source, local decnet database, National Institute of Health Guide On-line, RFCs, local network docs
plains.nodak.edu	134.129.111.64	apple, msdos, mac, amiga, ascii pics, comp.sys.handhelds, hp-28 listarchives
pokey.cs.wisc.edu	128.105.2.4	xproof (X11), gremlin (X10, X11)
polyslo.calpoly.edu	129.65.17.1	xtrek, top 2.0, spaceout, cnews, nethack, nntp, uucp, hosts, TR, RFCs, Conquer Docs, usenix tape files, short usenix files, Hitchhikers guide to the Internet, Internet Email list
portia.stanford.edu	36.21.0.69	unknown
postgres.berkeley.edu	128.32.149.1	University INGRES
power.eee.ndsu.nodak.edu	134.129.123.1	DECUS TeX, dvidriver package
pprg.unm.edu	129.24.13.10	bitmaps
primost.cs.wisc.edu	128.105.8.17	comp.compilers
princeton.edu	128.112.128.1	web
psuvax1.cs.psu.edu	128.118.6.2	network/hosts stuff
pyrite.rutgers.edu	128.6.4.15	Security mailing list archives

qed.rice.edu	128.42.4.38	GNU, X11R3, plot2ps sources
radio.astro.utoronto.ca	128.100.75.4	msdos, iris, SunUserGroup, UFGATE
rascal.ics.utexas.edu	128.83.144.1	main Kyoto Common Lisp distributor
relay.cdnnet.ca	128.189.97.41	CA domain registrations, fonts, MuTeX, raster files, RFCs, sun and usenet utils
research.att.com	192.20.225.2	TeX, gcc, ghostscript, f2c
rigel.efd.lth.se	130.235.48.3	VMS emacs, decwindows diffs
ringo.rutgers.edu	128.6.5.77	Omega sources
rlg-rt.stanford.edu	36.95.0.26	unknown
rml2.sri.com	128.18.22.20	unknown
rodan.acs.syr.edu	128.230.1.55	recursive listings of all known anonymous ftp sites
rogue.llnl.gov	128.115.2.99	DECnet security tools
rohini.telecomm.umn.edu	128.101.55.1	UMN hostables
roope.hut.fi	130.233.192.32	unknown
rover.umd.edu	128.8.2.73	unknown
rpi.edu	128.113.1.5	some stuff
rtsg.ee.lbl.gov	128.3.254.68	flex, compressed SLIP
rusmv1.rus.uni-stuttgart.de	129.69.1.12	RFCs, X11, atari, amiga, msdos, unix, mathematics (Fortran)
rutgers.edu	128.6.4.7	comp.sources.sun
sachiko.acc.stolaf.edu	130.71.128.17	unknown
safe.stanford.edu	36.44.0.193	3COM/Interlan 4.X BSD unix
sam.cs.cmu.edu	128.2.254.181	unknown
saqqara.cis.ohio-state.edu	128.146.8.98	unknown
sauna.hut.fi	130.233.251.253	GNU, unix, amiga, athena docs, some FTP dirs from US, security patches/docs, elm, nntp, news, X, jove, etc.
sayshell.umd.edu	128.8.2.88	version of KA9Q
sbcs.sunysb.edu	129.49.2.3	sun raster tools
scam.berkeley.edu	128.32.138.1	X sources, etc.
schizo.samsung.com	134.228.1.2	alt.sources, comp.sources.games, comp.sources.misc, comp.sources.sun, comp.sources.unix, comp.sources.x
science.utah.edu	128.110.192.2	TeX things, Hershey (tenex)
sct60a.sunyct.edu	192.52.220.2	amiga, msdos, gifs, compilers
sdcsvax.ucsd.edu	26.5.0.3	unknown
sds.sdsc.edu	132.249.20.22	supercomputer center info
sdsu.edu	130.191.229.14	GNU, M68K Xinu
serv1.cl.msu.edu	35.8.2.41	msu hosts files
sgi.com	192.58.91.2	IRIS stuff
sh.cs.net	192.31.103.3	NetLists, NetMaps, etc. (lots)

shambhala.berkeley.edu	128.32.132.54	xrn, xgraph
shemp.cs.ucla.edu	131.179.128.34	XWIP
shorty.cs.wisc.edu	128.105.2.8	Condor
sics.se	192.16.123.90	calc, ft1, gated, interviews, isode,mh, packet radio, ping, pmake, printmail, sps, Poskanzer bitmaps (runs whois server)
skippy.umiacs.umd.edu	128.8.120.23	sun-nets archive
skutt.cs.chalmers.se	129.16.2.7	unknown
slfs0.cs.rpi.edu	128.213.7.6	unknown
snow.white.toronto.edu	128.100.2.160	mg
sol.cs.ruu.nl	131.211.80.5	atari, GNU, HP-UX, TeX, Perl, UMFT, etc.
sol.ctr.columbia.edu	128.59.64.4	0background, ethernet stuff, GNUserv, hpgl2ps, DES
solar.stanford.edu	36.14.0.7	local Stanford info
soma.neuro.bcm.tmc.edu	128.249.50.12	unknown
sperm.ocean.washington.edu	128.95.252.7	RWVector, gcc, gdb, kermit, libg++, liblinpack, liboops, oopsV2R2+, plot5, spinup, sungraph, superfilters, xmodem, xyplot
sphere.mast.ohio-state.edu	128.146.7.200	phone (with bugs fixed)
spot.colorado.edu	128.138.238.1	netinfo: stuff, RFCs
squid.cs.ucla.edu	131.179.96.44	gifs
src.honeywell.com	129.30.1.10	PAX (read/write tar and cpio format)
ssyx.ucsc.edu	128.114.133.1	nothing worth mentioning
stat.wisc.edu	128.105.5.1	FACT, Statbib, S functions
stolaf.edu	130.71.128.1	news, anime, bitmaps
stout.atd.ucar.edu	128.117.80.30	unknown
styrofoam.cps.msu.edu	35.8.56.144	unknown
subcomm.ucs.indiana.edu	129.79.16.32	unknown
sumex-aim.stanford.edu	36.44.0.6	mac archives, Mycin (sun4), imap
sun.cnuce.cnr.it	192.12.192.4	atalk, ka9q, GNU
sun.soe.clarkson.edu	128.153.12.3	Packet Driver, X11 fonts, TeX, PCIP, Freemacs, LaTeX styles
sun1.ruf.uni-freiburg.de	132.230.1.1	unknown
suna.osc.edu	128.146.1.4	ape (animation production environment)
suned.zoo.cs.yale.edu	128.36.21.1	games, utils, other hacks
sunic.sunet.se	192.36.125.2	RFCs, nntp, news, sendmail, ntp, comp.sources.unix, comp.sources.games, comp.sources.misc, alt.sources, GNU
surya.waterloo.edu	129.97.129.72	tiff format, gif2ras
sutcase.case.syr.edu	128.230.32.2	zoo, tcp stuff

sutro.sfsu.edu	130.212.15.230	NeXT-related files, mazewar
svax.cs.cornell.edu	128.84.254.2	TransFig, Fig-FS, NetHack
swan.ulowell.edu	129.63.224.1	unknown
tacky.cs.olemiss.edu	130.74.96.13	3c505
tandem.com	130.252.10.8	ham radio
tank.uchicago.edu	128.135.136.2	mac, OzTex
tau.sm.luth.se	130.240.0.3	comp.binaries.ibm.pc
tcgould.tn.cornell.edu	128.84.248.35	transputer archives
tek4310.kent.edu	131.123.2.10	ESIX
terminator.cc.umich.edu	35.1.33.8	xscheme, msdos, atari, sysadmin archive
testarossa.mach.cs.cmu.edu	128.2.250.252	unknown
think.com	131.239.2.1	pmdc, X11.2 Interviews 3d
thor.acc.stolaf.edu	130.71.128.1	fj newsgroups, bible, GNU, some ps
thor.atd.ucar.edu	128.117.81.51	unknown
ti.com	128.247.159.141	Explorer compress & en, CLUE, CLX
titan.rice.edu	128.42.1.30	sun-spots, amiga ispell
tmc.edu	128.249.1.1	FUBBS bbs list
tolsun.oulu.fi	128.214.5.6	amiga, atari, c64, msdos, mac, irc
tomcat.gsfc.nasa.gov	128.183.10.100	G8BPQ
topaz.rutgers.edu	128.6.4.194	amiga, others, too much to list
trantor.harris-atd.com	26.13.0.98	unknown
trident.arc.nasa.gov	128.102.18.13	vms-nntp, trek73
trix.ai.mit.edu	128.52.32.6	
trout.nosc.mil	26.1.0.3	X11R3, benchmarks, popd, GNU emacs
trwind.trw.com	129.4.16.70	NNStat, cisco, ibmpc, isode, ka9q, mac, named, sendmail, sun-utils, traceroute, unix-utils
tuewsd.lso.win.tue.nl	131.155.2.8	unknown
tumtum.cs.umd.edu	128.8.128.49	NeWS pd software
turing.ctc.contel.com	131.131.11.100	modula2
tut.cis.ohio-state.edu	128.146.8.60	GNU, tcsh, lots of interesting things
tut.fi	128.214.1.2	Images, lots of misc. unix
twg.com	26.5.0.73	network stuff
tybalt.caltech.edu	131.215.139.100	GraphWidget
uafcseg.uark.edu	130.184.64.202	(login bbs. telnetable)
ub.d.umn.edu	131.212.32.6	unknown
uc.msc.umn.edu	128.101.1.3	unknown
ucbarpa.berkeley.edu	128.32.130.11	tn3270, pub/4.3, Exntended DCG Prolog
ucbvax.berkeley.edu	128.32.133.1	nntp, gnews, awm, empire
ucdavis.ucdavis.edu	128.120.2.1	dSLIP, POP2, NetHop, UCD whois, UCDMail, IETF-PPP records

ucece1.ece.uc.edu	129.137.32.106	unknown
uceng.uc.edu	129.137.33.1	VLSI Hardware Description Language
uclapp.physics.ucla.edu	128.97.64.122	unknown
ucsd.edu	128.54.16.1	graphics programs and images, ham radio stuff, MIDI programs and data, sound bites for Sparcstation, usenet sources
ug.utah.edu	128.110.4.24	not much
uhccux.uhcc.hawaii.edu	128.171.1.101	unknown
uhecs.helsinki.fi	128.214.4.1	unknown
uhura.cc.rochester.edu	128.151.224.17	nothing
uicbert.eecs.uic.edu	128.248.166.25	AT&T stuff, unix-pc
uicsle.csl.uiuc.edu	128.174.30.5	not much
uicvm.uic.edu	128.248.2.50	unknown
umaxc.weeg.uiowa.edu	128.255.64.80	NCSA telnet, sendmail
umd5.umd.edu	128.8.10.5	unknown
umigw.miami.edu	128.116.10.1	unknown
ummts.cc.umich.edu	35.1.1.43	atari st (cd PC7:)
umn-cs.cs.umn.edu	128.101.224.1	misc GNU, hypertext, news, japanese
umnstat.stat.umn.edu	128.101.51.1	XlispStat, S Bayes
unh.cs.cmu.edu	128.2.254.15	0cold-fusion paper /afs/cs/user/vac/ftp
unicorn.wwu.edu	192.35.140.10	GNU dbm (beta)
unido.informatik.uni-dortmund.de	129.217.64.60	unknown
unix.secs.oakland.edu	35.146.180.2	unknown
unix2.macc.wisc.edu	128.104.30.1	hosts.txt
unmvax.cs.unm.edu	129.24.16.1	getmaps
unsvax.nevada.edu	131.216.1.11	ftp-list
uoft02.utoledo.edu	131.183.1.4	VMSTPC
uokmax.ecn.uoknor.edu	129.15.20.2	tinymud log program
urth.acsu.buffalo.edu	128.205.7.9	unknown
usc.edu	128.125.1.45	amd (automounter)
utadnx.cc.utexas.edu	128.83.1.26	VMS sources (zetaps, laser, sxlps)
utsun.s.u-tokyo.ac.jp	133.11.7.250	Japanese PD, msdos, mac, unix, etc.
uunet.uu.net	192.48.96.2	usenet archives, much more
uvaarpa.virginia.edu	128.143.2.7	csound
uwasa.fi	128.214.12.3	mac, pc, suntools, unix, vms, os2
uwm.edu	129.89.2.1	info-tahoe
ux.acs.umn.edu	128.101.63.2	unknown
uxa.cso.uiuc.edu	128.174.2.3	mac, msdos (pcsig)
uxc.cso.uiuc.edu	128.174.5.50	games, misc, HitchHiker's Guide to the Internet, recipes, GIF
uxe.cso.uiuc.edu	128.174.5.54	amiga (Fish)
valhalla.ee.rochester.edu	128.151.160.11	RFCs, Network load balancer

van-bc.wimsey.bc.ca	128.189.233.155	interim (uupc), comp.archives archive
vax.cs.pitt.edu	130.49.2.1	ka9q
vax.ftp.com	128.127.25.100	FTP software, inc.
vaxa.isi.edu	128.9.0.33	clf-act, X, db
vaxb.acs.unt.edu	129.120.1.4	DOWN for VMS and other VMS utils
vega.hut.fi	130.233.200.42	msdos, mac, Kermit, fusion docs, food recipes (alt. gourmand), SF author lists, os2
venera.isi.edu	128.9.0.32	statspy (NNstat), GNU Chess
venus.ycc.yale.edu	130.132.1.5	SBTeX
vgr.brl.mil	192.5.23.6	info-iris, brl-cad, bump, ping+record route, ttcp, mon, pmon, images
vlsi.cs.umn.edu	128.101.230.15	PLP (Public line printer)
vm.utdallas.edu	129.110.102.2	lipphe ibm tcp/ip bit and k200 drivers
vm1.nodak.edu	134.129.111.1	fixes minix, fixes ev1188, QNS
vmd.cso.uiuc.edu	128.174.5.98	Hurricane Hugo GIF pictures
vms.ecs.rpi.edu	128.113.5.15	Message Exchange
vms2.ecs.rpi.edu	128.113.5.14	NEWSRDR
vmsd.oac.uci.edu	128.200.15.2	VMS stuff
watmath.waterloo.edu	129.97.128.1	lots of stuff
watmsg.waterloo.edu	129.97.129.9	GNU, pd BSD, uSystem docs, virus, cryptography
watsun.cc.columbia.edu	128.59.39.2	kermit
wb1.cs.cmu.edu	128.2.250.16	mach docs
weedeater.math.yale.edu	130.132.23.17	rayshade, misc. raytracing goodies
wheaties.ai.mit.edu	128.52.32.13	supdup, t3.1, tX11
whitechapel.media.mit.edu	18.85.0.125	OBVIUS, macnh
wilma.cs.brown.edu	128.148.32.66	Brown CS Field and Thread packages
winnie.princeton.edu	128.112.128.180	music software (unix & NeXT)
wpi.wpi.edu	130.215.24.1	dspl, anime, fusion, mac, GNU, ash, DES, misc Unix, TeX_DS3100, TeX_Umax, misc X
wsmr-simtel20.army.mil	26.2.0.74	msdos, unix, cpm, mac (tenex)
wuarchive.wustl.edu	128.252.135.4	GNU, X.11R3, GIF, IEN, RFCs, TeX, UUPC, info-mac, 4.3BSD-Tahoe, comp.binaries.amiga, comp.binaries.apple2, comp.binaries.atari.st, comp.binaries.ibm.pc, comp.sources.amiga, comp.sources.atari.st,

		comp.sources.games, comp.sources.misc, comp.sources.unix, comp.sources.x, msdos, simtel20 (24 hours/day)
xanth.cs.odu.edu	128.82.8.1	comp.sources.x, comp.sources.unix, comp.sources.misc, comp.sources.games, comp.sources.amiga, X, amiga
xlnvax.excelan.com	130.57.4.1	misc. (looking for suggestions)
xview.ucdavis.edu	128.120.1.150	unknown
ymir.claremont.edu	134.173.4.23	lots of VMS, TeX-for-VMS
z.andrew.cmu.edu	128.2.30.8	bugfixar + div
zaphod.ncsa.uiuc.edu	128.174.20.50	NCSA Telnet source, Mathematica
zariski.harvard.edu	128.103.1.107	macaulay
zerkalo.harvard.edu	128.103.40.201	traceroute
zeus.mgmt.purdue.edu	128.210.1.3	unknown
zurich.ai.mit.edu	18.26.0.176	liar, scheme

7.4 Manual for RN - A NEWSNET Program

This section represents an edited version of the Unix manual pages on the use of rn to read usenet newsletters.

Rn operates on three levels: the newsgroup selection level, the article selection level, and the paging level. Each level has its own set of commands, and its own help menu. At the paging level (the bottom level), rn behaves much like the more (1) program. At the article selection level, you may specify which article you want next, or read them in the default order, which is either in order of arrival on your system, or by subject threads. At the newsgroup selection level (the top level), you may specify which newsgroup you want next, or read them in the default order, which is the order that the newsgroups occur in your .newsrc file. (You will therefore want to rearrange your .newsrc file to put the most interesting newsgroups first. This can be done with the 'm' command on the Newsgroup Selection level.)

On any level, at *any* prompt, an 'h' may be typed for a list of available commands. This is probably the most important command to remember, so don't you forget it. Every prompt has a list of several plausible commands enclosed in square brackets. Pressing the space bar once will cause the first command in the list to be implemented. (All input is done in cbreak mode, so carriage returns should not be used to terminate anything except certain multi-character commands. Those commands will be obvious in the discussion below because they take an argument.)

Upon startup, rn will do several things:

1. It will look for your .newsrc file, which is your list of subscribed-to newsgroups. If rn does not find a .newsrc, it will create one. If it does find one, it will back it up under the name ".oldnewsrc."

2. It will input your .newsrc file, listing out the first several newsgroups with unread news.

3. It will perform certain consistency checks on your .newsrc. If your .newsrc is out of date in any way, rn will warn you and make the corrections, but you may have to wait a little longer for it to start up.

4. Rn will then check to see if any new newsgroups have been created, and give you the opportunity to add them to your .newsrc.

5. Rn then goes into the top prompt level—the newsgroup selection level.

Newsgroup Selection Level

In this section the words "next" and "previous" refer to the ordering of the newsgroups in your .newsrc file. On the newsgroup selection level, the prompt looks like this:

******** 17 unread articles in net.blurfl-read now? [ynq]

and the following commands may be given at this level:

y,SP Do this newsgroup now.

.command Do this newsgroup now, but execute command before displaying anything. The command will be interpreted as if given on the article selection level.

= Do this newsgroup now, but list subjects before displaying articles.

n Go to the next newsgroup with unread news.

N Go to the next newsgroup.

p Go to the previous newsgroup with unread news. If there is none, stay at the current newsgroup.

P Go to the previous newsgroup.

- Go to the previously displayed newsgroup (regardless of whether it is before or after the current one in the list).

1 Go to the first newsgroup.

^ Go to the first newsgroup with unread news.

$ Go to the end of the newsgroups list.

g newsgroup Go to newsgroup. If it is not currently subscribed to, you will be asked if you want to subscribe.

/pattern Scan forward for a newsgroup matching pattern. Patterns do globbing like filenames, i.e., use ? to match a single character, * to match any sequence of characters, and [] to specify a list of characters to match.

u Unsubscribe from current newsgroup.

l stringList newsgroups not subscribed to which contain the string specified.

L Lists the current state of the .newsrc, along with status information.

Status Meaning <number> Count of unread articles in newsgroup.

READ No unread articles in newsgroup.

UNSUB Unsubscribed newsgroup.

BOGUS Bogus newsgroup.

JUNK Ignored line in .newsrc (e.g. readnews "options" line).

m name Move the named newsgroup somewhere else in the .newsrc. If no name is given, the current newsgroup is moved. There are a number of ways to specify where you want the newsgroup-type h for help when it asks where you want to put it.

c Catch up-mark all unread articles in this newsgroup as read.

o pattern Only display those newsgroups whose name matches pattern.

a pattern Add new newsgroups matching pattern.

& Print out the current status of command line switches and any newsgroup restrictions.

&switch {switch} Set additional command line switches.

&& Print out the current macro definitions.

&&keys commands Define additional macros.

q Quit.

x Quit, restoring .newsrc to its state at startup of rn. The .newsrc you would have had you exited with 'q' will be called .newnewsrc, in case you did not really want to type 'x'.

^K Edit the global KILL file. This is a file that contains /pattern/j commands (one per line) to be applied to every newsgroup as it is started up; that is, when it is selected on the newsgroup selection level. The purpose of a KILL file is to mark articles as read on the basis of some set of patterns. This saves considerable wear and tear on your 'n' key. There is also a local KILL file for each newsgroup. Because of the overhead involved in searching for articles to kill, it is better to use a local KILL file whenever possible. Local KILL files are edited with a '^K' on the article selection level. There are also automatic ways of adding search commands to the local KILL file; see the 'K' command and the K search modifier on the article selection level.

Article Selection Level

On the article selection level, rn selects (by default) unread articles in numerical order (the order in which articles have arrived at your site). If you do a subject search (^N), the default order is modified to numericl within each subject thread. You may switch back and forth between numerical order and subject thread order at will. The -S switch can be used to make subject search mode the default.

On the article selection level you are not asked whether you want to read an article before the article is displayed. The rn simply displays the first page (or portion of a page, at low baud rates) of the article and asks if you want to continue. The normal article selection prompt comes at the end of the article (though article selection commands can also be given from within the middle of the article [the pager level] also). The prompt at the end of an article looks like this:

End of article 248 (of 257)-what next? [npq]

The following are the options at this point:

n,SP Scan forward for next unread article.
N Go to the next article.
^N Scan forward for the next article with the same subject, and make ^N default (subject search mode).
p Scan backward for previous unread article. If there is none, stay at the current article.
P Go to the previous article.
- Go to the previously displayed article (regardless of whether that article is before or after this article in the normal sequence).
^P Scan backward for the previous article with the same subject, and make ^N default (subject search mode).
^R Restart the current article.
v Restart the current article verbosely, displaying the entire header.
^L Refresh the screen.
^X Restart the current article, and decrypt as a rot13 message.
b Back up one page.
q Quit this newsgroup and go back to the newsgroup selection level.
^ Go to the first unread article.
$ Go to the last article (actually, one past the last article).
number Go to the numbered article.
range{,range} command{:command} Apply a set of commands to a set of articles. A range consists of either <article number> or <article number>-<article number>. A dot '.' represents the current article, and a dollar sign '$' represents the last article. Applicable commands include 'm' (mark as unread), 'M' (delayed mark as unread), 'j' (mark as read), "s dest" (save to a destination), "!command" (shell escape), "=" (print the subject) and "C" (cancel).
j Junk the current article-mark it as read. If this command is used from within an article, you are left at the end of the article, unlike 'n,' which looks for the next article.
m Mark the current article as still unread. (If you are in subject search mode you probably want to use M instead of m. Otherwise, the current article may be selected as the beginning of the next subject thread.)
M Mark the current article as still unread, but not until the newsgroup is exited. Until then, the current article will be marked as read. This is useful for returning to an article in another session, or in another newsgroup.
/pattern Scan forward for article containing pattern in the subject.
/pattern/h Scan forward for article containing pattern in the header.
/pattern/a Scan forward for article containing pattern anywhere in article.
/pattern/r Scan read articles also.
/pattern/c Make search case sensitive. Ordinarily, uppercase and lowercase are considered the same.
/pattern/modifiers:command{:command} Apply the commands list

ed to articles matching the search command (possibly with h, a, or r modifiers). Applicable commands include 'm' (mark as unread), 'M' (delayed mark as unread), 'j' (mark as read), "s dest" (save to a destination), "!command" (shell escape), "=" (print the subject) and "C" (cancel).

?pattern — Scan backward for article containing pattern in the subject. May be modified as the forward search is: ?pattern?modifiers[:commands]. It is likely that you will want an r modifier when scanning backward.

k — Mark as read all articles with the same subject as the current article.

K — Do the same as the k command, but also add a line to the local KILL file for this newsgroup to kill this subject every time the newsgroup is started up. For a discussion of KILL files, see the '^K' command below. See also the K modifier on searches above.

^K — Edit the local KILL file for this newsgroup. Each line of the KILL file should be a command of the form /pattern/j. (With the exception that rn will insert a line at the beginning of the form "THRU <number>," which tells rn the maximum article number that the KILL file has been applied to. You may delete the THRU line to force a rescan of current articles.) You may also have reason to use the m, h, or a modifiers. Be careful with the M modifier in a kill file; there are more efficient ways to never read an article. You might have reason to use it if a particular series of articles is posted to multiple newsgroups. In this case, M would force you to view the article in a different newsgroup.

r — Reply through net mail.

R — Reply, including the current article in the header file generated. (See 'F' command below). The YOUSAID environment variable controls the format of the attribution line.

f — Submit a followup article. If on a nonexistent article, such as the "End of newsgroup" pseudo- article (which you can get to with a '$' command), posts an original article (basenote).

F — Submit a followup article, and include the old article, with lines prefixed either by ">" or by the argument to a -F switch. Rn will attempt to provide an attribution line in front of the quoted article, generated from the From: line of the article. Unfortunately, the From: line does not always contain the right name; you should double check it against the signature and change it if necessary, or you may have to apologize for quoting the wrong person. The environment variables NEWSPOSTER, NEWSHEADER and ATTRIBUTION may be used to modify the posting behavior of rn (see environment section).

C — Cancel the current article, but only if you are the contributor or superuser.

c — Catch up in this newsgroup; i.e., mark all articles as read.

u — Unsubscribe to this newsgroup.

s destination — Save to a filename or pipe using sh. If only a directory name is specified, the environment variable SAVENAME is used to generate the actual name. If only a filename is specified (i.e., no directory), the environment variable SAVEDIR will be used to generate the actual directory. If nothing is specified, both variables will be used. Since the current directory for rn while doing a save command is your private news directory, saying "s ./filename" will force the file to your news directory.

w destination	The same as "s destination," but saves without the header.
W destination	The same as "S destination," but saves without the header.
&	Print out the current status of command line switches.
&switch {switch}	Set additional command line switches.
&&	Print out current macro definitions.
&&keys commands	Define an additional macro.
=	List subjects of unread articles.
#	Print last article number.

Pager Level

At the pager level (within an article), the prompt looks like this:

-MORE-(17%)

and a number of commands may be given:

SP	Display next page.
x	Display next page and decrypt as a rot13 message.
d,^D	Display half a page more.
CR	Display one more line.
q	Go to the end of the current article (don't mark it either read or unread). This leaves you at the "What next?" prompt.
j	Junk the current article. Mark it read and go to the end of the article.
^L	Refresh the screen.
X	Refresh the screen and decrypt as a rot13 message.
b,^B	Back up one page.
gpattern	Go to (search forward for) pattern within current article. Note that there is no space between the command and the pattern. If the pattern is found, the page containing the pattern will be displayed. The location on the page where the line matching the pattern goes depends on the value of the -g switch. By default, the matched line goes at the top of the screen.
G	Search for g pattern again.
^G	This is a special version of the 'g' command that is used for skipping articles in a digest. It is equivalent to setting "-g4" and then executing the command "g^Subject:"

The following commands skip the rest of the current article, then behave as if the "What next?" prompt at the end of the article had been used. See the documentation at the article selection level for these commands.

$ & / = ? c C f F k K ^K m M r R ^R u v Y ^ number range{,range} command{:command}

The following commands also skip to the end of the article, but have the additional effect of marking the current article as read:
n N ^N s S | w W

Options

Rn has a nice set of options to allow you to tailor the interaction to your liking. (You might like to know that the author swears by "-e -m -S -/.") These options may be set on the command line, via the RNINIT environment variable, via a file pointed to by the RNINIT variable, or from within rn via the & command. Options may generally be unset by saying "+switch." Options include: -c checks for news without reading news. If a list of newsgroups is given on the command line, only those newsgroups will be checked; otherwise, all subscribed- to newsgroups are checked. Whenever the -c switch is specified, a non-zero exit status from rn means that there is unread news in one of the checked newsgroups. The -c switch does not disable the printing of newsgroups with unread news; this is controlled by the -s switch. (The -c switch is not meaningful when given via the & command.)

-C<number> tells rn how often to checkpoint the .newsrc, in articles read. Actually, this number says when to start thinking about doing a checkpoint if the situation is right. If a reasonable checkpointing situation does not arise within 10 more articles, the .newsrc is checkpointed at random.

-d<directory name> sets the default save directory to something other than ~/News. The directory name will be globbed (via csh) if necessary (and if possible). Articles saved by rn may be placed in the save directory, or in a subdirectory thereof, depending on the command that you give and the state of the environment variables SAVEDIR and SAVENAME. Any KILL files (see the K command in the Article Selection section) also reside in this directory and its subdirectories, by default. In addition, shell escapes leave you in this directory.

-D <flags> enables debugging output. See common.h for flag values. Warning: normally, rn attempts to restore your .newsrc when an unexpected signal or internal error occurs. This is disabled when any debugging flags are set.

-e causes each page within an article to be started at the top of the screen, not just the first page. (It is similar to the -c switch of more(1).) You never have to read scrolling text with this switch. This is especially helpful at certain baud rates because you can start reading the top of the next page without waiting for the whole page to be printed. It works nicely in conjunction with the -m switch, particularly if you use half-intensity for your highlight mode. See also the -L switch.

-E<name>=<val> sets the environment variable <name> to the value specified. Within rn, "&-ESAVENAME=%t" is similar to "setenv SAVENAME '%t'" in csh, or "SAVENAME='%t'; export SAVENAME" in sh. Any environment variables set with -E will be inherited by subprocesses of rn.

-F<string> sets the prefix string for the 'F' followup command to use in prefixing each line of the quoted article. For example, "-F<tab>" inserts a tab on the front of each line (which, unfortunately, will cause long lines to wrap around), "-F>>>>" inserts ">>>>" on every line, and "-F" by itself causes nothing to be inserted, in case, for example, you want to reformat the text. The initial default prefix is ">."

-g<line> tells rn which line of the screen you want searched-for strings to show up on when you search with the 'g' command within an article. The lines are numbered starting with 1. The initial default is "-g1," meaning the first line of the screen. Setting the line to less than 1 or more than the number of lines on the screen will set it to the last line of the screen.

-h<string> hides (disables the printing) all header lines beginning with string. For instance, -hexp will disable the printing of the "Expires:" line. Case is insignificant. If <string> is null, all header lines except Subject are hidden, and you may then use +h to select those lines you want to see. You may wish to use the baud-rate switch modifier below to hide more lines at lower baud rates.

-H<string> works just like -h except that instead of setting the hiding flag for a header line, it sets the magic flag for that header line. Certain header lines have magic behavior that can be controlled this way. At present, the following actions are caused by the flag for the particular line: the Newsgroups line will only print when there are multiple newsgroups, the Subject line will be underlined, and the Expires line will always be suppressed if there is nothing on it. In fact, all of these actions are the default, and you must use +H to undo them.

-i=<number> specifies how long (in lines) to consider the initial page of an article. Normally this is determined automatically depending on baud rate. (Note that an entire article header will always be printed regardless of the specified initial page length. If you are working at low baud rate and wish to reduce the size of the headers, you may hide certain header lines with the h switch.)

-l disables the clearing of the screen at the beginning of each article, in case you have a bizarre terminal.
-L tells rn to leave information on the screen as long as possible by not blanking the screen between pages, and by using clear to end-of-line. (The more(1) program does this.) This feature works only if you have the requisite termcap capabilities. The switch has no effect unless the -e switch is set.

-m=<mode> enables the marking of the last line of the previous page printed, to help the user see where to continue reading. This is most helpful when less than a full page is going to be displayed. It may also be used in conjunction with the -e switch, in which case the page is erased, and the first line (which is the last line of the previous page) is highlighted. If -m=s is specified, the standout mode will be used, but if -m=u is specified, underlining will be used. If neither =s or =u is specified, standout is the default. Use +m to disable highlighting.

-M forces mailbox format in creating new save files. Ordinarily, you are asked which format you want.

-N forces normal (non-mailbox) format in creating new save files. Ordinarily you are asked which format you want.

-r causes rn to restart in the last newsgroup read during a previous session with rn. It is equivalent to a normal start up and then getting to the newsgroup with a g command.

-s with no argument suppresses the initial listing of newsgroups with unread news, whether -c is specified or not. Thus, -c and -s can be used together to "silently" test the status of news from within your .login file. If -s is followed by a number, the initial listing is suppressed after that many lines have been listed. Presuming that you have your .newsrc sorted into order of interest, -s5 will tell you the 5 most interesting newsgroups that have unread news. This is also a nice feature to use in your .login file, since it not only tells you whether there is unread news, but also how important the unread news is, without having to wade through the entire list of unread newsgroups. If no -s switch is given, -s5 is assumed, so just putting "rn -c" into your .login file is fine.

- Similarly, switches may be selected based on terminal type:
-=vt100+T set +T on vt100 -=tvi920-ETERM=mytvi get a special termcap entry -=tvi920-ERNMACRO=%./.rnmac.tvi set up special keymappings +=paper-v set verify mode if not hardcopy.

Some switch arguments, such as environment variable values, may require spaces in them. Such spaces should be quoted via ", ', or \ in the conventional fashion, even when passed via RNINIT or the & command.

The special percent escapes are similar to print percent escapes. These cause the substitution of various run-time values into the string. The following are currently recognized:

%a Current article number.

%A Full name of current article (%P/%c/%a). (On a Eunice system with the LINKART option, %P/%c/%a returns the name of the article in the current newsgroup, while %A returns the real name of the article, which may be different if the current article was posted to multiple newsgroups.) %b Destination of last save command, often a mailbox.

%B The byte offset to the beginning of the part of the article to be saved, set by the save command. The 's' and 'S' commands set it to 0, and the 'w' and 'W' commands set it to the byte offset of the body of the article.

%c Current newsgroup, directory form.

%C Current newsgroup, dot form.

%d Full name of newsgroup directory (%P/%c).

%D "Distribution:" line from the current article.

%f "From:" line from the current article, or the "Reply-To:" line if there is one. This differs from %t in that comments (such as the full name) are not stripped out with %f.

%F "Newsgroups:" line for a new article, constructed from "Newsgroups:" and "Followup-To:" lines of current article.

%h Name of the header file to pass to the mail or news poster, containing all the information that the poster program needs in the form of a message header. It may also contain a copy of the current article. The format of the header file is controlled by the MAILHEADER and NEWSHEADER environment variables. %H Host name (your machine's name).

%i "Message-I.D.:" line from the current article, with <> guaranteed.

%I The reference indication mark (see the -F switch.)

%l The news administrator's login name, if any.

%L Login name (yours).

%m The current mode of rn, for use in conditional macros.
i Initializing. n Newsgroup selection level. a Article selection level.
p Pager level. m Miscellaneous questions.

%M The number of articles marked to return via the 'M' command. If the same article is Marked multiple times, "%M" counts it multiple times in the current implementation.

%n "Newsgroups:" line from the current article.

%N Full name (yours).

%o Organization (yours).

%O Original working directory (from which you ran rn).

%p Your private news directory, normally ~/News.

%P Public news spool directory, normally /usr/spool/news.

%r Last reference on references line of current article (parent article I.D.).

%R References list for a new article, constructed from the references and article I.D. of the current article.

%s Subject, with all Re's and (nf)'s stripped off.

%S Subject, with one "Re:" stripped off.

%t "To:" line derived from the "From:" and "Reply-To:" lines of the current article. This always returns an Internet format address. %T "To:" line derived from the "Path:" line of the current article to produce a uucp path.

%u The number of unread articles in the current newsgroup.

%U The number of unread articles in the current newsgroup, not counting the current article.

%x The news library directory.

%X The rn library directory.

%z The length of the current article in bytes.

%~ Your home directory.

%. The directory containing your dot files, which is your home directory unless the environment variable DOTDIR is defined when rn is invoked.

%$ Current process number.

%/ Last search string.

%% A percent sign.

%{name} or %{name-default} The environment variable "name."

%[name] The value of header line "Name:" from the current article. The "Name: " is not included. For example, "%D" and "%[distribution]" are equivalent. The name must be spelled out in full.

%`command` Inserts the output of the command, with any embedded newlines translated to space.

%"prompt" Prints prompt on the terminal, then inputs one string, and inserts it.

%digit The digits 1 through 9 interpolate the string matched by the nth bracket in the last pattern match that had brackets. If the last pattern had alternatives, you may not know the numberof the bracket you want; %0 will give you the last bracket matched.

Modifiers: to capitalize the first letter, insert '^': "%^C" produces something like "Net.jokes." Inserting '_' causes the first letter following the last '/' to be capitalized: "%_c" produces "net/Jokes."

MACROS When rn starts up, it looks for a file containing macro definitions (see environment variable RNMACRO). Any sequence of commands may be bound to any sequence of keys, so you could remap your entire keyboard if you desire. Blank lines or lines beginning with # in the macro file are considered comments; otherwise rn looks for two fields separated by white space. The first field gives the sequence of keystrokes that trigger the macro, and the second field gives the sequence of commands to execute. Both fields are subject to % interpolation, which will also translate backslash and up-arrow sequences. (The keystroke field is interpreted at startup time, but the command field is interpreted at macro execution time, so that you may refer to % values in a macro.) For example, if you want to reverse the roles of carriage return and space in rn:

^J \040 ^M \040 \040 ^J

will do just that. By default, all characters in the command field are interpreted as the canonical rn characters, i.e., no macro expansion is done. Otherwise, the above pair of macros would cause an infinite loop. To force macro expansion in the command field, enclose the macro call with ^(... ^) thusly:

@s | mysavescript @w w^(@s^)

You can use the %() conditional construct to construct macros that work differently under varied circumstances. The current mode (%m) of rn could be used to make a command that only works at a particular level. For example:

^[[O %(%m=p?\040) will only allow the macro to work at the pager level.

%(%{TERM}=vt100?^[[O) /^J

will do the binding only if the terminal type is vt100, though if you have many of these it would be better to have separate files for each terminal.

If you want to bind a macro to a function key that puts a common garbage character after the sequence (such as the carriage return on the end of Televideo 920 function sequences), DO NOT put the carriage return into all the sequences or you will waste a *considerable* amount of internal storage. Instead of "^AF^M," use "^AF+1," which indicates to rn that it should gobble up one character after the F.

AUTHOR Larry Wall, Systems Development Corp., Santa Monica, CA <lwall@sdcrdcf.UUCP> Regular expression routines are borrowed from emacs, by James Gosling.

FILES %./.newsrc status of your news reading

%./.oldnewsrc backup copy of your .newsrc from start of session

%./.rnlock lock file so you do not screw up your .newsrc

%./.rnlast info from last run of rnP

%./.rnsoft soft pointers into /usr/lib/active to speed startup, synchronous with .newsrc

%./.rnhead temporary header file to pass to a mailer or news poster

%./.rnmac macro and keymap definitions

%p your news save directory, usually ~/News

%x/active the list of active newsgroups, usually /usr/lib/news/active

%P the public news spool directory, usually /usr/spool/news

%X/INIT system-wide default switches

7.5 A Primer on How to Work With the USENET Community

Chuq Von Rospach

You now have access to Usenet, a big network of thousands of computers. Other documents or your system administrator will provide detailed technical documentation. This message describes the Usenet culture and customs that have developed over time. All new users should read this message to find out how Usenet works. (Old users could read it, too, to refresh their memories.)

USENET is a large collection of computers that share data with each other. It is the people on these computers that make USENET worth the effort, and for USENET to function properly those people must be able to interact in productive ways. This paper is intended as a guide to using the net in ways that will be pleasant and productive for everyone.

This paper is not intended to teach you how to use USENET. Instead, it is a guide to using it politely, effectively, and efficiently. Communication by computer is new to almost everybody, and there are certain aspects that can make it a frustrating experience until you get used to them. This paper should help you avoid the worst traps.

The easiest way to learn how to use USENET is to watch how others use it. Start reading the news and try to figure out what people are doing and why. After a couple of weeks you will start understanding why certain things are done and what things shouldn't be done. There are documents available that describe the technical details of how to use the software. These vary depending on which programs you use to access the news. You can get copies of these from your system administrator. If you do not know who that person is, they can be contacted on most systems by mailing to account "usenet."

Never Forget that the Person on the Other Side is Human

Because your interaction with the network is through a computer, it is easy to forget that there are people "out there." Situations arise where emotions erupt into a verbal free-for-all that can lead to hurt feelings.

Please remember that people all over the world are reading your words. Do not attack people if you cannot persuade them with your presentation of the facts. Screaming, cursing, and abusing others only serves to make people think less of you and less willing to help you when you need it. Try not to say anything to others you would not say to them in person in a room full of people.

Be Brief

Never say in ten words what can be said in less. Say it succinctly and it will have a greater impact. Remember that the longer you make your article, the fewer people will bother to read it.

Your Postings Reflect Upon You — Be Proud of Them

Most people on USENET will know you only by what you say and how well you say it. They may someday be your co-workers or friends. Take some time to make sure each posting is something that will not embarrass you later. Minimize your spelling errors and make sure that the article is easy to read and understand. Writing is an art, and to do it well requires practice. Since much of how people judge you on the net is based on your writing, such time is well spent.

Use Descriptive Titles

The subject line of an article is there to enable a person with a limited amount of time to decide whether or not to read your article. Tell people what the article is about before they read it. A title like "Car for Sale" to rec.autos does not help as much as "66 MG Midget for sale: Beaverton OR." Don't expect people to read your article to find out what it is about because many of them won't bother. Some sites truncate the length of the subject line to 40 characters so keep your subjects short and to the point.

Think About Your Audience

When you post an article, think about the people you are trying to reach. Asking UNIX(*) questions on rec.autos will not reach as many of the people you want to reach if you asked them on comp.unix.questions or comp.unix.wizards. Try to get the most appropriate audience for your message, not the widest.

It is considered bad form to post both to misc.misc, soc.net-people, or misc.wanted and to some other newsgroup. If it belongs in that other newsgroup, it does not belong in misc.misc, soc.net-people, or misc.wanted.

If your message is of interest to a limited geographic area (apartments, car sales, meetings, concerts, etc...), restrict the distribution of the message to your local area. Some areas have special newsgroups with geographical limitations, and the recent versions of the news software allow you to limit the distribution of material sent to world-wide newsgroups. Check with your system administrator to see what newsgroups are available and how to use them.

If you want to try a test of something, do not use a world-wide newsgroup! Messages in misc.misc that say "This is a test" are likely to cause large numbers of caustic messages to flow into your mailbox. There are newsgroups that are local to your computer or area that should be used. Your system administrator can tell you what they are.

Be Careful with Humor and Sarcasm

Without the voice inflections and body language of personal communications, it is easy for a remark meant to be funny to be misinterpreted. Subtle humor tends to get lost, so take steps to make sure that people realize you are trying to be funny. The net has developed a symbol called the smiley face. It looks like ":-)" and points out sections of articles with humorous intent. No matter how broad the humor or satire, it is safer to remind people that you are being funny.

But also be aware that quite frequently satire is posted without any explicit indications. If an article outrages you strongly, you should ask yourself if it just may have been unmarked satire. Several self-proclaimed connoisseurs refuse to use smiley faces, so take heed or you may make a temporary fool of yourself.

Only Post a Message Once

Avoid posting messages to more than one newsgroup unless you are sure it is appropriate. If you do post to multiple newsgroups, do not post to each group separately. Instead, specify all the groups on a single copy of the message. This reduces network overhead and lets people who subscribe to more than one of those groups see the message once instead of having to wade through each copy.

Please Rotate Messages With Questionable Content

Certain newsgroups (such as rec.humor) have messages in them that may be offensive to some people. To make sure that these messages are not read unless they are explicitly requested, these messages should be encrypted. The standard encryption method is to rotate each letter by thirteen characters so that an "a" becomes an "n". This is known on the network as "rot13," and when you rotate a message, the word "rot13" should be in the "Subject:" line. Most of the software used to read usenet articles have some way of encrypting and decrypting messages. Your system administrator can tell you how the software on your system works, or you can use the Unix command "tr [a-z][A-Z] [n-z][a-m][N-Z][A-M]." (Note that some versions of Unix don't require the [] in the "tr" command. In fact, some systems will get upset if you use them in an unquoted manner. The following should work for everyone, but may be shortened on some systems: tr '[a-m][n-z][A-M][N-Z]' '[n-z][a-m][N-Z][A-M]' Don't forget the single quotes!

Summarize What You are Following Up

When you are following up someone's article, please summarize the parts of the article to which you are responding. This allows readers to appreciate your comments rather than trying to remember what the original article said. It is also possible for your response to get to some sites before the original article.

Summarization is best done by including appropriate quotes from the original article. Do not include the entire article since it will irritate the people who have already seen it. Even if you are responding to the entire article, summarize only the major points you are discussing.

When Summarizing, Summarize!

When you request information from the network, it is common courtesy to report your findings so that others can benefit as well. The best way of doing this is to take all the responses that you received and edit them into a single article that is posted to the places where you originally posted your question. Take the time to strip headers, combine duplicate information, and write a short summary. Try to credit the information to the people that sent it to you, where possible.

Use Mail, Don't Post a Follow-up

One of the biggest problems we have on the network is that when someone asks a question, many people send out identical answers. When this happens, dozens of identical answers pour through the net. Mail your answer to the person and suggest that they summarize to the network. This way the net will only see a single copy of the answers, no matter how many people answer the question.

If you post a question, please remind people to send you the answers by mail and offer to summarize them to the network.

Read All Follow-ups and Don't Repeat What Has Already Been Said

Before you submit a follow-up to a message, read the rest of the messages in the newsgroup to see whether someone has already said what you want to say. If someone has, don't repeat it.

Be Careful About Copyrights and Licenses

Once something is posted onto the network, it is effectively in the public domain. When posting material to the network, keep in mind that material that is UNIX-related may be restricted by the license you or your company signed with AT&T and be careful not to violate it. You should also be aware that posting movie reviews, song lyrics, or anything else published under a copyright could cause you, your company, or the net itself to be held liable for damages, so we highly recommend caution in using this material.

Cite Appropriate References

If you are using facts to support a cause, state where they came from. Don't take someone else's ideas and use them as your own. You don't want someone pretending that your ideas are theirs; show them the same respect.

Mark or Rotate Answers and Spoilers

When you post something (like a movie review that discusses a detail of the plot) which might spoil a surprise for other people, please mark your message with a warning so that they can skip the message. Another alternative would be to use the "rot13" protocol to encrypt the message so it cannot be read accidentally. When you post a message with a spoiler in it, make sure the word "spoiler" is part of the "Subject:" line.

Spelling Flames Considered Harmful

Every few months a plague descends on USENET called the spelling flame. It starts out when someone posts an article correcting the spelling or grammar in some article. The immediate result seems to be for everyone on the net to turn into a 6th grade English teacher and pick apart each other's postings for a few weeks. This is not productive and tends to cause people who used to be friends to get angry with each other.

It is important to remember that we all make mistakes, and that there are many users on the net who use English as a second language. If you feel that you must make a comment on the quality of a posting, please do so by mail, not on the network.

Don't Overdo Signatures

Signatures are nice, and many people can have a signature added to their postings automatically by placing it in a file called "$HOME/.signature." Don't overdo it. Signatures can tell the world something about you, but keep them short. A signature that is longer than the message itself is considered to be in bad taste. The main purpose of a signature is to help people locate you on the net, not learn your life story. Every signature should include your return address relative to a well-known site on the network. Your system administrator can give this to you.

Summary of Things to Remember

Never forget that the person on the other side is human.
Be brief.

Your postings reflect upon you; be proud of them.
Use descriptive titles.
Think about your audience.
Be careful with humor and sarcasm.
Only post a message once.
Please rotate material with questionable content.
Summarize what you are following up.
Use mail, don't post a follow-up.
Read all follow-ups and don't repeat what has already been said.
Be careful about copyrights and licenses.
Cite appropriate references.
When summarizing, summarize.
Mark or rotate answers or spoilers.
Spelling flames considered harmful.
Don't overdo signatures.

(*)UNIX is a registered trademark of AT&T.

Gene Spafford
Dept. of Computer Sciences, Purdue University, W. Lafayette IN 47907-2004

Internet: spaf@cs.purdue.edu uucp: ...!{decwrl,gatech,ucbvax}!purdue!spaf

7.6 List of USENET Newsletters Received by the Well

atl.general	Items of General interest in Atlanta, GA.
atl.jobs	Jobs in Atlanta, GA.
atl.test	Testing in Atlanta, GA.
aus.acsnet	Discussions of ACSnet (incl bug reports) [Australian]
aus.ai	AI discussions [Australian]
aus.auug	AUUG Inc — Australian Unix User Group [Australian]
aus.aviation	Planes, gliders, flying, etc. [Australian]
	aus.bicycle Push bikes[Australian]
aus.comms	Discussion about Academic Network Proposal [Australian]
aus.computers	Misc. computer types [Australian]
aus.computers.amiga	Discussions about Commodore Amiga computers [Australian]
aus.computers.ibm-pc	Discussions about the IBM pc & clones [Australian]
aus.conserve	Conservation issues. [Australian]

aus.films	Movies, cinema, TV [Australian]
aus.flame	Abusive noise, posted by morons. [Australian]
aus.followup	Followups to aus.general & aus.wanted articles [Austral]
aus.forsale	Announcements of items for sale. [Aus-tralian]
aus.fps	Fast Packet Switching [Australian]
aus.games	Discussions of games. [Australian]
aus.games.roleplay	Discussions of role playing games. [Australian]
aus.general	General information, announcements, etc [Australian]
aus.genstat	Genstat Stats Package [Australian]
aus.hi-fi	Hi-Fi/Stereo stuff [Australian]
aus.jobs	Jobs available & wanted [Australian]
aus.jokes	Jokes, humour, and boring trivia [Aus-tralian]
aus.jokes.d	Discussions of why that joke was no good [Australian]
aus.kermit	The KERMIT file transfer protocol [Australian]
aus.lp	Logic Programming [Australian]
aus.mac	The Apple Macintosh computer [Aus-tralian]
aus.mail	Mail systems, addressinc, &c [Australian]
aus.map	ACSnet maps (Moderated) [Australian]
aus.mbio	Molecular biology [Australian]
aus.music	Music and related issues. [Australian]
aus.netstatus	Status of local & international net links [Australian]
aus.news	The news system [Australian]
aus.parallel	Parallel processing [Australian]
aus.politics	Politics, debates, rational(?) arguments. [Australian]
aus.pyramid	Pyramid computers [Australian]
aus.radio	Amateur Radio [Australian]
aus.religion	Discussions of, or related to, religions [Australian]
aus.scheme	Scheme [Australian]
aus.sf	Discussion of SF&F literture, media, fandom [Australian]
aus.sources	Sources [Australian]
aus.spearnet	South Pacific Educational & Research Net [Australian]
aus.stats.s	The S data analysis and graphics software [Australian]
aus.sun-works	Sun Workstations [Australian]
aus.tex	The TeX typesetting system [Australian]
aus.wanted	Requests for sources, information, ... [Australian]
austin.general	Items of general interest in Austin, TX.
boulder.general	Items of general interest to Boulder, CO.
ca.driving	California freeways and backroads.
ca.earthquakes	What's shakin' in California.
ca.environment	Environmental concerns in California.
ca.general	Of general interest to readers in Calfornia only.
ca.news	USENET status and usage in California.
ca.news.group	Existing or proposed newsgroups for 'ca' distribution.

ca.politics	Political topics of interest to California readers only.
ca.test	Tests of 'ca' distribution articles.
ca.unix	Unix discussion/help.
ca.wanted	For Sale/Wanted postings throughout California.
can.ai	Artificial intelligence in Canada.
can.francais	The French language in Canada.
can.general	Items of general interest to Canadians.
can.jobs	Jobs in Canada.
can.politics	Canadian politics.
can.sun-stroke	Sun Microsystems Users in Canada.
can.usrgroup	/USR/GROUP related information in Canada.
can.uucp	Canadian uucp problems.
chi.ai	AI in Chicago, IL.
chi.eats	Dining in Chicago, IL.
chi.general	Items of general interest in Chicago, IL.
chi.mail	Electronic mail in the Chicago, IL area.
chi.places	Interesting places in the Chicago, IL area..
chi.test	Testing in Chicago, IL.
chi.wanted	Want ads for Chicago, IL.
chi.weather	Weather in Chicago, IL.
clari.biz	ClariNet UPI business news wiregroups
clari.biz.commodity	Commodity news and price reports (Moderated)
clari.biz.courts	Lawsuits and business related legal matters (Moderated)
clari.biz.economy	Economic news and indicators (Moderated)
clari.biz.features	Business feature stories (Moderated)
clari.biz.finance	Finance, currency, Corporate finance (Moderated)
clari.biz.finance.earnings	Earnings & dividend reports (Moderated)
clari.biz.finance.personal	Personal investing & finance (Moderated)
clari.biz.finance.services	Banks and financial industries (Moderated)
clari.biz.invest	News for investors (Moderated)
clari.biz.labor	Strikes, unions and labor relations (Moderated)
clari.biz.market	General stock market news (Moderated)
clari.biz.market.amex	American Stock Exchange reports and news (Moderated)
clari.biz.market.dow	Dow Jones NYSE reports (Moderated)
clari.biz.market.ny	NYSE reports (Moderated)
clari.biz.market.otc	NASDAQ reports (Moderated)
clari.biz.market.report	General market reports, S&P, etc. (Moderated)
clari.biz.mergers	Mergers and acquisitions (Moderated)
clari.biz.misc	Other business news (Moderated)
clari.biz.top	Top business news (Moderated)
clari.nb	ClariNet Newsbytes Information service Newsgroups
clari.nb.apple	Newsbytes Apple/Macintosh news (Moderated)
clari.nb.business	Newsbytes business & industry news (Moderated)
clari.nb.general	Newsbytes general computer news (Moderated)
clari.nb.govt	Newsbytes legal and government computer news (Moderated)
clari.nb.ibm	Newsbytes IBM PC World coverage (Moderated)

clari.nb.review	Newsbytes new product reviews (Moderated)
clari.nb.telecom	Newsbytes telecom & online industry news (Moderated)
clari.nb.trends	Newsbytes new developments & trends (Moderated)
clari.nb.unix	Newsbytes Unix news (Moderated)
clari.net	ClariNet non-news newsgroups
clari.net.admin	Announcements for news admins at ClariNet sites (Modera)
clari.net.announce	Announcements for all ClariNet readers (Moderated)
clari.net.products	New ClariNet products (Moderated)
clari.net.talk	Discussion of ClariNet
clari.news	ClariNet UPI general news wiregroups
clari.news.almanac	Daily almanac —quotes, "this date in history" etc. (Moderated)
clari.news.arts	Stage, drama and other fine arts (Moderated)
clari.news.aviation	Aviation industry and mishaps (Moderated)
clari.news.books	Books & publishing (Moderated)
clari.news.briefs	Regular news summaries (Moderated)
clari.news.bulletin	Major breaking stories of the week (Moderated)
clari.news.canada	News related to Canada (Moderated)
clari.news.children	Stories related to children and parenting (Moderated)
clari.news.consumer	Consumer news, car reviews etc. (Moderated)
clari.news.demonstration	Demonstrations around the world (Moderated)
clari.news.disaster	Major problems, accidents & natural disasters (Moderated)
clari.news.economy	General economic news (Moderated)
clari.news.election	News regarding both US and international elections (Moderated)
clari.news.entertain	Entertainment industry news & features (Moderated)
clari.news.environment	Environmental news, hazardous waste, forests (Moderated)
clari.news.europe	News related to Europe (Moderated)
clari.news.features	Unclassified feature stories (Moderated)
clari.news.fighting	Clashes around the world (Moderated)
clari.news.flash	Ultra-important once-a-year news flashes (Moderated)
clari.news.goodnews	Stories of success and survival (Moderated)
clari.news.gov	General Government related stories (Moderated)
clari.news.gov.agency	Government agencies, FBI etc. (Moderated)
clari.news.gov.budget	Budgets at all levels (Moderated)
clari.news.gov.corrupt	Government corruption, kickbacks etc. (Moderated)
clari.news.gov.international	International government-related stories (Moderated)
clari.news.gov.officials	Government officials and their problems (Moderated)

clari.news.gov.state	State government stories of national importance. (Moderated)
clari.news.gov.taxes	Tax laws, trials etc. (Moderated)
clari.news.gov.usa	U.S. Federal government news. (High volume) (Moderated)
clari.news.group	Special interest groups not covered in their own group)
clari.news.group.blacks	News of interest to black people (Moderated)
clari.news.group.women	Women's issues and abortion (Moderated)
clari.news.health	Disease, medicine, health care, sick celebs (Moderated)
clari.news.health.aids	AIDS stories, research, political issues (Moderated)
clari.news.interest	Human interest stories (Moderated)
clari.news.interest.animals	Animals in the news (Moderated)
clari.news.interest.history	Human interest stories and history in the making)
clari.news.interest.people	Famous people in the news (Moderated)
clari.news.interest.quirks	Unusual or funny news stories (Moderated)
clari.news.issues	Stories on major issues not covered in their own group.)
clari.news.issues.conflict	Conflict between groups around the world (Moderated)
clari.news.labor	Unions, strikes (Moderated)
clari.news.labor.strike	Strikes (Moderated)
clari.news.law	General group for law related issues (Moderated)
clari.news.law.civil	Civil trials and litigation (Moderated)
clari.news.law.crime	Major crimes (Moderated)
clari.news.law.crime.sex	Sex crimes and trials (Moderated)
clari.news.law.crime.trial	Trials for criminal actions (Moderated)
clari.news.law.crime.violent	Violent crime & criminals (Moderated)
clari.news.law.drugs	Drug related crimes and drug stories (Moderated)
clari.news.law.investigation	Investigation of crimes (Moderated)
clari.news.law.police	Police & law enforcement (Moderated)
clari.news.law.prison	Prisons, prisoners & escapes (Moderated)
clari.news.law.profession	Lawyers, Judges etc. (Moderated)
clari.news.law.supreme	U.S. Supreme court rulings & news (Moderated)
clari.news.lifestyle	Fashion, leisure etc. (Moderated)
clari.news.military	Military equipment, people & issues (Moderated)
clari.news.movies	Reviews, news and stories on movie stars. (Moderated)
clari.news.music	Reviews and issues concerning music and musicians. (Moderated)
clari.news.politics	Politicians and politics. (Moderated)
clari.news.religion	Religion, religious leaders, televangelists (Moderated)
clari.news.sex	Sexual issues, sex-related political stories (Moderated)
clari.news.terrorism	Terrorist actions and related news around the world (Moderated)
clari.news.top	Top U.S. news stories (Moderated)
clari.news.top.world	Top international news stories (Moderated)

clari.news.trends	Surveys and trends. (Moderated)
clari.news.trouble	Less major accidents, problems and mishaps (Moderated)
clari.news.tv	TV schedules, news, reviews and stars. (Moderated)
clari.news.urgent	Major breaking stories of the day (Moderated)
clari.news.weather	Weather and temperature reports (Moderated)
clari.sports	ClariNet UPI sports wiregroups
clari.sports.baseball	Baseball scores, stories, games, stats (Moderated)
clari.sports.basketball	Basketball coverage (Moderated)
clari.sports.features	Sports feature stories (Moderated)
clari.sports.football	Pro football coverage (Moderated)
clari.sports.hockey	NHL coverage (Moderated)
clari.sports.misc	Racing, Tennis and other sports, plus general sports news)
clari.sports.top	Top sports news (Moderated)
clari.tw	ClariNet UPI technology related news wiregroups
clari.tw.aerospace	Aerospace industry and companies (Moderated)
clari.tw.computers	Computer industry, applications and developments (Moderated)
clari.tw.defense	Defense industry issues (Moderated)
clari.tw.education	Stories involving Universities and colleges (Moderated)
clari.tw.electronics	Electronics makers and sellers (Moderated)
clari.tw.misc	General technical industry stories (Moderated)
clari.tw.nuclear	Nuclear power & waste (Moderated)
clari.tw.science	General science stories (Moderated)
clari.tw.space	NASA, Astronomy and spaceflight (Moderated)
clari.tw.telecom	Phones, satellites, media and general Telecom (Moderated)
co.general	Items of general interest to Colorado.
co.test	Testing in Colorado.
dc.dining	Dining in the Washington, DC area.
dc.forsale	Items for sale in the Washington, DC area.
dc.general	Items of general interest to the Washington, DC area.
dc.smithsonian	Smithsonian related events in the Washington, DC area.
dc.test	Testing in the Washington, DC area.
dfw.flame	Dallas, Fort Worth
dfw.forsale	Dallas, Fort Worth
dfw.general	Dallas, Fort Worth
dfw.news	Dallas, Fort Worth
dfw.test	Testing in Dallas, Fort Worth
essug.misc	ESS User Group
essug.telco	ESS User Group
fl.announce	Important announcements for everyone in Florida.
fl.attractions	Florida attractions and entertainment.
fl.comp	General computers in Florida.
fl.comp.rep	Technical computer repair or modifications in

	Florida.
fl.general	General topics in Florida.
fl.jobs	The Florida job market.
fl.mail	Mail systems, routers, paths in Florida.
fl.map	Map entries for Florida sites. (Moderated)
fl.news	News problems and features in Florida.
fl.sources	Distribution of source code or documentation in Florida.
fl.test	Testing workspace in Florida.
fl.travel	Travel within Florida.
fl.uug	UNIX user groups within Florida.
fl.yumyum	Reviews and advice on restaurants in Florida.
ga.forsale	Items for sale in Georgia.
ga.general	Items of general interest in Georgia.
ga.test	Testing in Georgia.
houston.eats	Dining in Houston, TX.
houston.general	Items of general interest in Houston, TX.
houston.news	USENET in Houston, TX.
la.eats	Dining in Los Angeles, CA.
la.general	Items of general interest in Los Angeles, CA.
la.news	USENET in Los Angeles, CA.
la.seminars	Seminars in Los Angeles, CA.
la.test	Testing in Los Angeles, CA.
mi.map	Michigan uucp map postings.
mi.misc	Miscelaneous postings of interest to Michigan.
mi.usrgroup	Minnesota /usr/group related postings.
milw.general	Milwaukee.
mn.archive	Archive sites in Minnesota.
mn.general	Items of general interest to Minnesota.
mn.map	Minnesota uucp map postings. (Moderated)
mn.sources	Minnesota program sources.
mn.test	Testing in Minnesota.
mn.traffic	Minnesota USENET traffic statistics.
ne.food	Dining in New England.
ne.forsale	New England Items for sale.
ne.general	Items of general interest in New England.
ne.housing	Housing in New England.
ne.jobs	Jobs in New England.
ne.news	USENET in New England.
ne.org.decus	DECUS related postings in the New England Area.
ne.seminars	Seminars in New England.
ne.wanted	New England want ads.
nj.events	Events in New Jersey.
nj.general	Items of general interest in N.J.
nj.test	Testing in New Jersey.
nj.wanted	New Jersey want ads.
nj.weather	Weather in New Jersey.
nwu.general	
ny.config	USENET Configuration in New York.
ny.general	Items of general interest in New York.

ny.nysernet.maps	NYSERNet maps.
ny.nysernet.nysertech	NYSERNet related information.
ny.test	Testing in New York.
ny.wanted	New York want ads.
oc.acm	Orange County, CA ACM related information.
oc.general	Items of general interest in Orange County, CA.
ont.archives	Archives in Ontario, Canada.
ont.events	Ontario, Canada happenings.
ont.general	Items of general interest in Ontario, Canada.
ont.jobs	Jobs in Ontario, Canada.
ont.micro	Microcomputer related postings in Ontario, Canada.
ont.sf-lovers	Science fiction lovers in Ontario, Canada.
ont.singles	Singles in Ontario, Canada.
ont.test	Testing in Ontario, Canada.
ont.uucp	UUCP related postings in Ontario, Canada.
or.forsale	Oregon want ads.
or.general	Items of general interest in Oregon.
pa.test	Pennsylvannia testing.
pnw.general	Items of general interest to the Pacific Northwest
seattle.general	General stuff in Seattle, Washington
stl.general	General interest items for St. Louis sites.
stl.jobs	St. Louis job information.
stl.news	St. Louis net information.
stl.rec	St. Louis recreational information.
su.admin	Stanford University
su.admin.tips	Stanford University
su.class.cs040	Stanford University
su.class.cs140	Concurrent programming (Stanford University)
su.class.cs143a	Stanford University
su.class.cs145	Stanford University
su.class.cs193c	Stanford University
su.class.cs221	Stanford University
su.class.cs227	AI programming in Prolog (Stanford University)
su.class.cs229	C.S. 229 bulletin board (Stanford University)
su.class.cs242	Stanford University
su.class.cs244	Computer Networks: Architecture and Implementation (Stanford University)
su.class.cs258	Introduction to Programming Language Theory (Stanford University)
su.class.cs306	Stanford University
su.class.cs309a	Federated Databases (Stanford University)
su.class.cs347	Stanford University
su.class.cs367a	Stanford University
su.class.cs374	Stanford University
su.class.cs378	Phenomenological Foundations of Cognition, Language and)
su.class.cscamp	Stanford University
su.computers	Stanford University
su.computers.rcc	Resident Computer Coordinators bulletin board (Stanford)

su.etc	Stanford University
su.events	Stanford University
su.gay	Stanford University
su.issues.china	Stanford University
su.jobs	Stanford University
su.macintosh	Stanford University
su.market	Stanford University
su.nethax	Stanford University
su.news	Stanford University
su.test	Stanford University Testing
su.vaxhax	Stanford University
su.vnews	Stanford University
tn.flame	Tennessee.
tn.talk	Tennessee.
tn.test	Testing in Tennessee.
tor.general	Items of general interest in Toronto, Canada.
tor.news	USENET in Toronto, Canada.
tor.news.stats	USENET Statistics in Toronto, Canada.
tor.test	Testing in Toronto, Canada.
tx.flame	Texas flames.
tx.general	Items of general interest in Texas.
tx.jobs	Jobs in Texas.
tx.news	USENET in Texas.
tx.politics	Politics in Texas.
tx.wanted	Texas want ads.
u3b.config	3B distribution configuration.
u3b.misc	3B miscellaneous discussions.
u3b.sources	Sources for AT&T 3B systems.
u3b.tech	3B technical discussions.
u3b.test	3B distribution testing.
uc.general	University of California general stuff.
uc.motss	Issues pertaining to homosexuality at University of California.
uc.news	University of California news.
uc.test	Testing for University of California.
uw.gnu	For GNU at WATERLU
uw.jsaw	For Japanese Student Association of Waterloo
clari.nb.index	For the weekly "Newsbytes Index" article.
bit.comserve	General information about COMSERVE.
bit.general	General BITNET info.NETMONTH, SERVERS.
bit.listserv.aaua-l	(Moderated)
bit.listserv.advise-l	For user services people, consultants, etc.
bit.listserv.aidsnews	Discussions about AIDS.
bit.listserv.aix-l	IBM AIX discussion list.
bit.listserv.allmusic	Discussion of all forms of music.
bit.listserv.anthro-l	
bit.listserv.apple2-l	Apple II discussions.
bit.listserv.applicat	Identify and document Bitnet applications.
bit.listserv.asm370	IBM System/370 Assemble Language.
bit.listserv.big-lan	Discussion of campus sized LANs.
bit.listserv.billing	Chargeback of computer resources.

bit.listserv.biosph-l	
bit.listserv.bitnews	News from BITNIC.
bit.listserv.brfc-l	Bitnet RFCs (Requests for Comment) discussed.
bit.listserv.c18-l	Eighteenth century discussion.
bit.listserv.c370-l	C Programming language on 370 machines.
bit.listserv.candle-l	Candle products discussion list.
bit.listserv.christia	Practical Christian life.
bit.listserv.cics-l	Discussion of CICS.
bit.listserv.cinema-l	Discussion of movies.
bit.listserv.cmspip-l	VM/SP CMS pipelines discussion list.
bit.listserv.commed	Computer mediated education.
bit.listserv.commodor	
bit.listserv.confer-l	An academic conferencing system.
bit.listserv.confocal	
bit.listserv.cumrec-l	Administrative computer users/programmers.
bit.listserv.cyber-l	CDC Cyber support, announcements, reviews.
bit.listserv.dbase-l	dBase programming language and dialects.
bit.listserv.db2-l	Discussion of IBM's Data Base.
bit.listserv.disarm-l	Discussion of disarmament.
bit.listserv.domain-l	Bitnet support of domain names.
bit.listserv.drp-l	Disaster recovery plan for comp services.
bit.listserv.earntech	Earn technical list.
bit.listserv.economy	
bit.listserv.edi-l	Electronic data interchange issues.
bit.listserv.edpolyan	Educational policy analysis.
bit.listserv.edtech	Educational technology.
bit.listserv.edusig-l	
bit.listserv.emflds-l	
bit.listserv.emusic-l	Technical discussion of electronic music.
bit.listserv.envbeh-l	Environment, design, and human behavior.
bit.listserv.erl-l	Educational Research List.
bit.listserv.esl-l	DECUS Education Software Library discussion.
bit.listserv.ethics-l	Ethical discussions.
bit.listserv.film-l	Film making and reviews.
bit.listserv.frac-l	Fractals.
bit.listserv.future-l	Future developments in Bitnet.
bit.listserv.games-l	Computer games list.
bit.listserv.gaynet	Discussion of gay and lesbian concerns.
bit.listserv.gddm-l	About IBM's GDDM graphics product.
bit.listserv.geodesic	
bit.listserv.gerinet	
bit.listserv.gguide	Guide to creating a Bitnet guide.
bit.listserv.gis-l	Discussion of graphics.
bit.listserv.govdoc-l	Government document issues.
bit.listserv.gutnberg	Machine readable texts.
bit.listserv.hellas	Hellenic discussion list.
bit.listserv.helpnet	Network emergency response planning.
bit.listserv.history	General history discussions.
bit.listserv.i-amiga	Info-Amiga list.
bit.listserv.ibm-hesc	Discussion of IBM's HESC program.
bit.listserv.ibm-main	IBM mainframe topics.

bit.listserv.ibm-nets	IBM networking.
bit.listserv.ibmtcp-l	TCP/IP on IBM equipment.
bit.listserv.ibm7171	The 7171 protocol converter.
bit.listserv.info-gcg	Computer aided molecular biology.
bit.listserv.infonets	
bit.listserv.ioob-l	Industrial Psychology.
bit.listserv.isn	The AT&T ISN system.
bit.listserv.jes2-l	JES2 discussion list.
bit.listserv.jnet-l	For discussion about JNET.
bit.listserv.l-hcap	Issues related to handicapped people.
bit.listserv.l-vmctr	VMCENTER software discussions.
bit.listserv.lawsch-l	Discussion of law schools.
bit.listserv.liaison	For user services people at Bitnet sites.
bit.listserv.license	Software licensing issues.
bit.listserv.linkfail	Bitnet link failure topics and announcements.
bit.listserv.literary	Discussions about literature.
bit.listserv.lstsrv-l	About Listserve machines.
bit.listserv.mail-l	Mail systems, user agents, etc.
bit.listserv.mailbook	Rice's MAILBOOK system.
bit.listserv.mba-l	Discussion of MBAs.
bit.listserv.mbu-l	
bit.listserv.mednews	Medical News.
bit.listserv.mexico-l	
bit.listserv.ministry-l	Careers in religious ministry.
bit.listserv.mon-l	Network monitoring.
bit.listserv.netmon-l	The NETMON program for monitoring the network.
bit.listserv.netnws-l	NETNEWS topics.
bit.listserv.new-list	Announcements of new discussion lists.
bit.listserv.newsb-l	College news bureau issues.
bit.listserv.netscout	
bit.listserv.next-l	NeXT computer list.
bit.listserv.nodmgt-l	Node management.
bit.listserv.notis-l	NOTIS/DOBIS discussions.
bit.listserv.novell	NOVELL Lan Interest Group.
bit.listserv.omrscan	Optical scanners.
bit.listserv.online-l	JBH Online.
bit.listserv.ozone	Save nature list.
bit.listserv.pacs-l	Library systems - CDROM, CAI, AI etc.
bit.listserv.page-l	IBM 3812/3820 tips and problems discussion.
bit.listserv.pagemakr	discussions about PageMaker.
bit.listserv.pmdf-l	Pascal Memo Distribution Facility for VAX/VMS.
bit.listserv.policy-l	BITNET policy issues.
bit.listserv.politics	Political discussions.
bit.listserv.power-l	
bit.listserv.procom-l	
bit.listserv.redist-l	Redistribution of ARPA lists and digests.
bit.listserv.relusr-l	Relay users forum.
bit.listserv.rexxlist	The REXX interpreter.
bit.listserv.rhetoric	Rhetoric, social movements, persuasion.
bit.listserv.rscsmods	Mods to RSCS.

bit.listserv.rscsv2-l	RSCS version 2.
bit.listserv.rustex-l	
bit.listserv.s-comput	Supercomputing topics.
bit.listserv.sas-l	SAS (Statistical Analysis System) discussions.
bit.listserv.saw-l	
bit.listserv.script-l	IBM and Waterloo Script.
bit.listserv.scuba-l	SCUBA Diving list.
bit.listserv.servers	Network file servers.
bit.listserv.simula	The simula language.
bit.listserv.snamgt-l	SNA networks.
bit.listserv.sos-data	Social science data discussions.
bit.listserv.spires-l	SPIRES information retrieval system.
bit.listserv.sportpsy	Exercise and sport psychology.
bit.listserv.spssx-l	The SPSSX Statistical package.
bit.listserv.sqlinfo	SQL system and language.
bit.listserv.stat-l	Statistical consulting.
bit.listserv.std-l	BITNET "standard" environments.
bit.listserv.tech-l	Technical working groups Preshare info.
bit.listserv.test	
bit.listserv.tex-l	The TEX typesetting language.
bit.listserv.tn3270-l	TN3270 protocol discussion list.
bit.listserv.trafic-l	Network traffic.
bit.listserv.trans-l	File tranfer topics for Bitnet sites.
bit.listserv.travel-l	About travel and tourism.
bit.listserv.ucp-l	The University Computer Project in SHARE.
bit.listserv.ug-l	Usage Guidelines - network abuse and etiquette.
bit.listserv.urep-l	UREP - the UNIX/RSCS emulator.
bit.listserv.usrdir-l	User directory services/servers.
bit.listserv.valert-l	Virus Alert - Urgent Virus Warnings.
bit.listserv.vector-l	IBM 3090-VF vector facility topics.
bit.listserv.vfort-l	VS FORTRAN discussion group.
bit.listserv.virus-l	Computer viruses.
bit.listserv.vm-util	
bit.listserv.vmslsv-l	
bit.listserv.vmxa-l	Installation, operation, maintenance of VM/XA.
bit.listserv.word-pc	Microsoft Word under DOS and Windows.
bit.listserv.wp50-l	Word Perfect 5.0.
bit.listserv.xcult-l	International intercultural newsletter.
bit.listserv.xedit-l	
bit.listserv.xerox-l	The Xerox Discussion List.
bit.listserv.xmailer	Crosswell Mailer issues.
bit.listserv.x400-l	X-400 mail topics.
bit.listserv.9370-l	IBM 9370 family and VM/IS packaging system.
bit.mailserv.word-mac	
bit.mailserv.word-pc	
bit.netmonth	Monthly newsletter.
bit.servers	Lists of servers accessible via BITNET.
bit.test	Simply for testing.
eunet.bugs.4bsd	Bug reports on 4.*bsd, limited (EUnet) "audience".

eunet.bugs.uucp	Bug reports on uucp, specifically EUUG uucp.
eunet.esprit	Discussion/info about Esprit projects.
eunet.euug	EUUG-related topics, announcements, etc.
eunet.general	General discussions.
eunet.followup	Followup group for eunet.general.
eunet.jokes	Jokes only Europeans can (do?) understand... :-)
eunet.micro.acorn	Discussion about Acorn micros.
eunet.newprod	Announcements of new products of European interest.
eunet.news	Group for news topics, limited to EUnet.
eunet.news.group	Discussion on and proposals for new eunet newsgroups.
eunet.politics	(European) political discussions (and flames!).
eunet.sources	EUnet-wide (only!) group for posting sources.
eunet.test	EUnet-wide test group.
eunet.works	Workstations (specifically European) topics.
alt.activism	Activities for activists.
alt.aquaria	The aquarium & related as a hobby.
alt.atheism	
alt.bbs	Computer BBS systems & software.
alt.callahans	Callahan's bar for puns and fellowship.
alt.co-ops	Discussion about co-operatives.
alt.cobol	
alt.config	Alternative subnet discussions and connectivity.
alt.conspiracy	
alt.cosuard	Council of Sysops & Users Against Rate Discrimination.
alt.cult-movies	Movies with a cult following (e.g., Rocky Horror PS)
alt.cyb-sys	Cybernetic systems.
alt.cyberpunk	High-tech low-life.
alt.cyberpunk.tech	Cyberspace and Cyberpunk technology.
alt.drugs	Recreational pharmaceuticals and related flames.
alt.exotic-music	Exotic music discussions.
alt.fan.dave_barry	
alt.fan.mike-jittlov	
alt.fandom.cons	
alt.fandom.misc	
alt.fax	Faxing documents — protocols, equipment, etc.
alt.fishing	Fishing as a hobby and sport.
alt.flame	Alternative, literate, pithy, succinct screaming.
alt.folklore.computers	
alt.fractals	
alt.gourmand	Recipes and cooking info. (Moderated)
alt.great-lakes	Discussions of the Great Lakes and adjacent places.
alt.hypertext	Discussion of hypertext — uses, transport, etc.
alt.individualism	Philosophies where individual rights are paramount.
alt.kids-talk	
alt.msdos.programmer	For the serious MS/DOS programmer (no for

	sale ads).
alt.mud	
alt.pagan	
alt.peeves	Discussion of peeves and related.
alt.postmodern	Postmodernism, semiotics, deconstruction, and the like.
alt.prose	Postings of original writings, fictional & otherwise.
alt.prose.d	Discussions about postings in alt.prose.
alt.recovery	12-step groups (such as AA, ACA, GA, etc)
alt.religion.computers	People who believe computing is "real life."
alt.restaurants	Serious consideration of the art of restauranting.
alt.rhode_island	Discussion of the great little state.
alt.rock-n-roll	Counterpart to alt.sex and alt.drugs....
alt.rock-n-roll.metal	
alt.romance	
alt.sewing	
alt.sex	Postings of a prurient nature.
alt.sex.bestiality	
alt.sex.bondage	Postings about dominance/submission.
alt.skate	
alt.skinheads	
alt.slack	Posting relating to the Church of the Subgenius.
alt.source-code	Source code ONLY!
alt.sources	Alternative source code, unmoderated. Caveat Emptor.
alt.sources.amiga	Technically-oriented Amiga PC sources.
alt.sources.d	Discussion of posted sources.
alt.sources.index	(Moderated)
alt.sources.patches	
alt.sys.sun	Unmoderated Sun "workstation" computers.
alt.test	Alternative subnetwork testing.
alt.tv.prisoner	
biz.clarinet	Announcements about ClariNet
biz.clarinet.sample	Samples of ClariNet newsgroups for the outside world
biz.comp.hardware	Generic commercial hardware postings.
biz.comp.services	Generic commercial service postings.
biz.comp.software	Generic commercial software postings.
biz.comp.telebit	Support of the Telebit modem.
biz.config	Biz Usenet configuration and administration.
biz.control	Control information and messages.
biz.dec	
biz.dec.ip	
biz.dec.workstations	
biz.misc	Miscellaneous postings of a commercial nature.
biz.stolen	Postings about stolen merchandise.
biz.test	Biz newsgroup test messages.
comp.ai	Artificial intelligence discussions.
comp.ai.digest	Artificial Intelligence discussions. (Moderated)
comp.ai.edu	Applications of Artificial Intelligence to Education.
comp.ai.neural-nets	All aspects of neural networks.

comp.ai.nlang-know-rep	Natural Language and Knowledge Representation. (Moderated)
comp.ai.shells	Artificial intelligence applied to shells. (Moderated)
comp.ai.vision	Artificial Intelligence Vision Research. (Moderated)
comp.arch	Computer architecture.
comp.archives	Descriptions of public access archives. (Moderated)
comp.binaries.amiga	Encoded public domain programs in binary. (Moderated)
comp.binaries.apple2	Binary-only postings for the Apple II computer.
comp.binaries.atari.st	Binary-only postings for the Atari ST. (Moderated)
comp.binaries.ibm.pc	Binary-only postings for IBM PC/MS-DOS. (Moderated)
comp.binaries.ibm.pc.d	Discussions about IBM/PC binary postings.
comp.binaries.mac	Encoded Macintosh programs in binary. (Moderated)
comp.binaries.os2	(Moderated)
comp.bugs.2bsd	Reports of UNIX* version 2BSD related bugs.
comp.bugs.4bsd	Reports of UNIX version 4BSD related bugs.
comp.bugs.4bsd.ucb-fixes	Bug reports/fixes for BSD Unix. (Moderated)
comp.bugs.misc	General UNIX bug reports and fixes (incl V7, uucp)
comp.bugs.sys5	Reports of USG (System III, V, etc.) bugs.
comp.cog-eng	Cognitive engineering.
comp.compilers	Compiler construction, theory, etc. (Moderated)
comp.databases	Database and data management issues and theory.
comp.dcom.lans	Local area network hardware and software.
comp.dcom.lans.hyperchannel	Hyperchannel networks within an IP network.
comp.dcom.lans.v2lni	Proteon Pronet/V2LNI Ring networks.
comp.dcom.modems	Data communications hardware and software.
comp.dcom.sys.cisco	
comp.dcom.telecom	Telecommunications digest. (Moderated)
comp.doc	Archived public-domain documentation. (Moderated)
comp.doc.techreports	Lists of technical reports. (Moderated)
comp.dsp	
comp.editors	Topics related to computerized text editing.
comp.edu	Computer science education.
comp.edu.composition	Writing instruction in computer-based classrooms.
comp.emacs	EMACS editors of different flavors.
comp.fonts	Typefonts — design, conversion, use, etc.
comp.graphics	Computer graphics, art, animation, image processing.
comp.graphics.digest	Graphics software, hardware, theory, etc. (Moderated)
comp.groupware	
comp.infosystems	Any discussion about information systems.
comp.ivideodisc	Interactive videodiscs — uses, potential, etc.
comp.lang.ada	Discussion about Ada*.
comp.lang.apl	Discussion about APL.

comp.lang.asm370	Programming in IBM System/370 Assembly Language.
comp.lang.c	Discussion about C.
comp.lang.c++	The object-oriented C++ language.
comp.lang.clu	The CLU language & related topics. (Moderated)
comp.lang.eiffel	The object-oriented Eiffel language.
comp.lang.forth	Discussion about Forth.
comp.lang.forth.mac	The CSI MacForth programming environment.
comp.lang.fortran	Discussion about FORTRAN.
comp.lang.icon	Topics related to the ICON programming language.
comp.lang.idl	IDL (Interface Description Language) related topics.
comp.lang.lisp	Discussion about LISP.
comp.lang.lisp.franz	The Franz Lisp programming language.
comp.lang.lisp.x	The XLISP language system.
comp.lang.misc	Different computer languages not specifically listed.
comp.lang.modula2	Discussion about Modula-2.
comp.lang.pascal	Discussion about Pascal.
comp.lang.perl	
comp.lang.postscript	The PostScript Page Description Language.
comp.lang.prolog	Discussion about PROLOG.
comp.lang.rexx	The REXX command language.
comp.lang.scheme	The Scheme Programming language.
comp.lang.scheme.c	The Scheme language environment.
comp.lang.sigplan	Info & announcements from ACM SIGPLAN. (Moderated)
comp.lang.smalltalk	Discussion about Smalltalk 80.
comp.lang.visual	Visual programming languages.
comp.laser-printers	Laser printers, hardware and software. (Moderated)
comp.lsi	Large scale integrated circuits.
comp.lsi.cad	Electrical Computer Aided Design.
comp.mail.elm	Discussion and fixes for ELM mail system.
comp.mail.headers	Gatewayed from the ARPA header-people list.
comp.mail.mh	The UCI version of the Rand Message Handling system.
comp.mail.misc	General discussions about computer mail.
comp.mail.multi-media	Multimedia Mail.
comp.mail.mush	The Mail User's Shell (MUSH).
comp.mail.sendmail	Configuring and using the BSD sendmail agent.
comp.mail.uucp	Mail in the uucp network environment.
comp.misc	General topics about computers not covered elsewhere.
comp.music	Applications of computers in music research.
comp.newprod	Announcements of new products of interest. (Moderated)
comp.object	
comp.org.decus	DEC* Users' Society newsgroup.
comp.org.fidonet	FidoNews digest, official news of FidoNet As-

	soc. (Moderated)
comp.org.ieee	Issues and announcements about the IEEE & its members.
comp.org.usenix	USENIX Association events and announcements.
comp.org.usenix.roomshare	
comp.org.usrgroup	News/discussion about/from the /usr/group organization.
comp.os.aos	Topics related to Data General's AOS/VS.
comp.os.cpm	Discussion about the CP/M operating system.
comp.os.cpm.amethyst	Discussion of Amethyst, CP/M-80 software package.
comp.os.eunice	The SRI Eunice system.
comp.os.mach	The MACH OS from CMU & other places.
comp.os.minix	Discussion of Tanenbaum's MINIX system.
comp.os.misc	General OS-oriented discussion not carried elsewhere.
comp.os.os2	Discussions about the os2 operating system.
comp.os.os9	Discussions about the os9 operating system.
comp.os.research	Operating systems and related areas. (Moderated)
comp.os.rsts	Topics related to the PDP-11 RSTS/E operating system.
comp.os.v	The V distributed operating system from Stanford.
comp.os.vms	DEC's VAX* line of computers & VMS.
comp.os.xinu	The XINU operating system from Purdue (D. Comer).
comp.parallel	Massively parallel hardware/software. (Moderated)
comp.periphs	Peripheral devices.
comp.periphs.printers	Information on printers.
comp.periphs.scsi	
comp.protocols.appletalk	Applebus hardware & software.
comp.protocols.ibm	Networking with IBM mainframes.
comp.protocols.iso	The ISO protocol stack.
comp.protocols.iso.dev-environ	The ISO Development Environment.
comp.protocols.iso.x400	X400 mail protocol discussions. (Moderated)
comp.protocols.iso.x400.gateway	X400 mail gateway discussions. (Moderated)
comp.protocols.kerberos	The Kerberos authentification server.
comp.protocols.kermit	Info about the Kermit package. (Moderated)
comp.protocols.misc	Various forms and types of FTP protocol.
comp.protocols.nfs	Discussion about the Network File System protocol.
comp.protocols.pcnet	Topics related to PCNET (a personal computer network).
comp.protocols.pup	The Xerox PUP network protocols.
comp.protocols.tcp-ip	TCP and IP network protocols.
comp.protocols.tcp-ip.domains	Topics related to domain style names.
comp.protocols.tcp-ip.ibmpc	TCP/IP for IBM(-like) personal computers.
comp.realtime	Issues related to real-time computing.

comp.risks	Risks to the public from computers and users. (Moderated)
comp.security.announce	Announcements from CERT. (Moderated)
comp.simulation	Simulation methods, problems, uses. (Moderated)
comp.society	The impact of technology on society. (Moderated)
comp.society.futures	Events in technology affecting future computing.
comp.society.women	Women's roles and problems in computing (Moderated)
comp.soft-sys.andrew	The Andrew system from CMU.
comp.software-eng	Software Engineering and related topics.
comp.sources.amiga	Source code-only postings for the Amiga. (Moderated)
comp.sources.atari.st	Source code-only postings for the Atari ST. (Moderated)
comp.sources.bugs	Bug reports, fixes, discussion for posted sources
comp.sources.d	For any discussion of source postings.
comp.sources.games	Postings of recreational software. (Moderated)
comp.sources.games.bugs	Bug reports and fixes for posted game software.
comp.sources.mac	Software for the Apple Macintosh. (Moderated)
comp.sources.misc	Posting of software. (Moderated)
comp.sources.sun	Software for Sun workstations. (Moderated)
comp.sources.unix	Postings of complete, UNIX-oriented sources. (Moderated)
comp.sources.wanted	Requests for software and fixes.
comp.sources.x	Software for the X windows system. (Moderated)
comp.specification	
comp.std.c	Discussion about C language standards.
comp.std.internat	Discussion about international standards.
comp.std.misc	Discussion about various standards.
comp.std.mumps	Discussion for the X11.1 committee on Mumps. (Moderated)
comp.std.unix	Discussion for the P1003 committee on UNIX. (Moderated)
comp.sw.components	Software components and related technology.
comp.sys.alliant	
comp.sys.amiga	Commodore Amiga: info and uses, but no programs.
comp.sys.amiga.hardware	
comp.sys.amiga.tech	Technical discussion about the Amiga.
comp.sys.apollo	Apollo computer systems.
comp.sys.apple2	
comp.sys.atari.8bit	Discussion about 8 bit Atari micros.
comp.sys.atari.st	Discussion about 16 bit Atari micros.
comp.sys.att	Discussions about AT&T microcomputers.
comp.sys.cbm	Discussion about Commodore micros.
comp.sys.cdc	Control Data Corporation Computers (e.g., Cybers).
comp.sys.celerity	Celerity Computers
comp.sys.concurrent	(Moderated)
comp.sys.dec	Discussions about DEC computer systems.
comp.sys.dec.micro	DEC Micros (Rainbow, Professional 350/380)

comp.sys.encore	Encore's MultiMax computers.
comp.sys.handhelds	Handheld computers and programmable calculators.
comp.sys.hp	Discussion about Hewlett-Packard equipment.
comp.sys.ibm.pc	Discussion about IBM personal computers.
comp.sys.ibm.pc.digest	The IBM PC, PC-XT, and PC-AT. (Moderated)
comp.sys.ibm.pc.programmer	
comp.sys.ibm.pc.rt	Topics related to IBM's RT computer.
comp.sys.intel	Discussions about Intel systems and parts.
comp.sys.intel.ipsc310	Anything related to Xenix on an Intel 310.
comp.sys.isis	The ISIS distributed system from Cornell.
comp.sys.laptops	
comp.sys.m6809	Discussion about 6809's.
comp.sys.m68k	Discussion about 68k's.
comp.sys.m68k.pc	Discussion about 68k-based PCs. (Moderated)
comp.sys.m88k	Discussion about 68k-based computers.
comp.sys.mac	Discussions about the Apple Macintosh and Lisa.
comp.sys.mac.digest	Apple Macintosh: info&uses, but no programs. (Moderated)
comp.sys.mac.hardware	Hardware related discussions about the macintosh.
comp.sys.mac.hypercard	The Macintosh Hypercard: info & uses.
comp.sys.mac.programmer	Discussion by people programming the Apple Macintosh.
comp.sys.mips	Systems based on MIPS chips.
comp.sys.misc	Discussion about computers of all kinds.
comp.sys.ncr	
comp.sys.next	Discussion about the new NeXT computer.
comp.sys.northstar	Northstar microcomputer users.
comp.sys.nsc.32k	National Semiconductor 32000 series chips.
comp.sys.proteon	Proteon gateway products.
comp.sys.pyramid	Pyramid 90x computers.
comp.sys.ridge	Ridge 32 computers and ROS.
comp.sys.sequent	Sequent systems, (Balance and Symmetry).
comp.sys.sgi	Silicon Graphics's Iris workstations and software.
comp.sys.sun	Sun "workstation" computers. (Moderated)
comp.sys.super	Supercomputers.
comp.sys.tahoe	CCI 6/32, Harris HCX/7, & Sperry 7000 computers.
comp.sys.tandy	Discussion about TRS-80's.
comp.sys.ti	Discussion about Texas Instruments.
comp.sys.ti.explorer	The Texas Instruments Explorer.
comp.sys.transputer	The Transputer computer and OCCAM language.
comp.sys.workstations	Various workstation-type computers. (Moderated)
comp.sys.xerox	Xerox 1100 workstations and protocols.
comp.sys.zenith	Heath terminals and related Zenith products.
comp.sys.zenith.z100	The Zenith Z-100 (Heath H-100) family of computers.
comp.terminals	All sorts of terminals.

comp.terminals.bitgraph	The BB&N BitGraph terminal.
comp.terminals.tty5620	AT&T Dot mapped display terminals (5620 and BLIT).
comp.text	Text processing issues and methods.
comp.text.desktop	Technology & techniques of desktop publishing.
comp.text.tex	TeX, LaTeX and related issues.
comp.theory	Theoretical Computer Science.
comp.theory.cell-automata	Discussion of all aspects of cellular automata.
comp.theory.dynamic-sys	Ergodic theory and dynamical systems.
comp.theory.info-retrieval	Information retrieval topics. (Moderated)
comp.theory.self-org-sys	Topics related to self-organization.
comp.unix	Discussion of UNIX* features and bugs. (Moderated)
comp.unix.aix	
comp.unix.aux	The version of UNIX for Apple Macintosh II computers.
comp.unix.cray	Cray computers and their operating systems.
comp.unix.i386	Versions of Unix running on Intel 80386-based boxes.
comp.unix.microport	Discussion of Microport's UNIX.
comp.unix.questions	UNIX neophytes group.
comp.unix.ultrix	Discussions about DEC's Ultrix.
comp.unix.wizards	Discussions, bug reports, and fixes on and for UNIX.
comp.unix.xenix	Discussion about the Xenix OS.
comp.virus	Computer viruses & security. (Moderated)
comp.windows.misc	Various issues about windowing systems.
comp.windows.ms	Window systems under MS/DOS.
comp.windows.news	Sun Microsystems' NeWS window system.
comp.windows.x	Discussion about the X Window System.
ddn.mgt-bulletin	The DDN Management Bulletin from NIC.DDN.MIL (Moderated)
ddn.newsletter	The DDN Newsletter from NIC.DDN.MIL (Moderated)
gnu.announce (Moderated)	Status and announcements from the Project.
gnu.bash.bug	Bourne Again SHell bug reports and suggested fixes.
gnu.chess	Announcements about the GNU chess program.
gnu.config	GNU's Not Usenet administration and configuration.
gnu.emacs	Editor/development environment and occasional sources.
gnu.emacs.bug	GNU Emacs bug reports and suggested fixes.
gnu.emacs.gnews	News reading under GNU Emacs using Weemba's Gnews.
gnu.emacs.gnus	News reading under GNU Emacs using GNUS (in English).
gnu.emacs.vms	VMS port of GNU Emacs.
gnu.g++	Announcements about the GNU C++ Compiler.
gnu.g++.bug	G++ and GDB+ bug reports and suggested fixes.

gnu.g++.lib.bug	G++ library bug reports and suggested fixes.
gnu.gcc	Announcements about the GNU C Compiler.
gnu.gcc.bug	GNU C Compiler bug reports and suggested fixes.
gnu.gdb.bug	GNU C/C++ DeBugger bug reports and suggested fixes.
gnu.ghostscript.bug	GNU Ghostscript interpreter bugs.
gnu.misc.discuss	Serious discussion about GNU and freed software.
gnu.test	GNU's Not Usenet alternative sub-network testing.
gnu.utils.bug	Bugs in GNU utility programs (e.g., gnumake, gawk).
mail.info-nets	Info-Nets mailing list.
misc.consumers	Consumer interests, product reviews, etc.
misc.consumers.house	Discussion about owning and maintaining a house.
misc.emerg-services	Forum for paramedics & other first responders.
misc.forsale	Short, tasteful postings about items for sale.
misc.handicap	Items of interest for/about the handicapped. (Moderated)
misc.headlines	Current interest: drug testing, terrorism, etc.
misc.headlines.unitex	International news from the UN and related. (Moderated)
misc.invest	Investments and the handling of money.
misc.jobs.misc	Discussion about employment, workplaces, careers.
misc.jobs.offered	Announcements of positions available.
misc.jobs.resumes	Postings of resumes and "situation wanted" articles.
misc.kids	Children, their behavior and activities.
misc.legal	Legalities and the ethics of law.
misc.misc	Various discussions not fitting in any other group.
misc.rural	Devoted to issues concerning rural living.
misc.security	Security in general, not just computers. (Moderated)
misc.taxes	Tax laws and advice.
misc.test	For testing of network software.Very boring.
misc.wanted	Requests for things that are needed (NOT software).
news.admin	Comments directed to news administrators.
news.announce.conferences	Calls for papers and conference announcements.
news.announce.important	General announcements of interest to all. (Moderated)
news.announce.newgroups	Calls for newgroups & announcements of same. (Moderated)
news.announce.newusers	Explanatory postings for new users. (Moderated)
news.config	Postings of system down times and interruptions.
news.groups	Discussions and lists of newsgroups.
news.lists	News-related statistics and lists. (Moderated)

news.lists.ps-maps	
news.misc	Discussions of USENET itself.
news.newusers.questions	Q & A for users new to the Usenet.
news.software.anu-news	VMS B-news software from Australian National University.
news.software.b	Discussion about B-news-compatible software.
news.software.nn	
news.software.nntp	The Network News Transfer Protocol.
news.software.notes	Notesfile software from the University of Illinois.
news.sysadmin	Comments directed to system administrators.
pubnet.config	Pubnet connectivity discussions.
pubnet.nixpub	The "nixpub" list of public access UNIXes.
pubnet.sources	Software of interest to BBS users and sysops.
pubnet.sysops	Discussions between sysops of BBS systems.
pubnet.talk	Miscellaneous BBS talk.
pubnet.test	Pubnet subnet testing.
pubnet.wanted	"Wanted" messages with a limited audience.
rec.aquaria	The aquarium & related as a hobby.
rec.arts.anime	Japanese animation fen discussion.
rec.arts.books	Books of all genres, and the publishing industry.
rec.arts.cinema	(Moderated)
rec.arts.comics	Comic books and strips, graphic novels, sequential art.
rec.arts.drwho	Discussion about Dr. Who.
rec.arts.erotica	(Moderated)
rec.arts.int-fiction	Discussions about interactive fiction.
rec.arts.misc	Discussions about the arts not in other groups.
rec.arts.movies	Discussions of movies and movie making.
rec.arts.movies.reviews	Reviews of movies. (Moderated)
rec.arts.poems	For the posting of poems.
rec.arts.sf-lovers	Science fiction lovers' newsgroup.
rec.arts.startrek	Star Trek, the TV shows and the movies.
rec.arts.startrek.info	(Moderated)
rec.arts.tv	The boob tube, its history, and past and current shows.
rec.arts.tv.soaps	Postings about soap operas.
rec.arts.tv.uk	Discussions of telly shows from the UK.
rec.arts.wobegon	"A Prairie Home Companion" radio show discussion.
rec.audio	High fidelity audio.
rec.audio.high-end	(Moderated)
rec.autos	Automobiles, automotive products and laws.
rec.autos.driving	
rec.autos.sport	Discussion of organized, legal auto competitions.
rec.autos.tech	Technical aspects of automobiles, et. al.
rec.aviation	Aviation rules, means, and methods.
rec.backcountry	Activities in the Great Outdoors.
rec.bicycles	Bicycles, related products and laws.
rec.birds	Hobbyists interested in bird watching.
rec.boats	Hobbyists interested in boating.

rec.equestrian	Discussion of things equestrian.
rec.folk-dancing	Folk dances, dancers, and dancing.
rec.food.cooking	Food, cooking, cookbooks, and recipes.
rec.food.drink	Wines and spirits.
rec.food.recipes	(Moderated)
rec.food.veg	Vegetarians.
rec.gambling	Discussions about games of chance (and mis-chance).
rec.games.board	Discussion and hints on board games.
rec.games.bridge	Hobbyists interested in bridge.
rec.games.chess	Chess and computer chess.
rec.games.empire	Discussion and hints about Empire.
rec.games.frp	Discussion about Fantasy Role Playing games.
rec.games.go	Discussion about Go.
rec.games.hack	Discussion, hints, etc. about the Hack game.
rec.games.misc	Games and computer games.
rec.games.moria	Comments, hints, and info about the Moria game.
rec.games.pbm	Discussion about Play by Mail games.
rec.games.programmer	Discussion of adventure game programming.
rec.games.rogue	Discussion and hints about Rogue.
rec.games.trivia	Discussion about trivia.
rec.games.vectrex	The Vectrex game system.
rec.games.video	Discussion about video games.
rec.gardens	Gardening, methods and results.
rec.guns	Discussions about firearms. (Moderated)
rec.ham-radio	Amateur radio practices, contests, events, rules, etc.
rec.ham-radio.packet	Discussion about packet radio setups.
rec.ham-radio.swap	Offers to trade and swap radio equipment.
rec.humor	Jokes and the like. May be somewhat offensive.
rec.humor.d	Discussions on the content of rec.humor articles.
rec.humor.funny	Jokes that are funny (in the moderator's opinion). (Moderated)
rec.mag	Magazine summaries, tables of contents, etc.
rec.mag.fsfnet	A science fiction "fanzine." (Moderated)
rec.mag.otherrealms	Edited science fiction & fantasy "magazine". (Moderated)
rec.misc	General topics about recreational/participant sports.
rec.models.rc	Radio-controlled models for hobbyists.
rec.models.rockets	
rec.motorcycles	Motorcycles and related products and laws.
rec.music.beatles	Postings about the Fab Four & their music.
rec.music.bluenote	Discussion of jazz, blues, and related types of music.
rec.music.cd	CDs — availability and other discussions.
rec.music.classical	Discussion about classical music.
rec.music.dementia	Discussion of comedy and novelty music.
rec.music.dylan	Discussion of Bob's works & music.
rec.music.folk	Folks discussing folk music of various sorts.

rec.music.gaffa	Progressive music (e.g., Kate Bush). (Moderated)
rec.music.gdead	A group for (Grateful) Dead-heads.
rec.music.makers	For performers and their discussions.
rec.music.misc	Music lovers' group.
rec.music.newage	"New Age" music discussions.
rec.music.synth	Synthesizers and computer music.
rec.nude	Hobbyists interested in naturist/nudist activities.
rec.org.sca	Society for Creative Anachronism.
rec.pets	Pets, pet care, and household animals in general.
rec.photo	Hobbyists interested in photography.
rec.puzzles	Puzzles, problems, and quizzes.
rec.radio.noncomm	
rec.radio.shortwave	
rec.railroad	Real and model train fans' newsgroup.
rec.scuba	Hobbyists interested in SCUBA diving.
rec.skiing	Hobbyists interested in snow skiing.
rec.skydiving	Hobbyists interested in skydiving.
rec.sport.baseball	Discussion about baseball.
rec.sport.basketball	Discussion about basketball.
rec.sport.football	Discussion about football.
rec.sport.hockey	Discussion about hockey.
rec.sport.misc	Spectator sports.
rec.sport.pro-wrestling	
rec.sport.soccer	
rec.travel	Traveling all over the world.
rec.video	Video and video components.
rec.windsurfing	
rec.woodworking	Hobbyists interested in woodworking.
sci.aeronautics	The science of aeronautics & related technology.
sci.astro	Astronomy discussions and information.
sci.bio	Biology and related sciences.
sci.bio.technology	Any topic relating to biotechnology.
sci.chem	Chemistry and related sciences.
sci.crypt	Different methods of data en/decryption.
sci.econ	
sci.edu	Science education.
sci.electronics	Circuits, theory, electrons and discussions.
sci.energy	Discussions about energy, science & technology.
sci.environment	Discussions about the environment and ecology.
sci.lang	Natural languages, communication, etc.
sci.lang.japan	The Japanese language, both spoken and written.
sci.logic	Logic — math, philosophy & computational aspects.
sci.math	Mathematical discussions and pursuits.
sci.math.num-analysis	Numerical analysis.
sci.math.stat	Statistics discussion.
sci.math.symbolic	Symbolic algebra discussion.
sci.med	Medicine and its related products and regulations.
sci.med.aids	AIDS: treatment, pathology/biology of HIV, prevention.

sci.med.physics	Issues of physics in medical testing/care.
sci.military	Discussion about science and the military. (Moderated)
sci.misc	Short-lived discussions on subjects in the sciences.
sci.nanotech	Self-reproducing molecular-scale machines. (Moderated)
sci.philosophy.meta	Discussions within the scope of "MetaPhilosophy."
sci.philosophy.tech	Technical philosophy: math, science, logic, etc.
sci.physics	Physical laws, properties, etc.
sci.physics.fusion	Info on fusion, esp. "cold" fusion.
sci.psychology	Topics related to psychology.
sci.psychology.digest	(Moderated)
sci.research	Research methods, funding, ethics, and whatever.
sci.skeptic	Skeptics discussing psuedo-science.
sci.space	Space, space programs, space related research, etc.
sci.space.shuttle	The space shuttle and the STS program.
sci.virtual-worlds	(Moderated)
soc.college	College, college activities, campus life, etc.
soc.couples	Discussions for couples (cf. soc.singles).
soc.culture.african	Discussions about Africa & things African.
soc.culture.arabic	Technological & cultural issues, *not* politics.
soc.culture.asean	
soc.culture.asian.american	Issues and discussion about Asian-Americans.
soc.culture.british	
soc.culture.celtic	Group about Celts (*not* basketball!).
soc.culture.china	About China and Chinese culture.
soc.culture.esperanto	The neutral international language Esperanto.
soc.culture.greek	Group about Greeks.
soc.culture.hongkong	Discussions pertaining to Hong Kong.
soc.culture.indian	Group for discussion about India and things Indian.
soc.culture.iranian	
soc.culture.japan	Everything Japanese, except the Japanese language.
soc.culture.jewish	Jewish culture & religion. (cf. talk.politics.mideast)
soc.culture.korean	Discussions about Korean and things Korean.
soc.culture.latin-america	Topics about Latin-America.
soc.culture.misc	Group for discussion about other cultures.
soc.culture.nordic	Discussion about culture up north.
soc.culture.pakistan	
soc.culture.polish	
soc.culture.sri-lanka	Things and people from Sri Lanka.
soc.culture.taiwan	Discussion about things Taiwanese.
soc.culture.turkish	Discussion about things Turkish.
soc.culture.vietnamese	
soc.feminism	Discussion of feminism and feminist issues. (Moderated)
soc.history	

soc.human-nets	Computer aided communications digest. (Moderated)
soc.men	Issues related to men, their problems and relationships.
soc.misc	Socially-oriented topics not in other groups.
soc.motss	Issues pertaining to homosexuality.
soc.net-people	Announcements, requests, etc. about people on the net.
soc.politics	Political problems, systems, solutions. (Moderated)
soc.politics.arms-d	Arms discussion digest. (Moderated)
soc.religion.christian	Christianity and related topics. (Moderated)
soc.religion.eastern	(Moderated)
soc.religion.islam	(Moderated)
soc.rights.human	Human rights and activism (e.g., Amnesty International).
soc.roots	Genealogical matters.
soc.singles	Newsgroup for single people, their activities, etc.
soc.women	Issues related to women, their problems and relationships.
talk.abortion	All sorts of discussions and arguments on abortion.
talk.bizarre	The unusual, bizarre, curious, and often stupid.
talk.origins	Evolution versus creationism (sometimes hot!).
talk.philosophy.misc	Philosophical musings on all topics.
talk.politics.guns	The politics of firearm ownership and (mis)use.
talk.politics.mideast	Discussion and debate over Middle Eastern events.
talk.politics.misc	Political discussions and ravings of all kinds.
talk.politics.soviet	Discussion of Soviet politics, domestic and foreign.
talk.politics.theory	Theory of politics and political systems.
talk.rape	Discussions on stopping rape; not to be cross-posted.
talk.religion.misc	Religious, ethical, & moral implications.
talk.religion.newage	Esoteric and minority religions and philosophies.
talk.rumors	For the posting of rumors.
unix-pc.bugs	Bug reports, fixes and workarounds.
unix-pc.general	General information and discussion.
unix-pc.sources	Source code to various programs.
unix-pc.test	Test group.
unix-pc.uucp	Configuration and management of uucp on Unix-PCs.
vmsnet.admin	Administrative stuff for VMSnet.
vmsnet.announce	General announcements of interest to all VMSnet readers)
vmsnet.announce.newusers	Orientation info for new users. (Moderated)
vmsnet.mail	Discussions of e-mail on VMS systems, OTHER than VMSnet.
vmsnet.mail.pmdf	Gatewayed to info-pmdf mailing list.

vmsnet.misc	Discussions of VMSnet itself, gatewayed to vmsnet maili.
vmsnet.sources	Source code postings for VMS systems (including VMSnet).
vmsnet.sources.d	Discussions and requests for same.
vmsnet.sources.games	Recreational software (optional).
vmsnet.sysmgt	
vmsnet.test	
vmsnet.uucp	
bionet.agroforestry	Discussion of agroforestry.
bionet.general	General BIONET announcements.
bionet.jobs	Scientific Job opportunities.
bionet.journals.contents	Contents of biology journal publications.
bionet.molbio.ageing	Discussions of cellular and organismal ageing.
bionet.molbio.bio-matrix	Computer applications to biological databases.
bionet.molbio.embldatabank	Info about the EMBL Nucleic acid database.
bionet.molbio.evolution	How genes and proteins have evolved.
bionet.molbio.genbank	Info about the GenBank Nucleic acid database.
bionet.molbio.genbank.updates	Hot off the presses... (Moderated)
bionet.molbio.gene-org	How genes are organized on chromosomes.
bionet.molbio.genome-program	Discussion of human genome project issues.
bionet.molbio.methds-reagnts	Requests for information and lab reagents.
bionet.molbio.news	Research news of interest to the community.
bionet.molbio.pir	Info about the PIR protein sequence database.
bionet.molbio.proteins	Research on proteins and protein databases.
bionet.molbio.swiss-prot	Discussion on the SWISS-PROT Database.
bionet.population-bio	Technical discussions about population biology.
bionet.sci-resources	Information about funding agencies, etc.
bionet.software	Information about software for biology.
bionet.technology.conversion	Use of techology to convert waste and biomass.
bionet.users.addresses	Who's who in biology
ba.food	Bay Area restaurants and eating places.
ba.general	Announcements of general interest to all readers.
ba.market.computers	For Sale/Wanted: computers and software.
ba.market.housing	For Sale/Rent/Wanted: housing, land, roommates.
ba.market.misc	For Sale/Wanted: miscellaneous.
ba.market.vehicles	For Sale/Wanted: autos, cycles, trucks, etc.
ba.motss	Newsgroup for Bay Area motss'ers.
ba.mountain-folk	Living in the hills and mountains around the Bay Area.
ba.music	Musical events in the Bay Area.
ba.news	General issues of 'ba' Usenet administration.
ba.news.config	Announcments and discussion of Bay Area connectivity.
ba.news.group	Meta-discussions about newsgroups in 'ba' distribution.
ba.news.stats	Bay Area USENET statistical and information postings.
ba.politics	Political topics of interest to Bay Area readers.
ba.seminars	Announcements of Bay Area seminars.

ba.singles	Local newsgroup for single people.
ba.sports	Discussion of sports in the Bay Area.
ba.test	Tests of 'ba' distribution. (Some sites autorespond.)
ba.transportation	Discussion of Bay Area transit/commute/driving issues.
ba.windows.x	X windows discussion/help.

OK:!wc /usr/lib/news/newsgroups
1153 (lines) 6518 (words) 60000 /usr/lib/news/newsgroups

7.7 BITNET Listserv Forums

The following list is a one line description of each bitnet listserv based discussion group or forum that was known at the time it was requested from a listserver, namely listserv@uccvma.bitnet. The list is about 2,400 lines long and growing. A peered discussion is one that is copied to another listserver, so that the actual distribution of information is slightly distributed and not completely centralized. In those cases you usually subscribe to the listserv nearest you. You can get a more up-to-date copy of this list by sending the command list global to a server near you.

List of all LISTSERV lists known to LISTSERV@UCCVMA on 26 Feb 1991 08:55

'AMALGAM'	AMALGAM@DSORUS1I	Dental AMALGAM and MERCURY Poisoning
'AMERSTDY'	AMERSTDY@MIAMIU	(Peered) American Studies
'CLIO-L'	CLIO-L@MIAMIU	(Peered) A description of your list goes here
'CUFS-L'	CUFS-L@MIAMIU	(Peered) A discussion of the CUFS system
'DARS-L'	DARS-L@MIAMIU	Degree Audit Reporting System Discussion List
'ECONET'	ECONET@MIAMIU	(Peered) A discussion of Ecological and Envir
'EDUCATIONAL-...	ERL-L@TCSVM	Educational Research List (TCSVM)
'I-AMIGA-UIUC...	I-AMIGA@UIUCVMD	Archive of I-AMIGA list elsewhere on net (Don
'IBM7171-MAIN'	IBM7171@TCSVM	(Peered) Protocol Converter list
'IBSCG'	IBSCG@MIAMIU	(Peered) International Business School computers
'KKY-L'	KKY-L@MIAMIU	(Peered) KKPsi/TBS Dis-

		tribution List
'MCUG-L'	MCUG-L@MIAMIU	(Peered) Alternative Colorful Postings
'MUMAIL-L'	MUMAIL-L@MIAMIU	(Peered) Miami University Mail exchange discu
'NEW-SUPERCOM...'	S-COMPUT@BNANDP11	(Peered) SuperComputers list (BNANDP11)
	S-COMPUT@TCSVM	(Peered) SuperComputers list (TCSVM)
	S-COMPUT@UGA	(Peered) SuperComputers List (UGA)
	S-COMPUT@USCVM	(Peered) SuperComputers list (USCVM)
'NIH-GUIDE'	NIHGUIDE@TCSVM	NIH Guide List (TCSVM)
	NIHGGC-L@UBVM	NIH Grants and Contracts Distribution List
'NIHDOC-L'	NIHDOC-L@LSUVM	NIH Guide List (LSUVM)
'PCSA-L'	LANWORKS@MIAMIU	(Peered) A discussion of Digital's PCSA products
'PHYSICS'	PHYSICS@MIAMIU	(Peered) Physics discussion list
'SGANET'	SGANET@DSORUS1I	SGANET ...
AAUA-L	AAUA-L@UBVM	American Association of University Administra
ACADDR-L	ACADDR-L@MCGILL1	Academic Computing Centre Directors Forum
ACADEMIC	ACADEMIC@BRUFMG	Forum de Ciencia Computacional
ACADV	ACADV@NDSUVM1	ACADV Academic Advising Forum
ACCY-L	ACCY-L@UHUPVM1	ACCY-L Accounting Distribution List
ACM-L	ACM-L@OHSTVMA	ACM-L List for Student Chapters of ACM
	ACM-L@UCF1VM	Florida ACM Student Chapter Discussion List
ACMSTCHP	ACMSTCHP@SUVM	ACM Student Chapters
ACS-L	ACS-L@POLYGRAF	IBM Advanced Control System Discussion list
ACS-SPI	ACS-SPI@UNCVM1	UNC/ACS List for SPIRES Users.
ACSALF	ACSALF@UQUEBEC	Association canadienne des sociologues et des
ACSCMS-L	ACSCMS-L@UNCVM1	UNC/ACS VM/XA CMS USERS LIST.
ACSOFT-L	ACSOFT-L@WUVMD	Academic Software Development
ACTION	ACTION@USCVM	USC-UCS IBM VM Problem Reports List
ACTIV-L	ACTIV-L@UMCVMB	Activists Mailing List
ACTNOW-L	ACTNOW-L@BROWNVM	College Activism/

		Information List
ACUA-L	ACUA-L@UVMVM	acua-l
ADMIN-L	ADMIN-L@ALBNYDH2	NYS DEPARTMENT OF HEALTH ADMIN INFOR
ADMINSEC	ADMINSEC@UTORONTO	Netnorth Administrative Secretary
ADMINVP	ADMINVP@IUBVM	Mailing list for staff of the VP for Finance
ADMRA-L	ADMRA-L@ALBNYDH2	ADIRONDACK MEDICAL RECORDS ASSOCIATION LIST
ADND-L	ADND-L@PUCC	(Peered) Advanced Dungeons and Dragons discus
	ADND-L@UTARLVM1	(Peered) Advanced Dungeons and Dragons discus
ADQ	ADQ@UQUEBEC	Association des demographes du Quebec
ADR-L	ADR-L@ALBNYVM1	ADR Database Products Discussion List
ADVANC-L	ADVANC-L@IDBSU	LISTSERV LIST 'ADVANC-L'
ADVICE-L	ADVICE-L@JPNTOHOK	Technical Assistance for Users at JPNTOHOK
ADVISE-L	MD4F@CMUCCVMA	(Peered) User Services List (ADVISE-L)
	ADVISE-L@EB0UB011	(Peered) User Services List
	ADVISE-L@UIUCVMD	ADVISE-L (log files only)
	ADVISE-L@UTORONTO	(Peered) User Services List
AELFLOW	AELFLOW@TECHNION	"Aerospace Eng. Fluid Group"
AESRG-L	AESRG-L@UMCVMB	Applied Expert Systems Research Group List
AFRICA-L	AFRICA-L@BRUFPB	FORUM PAN-AFRICA
AG-EXP-L	AG-EXP-L@NDSUVM1	AG-EXP-L Ag Expert Systems
AG-FORST	AG-FORST@IRLEARN	BIOSCI AgroForestry Bulletin Board
AGEING	AGEING@IRLEARN	BIOSCI Ageing Bulletin Board
AGFTECH	AGFTECH@DEARN	AGF-Subnetz-Koordinatoren
AGRIC-L	AGRIC-L@UGA	Agriculture Discussion
AIDS	AIDS@EB0UB011	(Peered) Sci.Med.AIDS Newsgroup
	AIDS@RUTVM1	(Peered) Sci.Med.AIDS Newsgroup
	AIDS@USCVM	(Peered) Sci.Med.AIDS

	Newsgroup	
AIDS_INTL	ICECA@RUTVM1	Intl Committee for Elec Comm on AIDS
AIDSNEWS	AIDSNEWS@EB0UB011	(Peered) AIDS/HIV News
	AIDSNEWS@RUTVM1	(Peered) AIDS/HIV News
	AIDSNEWS@USCVM	(Peered) AIDS/HIV News
AILIST	AILIST@DB0TUI11	(Peered) Artificial Intelligence List
	AILIST@FINHUTC	(Peered) Artificial Intelligence List
	AILIST@NDSUVM1	(Peered) AILIST Artificial Intelligence List
AIR-L	AIR-L@UNMVM	AIR-L - Institutional Researchers/University
AIX-IL	AIX-IL@TECHNION	Aerospace Eng. Test List
AIX-L	AIX-L@PUCC	IBM AIX Discussion List
AIX370-L	AIX370-L@UWAVM	AIX370 Discussion List
AJCUAVP	AJCUAVP@GUVM	AJCU Academic Vice Presidents
AJCUCOMM	AJCUCOMM@GUVM	AJCU Communications Committee
AJCUCOMP	AJCUCOMP@GUVM	AJCU Computer Center Directors
AJCUNEWS	AJCUNEWS@GUVM	AJCU News for those not on other AJCU lists
AJCUPRES	AJCUPRES@GUVM	AJCU Presidents
AKPAR-L	AKPAR-L@DEARN	Arbeitskreis Parallelrechner
ALBVMUG	ALBVMUG@RPIECS	Albany/Upstate New York VM User's Group
ALF-L	ALF-L@YORKVM1	Academic Librarian's Forum
ALL-L	ALL-L@BRLNCC	"USUARIOS DO SISTEMA BRLNCC (VM/XA)"
ALLDIST	ALLDIST@VTVM1	VCES Unit Office Mailing List
ALLIN1-L	ALLIN1-L@SBCCVM	ALL-IN-1 Managers and Users mailing list.
ALLMUSIC	ALLMUSIC@AUVM	Discussions on all forms of Music
	ALLMUSIC@UFRJ	ALLMUSIC PEERED LIST
ALPHA-L	ALPHA-L@LEPICS	L3 Alpha physics block analysis diagram group
ALTERNAT	ALTERNAT@NDSUVM1	Alternatives Journal
ALTLEARN	ALTLEARN@SJUVM	Alternative Approaches to Learning Discussion
AMBIENTE	AMBIENTE@UFRJ	Ambiente - Forum Para discussao sobre o meio

	AMFCH-L	
	AMFCH-L@UCHCECVM	Noticias Acerca de la Cooperacion Franco-Chil
AMI-HARD	AMI-HARD@UMAINECS	Re-distribution of Comp.sys.amiga.hardware fr
AMI-TECH	AMI-TECH@UMAINECS	Re-distribution of Comp.sys.amiga.tech group
AMIGA-A	AMIGA-A@FINHUTC	Amiga filelist archives (Do not try to subscr
AMIGA-D	AMIGA-D@FINHUTC	Digests of Comp.Sys.Amiga (Moderated)
AMIGA-S	AMIGA-S@FINHUTC	Sources & Binaries for Amiga (Moderated)
AMIGAHAR	AMIGAHAR@DHDURZ1	AMIGAGHARCOMP.SYS.AMIGA.HARDWARE re-dist.
AMLG-L	AMLG-L@IUBVM	AMLG Mail Distribution List
AMNESTY	AMNESTY@JHUVM	Amnesty International list
AMSSIS-L	AMSSIS-L@UAFSYSB	AMS Student Information System Forum
AMYMAIL	AMYMAIL@JPNKEKVM	AMY Mail list
ANIME-L	ANIME-L@VTVM1	Japanese animedia and other animation news.
ANNOUNCE	ANNOUNCE@JPNKISCI	fj.{announce,misc,meeting}
ANSAX-L	ANSAX-L@WVNVM	ANSAXNET Discussion Forum
ANSP-L	ANSP-L@BRUSPVM	Rede ANSP
ANTHRO-L	ANTHRO-L@UBVM	General Anthropology Bulletin Board
ANU-NEWS	ANU-NEWS@NDSUVM1	ANU-NEWS Discussion
ANYSUG-L	ANYSUG-L@ALBNYDH2	Albany New York SAS User's Group
AOBULL-L	AOBULL-L@ALBNYDH2	NEW YORK STATE DEPARTMENT OF HEALTH AREA OFFI
APASD-L	APASD-L@VTVM2	APA Research Psychology Network
APASPAN	APASPAN@GWUVM	APA Scientific Grassroots Network
APB-L	APB-L@LAVALVM1	Advancement of Paradigmatic Behaviorism
APB-UL-L	APB-UL-L@LAVALVM1	Avancement du behaviorisme paradigmatique - U

APICS	APICS@UBVM	UB A. P. I. C. S. Discussion List
APL-ERS	APL-ERS@IRLEARN	UCD APL Interest Group
APL-L	APL-L@UNBVM1	APL Language Discussion
APNET-L	APNET-L@JPNSUT00	Asia Pacific Network
APO-L	APO-L@PURCCVM	Alpha Phi Omega
APPLE2-L	APPLE2-L@BROWNVM	Apple II List
APPLICAT	APPLICAT@BITNIC	(Peered) Applications under BITNET
AQUA-L	AQUA-L@UOGUELPH	Aquaculture Discussion List
AQUIFER	AQUIFER@IBACSATA	Pollution and grondwater recharge
ARACHNET	ARACHNET@UTORONTO	An Association of Discussion Groups in the Hu
ARCLIB-L	ARCLIB-L@IRLEARN	Mailing List for Irish and UK Architectural L
AREXX-L	AREXX-L@UCF1VM	Amiga REXX Discussion List
ARIEL-L	ARIEL-L@USACHVM1	"Software Estadistico Ariel"
ARLIS-L	ARLIS-L@UKCC	ART LIBRARIES SOCIETY DISCUSSION LIST
ARMS-L	ARMS-L@BUACCA	Arms-L Mailing List
ARPABBS	ARPABBS@TCSVM	(Peered) Arpanet Bulletin-Boards
	ARPABBS@UBVM	(Peered) Arpanet Bulletin-Boards
ARRTECH	ARRTECH@TECHNION	Technion's architecture faculty general list
ARTCRIT	ARTCRIT@YORKVM1	Art Criticism Discussion Forum
AS-ACADE	AS-ACADE@UCHCECVM	Asociacion de Academicos Fac. de Cs. Fis. y M
ASA-L	ASA-L@TAMVM1	African Students Association Discussion List
ASANALCO	ASANALCO@ANDESCOL	Asamblea Nacional Constituyente
ASHE-L	ASHE-L@UMCVMB	Association for the Study of Higher Education
ASIANAD	ASIANAD@JPNSUT00	Asia(JP,KR,TW) Node Administrator
ASISAH	ASISAH@GWUVM	ASIS Discussion List
ASM-L	ASM-L@PCCVM	Student Chapters of ASM (Association of Syste
ASM370	ASM370@UIUCVMD	ASM370 (log files only)
ASRC-L	ASRC-L@LEPICS	Discussion of AXL3 Smallest Resolvable Cluste

ASSEMBLER-LIST	ASM370@DEARN	(Peered) IBM 370 Assembly Programming Discuss
	ASM370@EB0UB011	(Peered) IBM 370 Assembly Programming Discuss
ASSMPC-L	ASSMPC-L@USACHVM1	"Assembly for the IBM-PC"
ASTRA-UG	ASTRA-UG@ICNUCEVM	ASTRA Users Group Discussion List
ASTRA-WG	ASTRA-WG@ICNUCEVM	Gruppo di lavoro progetto ASTRA
ASTROL-L	ASTROL-L@BRUFPB	FORUM FOR ASTROLOGICAL DISCUSSION
ASYSM-L	ASYSM-L@UA1VM	Associate Members of the ASM (Association of
ATARST-L	ATARST-L@UIUCVMD	Atari ST discussions
ATLANT-L	ATLANT-L@UNBVM1	Atlantic Canada Region Computing Centre Staff
ATTEND	ATTEND@BITNIC	BITNET Technical Meeting Attendees
ATT386-L	ATT386-L@UIUCVMD	AT&T 6386 WGS computer discussion
AUDIO-L	AUDIO-L@VMTECMEX	Audio discussion list
AUTO-L	AUTO-L@TECHNION	Remote Autolog Software Problem List
AUTOCAD	AUTOCAD@OHSTVMA	AUTOCAD Autocad Discussion List
AUTOCAT	AUTOCAT@UVMVM	AUTOCAT: Library cataloging and authorities d
AUTORACE	AUTORACE@INDYCMS	AUTORACE a Discussion of Auto Racing
AVIATION	AVIATION@BRUFPB	General Aviation List
AVM-L	AVM-L@PURCCVM	AVMEDIA uses file server, but does not run a
AVSFORUM	AVSFORUM@TAMVM1	CSC Academic Vax Private Forum
AYN-RAND	AYN-RAND@UA1VM	Ayn Rand Philosophy Discussion List
AYUDA1	AYUDA1@USACHVM1	"Consultas y Soluciones"
AYUDA2	AYUDA2@USACHVM1	"Lista interna para la Unidad de Soporte Tecn
AYUDA4	AYUDA4@USACHVM1	"Lista para PRUEBAS de la Unidad de Soporte T
BACIS-L	BACIS-L@UKANVM	"KU BACIS Staff"
BALT-L	BALT-L@UBVM	(Peered) Baltic Republics Discussion List
	BALT-L@UKACRL	(Peered) Baltic Republics Discussion List
BANNER-L	BANNER-L@WVNVM	Student Information System Discussions

BANYAN	BANYAN-L@AKRONVM	Banyan Networks Discussion List
	BANYAN@WCU	BANYAN LANS
BATCH-L	BATCH-L@PURCCVM	Purdue BATCH discussion list
	BATCH-L@VTVM1	Virginia Tech Batch Facility Users List
BATCHX-L	BATCHX-L@UFRJ	BATCHX - Discussoes e Informacoes
BBSTEST	BBSTEST@NIHCUSV1	BBSTEST List
BCS-L	BCS-L@NMSUVM1	Business Computer Systems Class List
BEE-L	BEE-L@ALBNYVM1	Discussion of Bee Biology
BEER-L	BEER-L@UA1VM	Home Brewed Beer Discussion List
BEHAVIOR	BEHAVIOR@ASUACAD	Behavioral and Emotional Disorders in Childre
BELIEF-L	BELIEF-L@BROWNVM	(Peered) Personal Ideologies Discussion List
	BELIEF-L@UCF1VM	(Peered) Personal Ideologies Discussion List
BERWRO-L	BERWRO-L@UBVM	Discussion of Berkely/ Wroclaw Activities List
BETA-L	BETA-L@LEPICS	L3 Analysis Group Beta
BI-L	BI-L@BINGVMB	Bibliographic Instruction Discussion Group
BIG-LAN	BIG-LAN@EB0UB011	Campus-Size LAN Discussion Group
	BIG-LAN@IRLEARN	UCD Distribution of BIG-LAN
	BIG-LAN@TECMTYVM	Selected archives of the BIG-LAN discussion l
BILLING	BILLING@HDETUD1	Chargeback of (computer) resources
BIO-DOST	BIO-DOST@TREARN	Biyolojik Bilimlerde Calisan Turk Bilim Adaml
BIO-JRNL	BIO-JRNL@IRLEARN	BIOSCI Bio-Journals Bulletin Board
BIO-NAUT	BIO-NAUT@IRLEARN	BIOSCI Bionauts Bulletin Board
BIO-SOFT	BIO-SOFT@IRLEARN	BIOSCI Software Bulletin Board
BIOJOBS	BIOJOBS@IRLEARN	BIOSCI Employment Bulletin Board
BIOMATRX	BIOMATRX@IRLEARN	BIOSCI Bio-Matrix Bulletin Board
BIOMCH-L	BIOMCH-L@HEARN	Biomechanics and Movement Science listserver
BIOMED-L	BIOMED-L@MCGILL1	Assoc. of Biomedical

		Communications Directors
	BIOMED-L@NDSUVM1	BIOMED-L Biomedical Ethics
BIOMET-L	BIOMET-L@ALBNYDH2	BUREAU OF BIOMETRICS AT ALBNYDH2
BIONEWS	BIONEWS@IRLEARN	BIOSCI BioNews Bulletin Board
BIOSPH-L	BIOSPH-L@UBVM	Biosphere, ecology, Discussion List
BIOVOTE	BIOVOTE@IRLEARN	BIOSCI Ballot Box
BIPM-L	BIPM-L@FRORS12	Bureau International des Poids et Mesures
BIRD_RBA	BIRD_RBA@ARIZVM1	National Birding Hotline Cooperative
BIRDCHAT	BIRDCHAT@ARIZVM1	National Birding Hotline Cooperative (Chat Li
BIRDCNTR	BIRDCNTR@ARIZVM1	National Birding Hotline Cooperative (Central
BIRDEAST	BIRDEAST@ARIZVM1	National Birding Hotline Cooperative (East)
BIRDWEST	BIRDWEST@ARIZVM1	National Birding Hotline Cooperative (West)
BISEXU-L	BISEXU-L@BROWNVM	Bisexuality Discussion List
BITLIB-D	BITLIB-D@UTCVM	BITLIB Distribution List
BITLIB-L	BITLIB-L@UTCVM	BITLIB Discussion List
BITNET-L	BITNET-L@BRLNCC	"USUARIOS DE BITNET NO LNCC"
	BITNET-L@BRUFPB	(Peered) LISTA PARA OS USUARIOS DA BITNET
BITNET-2	BITNET-2@TCSVM	Discussion of BITNET II
BITNEWS	BITNEWS@BITNIC	(Peered) BITNET Network News List
	BITNEWS@DEARN	(Peered) BITNET News List
	BITNEWS@EB0UB011	(Peered) BITNET News List
	BITNEWS@FINHUTC	(Peered) BITNET News List
	BITNEWS@HEARN	(Peered) BITNET News List
	BITNEWS@MARIST	(Peered) BITNET News List
	BITNEWS@UGA	(Peered) BITNET News
BITNIC-LIAISON	LIAISON@TCSVM	(Peered) Network Site Liaisons
BITTECH	BITTECH@BITNIC	Meeting attendees
BITUSE-L	BITUSE-L@UMAB	Bitnet User's Group
BIXANET	BIXANET@JHUVM	Brainwave Systems users group

BLIND-L	BLIND-L@UAFSYSB	Computer Use by and for the Blind
BLOOMVP	BLOOMVP@IUBVM	Mailing list for staff of the VP for Blooming
BMDP-L	BMDP-L@MCGILL1	BMDP SOFTWARE USERS
BOARD-F	BOARD-F@FRMOP11	Bureau de l'association EARN-France
BOC-L	BOC-L@UBVM	Imaginitive Rock Music Discussion List
BRAS-CON	BRAS-CON@FRORS12	"Brazilian Interest List for Europe (Bras-net
BRAS-NET	BRAS-NET@BRUFMG	Brasileiros no Exterior
	BRAS-NET@BRUFPB	Brasileiros no Exterior
	BRAS-NET@UFRJ	Brasileiros no Exterior
BRFC-L	BRFC-L@PUCC	BITNET RFC Discussion List
BRIDGE	BRIDGE@FINHUTC	Bridge Communication products
BRINE-L	BRINE-L@UGA	Brine Shrimp Discussion List
BRIT-L	BRIT-L@KSUVM	Behavioral Research In Transplantation
BRS-L	BRS-L@USCVM	BRS/Search Full Text Retrieval Software Discu
BSRUSERS	BSRUSERS@PUCC	BSR Software discussion list.
BUDDHIST	BUDDHIST@JPNTOHOK	Forum on Indian and Buddhist Studies
BURC	BURC@TREARN	Bogazici University Graduates Communication L
BUSLIB-L	BUSLIB-L@IDBSU	LISTSERV LIST 'BusLib-L'
C-BOWL	C-BOWL@RICEVM1	College Bowl Teams and Officials
C-L	C-L@INDYCMS	Discussion of C Programming
	C-L@UIUCVMD	C (language) discussions
CA-L	CA-L@MITVMA	BITNET part of CA@Think.COM (Cellular Automat
CA-VMNET	CA-VMNET@UTORONTO	Canadian VMNET Backbone Group
CAACSALF	CAACSALF@UQUEBEC	Conseil d'administration de l'ACSALF
CACCS-L	CACCS-L@UOGUELPH	Canadian Association of Campus Computer Store
CACDE-L	CACDE-L@UOGUELPH	Canadian Association for Computers in Design
CACI-L	CACI-L@UALTAVM	Research and Advanced Study: Canada and Italy

CACUSS-L	CACUSS-L@UOGUELPH	Canadian Association of College & University
CADAM-L	CADAM-L@FINHUTC	(Peered) CADAM guru forum
CADLIST	CADLIST@FINHUTC	(Peered) CAD General Discussion Group
CAEDS-L	CAEDS-L@FINHUTC	(Peered) CAEDS guru forum
CAG-IGBP	CAG-IGBP@UOGUELPH	CAG_IBP Information Exchange
CALPAR	CALPAR@ICNUCEVM	CNUCE Reparto Calcolo Vettoriale e Parallelo
CANCER-L	CANCER-L@WVNVM	WVNET CANCER discussion list
CANDLE-L	CANDLE-L@UA1VM	Candle Products Discussion List
CANINE-L	CANINE-L@PCCVM	Discussion forum for Dog fanciers
CANOPUS	CANOPUS@FINHUTC	Canopus magazine
CANSPACE	CANSPACE@UNBVM1	Canadian Space Geodesy Forum
CARCH-L	CARCH-L@IBACSATA	Computer Architecture International Group
CARI-VOI	CARI-VOI@IGECUNIV	CARI-VOIComunicazioni agli utenti
CARO-DIR	CARO-DIR@ICNUCEVM	CNUCE Comunicazioni dei dipendenti col Dirett
CAROCISI	CAROCISI@IGECUNIV	CAROCISISuggerimenti-insulti-richieste di a
CARUL	CARUL@LAVALVM1	Club des administrateurs de reseaux locaux de
CASE-L	CASE-L@UCCVMA	Computer Aided Software Engineering
CATIA-L	CATIA-L@FINHUTC	(Peered) CATIA guru forum
CAUCE-L	CAUCE-L@UREGINA1	Canadian Association for University Continuin
CBA-LAB	CBA-LAB@UICVM	CBA PC Lab Faculty Support
CBDS-L	CBDS-L@FINHUTC	(Peered) CBDS guru forum
CC	CC@MCGILL1	Computing Centre Staff Names
CC-L	CC-L@NMSUVM1	NMSU Computer Center List
CCANET	CCANET@RPICICGE	Canadian Communication Association Network
	CCANET@RPIECS	Canadian Communication Association Network

CCCECS	CCCECS@ICNUCEVM	Commiss. per il Coord. dei Centri Erogatori p
CCES-L	CCES-L@UNBVM1	Congress of Canadian Engineering Students (Fo
CCHD-L	CCHD-L@UNCVM1	Carolina Consortium for Human Development.
CCIJLEX	CCIJLEX@UCHCECVM	Foro de Informatica Juridica.
CCNET-L	CCNET-L@UGA	Chinese Computing Network
CCNEWS	CCNEWS@BITNIC	Campus Computing Newsletter Editors
CCS	CCS@UKCC	Center for Computational Sciences
CDC-SE	CDC-SE@SEARN	Swedish EARN Node ADministrators - CDC system
CDCNAD-F	CDCNAD-F@FRMOP11	Liste des 'Node ADministators' CDC francais
CDROM-L	CDROM-L@UCCVMA	CD-ROM
CEC	CEC@QUCDN	Canadian Electro-Acoustics Community (CEC)
CEM-L	CEM-L@UTDALLAS	UTD Center for Engineering Mathematics
CEMS-L	CEMS-L@MARIST	Collegiate Emergency Medical Services
CENTAM-L	CENTAM-L@UBVM	Central America Discussion List
CENTER-L	CENTER-L@JPNTOHOK	Suggestion and Complaints to JPNTOHOK
CENTRG-L	CENTRG-L@UTORONTO	Central Region Directors
CGE	CGE@MARIST	Computer Graphics Education Newsletter
CHAT-L	CHAT-L@POLYGRAF	(Peered) Forum on the VM/CMS Chat program
	CHAT-L@SEARN	(Peered) Forum on the VM/CMS Chat program
CHEME-L	CHEME-L@PSUVM	Chemical Engineering List
CHEMED-L	CHEMED-L@UWF	Chemistry Education Discussion List
CHEMIC-L	CHEMIC-L@TAUNIVM	Chemistry in Israel List
CHEMSERV	CHEMSERV@UKANVM	"American Chemical Society"
CHEP91-C	CHEP91-C@JPNKEKVM	CHEP91 Scientific Advisory Committee
CHESS-L	CHESS-L@GREARN	The Chess Discussion List
CHEST-L	CHEST-L@IRLEARN	CHEST-L

CHILE-L	CHILE-L@PURCCVM	Discussion regarding Chile
	CHILE-L@UCHCECVM	Informaciones y Cultura acerca de CHILE.
CHILENET	CHILENET@UCHCECVM	(Peered) Lista de Informaciones para la Red A
	CHILENET@UTFSM	(Peered) Lista de Informaciones para la Red A
CHIMIECH	CHIMIECH@FRMOP11	Correspondants Scientifiques du GS Chimie Mol
CHIMIECT	CHIMIECT@FRMOP11	Correspondants Techniques du GS Chimie Molecu
CHIMIEGS	CHIMIEGS@FRMOP11	Groupement Scientifique Chimie Moleculaire
CHINA	CHINA@PUCC	Chinese Studies list
CHINA-ND	CHINA-ND@KENTVM	"China News Digest"
CHINA-NN	CHINA-NN@ASUACAD	China News Network
CHINA-NT	CHINA-NT@UGA	China-Net
CHINANET	CHINANET@TAMVM1	CHINANET: Networking In China
CHRISTIA	CHRISTIA@FINHUTC	Practical Christian Life
CHROM-22	CHROM-22@IRLEARN	BIOSCI Chromosome-22 Bulletin Board
CHUG-L	CHUG-L@BROWNVM	Brown University Computing in the Humanities
CIAMAA-L	CIAMAA-L@USACHVM1	"First Ibero-American Conference of the Atmos
CICS-KER	CICS-KER@LEHIIBM1	CICS-Kermit Discussion List
CICS-L	CICS-L@AKRONVM	(Peered) CICS Discussion List
	CICS-L@AWIIMC11	(Peered) CICS List
	CICS-L@BYUVM	(Peered) CICS List
	CICS-L@MARIST	(Peered) CICS List
	CICS-L@UALTAVM	(Peered) CICS List
	CICS-L@UGA	(Peered) CICS List
	CICS-L@UTARLVM1	(Peered) CICS List
CINEMA-L	CINEMA-L@AUVM	Discussions on all forms of Cinema
CISCO-L	CISCO-L@DEARN	CISCO Anwendergruppe
CISCOM-L	CISCOM-L@MCMVM1	CISCOM-L LIST
CISLIST	CISLIST@GWUVM	Computer and Information Systems List (Local
CISMVS-L	CISMVS-L@MCMVM1	CISMVS-L LIST
CISVM-L	CISVM-L@MCMVM1	CISVM-L LIST
CIVIL-L	CIVIL-L@BRUFPB	Lista sobre Engenharia Civil
	CIVIL-L@UNBVM1	Civil Engineering Reasearch & Education

CJUST-L	CJUST-L@IUBVM	Criminal Justice Discussion List
CLAN	CLAN@FRMOP11	Cancer Liaison and Action Network
CLASS-L	CLASS-L@SBCCVM	Classification, clustering, and phylogeny est
CLERICAL	CLERICAL@PURCCVM	CPT Clerical Staff
CLIC-L	CLIC-L@UHCCVM	CLIC staff
CLIMLIST	CLIMLIST@OHSTVMA	CLIMLIST List of Climatologists
CLIPPER	CLIPPER@BRUFPB	List for Clipper and DBMS systems for IBM PC
CLUB-USM	CLUB-USM@UTFSM	Lista de Informacion de la U.T.F.S.M y su que
CMC	CMC@RPICICGE	Computer Mediated Communication
	CMC@RPIECS	Computer Mediated Communication
CMDMEMO	CMDMEMO@UOTTAWA	CEMAID memo distribution
CMS-PIPELINES	CMSPIP-L@AWIIMC11	(Peered) VM/SP CMS Pipelines Discussion List
	CMSPIP-L@MARIST	(Peered) VM/SP CMS Pipelines Discussion List
CMSAPPL	CMSAPPL@UKACRL	CMSAPPL LIST
CMSR4-L	CMSR4-L@UIUCVMD	CMS release 4 discussions
CMSR5-L	CMSR5-L@UIUCVMD	CMS release 5 discussions
CMSUG-L	CMSUG-L@NDSUVM1	(Peered) CMSUG-L CMS List
	CMSUG-L@UIUCVMD	CMS Users Group
	CMSUG-L@UTARLVM1	(Peered) CMS User Guide List
CNEDUC-L	CNEDUC-L@TAMVM1	Computer Networking Education Discussion List
CNETIE-L	CNETIE-L@UALTAVM	International Centre Communication Network (C
CNFINFO	CNFINFO@CERNVM	List CNFINFO
CNG	CNG@ASUACAD	China News Group (ASU Local)
CNIDIR-L	CNIDIR-L@UNMVM	CNIDIR-L - Coalition for Networked Informatio
CNSF-L	CNSF-L@MITVMA	Cornell National Supercomputer Facilities Use
COAACAD	COAACAD@UBVM	SUNY COA Academic Subcommittee Discussion List

COASTGIS	COASTGIS@IRLEARN	Coastal GIS Distribution List
COCAMED	COCAMED@UTORONTO	Computers in Canadian Medical Education
COCO	COCO@PUCC	COCO - Tandy Color Computer List
COGS	COGS@UICVM	Computing on a Grand Scale List
COGSCI-L	COGSCI-L@MCGILL1	COGNITIVE SCIENCE CENTRE
	COGSCI-L@YORKVM1	Cognitive Science Discussion Group
COLA-L	COLA-L@UALTAVM	College on Location Analysis
COM-ALG	COM-ALG@NDSUVM1	COM-ALG - Commutative Algebra
COM-L	COM-L@ULKYVM	Communication discussion group
COMCIV-L	COMCIV-L@IUBVM	CompCiv-L:
COMCONF	COMCONF@RPICICGE	Experiment in inter-university cooperative ed
	COMCONF@RPIECS	Experiment in inter-university cooperative ed
COMDEV	COMDEV@RPIECS	Communication & international development
COMITE	COMITE@FRMOP11	Comite d'experts d'appel d'offres
COMLAW-L	COMLAW-L@UALTAVM	Computers and Legal Education
COMMCRD	COMMCRD@NERVM	NERDC Telecommunications Coordination list
COMMDIS	COMMDIS@RPICICGE	Speech disorders
	COMMDIS@RPIECS	Speech disorders
COMMED	COMMED@RPICICGE	Communication education
	COMMED@RPIECS	Communication education
COMMJOBS	COMMJOBS@RPICICGE	Position announcements in Communication Studi
	COMMJOBS@RPIECS	Position announcements in Communication Studi
COMMODOR	COMMODOR@UBVM	COMMODORE COMPUTERS DISCUSSION
COMMUNIK	COMMUNIK@UQUEBEC	Si les communications t'interessent (usagers,
COMP-CEN	COMP-CEN@UCCVMA	Computer Center Managers' Issues
COMP-SCI	COMP-SCI@TAUNIVM	Comp-Sci Distribution lis
COMPOS	COMPOS@FINHUTC	Composing Digest
COMSOC-L	COMSOC-L@BYUVM	(Computers and Society ARPA Digest)

COMSRV-L	COMSRV-L@YALEVM	Computer Support Services Discussion Group
CONFER-L	CONFER-L@NCSUVM	Academic Interactive Conferencing Discussion
CONFOCAL	CONFOCAL@UBVM	Confocal Microscopy List
CONS-L	CONS-L@MCGILL1	CONSULTANTS FORUM
CONSIM-L	CONSIM-L@UALTAVM	Conflict simulation Games
CONSLINK	CONSLINK@SIVM	Discussion on Biological Conservation
CONSULT	CONSULT@NERVM	NERDC Consulting - send questions here
	CONSULT@PURCCVM	PUCC Consultants
	CONSULT@WAYNEST1	C&IT/PaSS CONSULTING LIST
CONTEX-L	CONTEX-L@UOTTAWA	Ancient Texts Discussion Group List.
COORD-DE	COORD-DE@ICINECA	COORD-DE (GRUPPO DI COORDINAMENTO RETE DECNET
CORRYFEE	CORRYFEE@HASARA11	List of the Faculty of Economics, University
CORSI	CORSI@IGECUNIV	CORSINotizie su corsi, seminari, ecc.
COUPROG	COUPROG@UOGUELPH	PROGRAM COMMITTEE DISCUSSION
CPAC-L	CPAC-L@MARIST	ConnectPac(tm) Discussion list
CPR4-L	CPR4-L@UIUCVMD	CP release 4 discussions
CPR5-L	CPR5-L@UIUCVMD	CP release 5 discussions
CPT-L	CPT-L@PURCCVM	Mailing list for all CPT students
CPTCOOP	CPTCOOP@PURCCVM	CPT Co-op discussion list
CPTFAC-L	CPTFAC-L@PURCCVM	All CPT Faculty
CPTLAB-L	CPTLAB-L@PURCCVM	CPT Lab discussion list
CPTSTAFF	CPTSTAFF@PURCCVM	All CPT Faculty/Clerical/Admin Staff & PSTECH
CPTWIN-L	CPTWIN-L@PURCCVM	CPT Faculty Windows Users Group
CPT150-L	CPT150-L@PURCCVM	CPT 150 discussion list
CPT165-L	CPT165-L@PURCCVM	CPT 165 discussion list
CPT175-B	CPT175-B@PURCCVM	CPT 175 Section B discussion list
CPT175-E	CPT175-E@PURCCVM	CPT 175 Section E discussion list
CPT175-M	CPT175-M@PURCCVM	CPT 175 Section M discussion list
CPT244-L	CPT244-L@PURCCVM	CPT 244 discussion list
CPT265-L	CPT265-L@PURCCVM	CPT 265 discussion list
CPT365-L	CPT365-L@PURCCVM	CPT 365 discussion list

CPT487D	CPT487D@PURCCVM	CPT 487D discussion list
CPT488-L	CPT488-L@PURCCVM	CPT 488 discussion list
CRAY-L	CRAY-L@UTORONTO	Ontario Universities Cray Users Discussion Li
CRHLOG	CRHLOG@UIUCVMD	CSO Snack Bar Site On-line Logbook
CRIBBAGE	CRIBBAGE@INDYCMS	Cribbage.
CRTNET	CRTNET@FINHUTC	(Peered) Communication Research and Theory Ne
	CRTNET@PSUVM	(Peered) Communication Research and Theory Ne
CRYPTO-L	CRYPTO-L@JPNTOHOK	Forum on Cryptology and Related Mathematics
CSA-DATA	CSA-DATA@UICVM	Chinese Statistical Archive
CSAC	CSAC@UVMVM	CSAC: Computing Strategies Across the Curricu
CSAMIGA	CSAMIGA@DHDURZ1	CSAMIGA COMP.SYS.AMIGA.TECH redist.
CSEMLIST	CSEMLIST@HASARA11	List of the Society of Computer Science in Ec
CSG-L	CSG-L@UIUCVMD	Control Systems Group Network (CSGnet)
CSIS	CSIS@PACEVM	CSIS
CSLESL	CSLESL@PSUVM	Regional DEC CSLG/ESL Discussions
CSP-L	CSP-L@TREARN	Cross System Product Discussion List
CSR-L	CSR-L@UALTAVM	University of Alberta Center for Systems Rese
CSRNOT-L	CSRNOT-L@UIUCVMD	Center for the Study of Reading Contact list
CSUPDATE	CSUPDATE@INDYCMS	IUPUI Computing Services Announcements and Up
CSYS-AMI	CSYS-AMI@UMAINECS	Re-distribution of comp.sys.amiga group from
CS256	CS256@IPFWVM	CS256 COURSE DISCUSSION LIST
CUC-L	CUC-L@FRORS12	Comite des Utilisateurs du CIRCE
CUCOM-L	CUCOM-L@UNBVM1	Computer Users Committee List
CUGM-L	CUGM-L@TAMVM1	TAMU Computer Users Group Meeting list
CUMREC-L	CUMREC-L@NDSUVM1	CUMREC-L Administrative computer use

CUM90-L	CUM90-L@UBVM	CUMREC '90 Discussion List
CUR-L	CUR-L@MITVMA	Computer Usage Report List
CURRICUL	CURRICUL@PURCCVM	CPT Curriculum Mailing List
CW-EMAIL	CW-EMAIL@TECMTYVM	Campus-Wide Electronic Mail Systems discussio
CWIS-L	CWIS-L@WUVMD	Campus-Wide Information Systems
CWLOG	CWLOG@UIUCVMD	CSO CW Site Online Logbook
CYAN-TOX	CYAN-TOX@GREARN	The Cyanobacterial Toxins Discussion List
CYBER-L	CYBER-L@BITNIC	(Peered) CYBER List
	CYBER-L@DEARN	(Peered) CYBER List
	CYBER-L@EB0UB011	(Peered) CYBER Users Mailing List
	CYBER-L@FINHUTC	(Peered) CYBER List
	CYBER-L@UGA	(Peered) CDC Computer Discussion
CYBSYS-L	CYBSYS-L@BINGVMB	Cybernetics and Systems
CYRILLIC	CYRILLIC@ASUACAD	Russian Language List
C18-L	C18-L@PSUVM	18th Century Interdisciplinary Discussion
C370-L	C370-L@NCSUVM	C/370 Discussion List
	C370-L@UIUCVMD	C370-L (archive files only)
DAIRY-L	DAIRY-L@UMDD	Dairy Discussion List.
DAL-L	DAL-L@MITVMA	Data Access Language List (DAL, formerly CL/1
DANCE-L	DANCE-L@HEARN	International folkdance and traditional dance
DARGON-L	DARGON-L@NCSUVM	Dargon Project Writers Forum
DATUS-L	DATUS-L@DEARN	DATUS Anwendergruppe
DAVID-L	DAVID-L@UHCCVM	David Lassner's List
DBASE-L	DBASE-L@TECMTYVM	Discussion on the use of the dBase language a
DBCLASS	DBCLASS@PURCCVM	CPT 382/482 discussion list
DBL3-L	DBL3-L@LEPICS	Open forum on L3 Databases
DB2-L	DB2-L@AUVM	DB2 Data Base Discussion List
DCRLY-L	DCRLY-L@AUVM	Wash_DC Relay Mailing List
DEAF-L	DEAF-L@SIUCVMB	DEAF LIST
DEAR-BOD	DEAR-BOD@IRLEARN	EARN Directors - open submission

DEARN-ONLY-I-...	I-AMIGA@DEARN	- DELETED PEER of: Info-Amiga List
DEARNADM	DEARNADM@DEARN	Node administrators/ contacts of German EARN n
DEARNDIR	DEARNDIR@DEARN	Directors of German EARN nodes/sites
DEMO	DEMO@UQUEBEC	Liste de demonstration
DEMO-L	DEMO-L@JPNSUT10	demonstration for JPNSUT20
DENTAL	MEMBERS@UMAB	DENTAL TEST LIST
DENTALMA	DENTALMA@UCF1VM	For Dentistry related articles reports and te
DEPORTES	DEPORTES@ANDESCOL	Actividad Deportiva Mundial
DESERT-D	DESERT-D@PCCVM	Open Discussion forum on Operation Desert Sto
DESERT-L	DESERT-L@PCCVM	Open Discussion forum on Operation Desert Sto
DESIGN-L	DESIGN-L@PSUVM	Basic Design (Art and Architecture)
	DESIGN-L@UKANVM	"KU Computer Center Local Area Networking Des
DESQVIEW	DESQVIEW@BRUFPB	List for Desqview and Qemm users
DEVELCOM	DEVELCOM@RPICICGE	Communication and Human Development
	DEVELCOM@RPIECS	Communication and Human Development
DFNMVS	DFNMVS@DEARN	(Peered) DFN-Software Diskussionsforum MVS
DFNVM	DFNVM@DEARN	(Peered) DFN-Software Diskussionsforum VM
DFW-NET	DFW-NET@UTDALVM1	Dallas/Fort Worth networking issues list
DHAC	DHAC@PURCCVM	CPT Department Head's Advisory Committee
DHEP-L	DHEP-L@DEARN	DHEP-L
DHEPTC-L	DHEPTC-L@DEARN	DHEPTC-L
DIABETES	DIABETES@IRLEARN	International Research Project on Diabetes
DIABETIC	DIABETIC@PCCVM	Open Discussion forum for DIABETIC patient co
DIAL-L	DIAL-L@BRLNCC	"USUARIOS REMOTOS VIA LINHA DISCADA"
DIET	DIET@INDYCMS	Support and Discussion of Weight Loss
DIP-D	DIP-D@UWAVM	Diplomacy Digest (Moderated)
DIPL-L	DIPL-L@MITVMA	Discussion Group for

		the Game Diplomacy
DIS-L	DIS-L@IUBVM	DIS-L, a list of Drosophila workers to receiv
DISARM-D	DISARM-D@ALBNYVM1	Disarmament Discussion Monthly Digest
DISARM-L	DISARM-L@ALBNYVM1	Disarmament Discussion List
DISPRAC	DISPRAC@RPICICGE	Disciplinary practices in Communication Studi
	DISPRAC@RPIECS	Disciplinary Practices in Comm. Studies
DISSPLA	DISSPLA@TAUNIVM	DISSPLA List
DIST-CPM	DIST-CPM@RPICICGE	INFO-CPM Mailing List
	DIST-CPM@RPIECS	INFO-CPM Mailing List
DIST-HAM	DIST-HAM@RPICICGE	Info-Hams redistribution
	DIST-HAM@RPIECS	Info-Hams redistribution
DIST-MDM	DIST-MDM@RPICICGE	INFO-MODEMS Mailing List
	DIST-MDM@RPIECS	INFO-MODEMS Mailing List
DIST-MIC	DIST-MIC@RPICICGE	Info-Micro Mailing List
	DIST-MIC@RPIECS	Info-Micro Mailing List
DISTED	DISTED@UWAVM	Online Journal of Distance Ed. and Communications
DIV28	DIV28@GWUVM	APA's Division 28 Discussion List
DJ-L	DJ-L@NDSUVM1	DJ-L - Campus Radio Disk Jockeys
DNC-L	DNC-L@DEARN	DNC-L
DOEXP	DOEXP@USCVM	Electronic Library Consortium Requests ("The
DOHMEM-L	DOHMEM-L@ALBNYDH2	NEW YORK STATE DEPARMENT OF HEALTH MEMORANDA
DOMAIN	DOMAIN@ICNUCEVM	CNUCE Gestione Domini Posta Elettronica
DOMAIN-L	DOMAIN-L@BITNIC	(Peered) Domains Discussion Group
	DOMAIN-L@DEARN	(Peered) Domain discussion group
	DOMAIN-L@EB0UB011	(Peered) Domains discussion group
DOMAINIT	DOMAINIT@IBACSATA	Responsabili dei domini Italiani di Posta ele
DOMAINS	DOMAINS@UKACRL	
DORMS-L	DORMS-L@TECMTYVM	Dorms-l Residence Halls: Something more than
DOST	DOST@TREARN	Turkish Scientists' Discussion Group

DOSVSE-L	DOSVSE-L@LEHIIBM1	"DOS/VSE discussion list"
DOWNTIME	DOWNTIME@PURCCVM	Scheduled downtime information group
DPMA-L	DPMA-L@PURCCVM	Discussion list for Purdue chapter of DPMA
DPRB-L	DPRB-L@ALBNYDH2	Data Protection Review Board Correspondence
DRIV-L	DRIV-L@TAMVM1	The TUG DVI driver standards discussion list
DRP-L	DRP-L@UOGUELPH	Disaster Recovery Plan for Computing Services
DRUGABUS	DRUGABUS@UMAB	Drug Abuse Education Information and Research
DSI	DSI@MAINE	DSI - Employer/ Employee cross reference list
DTEP-L	DTEP-L@BRLNCC	"BITNET STAFF AT LNCC"
DTS-L	DTS-L@IUBVM	Dead Teachers Society Discussion List
DYNA-L	DYNA-L@TAMVM1	Dyanplan Discussion List
DYNSYS-L	DYNSYS-L@PTEARN	UNC/ACSDynamic Systems.
	DYNSYS-L@UNCVM1	UNC/ACS Dynamic Systems.
D20A-L	D20A-L@MITVMA	10 Player Diplomacy Game List (Sam Huntsman a
EAESPNET	EAESPNET@BNANDP11	EAESP Forum
EARLYM-L	EARLYM-L@AEARN	Early Music Discussion List
EARN-BOD	EARN-BOD@IRLEARN	EARN Board of Directors
EARN-IP	EARN-IP@FRMOP11	EARN-IP Special Interest List
EARN-IXI	EARN-IXI@FRMOP11	EARN-IXI Testing
EARN-MC	EARN-MC@IRLEARN	EARN Membership Committee
EARN-NOG	EARN-NOG@FRMOP11	Network Operations Group
EARN-OPG	EARN-OPG@IRLEARN	EARN Operating Procedures Group
EARN-RIF	EARN-RIF@FRULM11	Noeuds EARN Region Ile de France
EARN-RPG	EARN-RPG@FRMOP11	EARN Routing Project Group
EARN-RTC	EARN-RTC@IRLEARN	EARN RTC Users Group
EARN-SNA	EARN-SNA@FRMOP11	EARN-SNA Coordination
EARN-UG	EARN-UG@IRLEARN	EARN Users Group Dis-

		cussion List
EARN-X25	EARN-X25@IRLEARN	EARN X.25 Project Coordination and Technical
EARNBRUK	EARNBRUK@NOBIVM	List for EARN users i Norway.
EARNEWS	EARNEWS@FRMOP11	EARN News
EARNEXEC	EARNEXEC@IRLEARN	EARN Executive
EARNINFO	EARNINFO@FRMOP11	EARN Group on Information Services
EARNSTAT	EARNSTAT@DEARN	EARN Statistics Group
EARNTECH	EARNTECH@BITNIC	(Peered) EARN Technical Group
	EARNTECH@CEARN	(Peered) EARN Technical Group
EASI-EPC	EASI-EPC@DEARN	EASInet Project Committee
EASI-EUR	EASI-EUR@DEARN	EASInet EUropean Report List
EASI-REP	EASI-REP@DEARN	EASInet report list
EBCBBUL	EBCBBUL@HDETUD1	Computers in Biotechnology, Research and Education
EBCBCAT	EBCBCAT@HDETUD1	Catalogue of 'Biotechnological' software
ECCIRN-O	ECCIRN-O@HEARN	EuroCCIRN Open Distribution List
ECL3-L	ECL3-L@LEPICS	Open forum on the ECL3 program
ECONED-L	ECONED-L@UTDALLAS	Research in Economic Education
	ECONED-L@UTDALVM1	Research in Economic Education
ECONOMY	ECONOMY@TECMTYVM	Economic Problems in Less Developed Countries
ECP-MECH	ECP-MECH@FRECP12	Ecole d'ete de mecanique de l'Ecole Centrale
ECP-PIF	ECP-PIF@FRECP12	Programme International de Formation
ECP_NET	ECP_NET@FRECP12	Revue de Presse VIA — E.C.P., France
ECU-L	ECU-L@ECUVM1	East Carolina University User and Alumni List
EDAD-L	EDAD-L@WVNVM	Educational Administration Discussion List
EDD-L	EDD-L@KENTVM	"The EDD Data Editor List, rev 0"
EDI-L	EDI-L@UCCVMA	Electronic Data Interchange Issues
EDINFO-L	EDINFO-L@IUBVM	Educational Information list

EDNET6-L	EDNET6-L@IUBVM	K-12 Network Management Plan
EDPOLICY	EDPOLICY@PURCCVM	CPT Educational Policy Committee
EDPOLYAN	EDPOLYAN@ASUACAD	Professionals and Students Discussing Educati
EDSERV-L	EDSERV-L@UKANVM	"KU Educational Services Staff"
EDTECH	EDTECH@OHSTVMA	EDTECH - Educational Technology
EDUC	EDUC@UQUEBEC	Chercheurs en education
EDUCAI-L	EDUCAI-L@WVNVM	Educational Applications of Artificial Intell
EDUCOM-W	EDUCOM-W@BITNIC	EDUCOM-W - EDUCOM Women and Information Technology
EDUNET	EDUNET@FRMOP11	Comite de pilotage du serveur de logiciel
EDUNET-D	EDUNET-D@FRMOP11	Comite de pilotage du serveur de logiciel
EDUSIG-L	EDUSIG-L@UBVM	DECUS EDUSIG Discussion List
EDUTEL	EDUTEL@RPIECS	Education and information technologies
EEELOG	EEELOG@UIUCVMD	Engineering Workstation Lab at EE building
EEHLOG	EEHLOG@UIUCVMD	Engineering Workstation Lab at EH building
EELOG	EELOG@UIUCVMD	CSO EE Site Online Logbook
EEPG-L	EEPG-L@HEARN	Distribution list for the EEPG workinggroup o
EISSIG	EISSIG@ASUACAD	Executive Information Systems Special Interes
EJCREC	EJCREC@RPIECS	Electronic Journal of Communication
ELLASBIB	ELLASBIB@GREARN	List for the Greek Library Automation System.
ELN-L	ELN-L@UVVM	BC Electronic Library Network Project
EMACS	EMACS@TCSVM	(Peered) UNIX-EMACS distribution list
EMAIL-L	EMAIL-L@ALBNYDH2	NYDoH List for comments/problems/ suggestions
EMBL-DB	EMBL-DB@IRLEARN	BIOSCI EMBL-Databank Bulletin Board
EMBLGR	EMBLGR@GREARN	Greek EMBL Managment List.
EMELOG	EMELOG@UIUCVMD	Engineering Workstation Lab at ME building

EMFLDS-L	EMFLDS-L@UBVM	Electromagnetics in Medicine, Science & Comun
EMULPC-L	EMULPC-L@USACHVM1	"Emulation SW & HW on the IBM-PC"
EMUSIC-D	EMUSIC-D@AUVM	Electronic Music Digest
EMUSIC-L	EMUSIC-L@AUVM	Electronic Music Discussion List
ENERGY-L	ENERGY-L@TAUNIVM	Energy List
ENEWS	ENEWS@NCSUVM	NCSU Computing Center Electronic Newsletter
ENGLISH	ENGLISH@UTARLVM1	Dept. of English Discussion
ENVBEH-L	ENVBEH-L@POLYGRAF	Forum on Environment and Human Behavior
EPID-L	EPID-L@QUCDN	Topics in Epidemiology and Biostatistics
EPP-L	EPP-L@BUACCA	Albert Einstein Papers Project and Discussion
ERIC-L	ERIC-L@IUBVM	Experimental list for teaching and study of L
ESC-L	ESC-L@SNYCENVM	Empire State College CMS Users
ESE-L	ESE-L@SBCCVM	Expert Systems Environment mailing list.
ESL-L	ESL-L@UBVM	DECUS Education Software Library Discussion List
ESPER-L	ESPER-L@TREARN	Esperanto List
ESTAFF	ESTAFF@OHSTVMA	ESTAFF Educational Studies Staff
ESTFAC	ESTFAC@OHSTVMA	ESTFAC Educational Studies Faculty
ETC-L	ETC-L@UKANVM	"KU Academic User Services Open Discussion"
ETHICS-L	ETHICS-L@DEARN	(Peered) Discussion of Ethics in Computing
	ETHICS-L@MARIST	(Peered) Discussion of Ethics in Computing
	ETHICS-L@POLYGRAF	(Peered) Discussion of Ethics in Computing
	ETHICS-L@TWNMOE10	Ethics in computing discussion list
	ETHICS-L@UGA	(Peered) Discussion of Ethics in Computing
ETHMUS-L	ETHMUS-L@UMDD	EthnoFORUM, a global ethnomusicology forum.
ETHNO	ETHNO@RPICICGE	Ethnomethodology/ conversation analysis
	ETHNO@RPIECS	Ethnomethodology/ conversation analysis

ETHOLOGY	ETHOLOGY@FINHUTC	Ethology
ETHTECHL	ETHTECHL@NASVM	COSEPUP Teleconferencing list
EU-SOAR	EU-SOAR@HEARN	EU-SOAR European SOAR research communications
EUDORA	EUDORA@UIUCVMD	Eudora mailing list
EUROMAT	EUROMAT@FRMOP11	Euro Materiaux
EWM	EWM@ICNUCEVM	EWM European Women in Mathematics
EXECSEC	EXECSEC@UTORONTO	Netnorth Executive Secretary
EXEC28	EXEC28@GWUVM	APA's Division 28 Executive Board Discussion
EXPER-L	EXPER-L@TREARN	Experiences on Viral Attacks
EXTECH-L	EXTECH-L@VTVM1	Extension Technology Conference
EXTSTAFF	EXTSTAFF@VTVM1	All Extension Staff (EXTSTAFF)
EZT-L	EZT-L@MITVMA	EASYTRIEVE PLUS and EZ/KEY Info Exchange
FACAFF	FACAFF@PURCCVM	CPT Faculty Affairs Committee
FACDEV-L	FACDEV-L@UNBVM1	AAU Faculty Development Committee
FACILITY	FACILITY@PURCCVM	CPT Computer Coordinating Committee
FACSEN-L	FACSEN-L@UBVM	UB Faculty Senate Discussion List
FACSER-L	FACSER-L@WVNVM	Facilities and Services Discussion List
FALBTI-L	FALBTI-L@UTDALLAS	BTI/K200/NECU driver distribution list
	FALBTI-L@UTDALVM1	BTI/K200/NECU driver distribution list
FAMCOMM	FAMCOMM@RPICICGE	Marital/family & relational communication
	FAMCOMM@RPIECS	Marital/family & relational communication
FAMILY-L	FAMILY-L@UMCVMB	Delivery of Family Practice and Clinical Medi
FAMLYSCI	FAMLYSCI@UKCC	Family Science Network
FAMSTECH	FAMSTECH@ASUACAD	Financial Aid Systems - Technical Discussion
FARLOG	FARLOG@UIUCVMD	CSO FAR Site Online Logbook
FASTBS-L	FASTBS-L@UALTAVM	FASTBUS Discussion
FASTLN-L	FASTLN-L@VTVM1	(Peered) Virginia Tech Computing Center News
	FASTLN-L@VTVM2	(Peered) Virginia Tech

		Computing Center News
FELINE-L	FELINE-L@PCCVM	Discussion forum for Cat fanciers
FICINO	FICINO@UTORONTO	FICINO Discussion - Renaissance and Reformati
FIGI-L	FIGI-L@SCFVM	Forth Interest Group International List
FILM-L	FILM-L@VMTECMEX	Film making and reviews list.
FINE-ART	FINE-ART@EB0UB011	(Peered) Fine-Art Forum
	FINE-ART@RUTVM1	(Peered) Fine-Art Forum
FINTF	FINTF@BITNIC	Name of list: FinTF
FIREARMS	FIREARMS@UTARLVM1	FIREARMS Discussion List
FISC-L	FISC-L@NDSUVM1	FISC-L Fee-Based Info Serv Centers in Academi
FISICA-L	FISICA-L@BRUFMG	(Peered) Forum FISICA-L
	FISICA-L@BRUFPB	(Peered) Forum FISICA-L
	FISICA-L@BRUFSC	(Peered) Forum FISICA-L
	FISICA-L@UFRJ	(Peered) Forum FISICA-L
	FISICA-L@UKACRL	(Peered) Forum FISICA-L
FLAIRS	FLAIRS@UCF1VM	FLorida Artificial Intelligence Research Symp
FLYFISH	FLYFISH@UMAB	Fly Fishing Digest
FOCUS-L	FOCUS-L@ASUACAD	FOCUS-L
FOLKLORE	FOLKLORE@TAMVM1	Folklore Discussion List
FORAGE	FORAGE@ORSTVM	FORAGE WORKERS LIST
FOREIGN	FOREIGN@JPNKISCT	Foreigner students group list of K.I.T
FOREIGNS	FOREIGNS@JPNKISCI	(Peered) Open discussion for Foreigner studen
	FOREIGNS@JPNKISCT	(Peered) Open discussion for Foreigner students
FORUMBIO	FORUMBIO@BNANDP11	Forum on molecular biology
FOTO-L	FOTO-L@UFRJ	Foto-L - Forum for talk about Photography
FR-SNA	FR-SNA@FRMOP11	reseau SNA Francais
FRAC-A	FRAC-A@UIUCVMD	FRAC-A (archive files only)
FRAC-L	FRAC-L@GITVM1	"FRACTAL" discussion list
FRANKLIN	FRANKLIN@NCSUVM	Benjamin Franklin Scholars List
FREETALK	FREETALK@KRSNUCC1	A list for free-talking
FUNDLIST	FUNDLIST@JHUVM	List for the discussion of university fund ra

FUSION	FUSION@NDSUVM1	Fusion - Redistribution of sci.physics.fusion
FUTURE-L	FUTURE-L@BITNIC	(Peered) BITNET Futures List
	FUTURE-L@DEARN	(Peered) Discussion about the future of BITNET
	FUTURE-L@EB0UB011	(Peered) Future Developments List
	FUTURE-L@FINHUTC	(Peered) Discussion about the future of BITNET
	FUTURE-L@HEARN	(Peered) Discussion about the future of BITNET
	FUTURE-L@MARIST	(Peered) Discussion about the future of BITNET
	FUTURE-L@UGA	(Peered) Future Developments
FWAKE-L	FWAKE-L@IRLEARN	Finnegans Wake (by James Joyce) Discussion List
FWAKEN-L	FWAKEN-L@IRLEARN	Finnegans Wake - Textual Notes
FYS-INFO	FYS-INFO@FINHUTC	Fysiikan tapahtumakalenteri
GAELIC-L	GAELIC-L@IRLEARN	GAELIC Language Bulletin Board
GAMES-L	GAMES-L@BROWNVM	(Peered) Computer Games List
	GAMES-L@KRSNUCC1	(Peered) Computer Games List
	GAMES-L@LEHIIBM1	(Peered) Computer Games List
	GAMES-L@UTARLVM1	(Peered) Computer Games List
GARR$IP	GARR$IP@ICNUCEVM	GARR-IP Gruppo di Lavoro sulle reti IP per la
GARR-IP	GARR-IP@ICNUCEVM	GARR-IP Gruppo di Lavoro sulle reti IP per la
GARR-PE	GARR-PE@IBACSATA	(Peered) GARR (Research Networks Harmonization
	GARR-PE@ICNUCEVM	(Peered) GARR (Research Networks Harmonization
GBRC-L	GBRC-L@LEPICS	L3 Analysis Group Beta Resource Commitment
GCS-L	GCS-L@UIUCVMD	GCS discussions
GCSCHE-L	GCSCHE-L@UNBVM1	Graduate CSCHE chap-

		ters list
GDDM-L	GDDM-L@POLYGRAF	The GDDM Discussion list
GEL2D	GEL2D@FRULM11	Groupe des utilisateurs d'electrophorese bidi
GEN	GEN@UIUCVMD	Name
GENBANKB	GENBANKB@IRLEARN	BIOSCI GENBANK-BB Bulletin Board
GENDER	GENDER@RPICICGE	Communication and gender
	GENDER@RPIECS	Study of communication and gender
GENE-ORG	GENE-ORG@IRLEARN	BIOSCI Genomic-Organization Bulletin Board
GEODESIC	GEODESIC@UBVM	List for the discussion of Buckminster Fuller
GEOGRAPH	GEOGRAPH@FINHUTC	Geography
GERINET	GERINET@UBVM	Geriatric Health Care Discussion Group
GFULMED	GFULMED@NDSUVM1	GFULMED Grateful Med via BITNET
GGUIDE	GGUIDE@BITNIC	(Peered) BITNET User's Guide List
	GGUIDE@DEARN	(Peered) Users Guide list
	GGUIDE@EB0UB011	(Peered) Users Guide List
	GGUIDE@FINHUTC	(Peered) Users Guide List
	GGUIDE@HEARN	(Peered) Users Guide list
	GGUIDE@MARIST	(Peered) Users Guide list
	GGUIDE@UGA	(Peered) BITNIC GGUIDE List
GIF-L	GIF-L@VMTECMEX	GIF Graphics and applications list.
GIS-L	GIS-L@UBVM	Geographic Information Systems Discussion Lis
GMAIL-D	GMAIL-D@UBVM	GMAIL Distribution List
GMAST-L	GMAST-L@UTCVM	Gamemasters Interest Group
GML-L	GML-L@DB0FUB11	GML discussion list
GNOME-PR	GNOME-PR@IRLEARN	BIOSCI Human Genome Program Bulletin Board
GNUEMACS	GNUEMACS@FINHUTC	Gnu-Emacs bugs & info
GONE-L	GONE-L@TAUNIVM	GONE Rexx EXEC discussion list
GOULDBUG	GOULDBUG@CLVM	Gould CSD User's List
GOVDOC-L	GOVDOC-L@PSUVM	Discussion of Government Document Issues
GRADCOLL	GRADCOLL@UVMVM	GRADCOLL: Graduate College News List
GRADREF	GRADREF@TEMPLEVM	CAS GRADREF INFORMATION

GRAFIK-L	GRAFIK-L@DEARN	GRAFIK-L
GRAFOS-L	GRAFOS-L@UFRJ	GRAFOS-L Aspectos matematicos e computacionai
GRANOLA	GRANOLA@BROWNVM	GRANOLA: Vegetarian Discussion List
GRANT-L	GRANT-L@UA1VM	OSP Funding Alert List
GRANTS-L	GRANTS-L@JHUVM	NSF Grants & Contracts Bulletin Board Bitnet
GRAPH-L	GRAPH-L@BRUFPB	Lista sobre Computacao Grafica
	GRAPH-L@YALEVM	Yale University Graphics Users
GRAPHICS	GRAPHICS@OHSTVMA	GRAPHICS OSU Computer Graphics Discussion Lis
GRAPHNET	GRAPHNET@NDSUVM1	GRAPHNET - Graph Theory
GRAVITY	GRAVITY@UWF	Gravity Topics for Spacetime Course - Spaceti
GRLINKFL	GRLINKFL@GREARN	Greek EARN Linkfail List
GRTECH	GRTECH@GREARN	Greek EARN Technical Group List
GRUNGE-L	GRUNGE-L@UBVM	Grunge Rock Discussion List
GUASTITP	GUASTITP@ICNUCEVM	CNUCE Reparto Infrastrutture di Rete per la R
GUM	GUM@BRUFMG	Grupo de Usuarios MUSIC do Brasil (GUM)
GUT	GUT@FRULM11	Groupe francophone des Utilisateurs TeX
GWCOMM	GWCOMM@GWUVM	GWU's GWCOMM Discussion List
GWDG-NEU	GWDG-NEU@DGOGWDG1	Mitteilungen der GWDG
GWTESTL	GWTESTL@GWUVM	Test list for LISTSERV at GWU
HAM-FCC	HAM-FCC@UIUCVMD	HAM-FCC Ham Radio FCC relations
HAM-TCP	HAM-TCP@UIUCVMD	Ham-Tcp (log files only)
HAM-UNIV	HAM-UNIV@UIUCVMD	HAM-UNIV Ham Radio University Clubs mailing l
HAMLICEN	HAMLICEN@UIUCVMD	HAMLICEN Ham Radio Licensing Discussion
HARLIC-L	HARLIC-L@RICELIBR	HARLIC Libraries discussion group
HCDB-L	HCDB-L@LEPICS	Open forum on the Hadron Calorimeter Data Bas
HD-MGRS	HD-MGRS@MITVMA	IS Help Desk Managers
HDESK-L	HDESK-L@WVNVM	Help Desk Discussions
HDR-PPL	HDR-PPL@MARIST	Header-People Dis.

	HDR-PPL@UIUCVMD	Hdr-Ppl (log files only)
HEALTH-L	HEALTH-L@IRLEARN	International Discussion on Health Research
HEALTHCO	HEALTHCO@RPICICGE	Communication in health/medical context
	HEALTHCO@RPIECS	Communication in health/medical context
HEAVY-L	HEAVY-L@LEPICS	Heavy Monte-Carlo Flavours Subgroup
HEDSDIRS	HEDSDIRS@BITNIC	HEDSDIRS - HEDS Board of Directors and Staff
HEGEL	HEGEL@VILLVM	Discussion list for HEG-EL society.
HELLAS	HELLAS@AUVM	(Peered) The Hellenic Discussion List
	HELLAS@BROWNVM	(Peered) The Hellenic Discussion List
	HELLAS@GREARN	(Peered) The Hellenic DiscussionList
HELP-NET	HELP-NET@TEMPLEVM	BITNET/CREN/ INTERNET Help Resource.
HELPDESK	HELPDESK@TAMVM1	Texas A&M University HELPDESK List
HELPNET	HELPNET@NDSUVM1	HELPNET Network Emergency Response Planning
HEPNET-J	HEPNET-J@JPNKEKVM	Japanese HEPnet Discussion List
HEPVM	HEPVM@CEARN	HEPVM List
	HEPVM@EB0UB011	CEARN HEPVM Redistribution List
HGML-L	HGML-L@YALEVM	Human Gene Mapping Library
HHI-RES	HHI-RES@UTARLVM1	HHI Research Findings
HIRIS-L	HIRIS-L@IVEUNCC	HIgh Resolution Infrared Spectroscopy - List
HIROKO	HIROKO@JPNKISCI	(Peered) Taniyama.Hiroko list group (Using KA
	HIROKO@JPNSUT30	(Peered) Taniyama Hiroko list group
HISTORY	HISTORY@FINHUTC	History
HIT	HIT@UFRJ	Highly Imaginative Tech. - Science Fiction
HLPCMD-L	HLPCMD-L@BROWNVM	HELP Commands for VM/CMS
HOCKEY-L	HOCKEY-L@MAINE	College Hockey discussion list
HOMESAT	HOMESAT@NDSUVM1	HOMESAT - Home Satel-

		lite Technology
HONORS	HONORS@GWUVM	GWU's Honors Program Discussion List
HORROR	HORROR@PACEVM	Horror
HORT-L	HORT-L@VTVM1	Va Tech Horticulture Dept. - Monthly Releases
HP-28	HP-28@NDSUVM1	HP-28 - HP-28C and HP-28S Calculators
HP-48	HP-48@NDSUVM1	HP-48 - HP-48sx Hand Held System
HPMINI-L	HPMINI-L@UAFSYSB	Hewlett-Packard 9000 Series MiniComputer Disc
HP3000-L	HP3000-L@UTCVM	HP-3000 Systems Dis
HRD-L	HRD-L@UMCVMB	Human Resource Development Group List
HRI-L	HRI-L@HEARN	High Resolution Imaging in Astronomy, Discuss
HRIS-L	HRIS-L@UALTAVM	Human Resources Information (Canada)
HRMS-L	HRMS-L@UKANVM	"KU Student Records Information System Staff"
HRMS-TLS	HRMS-TLS@SNYCENVM	SUNY HRMS Technical users list
HRMS-ULS	HRMS-ULS@SNYCENVM	SUNY HRMS Users LIST
HSPNET-D	HSPNET-D@ALBNYDH2	Hospital Computer Network Discussion Group an
HSPNET-L	HSPNET-L@ALBNYDH2	Hospital Computer Network Discussion Group an
HULINTRO	HULINTRO@HARVARDA	HULINTRO - Harvard University Library Intro
HUMANETS	HUMANETS@RUTVM1	Human Nets Digest
HUMANIST	HUMANIST@BROWNVM	HUMANIST Discussion
HUMBUL	HUMBUL@UKACRL	HUMBUL
HUNGARY	HUNGARY@UCSBVM	Hungarian Discussion List
HYPBAR-L	HYPBAR-L@TECHNION	HyperBaric & Diving Medicine List
HYPERCRD	HYPERCRD@PURCCVM	Hypercard Discussion List
HYPERMED	HYPERMED@UMAB	Biomedical Hypermedia Instructional Design
I-AMIGA	I-AMIGA@FINHUTC	(Peered) Info-Amiga List
	I-AMIGA@RUTVM1	(Peered) Info-Amiga List
	AMIGA-L@UALTAVM	(Peered) Info-Amiga List
I-IBMPC	I-IBMPC@UIUCVMD	IBM PC discussions
I-PACRAD	I-PACRAD@UIUCVMD	Packet Radio
I-UNIX	I-UNIX@TCSVM	Info-Unix distribution list

I-VIDTEK	I-VIDTEK@UIUCVMD	VideoTech
IA-ADS	IA-ADS@MARIST	IA's ADS Discussion
IA-FRS	IA-FRS@MARIST	IA's FRS Discussion
IA-HRS	IA-HRS@MARIST	IA's HRS Discussion
IA-SIS	IA-SIS@MARIST	IA's SIS Discussion
IAIMU-L	IAIMU-L@ULKYVM	IDMS-based I/A software discussion list
IAMEX-L	IAMEX-L@TECMTYVM	Iamex-l Artificial Intelligence list of ITESM
IAPSY-L	IAPSY-L@ALBNYVM1	Interamerican Psychologists List (SIPNET)
IBM-HESC	IBM-HESC@PSUORVM	IBM Higher Education Consortium
IBM-KERM	IBM-KERM@CUVMA	IBM mainframe KERMIT developers
IBM-MAIN	IBM-MAIN@AKRONVM	(Peered) IBM Mainframe Discussion List
	IBM-MAIN@DEARN	(Peered) IBM Mainframe Discussion List
	IBM-MAIN@EB0UB011	(Peered) IBM Mainframe Discussion List
IBM-NETS	IBM-NETS@BITNIC	BITNIC IBM-NETS List
	IBM-NETS@FINHUTC	(Peered) IBM networking
	IBM-NETS@UGA	IBM Networking
IBM-SRD	IBM-SRD@NDSUVM1	IBM-SRD Screen Reader
IBMSYS-L	IBMSYS-L@UHCCVM	UHCC IBM Mainframe System Discussion List
IBMTCP-L	IBMTCP-L@PUCC	IBM TCP/IP List
	IBMTCP-L@UIUCVMD	IBMTCP-L (log files only)
IBM7171	IBM7171@IRLEARN	Protocol Converter List
	IBM7171@UIUCVMD	Log files only
IBYCUS-L	IBYCUS-L@USCVM	The Ibycus Scholarly Computer discussion list
ICEC-NET	MD40@CMUCCVMA	ICEC-Net Mailing List
ICRC-L	ICRC-L@IRLEARN	22nd Int'l Cosmic Ray Conference List
ICU-L	ICU-L@UBVM	Instruction Computing Update Newsletter List
IDFORUM	IDFORUM@YORKVM1	Industrial Design Forum
IDMS-L	IDMS-L@UGA	Cullinet IDMS Discussion
IDRISI-L	IDRISI-L@UOGUELPH	idrisi digest
IEEE-L	IEEE-L@USACHVM1	"Eventos en Ingenieria Electrica e Informatic
IERGNRL	IERGNRL@TECHNION	I.E.& M. - General User Group
IERLIST	IERLIST@TECHNION	I.E.& M. - Faculty
IFIP-MMM	IFIP-MMM@IBACSATA	IFIP Multimedia Multimode Messaging

IFIP84	IFIP84@UKACRL	IFIP84
IFPHEN-L	IFPHEN-L@WSUVM1	Interfacial Phenomena Interest List
IFPS-L	IFPS-L@VTVM2	Interactive Financial Planning System
IIESCNET	IIESCNET@ASUACAD	IIE Student Communications Network
ILL-L	ILL-L@UVMVM	ILL-L: Interlibrary Loan discussion group
IMAGEN-L	IMAGEN-L@UOGUELPH	IMAGEN Laser Printer Discussion
INCLEN-L	INCLEN-L@MCMVM1	INCLEN-L LIST
INDIA	INDIA@PCCVM	The India List
INDIA-D	INDIA-D@TEMPLEVM	(Peered) The Indian Interest Group
	INDIA-D@UKCC	(Peered) The Indian Interest Group
	INDIA-D@UTARLVM1	(Peered) The Indian Interest Group
INDIA-L	INDIA-L@UTARLVM1	The India News Network
INDIANWS	INDIANWS@PCCVM	The India List (NeWS)
INDNOTIS	INDNOTIS@INDYCMS	NOTIS implementation within the IU Library Sy
INDVIRUS	INDVIRUS@PURCCVM	Virus Info for Universities in Indiana
INDYMAIN	INDYMAIN@INDYCMS	IUPUI Mainframe Discussion List
INDYSAS	INDYSAS@INDYCMS	SAS at IUPUI
INDYSPSS	INDYSPSS@INDYCMS	SPSSx at IUPUI
INET91-L	INET91-L@NEUVM1	Information on the INET'91 conference
INF-Z100	INF-Z100@CLVM	Heath/Zenith Z100 Information Mailing List
INFINITE	INFINITE@FINHUTC	Info-Finite
INFO-ADA	INFO-ADA@FINHUTC	(Peered) Ada programming language (INFO-ADA)
	INFO-ADA@NDSUVM1	(Peered) Ada programming language (INFO-ADA)
INFO-APP	INFO-APP@NDSUVM1	INFO-APP Info-Apple List
INFO-ATARI16	INFO-A16@FINHUTC	(Peered) Atari ST users forum (INFO-ATARI16)
	INFO-A16@MARIST	(Peered) INFO-ATARI16 Discussion
	INFO-A16@TCSVM	(Peered) INFO-ATARI16 Discussion
	INFO-A16@UOGUELPH	(Peered) INFO-ATARI16 Discussion

INFO-ATARI8	INFO-A8@MARIST	(Peered) INFO-ATARI8 Discussion
INFO-AUX	INFO-AUX@PUCC	LISTSERV list for A/UX discussion and softwar
INFO-A8	INFO-A8@TCSVM	(Peered) INFO-ATARI8 Discussion
INFO-C	INFO-C@NDSUVM1	Info-C List
	INFO-C@UIUCVMD	INFO-C (log files only)
INFO-DEC	MD4J@CMUCCVMA	Info-DEC-Micro Mailing List
INFO-GCG	INFO-GCG@UTORONTO	INFO-GCG: GCG Genetics Software Discussion
INFO-GNU	INFO-GNU@FINHUTC	Gnu information
INFO-IBMPC	IBMPC-L@BNANDP11	(Peered) INFO-IBMPC Digest
	IBMPC-L@CEARN	(Peered) Info-IBMPC Digest
	IBMPC-L@DEARN	(Peered) IBMPC-L
	IBMPC-L@EB0UB011	(Peered) Info-IBMPC Digest
	IBMPC-L@FINHUTC	(Peered) Info-IBMPC Digest
	IBMPC-L@HEARN	(Peered) IBMPC-L
	IBMPC-L@POLYGRAF	(Peered) INFO-IBMPC Digest
	$$INFOPC@RICEVM1	(Peered) Info-IBMPC redistribution list
	IBMPC-L@TAMVM1	(Peered) INFO-IBMPC Digest
	IBMPC-L@TAUNIVM	(Peered) Info-IBMPC Digest
	IBMPC-L@UBVM	(Peered) INFO-IBMPC Digest
	IBMPC-L@UGA	(Peered) INFO-IBMPC Digest
	IBMPC-L@UTORONTO	(Peered) IBMPC Digest
	IBMPC-L@VTVM1	(Peered) INFO-IBMPC Digest
	IBMPC-L@VTVM2	(Peered) INFO-IBMPC Digest
INFO-KERMIT	I-KERMIT@BNANDP11	(Peered) INFO-KERMIT Digest
	I-KERMIT@CLVM	(Peered) INFO-KERMIT Digest
	I-KERMIT@CUVMA	(Peered) INFO-KERMIT Digest
	I-KERMIT@DEARN	(Peered) INFO-KERMIT Digest
	I-KERMIT@EB0UB011	(Peered) INFO-KERMIT Digest
	IKD@FINHUTC	(Peered) Info-Kermit Di-

		gest
	I-KERMIT@HEARN	(Peered) INFO-KERMIT Digest
	I-KERMIT@MARIST	(Peered) INFO-KERMIT Digest
	I-KERMIT@RUTVM1	(Peered) INFO-KERMIT Digest
	I-KERMIT@UTORONTO	(Peered) INFO-KERMIT Digest
	I-KERMIT@VTVM1	(Peered) INFO-KERMIT Digest
	I-KERMIT@VTVM2	(Peered) INFO-KERMIT Digest
INFO-MAC	INFO-MAC@BNANDP11	(Peered) INFO-MAC Digest
	INFO-MAC@CEARN	(Peered) INFO-MAC Digest
	INFO-MAC@DEARN	(Peered) INFO-MAC Digest
	INFO-MAC@ICNUCEVM	Informazioni sul Macintosh
	INFO-MAC@IRLEARN	INFO-MAC list
	INFO-MAC@RICEVM1	(Peered) INFO-MAC Digest
	INFO-MAC@UIUCVMD	(Peered) INFO-MAC Digest
	INFO-MAC@UTORONTO	(Peered) INFO-MAC Digest
INFO-M2	INFO-M2@UCF1VM	Modula2 List
INFO-NETS	INFONETS@BITNIC	(Peered) Info-Nets List
	INFONETS@DEARN	(Peered) Info-Nets List
	INFONETS@EB0UB011	(Peered) General network forum
	INFONETS@FINHUTC	(Peered) General network forum
	INFONETS@HEARN	(Peered) Info-Nets List
	INFONETS@MARIST	(Peered) Info-Nets List
INFO-PC	INFO-PC@IRLEARN	Distribution of Info-IBMPC
INFO-TI	INFO-TI@FINHUTC	TI Explorer
INFO-VAX	INFO-VAX@BNANDP11	(Peered) INFO-VAX Discussion
	MD4I@CMUCCVMA	(Peered) INFO-VAX Discussion
	INFO-VAX@DEARN	(Peered) Info Vax
	INFO-VAX@HEARN	(Peered) Info Vax
	INFO-VAX@IRLEARN	VAX Information Distribution List
	INFO-VAX@MARIST	(Peered) INFO-VAX Discussion
	INFO-VAX@TAMVM1	(Peered) INFO-VAX Dis-

		cussion
	INFO-VAX@TWNMOE10	INFO-VAX DEC VAX discussion group
	INFO-VAX@UBVM	(Peered) INFO-VAX Discussion
	INFO-VAX@UGA	(Peered) INFO-VAX Discussion
	INFO-VAX@VTVM2	(Peered) INFO-VAX Discussion
INFOCPM	INFOCPM@FINHUTC	CP/M operating system distribution list
INFOHAMS	INFOHAMS@TAUNIVM	INFOHAMS redistribution list
	INFOHAMS@UIUCVMD	InfoHams (log files only)
INFOSYS	INFOSYS@HDETUD1	Mailing list of information systems
INFO1100	INFO1100@FINHUTC	XEROX Lisp Machine Users List
INGRES-L	INGRES-L@HDETUD1	Discussion on the RDBMS INGRES
INGRESNL	INGRESNL@HDETUD1	Rotterdam/Delft INGRES-lijst
INNOPAC	INNOPAC@MAINE	III Online Public Access Catalog Discussion L
INSERM-L	INSERM-L@FRULM11	Conference electronique a l'INSERM
INTER-L	INTER-L@VTVM2	INTER-L is a Listerv operated by VPI&SU for N
INTERCUL	INTERCUL@RPICICGE	Cross-cultural communication
	INTERCUL@RPIECS	Study of intercultural communication
INTERF-L	INTERF-L@TAUNIVM	Israeli Group on Interfacial Phenomena
INTERNET	INTERNET@ICNUCEVM	ARPA-Internet News
INTERNS	INTERNS@GECRDVM1	CRD Interns List
INTERPER	INTERPER@RPICICGE	Interpersonal/small group communication
	INTERPER@RPIECS	Interpersonal/small group communication
INTGROUP	INTGROUP@NDSUVM1	INTGROUP - DATABASE Searchable Copy of INTERE
	INTGROUP@TECMTYVM	DATABASE Searchable Copy of INTEREST GROUPS L
INTLBU-L	INTLBU-L@TEMPLEVM	INTLBU-L International Business List
INTRPHYS	INTRPHYS@IDBSU	INTRPHYS (Interactive physics Teaching: MBL &
INTUDM-L	INTUDM-L@UTEPA	Using Intuition in Deci-

		sion Making
IOOB-L	IOOB-L@UGA	Industrial Psychology
IOOBF-L	IOOBF-L@UGA	Industrial Psychology Forum
IOUDAIOS	IOUDAIOS@YORKVM1	First Century Judaism Discussion Forum
IR-L	IR-L@UCCVMA	Information Retrieval List
IR-LIST	IR-LIST@IRLEARN	Information Retrieval Distribution List
IRCRETE	IRCRETE@IBACSATA	IRC Rete Interregionale IATINET
IRL-NET	IRL-NET@IRLEARN	Worldwide Irish-Interest Research Net
IRLIST-L	IRLIST-L@VTVM2	No title defined
IRSS-L	IRSS-L@UNCVM1	IRSS Staff and Users List.
ISCAMI	ISCAMI@GREARN	Computer Assist. Management & Manipulation of
ISCSTAFF	ISCSTAFF@JPNKISCI	(Peered) ISC staff list
	ISCSTAFF@JPNKISCT	(Peered) ISC staff list (staff only)
ISDS	ISDS@UIUCVMD	ISDS Illini Space Development Society List
ISE-L	ISE-L@NMSUVM1	ISE LIST
ISETL-L	ISETL-L@CLVM	ISETL (Interpretive SETL) Discussion List
ISN	ISN@RITVM	ISN Data Switch Technical Discussion Group
ISO-MSGS	ISO-MSGS@IBACSATA	ISO WG4 Messaging
ISODE	ISODE@IRLEARN	ISO/OSI Protocol Development Environment Disc
ISO10646	ISO10646@JHUVM	Multi-byte Code Issues
ISO8859	ISO8859@JHUVM	ASCII/EBCDIC character set related issues
ISPF-L	ISPF-L@DB0FUB11	ISPF discussion list
ISRLOG	ISRLOG@UIUCVMD	CSO ISR Site Online Logbook
ISTAFF	ISTAFF@JPNKISCI	ISC iizuka staff list
ITALIC-L	ITALIC-L@IRLEARN	ITALIC-L - The Irish Tex And Latex Interest C
ITEX-L	ITEX-L@TAUNIVM	ITEX Discussion List
ITRDBFOR	ITRDBFOR@ASUACAD	Dendrochronology Forum for the International
IUTINFO	IUTINFO@FRULM11	Messagerie des Departements Informatique des
IVCF-L	IVCF-L@UBVM	Intervarsity Christian Fellowship Discussion
IVRITEX	IVRITEX@TAUNIVM	Hebrew TeX list
IVY+	IVY+@MITVMA	Ivy+ Administrative

		Computing Group
IXI-APM	IXI-APM@HEARN	Distribution list for IXI Access Point Manage
J-FOOD-L	J-FOOD-L@JPNKNU10	Japanese food & culture discussion list
JANET	JANET@GWUVM	Waterloo Janet Network Discussion List
JAPAN	JAPAN@FINHUTC	Info-Japan
JCGLIST	JCGLIST@UKACRL	
JCGTEST	JCGTEST@UKACRL	JCGTEST
JCMT-L	JCMT-L@UALTAVM	James Clerk Maxwell Telescope
JCPC-L	JCPC-L@IRLEARN	RARE/EARN 90 Conference Programme Committee
JES2-L	JES2-L@CEARN	(Peered) JES2 discussion group
	JES2-L@NDSUVM1	(Peered) JES2 discussion group
JES3-L	JES3-L@UGA	JES3 Systems Programmers List
JNC90-L	JNC90-L@IRLEARN	Earn/Rare '90 organisation committee
JNET-L	JNET-L@BITNIC	(Peered) JNET Discussion Group
	JNET-L@DEARN	(Peered) JNET Discussion Group
	JNET-L@UGA	(Peered) BITNIC JNET-L List
	JNET-L@UIUCVMD	JNET-L (log files only)
JOB-LIST	JOB-LIST@FRORS12	Job offers from EARN Institute members
JOURNET	JOURNET@QUCDN	Discussion List for Journalism Education
JPATTEND	JPATTEND@JPNSUT10	Japan BITNET Meeting Attendees
JPBIT-L	JPBIT-L@JPNSUT00	discussion about Japan BITNET
JPBOARD	JPBOARD@JPNSUT00	Japan BITNET Board meeting
JPDECNET	JPDECNET@JPNKEKVM	Japan HEP/SPAN DECnet meeting
JPINFO-L	JPINFO-L@JPNSUT00	Information list about Japan
JPNAD-L	JPNAD-L@JPNSUT00	Japan Node Administrator's discussion list
JR-NET	JR-L@UFRJ	JR-NET - Junior Entreprise
JTEM-L	JTEM-L@UGA	Japanese Through Electronic Media
JUDAICA	JUDAICA@TAUNIVM	(Peered) Judaic Studies

		Newsletter
	JUDAICA@UMINN1	(Peered) JUDAICA Jewish & Near Eastern Studie
JUDICI-L	JUDICI-L@BINGVMB	Campus Judicial Affairs
JUGGLING	JUGGLING@INDYCMS	Juggling - For Jugglers of all abilities.
JULY1990	JULY1990@USCVM	USCInfo Development Team Coordination List
KBASE-L	KBASE-L@VTVM2	This is a private list for knowledgebase.
KEKMAC-L	KEKMAC-L@JPNKEKVM	KEKMAC-L MAC USER'S LIST
KERMIT-A	KERMIT-A@UIUCVMD	KERMIT-A (archive files only)
KERMIT-L	KERMIT-L@JPNSUT30	Kermit discussion list
KIDCAFE	KIDCAFE@NDSUVM1	KIDCAFE Kids-91 Dialog
KIDPEACE	KIDPEACE@NDSUVM1	KIDPEACE Kids and War
KIDPLAN	KIDPLAN@NDSUVM1	KIDPLAN Project Planning
KIDS-91	KIDS-91@NDSUVM1	KIDS-91 Project List
KLEIO-L	KLEIO-L@DGOGWDG1	List for Users of Kleio-Software
KNET-L	KNET-L@TAMVM1	The KNET discussion list
KNUG	KNUG@KENTVM	"The Kent Network Users Group"
KONFER-L	KONFER-L@TREARN	Conference Announcements lists
	KONFER-L@UBVM	Conference Announcements lists
KUBIB-L	KUBIB-L@UKANVM	"KU Library Bibliographers"
KUFUSE-L	KUFUSE-L@UKANVM	"KU Focus Users Group"
KULALA-L	KULALA-L@UKANVM	"KU Libraries ALA Conference Discussion List"
KULIB-L	KULIB-L@UKANVM	"KU Library Staff"
KUVAX-L	KUVAX-L@UKANVM	"KU VAX Information List"
KUVM-L	KUVM-L@UKANVM	"KU VM Information List"
KYACAD-L	KYACAD-L@ULKYVM	Kentucky Academic Computing Discussion
KYUCC	KYUCC@JPNKISCI	kyushu-u.cc
KYUSHU	KYUSHU@JPNKISCI	kyushu.{general,misc}
L-ARTECH	L-ARTECH@UQAM	Les Arts et les nouvelles technologies/Arts a
L-CHA	L-CHA@UQAM	Canadian Hist. Association Conference on Comp
L-ETHO	L-ETHO@UQAM	Ethologistes/Ethologists
L-HCAP	L-HCAP@NDSUVM1	L-HCAP List

L-OHACAD	L-OHACAD@AKRONVM	OHECC Academic Discussion List
L-ORACLE	L-ORACLE@UQAM	Usagers Oracle/Oracle's Users
L-SHC	L-SHC@UQAM	Comite de l'informatique de la SHC
LABOR-L	LABOR-L@YORKVM1	Discussion Forum on the emerging North Americ
LACROS-L	LACROS-L@VILLVM	Lacrosse Information List
LAFFAC	LAFFAC@PURCCVM	Lafayette CPT Faculty
LAFSTAFF	LAFSTAFF@PURCCVM	All Lafayette CPT Faculty/Clerical/Admin Staf
LAI571	LAI571@UBVM	LAI571 Class List
LAI672	LAI672@UBVM	LAI672 Class List
LANGUES	LANGUES@UQUEBEC	LANGUES Enseignement du francais par ordinate
LANTRA-L	LANTRA-L@FINHUTC	Interpreting (and) translation
LARC-L	LARC-L@UFRJ	Laboratorio Nacional de Redes de Computadores
LASER	LASER@BNANDP11	(Peered) Laser Lovers
	LASER@FINHUTC	(Peered) Laser Lovers
LASER-L	LASER-L@IRLEARN	Laser Printer Information Distribution List
LASMED-L	LASMED-L@TAUNIVM	Laser Medicine
LASPAU-L	LASPAU-L@HARVARDA	"LATIN AMERICAN SCHOLARSHIP PROGRAM OF AMERIC
LAWSCH-L	LAWSCH-L@AUVM	Law School Discussion List
LCC-L	LCC-L@BRUFMG	Lista para intercambio de informacoes entre o
LCOORD-L	LCOORD-L@CEARN	Listserv Coordination Board
LCUG	LCUG@SUVM	LCUG List
LDS-REQ	LDS-REQ@BYUVM	LDS Discussions
LEPICSP3	LEPICSP3@LEPICS	LEPICS Parallel Processing Project Group
LEXX-L	LEXX-L@IRISHVMA	LEXX editor discussions
LGA-L	LGA-L@UREGINA1	Local Government Administration List
LHLOG	LHLOG@UIUCVMD	CSO LH Site Online Logbook
LIAISON	LIAISON@BITNIC	(Peered) Network Site Liaisons
	LIAISON@DEARN	(Peered) Network Sites Liaison
	LIAISON@EB0UB011	(Peered) Network Site Liaisons
	LIAISON@UGA	(Peered) BITNIC LIAISON

LIBADMIN	LIBADMIN@UMAB	Library Administration and Management
LIBER	LIBER@UVMVM	LIBER: Libraries/Media Services Communication
LIBERNET	LIBERNET@UIUCVMD	LIBERNET (log files only)
LIBPLN-L	LIBPLN-L@QUCDN	University Library Planning Discussion
LIBREF-L	LIBREF-L@KENTVM	"Discussion of Library Reference Issues"
LIBRES	LIBRES@KENTVM	"Discussion of Library Research "establishing
LICENSE	LICENSE@BITNIC	(Peered) Software Licensing List
	LICENSE@DEARN	(Peered) Software Licensing List
	LICENSE@EB0UB011	(Peered) Software Licensing
	LICENSE@FINHUTC	(Peered) Software Licensing List
	LICENSE@HEARN	(Peered) Software Licensing List
	LICENSE@MARIST	(Peered) Software Licensing List
	LICENSE@UGA	(Peered) Software Licensing List
LICENT-L	LICENT-L@HEARN	Informatie over softwarelicenties voor instel
LING417	LING417@RICEVM1	Test List
LINK-L	LINK-L@GSUVM1	GSU Wells Computer Center newsletter discussi
LINKFAIL	LINKFAIL@BITNIC	(Peered) Link failure announcements
	LINKFAIL@CEARN	(Peered) Link failure announcements
	LINKFAIL@DEARN	(Peered) Link failure announcements
	LINKFAIL@EB0UB011	(Peered) Link failure announcements
	LINKFAIL@FINHUTC	(Peered) Link failure announcements
	LINKFAIL@FRULM11	(Peered) Link failure announcements
	LINKFAIL@HEARN	(Peered) Link failure announcements
	LINKFAIL@IRLEARN	(Peered) Link failure announcements
	LINKFAIL@MARIST	(Peered) Link failure announcements
	LINKFAIL@TAUNIVM	(Peered) Link failure announcements

	LINKFAIL@UGA	(Peered) Link failure announcements
LISTA	LISTA@NIHCUSV1	A-th List
LISTB	LISTB@NIHCUSV1	B-th List
LISTC	LISTC@NIHCUSV1	C-th List
LISTTECH	LISTTECH@TREARN	LISTSERV Programmers Discussion Group
LITERA-L	LITERA-L@TECMTYVM	Literat-l Literature in English & Spanish.
LITERARY	LITERARY@UCF1VM	Discussions about Literature
LIVE-EYE	LIVE-EYE@YORKVM1	Color and Vision Discussion Forum
LLTI	LLTI@DARTCMS1	Language Learning and Technology Internationa
LN	LN@FRMOP11	Langage Naturel
LOG	LOG@UIUCVMD	LOG (log files only)
LOLA-L	LOLA-L@LSUVM	LOLA Users
LORE	LORE@NDSUVM1	LORE - Folklore List
LPN-L	LPN-L@BROWNVM	Laboratory Primate Newsletter List
LS-ZAMBS	LS-ZAMBS@DJUKFA11	ZAM Betriebssystem Gruppe
LSTERN-L	LSTERN-L@FRMOP11	LISTEARN Discussion List
LSTFUT-L	LSTFUT-L@UIUCVMD	List server future discussions
LSTOWN-L	LSTOWN-L@INDYCMS	ListServ list owners list
LSTSRV-L	LSTSRV-L@POLYGRAF	(Peered) Forum on LISTSERV release 1.6
	LSTSRV-L@RUTVM1	(Peered) Forum on LISTSERV release 1.6
	LSTSRV-L@SEARN	(Peered) Forum on LISTSERV release 1.6
	LSTSRV-L@UGA	(Peered) Forum on LISTSERV release 1.6
LSTSRV-M	LSTSRV-M@SEARN	Revised LISTSERV Maintainers
LSTSRV-N	LSTSRV-N@SEARN	Working group on LISTSERV support for the new
LTEST-L	LTEST-L@UCLACN1	Language Testing Research and Practice
LWUSERS	LWUSERS@NDSUVM1	LWUsers LANWatch User List
L3ANA-L	L3ANA-L@LEPICS	L3 Analysis Group A
L3ANB-L	L3ANB-L@LEPICS	L3 Analysis Group B
L3GRAF-L	L3GRAF-L@LEPICS	L3 Graphics/Interactivity Group
MAC-CONF	MAC-CONF@UVMVM	Mac-Conf The Macintosh Computer in the Univer

MAC-L	MAC-L@YALEVM	Macintosh News and Information
MAC-TEL	MAC-TEL@IRLEARN	EARN Macintosh Users List - Extension for Mac
MAC-USER	MAC-USER@IRLEARN	EARN Macintosh Users List
MACAPPLI	MACAPPLI@DARTCMS1	A list for posting news and usage tips about
MACGIL-L	MACGIL-L@MCGILL1	McGill Macintosh Users Group
MACHRDWR	MACHRDWR@DARTCMS1	A list for posting advice about Macintosh har
MACIME-L	MACIME-L@BRUSPVM	Ciencia da Computacao
MACLAB-L	MACLAB-L@UHCCVM	MacLab staff
MACMAIL	MACMAIL@UTORONTO	MAC Mail Discussion List
MACNET-L	MACNET-L@YALEVM	Macintosh Networking Issues
MACSYSTM	MACSYSTM@DARTCMS1	A list for posting advice about Macintosh sys
MACTURK	MACTURK@TREARN	Turkish Macintosh Users Group
MAGAZINE	MAGAZINE@RPIECS	Magazines
MAIL-ITA	MAIL-ITA@IBACSATA	(Peered) Electronic Mail Future developements
	MAIL-ITA@ICNUCEVM	(Peered) Electronic Mail Future developements
MAIL-L	MAIL-L@BITNIC	(Peered) Mail Transfer/ User Agents
	MAIL-L@DEARN	(Peered) Mail Discussion List
	MAIL-L@EB0UB011	(Peered) Mail Discussion List
	MAIL-L@IRLEARN	Network Mail Discussion
	MAIL-L@MARIST	(Peered) Mail Discussion List
	MAIL-L@UGA	(Peered) BITNIC MAIL-L List
MAIL-USF	MAIL-USF@CFRVM	E-Mail Discussion List
MAILBOOK	MAILBOOK@CLVM	(Peered) MAIL/ MAILBOOK subscription list
	MAILBOOK@DEARN	(Peered) MAIL/ MAILBOOK subscription list
	MAILBOOK@EB0UB011	(Peered) MAIL/ MAILBOOK subscription list
MAILCNR	MAILCNR@ICNUCEVM	MAILCNRCNR GARR WG ON ELECTRONIC MAIL
MAKE-L	MAKE-L@UREGINA1	MAKE-L LIST

MAPS-L	MAPS-L@UGA	Maps and Air Photo Systems Forum
MARKET-A	MARKET-A@UHUPVM1	Financial markets research in Accounting and
MARKET-L	MARKET-L@UCF1VM	For marketing academics and practitioners.
MASSCOMM	MASSCOMM@RPICICGE	Mass comm. and new technologies
	MASSCOMM@RPIECS	Mass comm. and new technologies
MAT-DSGN	MAT-DSGN@JPNTOHOK	Forum on Materials Design by Computer
MATERI-L	MATERI-L@TAUNIVM	Material List
MATHDEP	MATHDEP@IRLEARN	UCD Maths Department Distribution List
MBA-L	MBA-L@MARIST	MBA Student curriculum discussion
MCLR-L	MCLR-L@MSU	MIDWEST CONSORTIUM FOR LATINO RESEARCH
MCRIT-L	MCRIT-L@HEARN	Multicriteria Discussion List
MDPHD-L	MDPHD-L@UBVM	Dual Degree Programs Discussion List
MDPIT-L	MDPIT-L@WUVMD	MDPIT-L list
MDS32-L	MDS32-L@INDYCMS	MDS32 Menu Definition System for Vax/VMS by E
MECH-L	MECH-L@UTARLVM1	Mechanical Engineering Discussion List
MEDCONS	MEDCONS@FINHUTC	Medcons (Medical consulting and case descript
MEDIA-L	MEDIA-L@BINGVMB	Media in Education
MEDIMAGE	MEDIMAGE@POLYGRAF	Medical Imaging Discussion List
MEDINF-L	MEDINF-L@DEARN	MEDINF-L
	MEDINF-L@YALEVM	Biomedical Informatics Discussion Group
MEDLIB-L	MEDLIB-L@UBVM	Medical Libraries Discussion List
MEDNETS	MEDNETS@NDSUVM1	MEDNETS Medical Telecommunications Networks
MEDNEWS	MEDNEWS@ASUACAD	MEDNEWS - Health Info-Com Network Newsletter
MEMOLIST	MEMOLIST@NERVM	NERDC Memo System distribution list
METALIB	METALIB@JPNTOHOK	Metallibrary
METHO	METHO@UQUEBEC	Methodologie quantitative, sciences sociales

METHODS	METHODS@IRLEARN	BIOSCI Methods-and-Reagents Bulletin Board
	METHODS@RPICICGE	Research methodology
	METHODS@RPIECS	Research methodology
MEXICO	MEXICO@VMTECMEX	Lista de distribucion "Mexico".
MEXICO-L	MEXICO-L@TECMTYVM	Knowing Mexico: people, places, culture.
MGSFAC	MGSFAC@UBVM	UB Management Science Faculty List
MGSGRAD	MGSGRAD@UBVM	UB Management Science Graduate Students List
MGSNEWS	MGSNEWS@UBVM	UB Management Science Discussion List
MGT190	MGT190@GWUVM	MGT 190 Discussion List
MHSNEWS	MHSNEWS@IBACSATA	MHS News
MIBSRV-L	MIBSRV-L@UA1VM	MIBSRV IBM Antiviral Update List (announcemen
MICNEWS	MICNEWS@UCLACN1	UCLA Micro Information Center News
MICRO-EL	MICRO-EL@TAUNIVM	MICROELECTRONICS INISRAEL List
MICROC-L	MICROC-L@YALEVM	Microcomputer Coordination Committee
MICROLAB	MICROLAB@TAMVM1	CSC Microcomputer Support Group Private List
MICRONET	MICRONET@UOGUELPH	Fungus and Root Interaction Discussion
MICS-L	MICS-L@HDETUD1	Morino's MVS Information Control System
MIDEUR-L	MIDEUR-L@UBVM	Discussion of Middle Europe topics
MIDNET-L	MIDNET-L@KSUVM	MIDnet Discussion Group
MIDNET-R	MIDNET-R@KSUVM	MIDnet Reconfiguration Discussion Group
MIDNET-T	MIDNET-T@KSUVM	MIDnet Technical Discussion
MIDNET-U	MIDNET-U@KSUVM	MIDnet User Services Discussion Group
MIDNET-X	MIDNET-X@KSUVM	Midnet Executive Committee
MINCON	MINCON@UKCC	Conference on Minority Recruitment and Retent
MINIX-L	MINIX-L@DEARN	(Peered) Minix operating system
	MINIX-L@FINHUTC	(Peered) Minix operating system
	MINIX-L@NDSUVM1	(Peered) Minix operating system

MIS-L	MIS-L@ALBNYDH2	NYS DEPARTMENT OF HEALTH MANAGE-MENT INFORMATI
MITVIRUS	MITVIRUS@MITVMA	MIT Virus Notification Service
MLA-L	MLA-L@IUBVM	Mailing list for the Music Library Associatio
MMEDIA-L	MMEDIA-L@VMTECMEX	Multimedia discussion list
MOD-KI	MOD-KI@DB0TUI11	Local redistribution of mod-ki@gmdzi.UUCP
MODULA-L	MODULA-L@UALTAVM	Modula-2 (language) dis-cussions
	MODULA-L@UIUCVMD	Modula-2 (language) dis-cussions
MOL-EVOL	MOL-EVOL@IRLEARN	BIOSCI Molecular-Evolution Bulletin Board
MON-L	MON-L@BITNIC	(Peered) BITNET Moni-toring List
	MON-L@DEARN	(Peered) BITNET Moni-toring List
	MON-L@EB0UB011	(Peered) BITNET Moni-toring List
	MON-L@UGA	(Peered) BITNIC MON-L List
MORIA-L	MORIA-L@CMUCCVMA	MORIA Discussion
MORRIS	MORRIS@SUVM	Morris Dancing Discus-sion List
MORTAR-L	MORTAR-L@UMCVMB	Mortar Board, Inc. Dis-cussion Group
MOSSBA-L	MOSSBA-L@USACHVM1	"Mossbauer Spectrosco-py, Software & Forum"
MOUNT-L	MOUNT-L@TRMETU	Mountaineering Discus-sion List 'MOUNT-L'
MPG-L	MPG-L@YALEVM	Yale MultiProtocol Gate-way Discussion Group
MSDOS-L	MSDOS-L@UKANVM	"KU MS-DOS Informa-tion List"
MSLIST-L	MSLIST-L@NCSUVM	MS Mailing List
MSSQL-L	MSSQL-L@DUKEVM	Microsoft SQL Server Discussion List
MT3270-L	MT3270-L@BROWNVM	Macintosh TN3270 Beta-test List
MUCO-FR	MUCO-FR@FRMOP11	Cystic Fibrosis list - France (MucoViscidose)
MUG	MUG@MARIST	(Peered) MUSIC/SP dis-cussion list
	MUG@TCSVM	(Peered) MUSIC-SP dis-cussion list
	MUG@UGA	(Peered) Marist MUG List

MULNAD-F	MULNAD-F@FRMOP11	Liste des 'Node ADministators' MULTICS franca
MULTAS-L	MULTAS-L@TREARN	Multitasking programming for PC
MULTI-L	MULTI-L@BARILVM	Language and Education in Multi-Lingual Setti
MUL3-L	MUL3-L@LEPICS	L3 Muon Reconstruction Software Forum
MUMPS-L	MUMPS-L@UGA	(Peered) MUMPS List
	MUMPS-L@VTVM2	(Peered) MUMPS List
MUSIC	MUSIC@FINHUTC	Music-Research
MUSIC-ED	MUSIC-ED@UMINN1	MUSIC-ED Music Education
MUSIC-L	MUSIC-L@MARIST	(Peered) MUSIC/SP User discussion list
	MUSIC-L@TCSVM	(Peered) MUSIC/SP User discussion list
	MUSIC-L@UGA	(Peered) MUSIC/SP User discussion list
MVS-SE	MVS-SE@SEARN	Swedish EARN Node ADministrators - MVS system
MVSNAD-F	MVSNAD-F@FRMOP11	Liste des 'Node ADministators' MVS francais
MVSTCPIP	MVSTCPIP@USCVM	TCP/IP for MVS Discussions
M2-IBM	M2-IBM@DB0TUI11	Modula-2 on /370 mailing list
	M2-IBM@EB0UB011	Modula-2 on /370 mailing list
M204	M204-L@AKRONVM	Model 204 Database Discussion List
NAC	NAC@NDSUVM1	NAC - News Announce Conferences
NACUBO	NACUBO@BITNIC	NACUBO College and University Business Office
NAD-F	NAD-F@FRMOP11	Liste des 'Node ADministators' francais
NAD-IE	NAD-IE@IRLEARN	EARN Node Administrators - Ireland
NAD-SE	NAD-SE@SEARN	Swedish EARN Node ADministrators - all operat
NADJ2-D	NADJ2-D@DEARN	German Node Administrators (NAD) JES2
NADJ3-D	NADJ3-D@DEARN	German Node Administrators (NAD) JES3
NADUNX-D	NADUNX-D@DEARN	German Node Administrators (NAD) UNIX/UREP

NADVAR-D	NADVAR-D@DEARN	German Node Administrators (NAD) for VARious
NADVM-D	NADVM-D@DEARN	German Node Administrators (NAD) VM
NADVMS-D	NADVMS-D@DEARN	German Node Administrators (NAD) VMS
NANET	NANET@FINHUTC	NaNet
NATIVE-L	NATIVE-L@TAMVM1	NATIVE-L
NATURA	NATURA@FRMOP11	Reseau NATURA
NATURA-L	NATURA-L@UCHCECVM	Ecologia y Proteccion de la Naturaleza en Chi
NB-L	NB-L@DGOGWDG1	Testliste (!!) fuer Nota-Bene-Benutzer
NCBIT-L	NCBIT-L@NCSUVM	North Carolina BITNET Site Contacts
NCE-L	NCE-L@UFRJ	Sugestoes e Servicos
NCS-L	NCS-L@UMDD	National Crime Survey Discussion
NCSA-L	NCSA-L@MITVMA	NCSA Supercomputer Center Users List
NCSMVS-L	NCSMVS-L@NCSUVM	TUCC to NCSU MVS Migration Information
NCVTX-L	NCVTX-L@NCSUVM	North Carolina DEC VTX Discussion List
NDNNET-I	NDNNET-I@FINHUTC	NORDUnet network project information
NDRG-L	NDRG-L@WVNVM	Nonlinear Dynamics Research Group
NDS-KONT	NDS-KONT@DGOGWDG1	Niedersaechsisches Kontingentierungssystem
NESUG-L	NESUG-L@UMAB	NorthEast SAS Users Group List
NET-INFO	NET-INFO@UVMVM	Net-Info: UVM Campus Network Information Cent
NET-TEAM	NET-TEAM@GREARN	Network Team Discussion LIst
NETADV-L	NETADV-L@MCGILL1	Network Advisory Committee
NETCON-L	NETCON-L@NCSUVM	Netcon 89 Info list
	NETCON-L@UTORONTO	Netnorth Transport Service Technical Contacts
NETDATAK	NETDATAK@JPNKEKVM	NETDATAK Discussion list
NETDIR-L	NETDIR-L@UTORONTO	Netnorth Directors
NETINFO	NETINFO@WSUVM1	WSU Network Information
NETMON-L	NETMON-L@BITNIC	(Peered) Discussion of NETMON
	NETMON-L@DEARN	(Peered) Discussion of

		NETMON
	NETMON-L@EB0UB011	(Peered) Discussion of NETMON
	NETMON-L@UGA	(Peered) Discussion of NETMON
NETMONTH	NETMONTH@MARIST	NetMonth Magazine
NETNORTH	NETNORTH@UOGUELPH	NETNORTH Communications Discussion
NETNWS-L	NETNWS-L@NDSUVM1	NETNWS-L Netnews List
NETONE	NETONE@UKCC	U-B Net_One Discussion Group
NETPST-L	NETPST-L@UTORONTO	Netnorth Mail Application Technical Contacts
NETREP-L	NETREP-L@UTORONTO	Netnorth Representatives
NETSCOUT	NETSCOUT@VMTECMEX	The BITnet/Internet scouts.
NETSRV-L	NETSRV-L@CEARN	NETSRV-L LIST
NETSRV-M	NETSRV-M@HEARN	NETSERV Maintainers
NETWORK	NETWORK@JPNKISCI	NetWork
NETWORKS	NETWORKS@ARIZVM1	UNIVERSITY OF ARIZONA Networking Discussion
NETWRK-L	NETWRK-L@MCGILL1	CC Network Group
NEURO1-L	NEURO1-L@UICVM	Neuroscience Information Forum
NEW-LIST	NEW-LIST@IRLEARN	(Peered) NEW-LIST - New List Announcements
	NEW-LIST@NDSUVM1	(Peered) NEW-LIST - New List Announcements
NEWBOOKS	NEWBOOKS@RPIECS	New Books in Communication
NEWCROPS	NEWCROPS@PURCCVM	Discussion list for New Crops
NEWLTEST	NEWLTEST@NDSUVM1	(Peered) NEWLTEST - Special Test List
NEWS-L	NEWS-L@ALBNYDH2	NYS DEPARTMENT OF HEALTH NEWS
NEWSE-D	NEWSE-D@INDYCMS	News of the Earth distribution
NEWSE-L	NEWSE-L@INDYCMS	News of the Earth letters
NEWSE-S	NEWSE-S@INDYCMS	News of the Earth supplements
NEWSLINE	NEWSLINE@RPICICGE	ComServe News Service
	NEWSLINE@RPIECS	Comserve News Service
NEXT-L	NEXT-L@BROWNVM	(Peered) NeXT Computer List
	NEXT-L@GREARN	(Peered) NeXT Computer List

	NEXT-L@MITVMA	NeXT Computer Info Exchange List
NIC-INFO	NIC-INFO@FRMOP11	Numerically Intensive Computing (General Info
NIC-USF	NIC-USF@CFRVM	NIC Computing Discussion List
NICLIST	NICLIST@NERVM	Numerically Intensive Computing
NIH-L	NIH-L@WSUVM1	WSU OGRD NIH Redistribution List
NIHDIS-L	NIHDIS-L@JHUVM	NIH Guide Discussion List
NIHGDE-L	NIHGDE-L@JHUVM	NIH Guide Primary Distribution
NIHGUIDE	NIHGUIDE@UMAB	NIH Listing of Available Grants and Contracts
	NIHGUIDE@UWAVM	NIH Guide U of Washington Distribution
NIHONGO	NIHONGO@FINHUTC	Nihongo
	NIHONGO@MITVMA	Japanese Language Discussion List
NL-KR	NL-KR@DB0TUI11	Local redistribution of NL-KR@CS.ROCHESTER.ED
	NL-KR@FINHUTC	(Peered) Natural Language List
	NL-KR@RPICICGE	Natural Language and Knowledge Representation
	NL-KR@RPIECS	Natural Language and Knowledge Representation
NL-KR-L	NL-KR-L@TAUNIVM	(Peered) Natural Language & Knowledge Represe
NLSNEWS	NLSNEWS@OHSTVMA	NLSNEWS NLS Newsletter Subscription List
NLSUPDAT	NLSUPDAT@OHSTVMA	NLSUPDAT NLS Data Update Service
NMBMKT-L	NMBMKT-L@UTORONTO	NRNET Marketing
NMBRTHRY	NMBRTHRY@NDSUVM1	Number Theory List
NMP-L	NMP-L@IUBVM	NACO Music Project
NMUSIC-L	NMUSIC-L@NCSUVM	New Music Discussion List
NN-TEST	NN-TEST@PURCCVM	Test list for VMNET-NEWS postings
NNDIRONT	NNDIRONT@UTORONTO	Netnorth Directors in Ontario (NNDIRONT)
NNEARN	NNEARN@BLEKUL11	NNEARN LIST : Virtual NETNEWS feed

		THROUGH LI
	NNEARN@FRMOP11	NNEARN LIST : Virtual NETNEWS feed through LI
NNWESTDOWN	DOWN-L@UALTAVM	NetNorth West System Down Announcements.
NNWESTVIP	NNWEST-L@UALTAVM	NetNorth West VIP's
NO-ARG-B	NO-ARG-B@UKACRL	NO-ARG-B (not yet operational)
NO-CLASS	NO-CLASS@JPNKISCI	No class information list (Test version)
NO-L-ARG	NO-L-ARG@UKACRL	NO-L-ARG : Nitric Oxide/L-Arginine discussion
NODAK-L	NODAK-L@NDSUVM1	NODAK-L North Dakota Issues
NODAPPLS	NODAPPLS@JPNSUT30	student's discussion list at Noda campus
NODMGT-L	NODMGT-L@BITNIC	(Peered) Node Management Discussion
	NODMGT-L@DEARN	(Peered) Node Management Discussion
	NODMGT-L@EB0UB011	(Peered) Node Management List
	NODMGT-L@FINHUTC	(Peered) Node Management Discussion
	NODMGT-L@HEARN	(Peered) Node Management Discussion
	NODMGT-L@MARIST	(Peered) Node Management Discussion
	NODMGT-L@UGA	(Peered) Node Management
NODUPD-D	NODUPD-D@BYUVM	Monthly update file distribution
NOEARN-L	NOEARN-L@NOBIVM	Drift og planlegging av EARN i Norge.
NOMAD2-L	NOMAD2-L@TAMVM1	The NOMAD2 Discussion List
NOMINATE	NOMINATE@BITNIC	NOMINATE - CREN Nominating Committe List
NOTABENE	NOTABENE@TAUNIVM	Nota Bene List
NOTIEXT	NOTIEXT@UNAMVM1	Servicio de noticias para Instituciones exter
NOTIS-L	NOTIS-L@TCSVM	NOTIS/DOBIS discussion group list
NOTISACQ	NOTISACQ@ULKYVM	NOTIS Acquisitions Discussion Group
NOTIUNAM	NOTIUNAM@UNAMVM1	Servicio de noticias UNAM para usuarios BITNE

NOTMUS-L	NOTMUS-L@UBVM	NOTIS MUSIC LIBRARY LIST
NOTRBCAT	NOTRBCAT@INDYCMS	rare book and special collections catalogers
NOVELL	NOVELL@SUVM	Novell LAN Interest Group
	NOVELL@TWNMOE10	NOVELL (PC/LAN) redistribution list
	NOVELL@UIUCVMD	NOVELL from SUVM (log files only)
NOVOPS	NOVOPS@SUVM	Novell Technology Operations List
NOVTTP	NOVTTP@SUVM	Novell Technology Transfer Partners List
NRV	NRV@DCZTU1	Niedersaechsischer Rechnerverbund
NSNNEWS	NSNNEWS@FINHUTC	Nsn/News
NSP-L	NSP-L@RPICICGE	Noble Savage Philosphers mailing list
	NSP-L@RPIECS	Noble Savage Philosphers mailing list
NUSLIST	NUSLIST@NUSVM	NUSVM General Discussion Group
NUTS	NUTS@FINHUTC	Traditional Nutty Stuff
NUTWORKS	NUTWORKS@TCSVM	NutWorks Distribution list
NYSERTEC	NYSERTEC@POLYGRAF	NYSERNet Technical List
OBSERVER	OBSERVER@RPICICGE	COMCONF Observers
	OBSERVER@RPIECS	COMCONF Observers
ODP-L	ODP-L@TAMVM1	Ocean Drilling Program Open Disscussion List
ODVC-L	ODVC-L@UNCVM1	Office of Data and Video Communications.
OFFICE-L	OFFICE-L@UKANVM	"KU OFFICE Users"
OH-ADMN	OH-ADMN@AKRONVM	OHECC Administrative Discussion List
OHEUG-L	OHEUG-L@UMDD	ORACLE Higher Education Users Group
OITT-L	OITT-L@HARVARDA	OIT Test List
OMNBUS-L	OMNBUS-L@YALEVM	Omnibus Production Committee
OMRSCAN	OMRSCAN@UOGUELPH	OMR Scanner Discussion
ONT-VIS	ONT-VIS@YORKVM1	Ontario Vision Researchers Forum Announcement
OPGRP-L	OPGRP-L@VTVM2	Virginia Tech Vax Operations Group/LUG
OPTICOMP	OPTICOMP@TAUNIVM	Optical Computing and Holography List
OPTICS-L	OPTICS-L@TAUNIVM	Optics Newsletter
OR-L	OR-L@UALTAVM	An Informal List for Offi-

		cial Representatives
ORACLE-L	ORACLE-L@SBCCVM	ORACLE database mailing list.
OREBAN-L	OREBAN-L@PSUORVM	Oregon Banner List
ORELOG	ORELOG@UIUCVMD	CSO OREGON Site Online Logbook
ORGCOMM	ORGCOMM@RPICICGE	Communication in organizations
	ORGCOMM@RPIECS	Communication in organizations
OS-2	OS-2@BLEKUL11	Moderated discussion forum on OS/2
OSC	L-OSC@AKRONVM	Ohio SuperComputing Discussion List
OTS-L	OTS-L@YALEVM	Organization for Tropical Studies at Yale Uni
OUSSS-L	OUSSS-L@UTORONTO	Ontario University Systems Software Support G
OWNER-L	OWNER-L@UKANVM	"KU Listserv Owners"
PA_NET	PA_NET@SUVM	Public Administration Network
PABXB-L	PABXB-L@HEARN	Project "Koppeling PABX'en"
PABXPROJ	PABXPROJ@HEARN	Distributielijst t.b.v. project "Koppeling PA
PABXT-L	PABXT-L@HEARN	Workinggroup on technical aspects within proj
PACARC-L	PACARC-L@WSUVM1	Pacific Rim Archaeology Interest List
PACK-L	PACK-L@DB0FUB11	List for package announcement
PACKRAD	PACKRAD@FINHUTC	Packet-radio list
PACS-L	PACS-L@TWNMOE10	PACS-L public access computer system
	PACS-L@UHUPVM1	Public-Access Computer Systems Forum
PAGE-L	PAGE-L@UCF1VM	IBM 3812/3820 Tips and Problems Discussion Li
PAGEMAKR	PAGEMAKR@INDYCMS	PageMaker for Desktop Publishers
PANIC	PANIC@UCHCECVM	Avisos de Condiciones de Error en los Servers
PAR-L	PAR-L@UTORONTO	Parallel Computing Taskforce
PARA-DAP	PARA-DAP@IRLEARN	"Parallel Computing / AMT DAP mailing list"
PARADOX	PARADOX@BRUFPB	List for Borland Paradox users
PAROUTE	PAROUTE@BITNIC	Pathalias Routing Mailing List
PASCAL-L	PASCAL-L@TREARN	Pascal Language Discus-

		sion List
	PASCAL-L@TWNMOE10	Pascal language DISCUSSION GROUP REDISTRIBUTI
	PASCAL-L@UIUCVMD	Pascal (language) discussions
	PASCAL-L@YALEVM	Borland Pascal Discussion Group
PC-EVAL	PC-EVAL@IRLEARN	Personal Computer Evaluation
PC-FORUM	PC-FORUM@TAUNIVM	Tel Aviv University PC Forum
PC-IP	PC-IP@FINHUTC	TCP/IP Implementations for PC:s
PC-L	PC-L@UFRJ	Forum IBM PC
PC-REXX	PC-REXX@UCF1VM	Personal REXX Discussion List
PCC-OPEN	PCC-OPEN@PCCVM	Open Discussion forum on PCCVM
PCCNEWS	PCCNEWS@PCCVM	Portland Community College IBM Laboratory New
PCIP	PCIP@IRLEARN	TCP/IP Protocol Implementations for PC Discussion
PCIP-L	PCIP-L@BYUVM	(Peered) PCIP
	PCIP-L@OHSTVMA	(Peered) PCIP
	PCIP-L@TAMVM1	(Peered) PCIP
PCSERV-L	PCSERV-L@RPICICGE	Public domain software servers
	PCSERV-L@RPIECS	Public domain software servers
	PCSERV-L@UALTAVM	Public domain software servers
PCSUPT-L	PCSUPT-L@YALEVM	Forum for the discussion of PC user support i
PCTECH-L	PCTECH-L@TREARN	MS-DOS Compatibles Support Group
PCTRAN-L	PCTRAN-L@YALEVM	PCTrans Issues
PCUGSC	PCUGSC@UIUCVMD	PC User's Group Steering Committee Mailing Li
PC9801	PC9801@JPNSUT30	NEC PC-9800 series discussion list
PDUSIG	PDUSIG@UIUCVMD	PC USER'S GROUP PUBLIC DOMAIN & UTILITIES SIG
PENPAL-L	PENPAL-L@UNCCVM	UNCC PENPAL-L Discussion
PERSON-L	PERSON-L@IRLEARN	Personal and Micro Computer Users Distribution

PETS-L	PETS-L@VMTECMEX	Domestic animal care and education list.
PETUALTAVM	PETNET-L@UALTAVM	PET Users List
PFCOOR	PFCOOR@ICNUCEVM	Progetto Finalizzato Sistemi Informatici e Ca
PFSICP-1	PFSICP-1@ICNUCEVM	1 - CALCOLO SCIENTIFICO PER GRANDI SISTEMI
PFSICP-2	PFSICP-2@ICNUCEVM	2 - Processori Dedicati
PFSICP-3	PFSICP-3@ICNUCEVM	3 - Architetture Parallele
PFSICP-4	PFSICP-4@ICNUCEVM	4 - Linguaggi di nuova concezione
PFSICP-5	PFSICP-5@ICNUCEVM	5 - Sistemi evoluti p er basi di dati
PFSICP-6	PFSICP-6@ICNUCEVM	6 - Metodi e strumenti per la progettazione d
PFSICP-7	PFSICP-7@ICNUCEVM	7 - Sistemi di supporto al lavoro intellettua
PFSICP-8	PFSICP-8@ICNUCEVM	8 - Iniziative di supporto per il calc. paral
PFUG-L	PFUG-L@JHUVM	Parallel FORTRAN Users' Group newsletter
PHIGS-L	PHIGS-L@FINHUTC	(Peered) PHIGS guru forum
PHILCA	PHILCA@YORKVM1	Canadian Philosophy Discussion Forum
PHILCOMM	PHILCOMM@RPICICGE	Philosophy of communication
	PHILCOMM@RPIECS	Philosophy of communication
PHILONCA	PHILONCA@YORKVM1	Philosophy Announcement Forum for Philosopher
PHILOSOP	PHILOSOP@YORKVM1	Philosophy Discussion Forum
PHOTO-GR	PHOTO-GR@GREARN	Ellhnikh Fotografikh Lesxh
PHOTO-L	PHOTO-L@BUACCA	Photography Phorum
PHOTOSYN	PHOTOSYN@TAUNIVM	Photosynthesis Researchers' List
PHOTREAC	PHOTREAC@JPNTOHOK	Electro- and Photo-Nuclear Reaction Discussio
PHYS-L	PHYS-L@UCF1VM	Forum for Physics Teachers
PHYS-STU	PHYS-STU@UWF	Physics Student Discussion List
PHYSIC-L	PHYSIC-L@TAUNIVM	Physics List
PHYSICS	PHYSICS@EB0UB011	(Peered) Physics Discussion
	PHYSICS@MARIST	(Peered) Physics Discus-

		sion
	PHYSICS@RICEVM1	(Peered) Physics Discussion
	PHYSICS@UBVM	(Peered) Physics Discussion
PITSREG2	PITSREG2@UBVM	BITNET2 Mid-Eastern U.S. List
PLAINS-L	PLAINS-L@NDSUVM1	Great Plains BITNET Topology
PLEARN-L	PLEARN-L@UBVM	Discussion of Polish EARN topics
PL1-L	PL1-L@UIUCVMD	PL1 (language) discussions
PL1KURS	PL1KURS@TRITU	PL/I Programmers Assistance List
PMC-LIST	PMC-LIST@NCSUVM	Postmodern Culture
PMC-TALK	PMC-TALK@NCSUVM	PMC-Talk
PMDF-L	PMDF-L@IRLEARN	PMDF Distribution List
POD-L	POD-L@TAMVM1	Professional Organizational Developement disc
POLAND-L	POLAND-L@UBVM	Discussion of Polish Culture list
POLCAN	POLCAN@YORKVM1	POLCAN Canadian Political Science Discussion
POLCOMM	POLCOMM@RPICICGE	Political communication
	POLCOMM@RPIECS	Study of political communication
POLI-SCI	POLI-SCI@RUTVM1	Political Science Digest
POLICY-L	POLICY-L@BITNIC	(Peered) Discussion about BITNET policies
	POLICY-L@DEARN	(Peered) Discussion about BITNET policies
	POLICY-L@EB0UB011	(Peered) Discussion about BITNET policies
	POLICY-L@UIUCVMD	POLICY-L (log files only)
POLITICA	POLITICA@UFRJ	POLITICA - Discussoes sobre a Politica Nacion
POLITICS	POLITICS@OHSTVMA	(Peered) Forum for the Discussion of Politics
	POLITICS@UCF1VM	(Peered) Forum for the Discussion of Politics
POLYMERP	POLYMERP@HEARN	(Peered) Polymer Physics discussions
	POLYMERP@RUTVM1	(Peered) Polymer Physics discussions
POP-BIO	POP-BIO@IRLEARN	BIOSCI Population Biology Bulletin Board
POSAB-L	POSAB-L@VTVM1	Professional Office Staff Advisory Board
POSTMAST	POSTMAST@PURCCVM	Postmasters

	POSTMAST@UICVM	UICVM Postmaster
	POSTMAST@UREGINA1	POSTMASTER INFOMA-TION.
POWER-L	POWER-L@MCGILL1	Power Outages Distribution List
	POWER-L@NDSUVM1	POWER-L IBM RS/6000 POWER Family
PRACTICE	PRACTICE@ASUACAD	PRACTICE
PRENAT-L	PRENAT-L@ALBNYDH2	PERINATAL OUTCOMES
PRIMES-L	PRIMES-L@FRULM11	Liste des ITA revendiquant la prime aux infor
PRINCIPL	PRINCIPL@FRMOP11	EARN policy and basic non technical EARN matt
PRIPROM	PRIPROM@PURCCVM	CPT Primary Promotions Sub-Comm
PRNTNG-L	PRNTNG-L@YALEVM	Printing Task Discussion Group
PROFILE	PROFILE@JPNKISCI	Self Introduction .....
PROFS-L	PROFS-L@DEARN	(Peered) PROFS discussion
	PROFS-L@IUBVM	Discussion list for PROFS users on the IU-BUS
	PROFS-L@MARIST	(Peered) PROFS discussion
	PROFS-L@RUTVM1	(Peered) PROFS discussion
	PROFS-L@TCSVM	(Peered) PROFS discussion
PROFSALT	PROFSALT@PCCVM	PROFS Alternatives
PROG-A16	PROG-A16@UOGUELPH	INFO-ATARI16 Programs
PROGRESS	PROGRESS@PURCCVM	CPT Promotion Progress & Contract Renewal Com
PROINFO	PROINFO@IBACSATA	LISTA SERVIZI DI INFORMAZIONI DI PROMOZIONE
PROJECTA	PROJECTA@RPICICGE	Comserve special projects: Working Group A
PROJECTB	PROJECTB@RPICICGE	Comserve special projects: Working Group B
PROJECTC	PROJECTC@RPICICGE	Comserve special projects: Working Group C
PROJECTD	PROJECTD@RPICICGE	Comserve special projects: Working Group D
PROJECTE	PROJECTE@RPICICGE	Comserve special projects: Working Group E
PROMPT-L	PROMPT-L@NCSUVM	NCSU Computing Center PROMPT Newsletter
PROP-L	PROP-L@UTARLVM1	Programmable Operator

		List
PROPRIO	PROPRIO@UQUEBEC	Proprietaires de listes.
PROTEINS	PROTEINS@IRLEARN	BIOSCI Protein-Analysis Bulletin Board
PROTOCOL	PROTOCOL@UIUCVMD	Computer Protocol Discussion
PSCRIPT	PSCRIPT@BNANDP11	(Peered) Postscript forum
	PSCRIPT@FINHUTC	(Peered) Postscript forum
PSI-L	PSI-L@RPICICGE	Parapsychology Discussion Forum
	PSI-L@RPIECS	Parapsychology Discussion Forum
PSRT-L	PSRT-L@UMCVMB	Political Science Research and Teaching List
PSTAT-L	PSTAT-L@IRLEARN	Discussion of Stats and Programming relating
PSUTOOLS	PSUTOOLS@PSUVM	Discussion of the programs in the PSUTOOLS Fi
PSYC	PSYC@PUCC	Psychology Newsletter list
PUAD220G	PUAD220G@USCVM	Mail service list for USC Public Administrati
PUBHEADS	PUBHEADS@UKANVM	"KU Library Public Service Dept. Heads"
PUMP-L	PUMP-L@UVVM	PUMP Discussion List
PURTOPOI	PURTOPOI@PURCCVM	Rhetoric, Language, Prof Writing
PURWCLAS	PURWCLAS@PURCCVM	Purdue Professional Writing Class Discussions
PURWRITE	PURWRITE@PURCCVM	Purdue Writing Majors and Alumni
PVM-L	PVM-L@DB0FUB11	Pass-Through Virtual Machines discussion list
PWRUSR-L	PWRUSR-L@MCGILL1	Power Users Group
P4200	P4200@IRLEARN	P4200-series Gateway Products Discussion Grou
Q-AND-A	Q-AND-A@JPNKISCI	Q and A — Postings for questions and answer
QADATA-L	QADATA-L@ALBNYDH2	New York State Department of Health: Data Qua
QMAIL-L	QMAIL-L@NCSUVM	QMail Information List
QNTEVA-L	QNTEVA-L@PSUVM	Quantitative Methods: Theory and Design. A TI
QTEMP	QTEMP@KENTVM	"Temporary Q Methodology Network"

QUAKE-L	QUAKE-L@NDSUVM1	QUAKE-L Discussion List
QUATRO-L	QUATRO-L@YALEVM	Borland Quattro Discussion Group at Yale
QUEENS-L	QUEENS-L@DEARN	QUEENS-L LIST
QUESTION	QUESTION@IPFWVM	IPFW User Question and Answer List
RADSIG	RADSIG@UWAVM	Radiology Special Interest Group
RAILROAD	RAILROAD@PCCVM	The Railroad List
RARE-EC	RARE-EC@IRLEARN	RARE Executive Committee Archive
RARE-L	RARE-L@IRLEARN	RARE Information & Discussion Distribution Li
RARE-MME	RARE-MME@IBACSATA	RARE Working Group 1 Multi Media Environment
RARE-WG1	RARE-WG1@IBACSATA	RARE Working Group 1
RARE-WG4	RARE-WG4@HEARN	RARE Working Group 4
RARE-WG8	RARE-WG8@HEARN	RARE Working Group 8
RARECOA	RARECOA@IRLEARN	Rare COA mailing list
RAREEXEC	RAREEXEC@IRLEARN	RARE Executive Committee
RBMI	RBMI@FRULM11	Groupe de Recherche en Biologie Moleculaire e
RC-LIST	RC-LIST@UCF1VM	Reevaluation Co-counseling discussion list
RCUG	RCUG@IRLEARN	Real COKE Users Group
RE-FORUM	RE-FORUM@UTARLVM1	Real Estate Forum
RECYCLE	RECYCLE@UMAB	Recycling in Practice
RED-BUG	RED-BUG@TREARN	Red File Server Users Group Bug Reports List
RED-SYS	RED-SYS@TREARN	Red File Server System Performance Discussion
RED-UG	RED-UG@DB0FUB11	(Peered) Red File Server Users Group
	RED-UG@HEARN	(Peered) Red File Server Users Group on Provi
	RED-UG@PTEARN	(Peered) Red Users Group on Provided Software
	RED-UG@TREARN	(Peered) Red Users Group on Provided Software
REDADMIN	REDADMIN@UCHCECVM	Administracion Red
REDALC	REDALC@FRMOP11	Reseau Amerique Latine et Caraibes
REDIST-L	REDIST-L@EB0UB011	(Peered) ARPA Re-Distribution
	REDIST-L@FINHUTC	(Peered) ARPA Re-

		Distribution
	REDIST-L@UGA	(Peered) ARPA Re-Distribution
REDTEC	REDTEC@UCHCECVM	Administracion Tecnica de la red REUNA.
REDUCE-L	REDUCE-L@DEARN	reduce-forum
REDUL	REDUL@FRMOP11	Coordination projet RE-DALC
REDULC	REDULC@FRMOP11	Groupes de contrepar-ties projet REDALC
REED-L	REED-L@UTORONTO	REED-L: Records of Ear-ly English Drama Discus
REGS-L	REGS-L@ALBNYDH2	Title 10 Rules and Regu-lations
RELATIV1	RELATIV1@UWF	Group 1 - Special Rela-tivity
RELATIV2	RELATIV2@UWF	Group 2 - Special Rela-tivity
RELIGCOM	RELIGCOM@UKCC	RELIGCOM —A Discus-sion forum re: RELigious C
RELUSR-L	RELUSR-L@NCSUVM	(Peered) Relay Users Forum
	RELUSR-L@UALTAVM	(Peered) Relay Users Forum
REL3-L	REL3-L@LEPICS	L3 reconstruction soft-ware forum
REMBAKUP	REMBAKUP@MITVMA	Remote Disk Backup Discussion List
RENPAC-L	RENPAC-L@BRLNCC	"USUARIOS REMOTOS VIA RENPAC"
REPARCHI	REPARCHI@ICNUCEVM	CNUCE Reparto Architet-ture Hardware e Softwar
RESEARCH	RESEARCH@TEMPLEVM	Research News
RESMON-L	RESMON-L@UAFSYSB	VMRESMON Maintainers List
RESP-DEC	RESP-DEC@ICINECA	RESP-DEC Discussioni su organizzazione e prob
REUNIR	REUNIR@FRMOP11	Liste des participants aux projets de REUNIR
REUNIRCT	REUNIRCT@FRMOP11	Coordination Technique de REUNIR
REVES	REVES@FRMOP11	Network on Helth Ex-pectancy
REXX-L	REXX-L@UIUCVMD	Rexx (language) discus-sions
REXXCOMP	REXXCOMP@UCF1VM	Rexx Compiler Discus-sion List
REXXLIST	REXXLIST@DEARN	(Peered) VM/SP REXX Language Discussion List
	REXXLIST@EB0UB011	(Peered) VM/SP REXX

		Language Discussion List
	REXXLIST@OHSTVMA	(Peered) General REXX Discussion List
	REXXLIST@POLYGRAF	(Peered) The REXX Language Discussion List
	REXXLIST@TWNMOE10	REXX discussion list
	REXX-L@UALTAVM	(Peered) The Rexx Language Discussion List
	REXXLIST@UCF1VM	(Peered) General REXX Language Discussion Lis
	REXXLIST@UGA	(Peered) REXX Programming discussion list
RHETORIC	RHETORIC@RPICICGE	Rhetoric, social movements, persuasion
	RHETORIC@RPIECS	Rhetoric, social movements, persuasion
RIRR	RIRR@ICNUCEVM	CNUCE Reparto Infrastrutture di Rete per la R
RIRRPRIV	RIRRPRIV@ICNUCEVM	CNUCE Reparto Infrastrutture di Rete per la R
RISKS	RISKS@CMUCCVMA	(Peered) Risks List
	RISKS@FINHUTC	(Peered) Risks in the use of computer systems
	RISKS@MARIST	(Peered) Risks List
RISKS-L	RISKS-L@IRLEARN	Discussion of Risks to Public in the Use of C
RLGLOC-L	RLGLOC-L@BINGVMB	RLG Library Systems Officer Forum
RNP-BIT	RNP-BIT@BRUFMG	Forum de discussao dos NAD's (Node ADministration
RNP-IBM	RNP-IBM@UFRJ	Discussao de sistemas IBM na RNP
RNPADM-L	RNPADM-L@BRLNCC	"ADMINISTRADORES DE NOS DA RNP"
ROBOTECH	ROBOTECH@USCVM	Robotech Mecha Listserv Group
ROOTS-L	ROOTS-L@NDSUVM1	ROOTS-L Genealogy List
ROUTTAB	ROUTTAB@BITNIC	ROUTTAB Test Sites List
RPCENTER	RPCENTER@PUCC	Rutgers-Princeton Center
RPDISTRB	RPDISTRB@PUCC	Rutgers-Princeton Center Distribution List.
RPIANN-L	RPIANN-L@RPICICGE	Rensselaer Announcements
	RPIANN-L@RPIECS	Rensselaer Announcements
RQSS	RQSS@UQUEBEC	Regroupement quebecois des sciences sociales
RSCS-L	RSCS-L@PUCC	RSCS Discussion List
RSCSMODS	RSCSMODS@EB0UB011	(Peered) The RSCS mod-

		ifications list
	RSCSMODS@FINHUTC	(Peered) The RSCS modifications list
	RSCSMODS@OHSTVMA	(Peered) The RSCS modifications list
RSCSV2-L	RSCSV2-L@BITNIC	(Peered) The RSCS version 2 List
	RSCSV2-L@DEARN	(Peered) The RSCS Version 2 List
	RSCSV2-L@EB0UB011	(Peered) The RSCS Version 2 List
	RSCSV2-L@FINHUTC	(Peered) The RSCS Version 2 List
	RSCSV2-L@HEARN	(Peered) The RSCS Version 2 List
	RSCSV2-L@UGA	(Peered) BITNIC RSCSV2-L List
RSTRAN-L	RSTRAN-L@YALEVM	RSCS Transparent Line Drivers for IBM 7171
RS1-L	RS1-L@NDSUVM1	RS1-L RS/1 List
RURALDEV	RURALDEV@KSUVM	Community and Rural Economic Development Inte
RUSTEX-L	RUSTEX-L@UBVM	Russian TeX and Cyrillic text processing list
R2B2	R2B2@UBVM	BITNET II REGION 2 INFORMATION LIST
SAD-L	SAD-L@UOGUELPH	Student Affairs Division: C.A.C.U.S.S.
SAFETY	SAFETY@UVMVM	Safety
SAG-L	SAG-L@UAFSYSB	Software AG Discussion List
SAME	SAME@FRULM11	SAME : Symbolic and Algebraic Manipulation in
SAMP-L	SAMP-L@UVMVM	samp-l
SAMPLE	SAMPLE@STLAWU	Experimental
SAO-L	SAO-L@UHCCVM	Student Affairs Officers — Discussion List (
SAS-GE	SAS-GE@IGECUNIV	SAS-GELista utilizzatori SAS
SAS-L	SAS-L@AWIIMC11	(Peered) SAS(r) Discussion
	SAS-L@FINHUTC	(Peered) SAS(r) Discussion
	SAS-L@MARIST	(Peered) SAS(r) Discussion
	SAS-L@OHSTVMA	(Peered) SAS(r) Discussion
	SAS-L@TCSVM	(Peered) SAS(r) Discussion (TCSVM)
	SAS-L@TWNMOE10	SAS discussion group in

	SAS-L@UALTAVM	Ministry of Education (Peered) SAS(r) Discussion
SAS-OSU	SAS-OSU@OHSTVMA	SAS-OSU OSU SAS Discussion List
SASPAC-L	SASPAC-L@UMSLVMA	SAS Public Access Consortium - SASPAC-L
SAS606-L	SAS606-L@UNCVM1	UNC ACS SAS 6.06 information list.
SAW-L	SAW-L@UBVM	SAW Discussion List
SBC-GRAF	SBC-GRAF@UFRJ	Comissao Especial de Computacao Grafica da SB
SBIEEE-L	SBIEEE-L@SBCCVM	SUNY/Stony Brook IEEE Local Chapter
SBPC-L	SBPC-L@SBCCVM	SUNY/Stony Brook PC Interest Group
SBPRLG-L	SBPRLG-L@SBCCVM	SUNY/Stony Brook Prolog Interest Group
SBRHYM-L	SBRHYM-L@SBCCVM	SUNY/Stony Brook Literary Underground
SBSTAT-L	SBSTAT-L@SBCCVM	SUNY/Stony Brook Statistical Software Interes
SBSWE-L	SBSWE-L@SBCCVM	Society of Women Engineers - Student Section
SCC-L	MD48@CMUCCVMA	soc.culture.china (Bitnet Distribution)
SCHEME	SCHEME@BNANDP11	(Peered) Scheme Programming Language
	SCHEME@FINHUTC	(Peered) Scheme programming language
SCHOOL-L	SCHOOL-L@IRLEARN	
SCI-RES	SCI-RES@IRLEARN	BIOSCI Science-Resources Bulletin Board
SCIFRAUD	SCIFRAUD@ALBNYVM1	Discussion of Fraud in Science
SCIT-L	SCIT-L@QUCDN	Studies in Communication and Information Tech
SCODAE	SCODAE@UMAB	Communications Network for Pharmacy-School-Ba
SCOUTS-L	SCOUTS-L@NDSUVM1	SCOUTS-L Youth Groups Discussion List
SCRIPT-L	SCRIPT-L@DEARN	(Peered) IBM vs Waterloo SCRIPT discussion gr
	SCRIPT-L@IRLEARN	SCRIPT-L Bulletin Board
	SCRIPT-L@RICEVM1	(Peered) IBM vs Waterloo SCRIPT discussion gr
	SCRIPT-L@UGA	(Peered) IBM vs Water-

		loo SCRIPT discussion gr
SCR97-D	SCR97-D@TAMVM1	The SCRIPT/9700 Distribution List
SCR97-L	SCR97-L@TAMVM1	The SCRIPT/9700 Information List
SCSE	SCSE@UQUEBEC	Societe canadienne de science economique
SCTF-L	SCTF-L@RICEVM1	Supercomputing Task Force
SCUBA-L	SCUBA-L@GUVM	Scuba diving discussion list
SCUG-G	SCUG-G@DGOGWDG1	Systems Center User Group - German
SCUG-L	SCUG-L@MITVMA	Supercomputer Users List
SCUP	SCUP@BITNIC	SCUPNEWS - Society for College and University
SCUPMA-L	SCUPMA-L@AUVM	Mid-Altantic SCUP Newsletter
SCUPNEWS	SCUPNEWS@UCBCMSA	SCUPNEWS - Society for College & University P
SDA-L	SDA-L@LLUVM	Seventh-Day Adventists
SDNET	SDNET@USCVM	International System Dynamics Society (SDNET)
SEARCH-L	SEARCH-L@PURCCVM	CPT Faculty Search & Screen Committee
SECURITY	SECURITY@FINHUTC	(Peered) Security mailing list
	SECURITY@MARIST	(Peered) SECURITY Digest
	SECURITY@OHSTVMA	(Peered) SECURITY Digest
	SECURITY@TCSVM	(Peered) SECURITY Digest
SECUSS-L	SECUSS-L@UBVM	SECUSSA Discussion List
SEDS-L	SEDS-L@TAMVM1	Students for Exploration and Development of S
SEDSNEWS	SEDSNEWS@TAMVM1	Students for Exploration and Development of S
SEGINEWS	SEGINEWS@BLIULG11	Title of seginews list
SEISM-L	SEISM-L@BINGVMB	Seismological Data Distribution
SEISMD-L	SEISMD-L@BINGVMB	Seismological Discussion
SERIALST	SERIALST@UVMVM	SERIALST: SERIALS in libraries - A user discu
SERVER-L	SERVER-L@IRLEARN	EARNTECH Servers Discussion
SERVERS	SERVERS@BNANDP11	Servers Machine Discussion List
SF-LIST	SF-LIST@JPNKISCI	SF author lists

SFER-L	SFER-L@UCF1VM	South Florida Environmental Reader
SFLOVERS	SFLOVERS@RUTVM1	(Peered) SF-Lovers List
	SFLOVERS@TCSVM	(Peered) SF-Lovers List
	SFLOVERS@UGA	(Peered) SF-Lovers List
SGAN-SAV	SGAN-SAV@VTVM1	SGANet - Student Association of Virginia (SAV
SGANET	SGANET@VTVM1	STUDENT GOVERNMENT GLOBAL MAIL NETWORK
SGANET-A	SGANET-A@VTVM1	Student Government Asian/Australian Mail Netw
SGANET-E	SGANET-E@VTVM1	Student Government European Mail Network
SGANET-N	SGANET-N@VTVM1	Student Government North American Mail Networ
SGANET-S	SGANET-S@VTVM1	STUDENT GOVERNMENT LATIN AMERICAN MAIL NETWOR
SGANET-T	SGANET-T@VTVM1	SGANet Technical Discussion Group
SGML-L	SGML-L@DHDURZ1	SGML-L Mailing list
SHAKER	SHAKER@UKCC	Shaker - A forum on the United Society of Bel
SHAKSPER	SHAKSPER@UTORONTO	Shakespeare Electronic Conference
SHAPE-L	SHAPE-L@DB0TUI11	Shape discussion list
SHARE-L	SHARE-L@FRORS12	Spectroscopic Happenings on Actinides and Rar
SHOGI-L	SHOGI-L@TECHNION	The Shogi Discussion List
SHOPTALK	SHOPTALK@MCGILL1	Micro Computer Users Forum
SIGAC-L	SIGAC-L@UNCVM1	ADCIS Academic Computing SIG.
SIGUCCS	SIGUCCS@OHSTVMA	SIGUCCS 90 Planning Committee
SILGRA-L	SILGRA-L@WSUVM1	Silicon Graphics Workstations List
SIMULA	SIMULA@BITNIC	(Peered) The SIMULA Language List
	SIMULA@DEARN	(Peered) The SIMULA Language List
SINAPE-L	SINAPE-L@BRLNCC	"SIMPOSIO NACIONAL DE PROBABILIDADE E ESTATIS
SINFONIA	SINFONIA@ASUACAD	Phi Mu Alpha Sinfonia discussion group

SIR-L	SIR-L@UREGINA1	SIR/DBMS(r) Software Discussion List
SIS-COM	SIS-COM@UVMVM	SIS-COM: Student Information Systems Committe
SITEMGRS	SITEMGRS@UIUCVMD	CSO Student Site Management
SITENEWS	SITENEWS@UIUCVMD	CSO Operators Site Information Mailing List
SKEPTIC	SKEPTIC@YORKVM1	SKEPTIC Discussion Group
SKIVT-L	SKIVT-L@UVMVM	SKIVT-L: Ski Vermont — Area Snow Reports and
SLART-L	SLART-L@PSUVM	Second Language Acquisition Research and Teac
SLOVAK-L	SLOVAK-L@UBVM	Discussion of Slovak issues
SM-RUM	SM-RUM@ICNUCEVM	SMall Ruminant Discussion List
SM-WG	SM-WG@ICNUCEVM	SM-WG CNUCE Servizio Erogazione Calcolo
SMALK	SMALK@FINHUTC	SmallTalk discussion
SMS-L	SMS-L@VTVM1	System-Managed Storage Discussion List
SNAMGT-L	SNAMGT-L@UMRVMB	SNA Network Management Discussion
SN3-L	SN3-L@HEARN	Distribution list for High Speed Internetwork
SN3BEV-L	SN3BEV-L@HEARN	Distribution list for the SURFnet-3 project w
SN3GEB-L	SN3GEB-L@HEARN	Distribution list for the SURFnet-3 project w
SN3TEC-L	SN3TEC-L@HEARN	Distribution list for the SURFnet-3 project w
SOCCER-L	SOCCER-L@UKCC	Soccer Boosters List
SOCORG-K	SOCORG-K@U	TORONTO Social Organization of Knowledge Discussion &
SOCWORK	SOCWORK@UMAB	Social Work Discussion List
SOFT-ENG	SOFT-ENG@BYUVM	(Soft-Eng. Arpa Discussions)
SOFT-L	SOFT-L@UCHCECVM	Lista de Software para Microcomputadores y ot
SOFTRB-L	SOFTRB-L@YALEVM	Yale Project Eli Software Review Board
SOS-DATA	SOS-DATA@UNCVM1	Social Science Data List.
	SOS-DATA@UNCXA1	Social Science Data List.
SOSAIN	SOSAIN@JPNKISCT	SOSAIN communication list
SPACE	SPACE@FINHUTC	(Peered) Space discus-

		sions forum
	SPACE@TCSVM	(Peered) SPACE Digest
	SPACE@UBVM	(Peered) SPACE Digest
	SPACE@UGA	(Peered) SPACE Digest
SPACE-IL	SPACE-IL@TAUNIVM	Israeli Space & Remote Sensing List
SPAD	SPAD@FRULM11	SPAD : GROUPE DE DISCUSSION AUTOUR DE SCRATCH
SPCEDS-L	SPCEDS-L@UBVM	SUNY/Buffalo Special Education (Students) Dis
SPEEDE-L	SPEEDE-L@VTVM1	AACRAO electronic transcript discussion
SPHALB-L	SPHALB-L@ALBNYDH2	SUNYA/DOH/AMC SCHOOL OF PUBLIC HEALTH
SPILIB-L	SPILIB-L@SUVM	SPIRES Library Discussion Group
SPIRES-L	SPIRES-L@BITNIC	(Peered) SPIRES Conference List
	SPIRES-L@DEARN	(Peered) SPIRES Conference List
	SPIRES-L@EB0UB011	(Peered) SPIRES Conference List
SPITEK-L	SPITEK-L@UNCVM1	List for SPIRES Technical Personnel.
SPORTPSY	SPORTPSY@TEMPLEVM	Exercise and Sports Psychology
SPRINT-L	SPRINT-L@NDSUVM1	SPRINT-L Borland Sprint Word Processor Discus
SPSSX-L	SPSSX-L@MARIST	(Peered) SPSSX(r) Discussion
	SPSSX-L@OHSTVMA	(Peered) SPSSX(r) Discussion
	SPSSX-L@TWNMOE10	SPSSX(r) redistribution from UGA
	SPSSX-L@UALTAVM	(Peered) SPSSX(r) Discussion
	SPSSX-L@UGA	(Peered) SPSSX(r) Discussion
SPSS90-L	SPSS90-L@MCGILL1	SPSS 90 Conference List
SPSS91-L	SPSS91-L@MCGILL1	SPSS 91 Conference List
SQL-L	SQL-L@DB0FUB11	(Peered) SQL discussion list
	SQL-L@FINHUTC	(Peered) SQL discussion list
	SQL-L@MITVMA	SQL Info Exchange
SQLINFO	SQLINFO@UICVM	Forum for SQL/DS and Related Topics
SQSP	SQSP@UQUEBEC	Societe quebecoise de science politique

SRCMSL-L	SRCMSL-L@MCMVM1	SRCMSL-L LIST
SRIS-L	SRIS-L@UKANVM	"KU Student Records Information System Staff"
SRVNOT-L	SRVNOT-L@YALEVM	Service Notes Group
SSA-TF	SSA-TF@UVMVM	SSA-TF: Support Services and Administration T
SSCNEWS	SSCNEWS@UTARLVM1	News from the Superconducting Super Collider
ST-AUDIT	ST-AUDIT@UWF	Spacetime Topics for Bitnet (Audit List)
STAMPS	STAMPS@PCCVM	The Stamps List
STARDATA	STARDATA@HASARA11	Sociaal Wetenschappelijke Databestanden
STARGAME	STARGAME@PCCVM	STARTREK Role Playing game list
STAT-GEO	STAT-GEO@UFRJ	Forum of Quantitative Methods in Geosciences.
STAT-L	STAT-L@MCGILL1	STATISTICAL CONSULTING
STATEPOL	STATEPOL@UMAB	Politics in the American States
STATLG-L	STATLG-L@SBCCVM	Bitnet Baseball League and Sports Discussion
STD-L	STD-L@BITNIC	(Peered) BITNET Standards List
	STD-L@DEARN	(Peered) BITNET Standards List
	STD-L@EB0UB011	(Peered) BITNET Standard Environments
	STD-L@FINHUTC	(Peered) BITNET Standards List
	STD-L@HEARN	(Peered) BITNET Standards List
	STD-L@MARIST	(Peered) BITNET Standards List
	STD-L@UGA	(Peered) BITNIC STD-L List
STD-UNIX	STD-UNIX@TCSVM	STD-UNIX redistribution list
STINGCRN	STINGCRN@CERNVM	List STINGCRN
STKACS-L	STKACS-L@USCVM	Storage Tek Automated Cartridge System Discus
STLHE-L	STLHE-L@UNBVM1	Forum for Teaching & Learning in Higher Educ.
STOPRAPE	STOPRAPE@BROWNVM	Sexual Assault Activist List
STORM-L	STORM-L@UIUCVMD	STORM-L Storms and weather related info
STORM-W	STORM-W@UIUCVMD	STORM-W Storms and Weather Watches
STREK-L	STREK-L@HEARN	(Peered) Star Trek Fan

		Club list
	STREK-L@PCCVM	(Peered) Star Trek Fan Club list
STUDENTS	STUDENTS@JPNTOHOK	Tohoku Univ Students Forum
STUDSRVC	STUDSRVC@PURCCVM	CPT Student Services Commmittee
STUTT-L	STUTT-L@TEMPLEVM	Stuttering: Research and Clinical Practice
SUEARN-L	SUEARN-L@UBVM	Connecting the USSR to Internet digest
SUG-L	SUG-L@UNCVM1	RTPNC SAS Users Group.
SUGGEST	SUGGEST@TEMPLEVM	Temple's mainframe discussion
SUNIBI-L	SUNIBI-L@YALEVM	Focus/Sun Discussion Group
SUNSPOTS	SUNSPOTS@FRULM11	(Peered) Sun Spots Discussion
	SUNSPOTS@RICEVM1	(Peered) Sun Microsystems Hardware and Softwa
	SUNSPOTS@UBVM	(Peered) Sun Spots Discussion
SUNYDEC	SUNYDEC@UBVM	SUNY DEC Local Users Group Mailing List
SUNYEC-L	SUNYEC-L@BINGVMB	SUNY Educational Communications Centers
SUNYLA-L	SUNYLA-L@BINGVMB	SUNY Library Association Listserv
SUNYSPHL	SUNYSPHL@ALBNYDH2	State University of New York School of Public
SUNYT1-L	SUNYT1-L@SNYCENVM	SUNY T1 Project Status list
SUNY2D-L	SUNY2D-L@UBVM	SUNY Title IID Grant Discussion List
SUP-COND	SUP-COND@TAUNIVM	SuperConductivity List
SUP-L	SUP-L@UKACRL	
SUPER	SUPER@BLEKUL11	Super list
SUPER-L	SUPER-L@BRUSPVM	Supercomputadores
	SUPER-L@MCGILL1	Super Computer Users Forum
SUPER-U	SUPER-U@UNCVM1	UNC/ACS Super Computer Users.
SUPERC	SUPERC@FRMOP11	European Superconductivity
SUPERSFT	SUPERSFT@PSUVM	Announcement list of available IBM 3090 softw
SUPERSIG	SUPERSIG@UTORONTO	Super Computing Special Interest Group
SUPEUR	SUPEUR@FRMOP11	Supercomputing in Eu-

		rope (user's group)
SUPPOR-L	SUPPOR-L@ULKYVM	Support Center Testing Group
SUPSTEER	SUPSTEER@FRMOP11	Supeur Steering Committee
SURFIS	SURFIS@HDETUD1	SURFiS
SUTPPLS	SUTPPLS@JPNSUT10	student's discussion list
SUTTOOLS	SUTTOOLS@JPNSUT00	SUT tool's discussion list
SWIX	SWIX@CERNVM	No title defined
SWL-L	SWL-L@CUVMA	(Peered) Short Wave Listener's List
	SWL-L@OHSTVMA	(Peered) Short Wave Listener's List
SWNL	SWNL@UVMVM	swnl Social Work Newsletter
SWVW	SWVW@CERNVM	No title defined
SXUNIX-L	SXUNIX-L@HEARN	SUPER-UNIX User group
SYNTH-L	SYNTH-L@AUVM	Redistribution of rec.music.synth
TAG-L	TAG-L@NDSUVM1	TAG-L Talented and Gifted Education
TAINS-L	TAINS-L@JPNTOHOK	Forum on Tohoku Univ OSI Network
TASM-L	TASM-L@BRUFPB	Borland Turbo Assembler and Debugger List
TASP-L	TASP-L@TTUVM1	TASP-L
TAXACOMA	TAXACOMA@MSU	TAXACOM ANNOUNCEMENTS
TAXACOMP	TAXACOMP@MSU	TAXACOM PROGRAMMERS
TAXACOMT	TAXACOMT@MSU	TAXACOM TECHNICAL
TCP-IP	TCP-IP@TWNMOE10	ARPA TCP-IP Discussion Redistribution
	TCP-IP@UTDALLAS	ARPA TCP-IP Discussion Redistribution
	TCP-IP@UTDALVM1	ARPA TCP-IP Discussion Redistribution
TCP-IP-L	TCP-IP-L@BLEKUL10	tcp-ip-l local list
	TCP-IP-L@UIUCVMD	TCP-IP discussion from SRI-NIC
TCP-ITA	TCP-ITA@ICNUCEVM	TCP-ITA Problematiche delle reti Internet in
TCPIP-L	TCPIP-L@IRLEARN	TCPIP Information Distribution List
	TCPIP-L@UIUCVMD	TCP-IP Bitnet discussions
TCPLUS-L	TCPLUS-L@UCF1VM	TURBO C++ Discussion group.
TEACHEFT	TEACHEFT@WCU	Teaching Effectiveness
TECH-L	TECH-L@BITNIC	(Peered) TECH-L List
	TECH-L@DEARN	(Peered) TECH-L List

	TECH-L@EB0UB011	(Peered) Technical Working Groups
	TECH-L@FINHUTC	(Peered) TECH-L List
	TECH-L@UGA	(Peered) BITNIC TECH-L List
TECHNEWS	TECHNEWS@BITNIC	BITNET Technical News List
TECSUN-L	TECSUN-L@MITVMA	SUN Computer Technical Users List
TEI-L	TEI-L@UICVM	Text Encoding Initiative public discussion li
TEL	TEL@USCVM	The Turkish Electronic Mail List
TELCOM-L	TELCOM-L@UKANVM	"KU Telecommunications Discussion Group"
TELEMED	TELEMED@FRMOP11	Network for the TELEMED project
TELEX	TELEX@CEARN	TELEX Users List
TESLA	TESLA@NERVM	Technical Standards for Library Automation
TEST	TEST@BLEKUL10	Test list
	TEST@FRMOP11	Liste de Test
	TEST@KENTVM	"The test list"
	TEST@PURCCVM	Test list
	TEST@TAUNIVM	Test list only
	TEST@TREARN	(Peered) This is a test
	TEST@TREGE1	(Peered) This is a test
TEST-L	TEST-L@FRULM11	TEST List
	TEST-L@GREARN	A list for LISTMAN (List Manager) tests
	TEST-L@KRKOREA1	Test list for newly installed LISTSERV.
	TEST-L@MCGILL1	TEST-l
	TEST-L@MCMVM1	TEST LIST
	TEST-L@NMSUVM1	Test list
	TEST-L@PUCING	Lista de prueba
	TEST-L@SNYCENVM	SUNY Test List
	TEST-L@UHUPVM1	No title defined
	TEST-L@UIUCVMD	(Peered) Test list
	TEST-L@VTVM1	Test list - not for real use
	TEST-L@VTVM2	test list
	TEST-L@YALEADS	Test Distribution List
TESTE-L	TESTE-L@BRUFMG	Lista de teste do LCC
TESTS-L	TESTS-L@TECHNION	TESTS-L
TESTUWF	TESTUWF@UWF	UWF Test Listserv List
TEST1-L	TEST1-L@GSUVM1	TEST1-L: Wells Computer Center local test lis
	TEST1-L@UNCCVM	Test List to Check LISTSERV
TEST2	TEST2@TREARN	(Peered) This is a test - 2 list

TEST2-L	TEST2-L@UNCCVM	Test LISTSERV List 2
TEX-D-L	TEX-D-L@DEARN	German TeX Users Communication List
TEX-ED	TEX-ED@UICVM	TeX Education Forum List
TEX-EURO	TEX-EURO@DHDURZ1	TeX-EuroDistribution List for European TeX
TEX-HAX	TEX-HAX@JPNKISCI	LISTSERV:TEXHAX TeXhax local distribution lis
TEX-IBM	TEX-IBM@DHDURZ1	TEX-IBM Distribution list
TEX-L	TEX-L@BNANDP11	(Peered) The TeXnical topics list
	TEX-L@CLVM	(Peered) The TeXnical topics list
	TEX-L@FRULM11	TeX-L : TeXhax redistribution from ASTON
	TEX-L@HEARN	(Peered) The TeXnical topics list
	TEX-L@MARIST	(Peered) The TeXnical topics list
	TEXHAX@UWAVM	(Peered) TeXhax Distribution List
TEX-NL	TEX-NL@HEARN	TEX-NL
TEXHAX-L	TEXHAX-L@IRLEARN	TeX Information Distribution List
TEXIS-L	TEXIS-L@UTDALLAS	A Texas IS Faculty Research Forum
	TEXIS-L@UTDALVM1	A Texas IS Faculty Research Forum
TEXMAG-L	TEXMAG-L@BYUVM	(Peered) (TeXMaG)
	TEXMAG-L@DEARN	(Peered) TeXMaG list
	TEXMAG-L@HEARN	(Peered) (TeXMaG)
	TEXMAG-L@IRLEARN	(Peered) TeXMaG - Magazine for TeX Enthusiast
	TEXMAG-L@PUCC	(Peered) (TeXMaG)
	TEXMAG-L@TCSVM	(Peered) (TeXMaG)
	TEXMAG-L@UICVM	(Peered) (TeXMaG)
	TEXMAG-L@UTORONTO	(Peered) (TeXMaG)
TEXROX-L	TEXROX-L@TAMVM1	The TeXrox Information List
TEXT-SRV	TEXT-SRV@GREARN	A T.E.X.T. Consortium Info Center
THEATRE	THEATRE@GREARN	The Theatre Discussion List
THEORY	THEORY@JPNKISCI	LISTSERV:Theorynet local distribution list
THEORY-A	THEORY-A@NDSUVM1	Theory-A - TheoryNet World-Wide Events
THEORY-B	THEORY-B@NDSUVM1	Theory-B - TheoryNet Ongoing Seminars and Lec

THEORY-C	THEORY-C@NDSUVM1	Theory-C - TheoryNet General Discussions
THEORYNT	THEORYNT@NDSUVM1	TheoryNet List
	THEORYNT@UICVM	Computer Science Theory Net
THETAXI	THETAXI@GITVM1	Discussion list for Theta Xi Fraternity
THPHYSIO	THPHYSIO@FRMOP11	Thermal Physiology
THYST-L	THYST-L@BROWNVM	Thistle Discussion List
TIGER-L	TIGER-L@UKANVM	"TIGER Test Project"
TIMECLCK	TIMECLCK@UIUCVMD	CSO South Site Timeclock Logbook
TINCAN-L	TINCAN-L@YALEVM	Macintosh Terminal Emulator Issues
TKRING_U	TKRING_U@UNAMVM1	Lista de usuarios de la red TOKEN RING
TML-L	TML-L@IUBVM	Thesaurus Musicarum Latinarum Database for La
TNT-L	TNT-L@UMAB	TNT Discussion Group
TN3270-L	TN3270-L@RUTVM1	tn3270 protocol discussion list
TOPOLOGY	TOPOLOGY@UCBCMSA	Computational Topology
TOSCA-L	TOSCA-L@HEARN	TOSCA-L
TPRINT-L	TPRINT-L@YALEVM	TPrint Issues
TPS-L	TPS-L@INDYCMS	talk.politics.soviet via ListServ
TR-GRP-L	TR-GRP-L@UIUCVMD	
TR-L	TR-L@DB0FUB11	Token Ring discussion-list
TRACK-D	TRACK-D@AWIIMC11	(Peered) "TRACK Distribution List"
	TRACK-D@MARIST	(Peered) "TRACK Distribution List"
	TRACK-D@PUCC	(Peered) "TRACK Distribution List"
TRACK-L	TRACK-L@AWIIMC11	(Peered) "TRACKers forum"
	TRACK-L@MARIST	(Peered) "TRACKers forum"
	TRACK-L@PUCC	(Peered) "TRACKers forum"
TRAFIC-L	TRAFIC-L@BITNIC	(Peered) Traffic Monitoring List
	TRAFIC-L@DEARN	(Peered) Traffic monitoring list
	TRAFIC-L@EB0UB011	(Peered) Traffic Monitoring List
	TRAFIC-L@FINHUTC	(Peered) Traffic Monitoring List
	TRAFIC-L@HEARN	(Peered) Traffic monitor-

		ing list
	TRAFIC-L@MARIST	(Peered) Traffic monitoring list
	TRAFIC-L@UGA	(Peered) Traffic Monitoring List
TRANS-L	TRANS-L@BITNIC	(Peered) File transfer list
	TRANS-L@DEARN	(Peered) File transfer list
	TRANS-L@EB0UB011	(Peered) File Transport List
	TRANS-L@FINHUTC	(Peered) File Transfer List
	TRANS-L@UGA	(Peered) BITNIC TRANS-L List
TRANSGEN	TRANSGEN@BROWNVM	Transsexuality/ Transvestism/ Transgender List
TRANSIT	TRANSIT@GITVM1	Transit Issues Discussion List
TRAOM-L	TRAOM-L@AEARN	TRends in Angular Overlap Model
TRAVEL-L	TRAVEL-L@TREARN	Tourism Discussions..
TRC-L	TRC-L@ULKYVM	Telecommunications Research Center List
TRIREF-L	TRIREF-L@UNCVM1	Triangle Reference Librarians.
TSAA-L	TSAA-L@PURCCVM	Turkish Students Assistance Association
TSCCOM-L	TSCCOM-L@UIUCVMD	Tunisian Scientific Coordination Committee
TSMCOM-L	TSMCOM-L@UIUCVMD	Tunisian Scientific Magazine Committee
TSO-REXX	TSO-REXX@UCF1VM	TSO REXX Discussion List
TSSNEWS	TSSNEWS@PSUVM	Tunisian Scientific Society News
TSTAFF	TSTAFF@JPNKISCT	All staffs of ISC TOBATA K.I.T
TUG-Q	TUG-Q@TAMVM1	TUG Conference question list
TUNISNET	TUNISNET@PSUVM	The Tunisia Network
TURBOC-L	TURBOC-L@TREARN	(Peered) TURBO C Discussion group.
	TURBOC-L@TWNMOE10	BORLAND TURBO C DISCUSSION GROUP REDISTRIBUTI
	TURBOC-L@UCF1VM	(Peered) TURBO C Discussion group.
	TURBOC-L@UTFSM	(Peered) TURBO C Discussion group, Peer en UT
	TURBOC-L@YALEVM	Borland Turbo C Discus-

		sion Group at Yale
TV-L	TV-L@TREARN	TV Discussions....
TWNAD-L	TWNAD-L@TWNMOE10	TWNAD-L Taiwan BITNET NODE administration dis
TWUNIV-L	TWUNIV-L@TWNMOE10	Chinese Scholars and students discussion list
TXBITNET	TXBITNET@UTDALLAS	Texas BITNET issues list
	TXBITNET@UTDALVM1	Texas BITNET issues list
UACSR-L	CAPDU-L@UALTAVM	Canadian Association of Public Data Users
UAHELP	UAHELP@ARIZVM1	University of Arizona On-Line Consulting
UA2PRIME	UA2PRIME@CERNVM	UA2 Collaboration
UC-STUDY	UC-STUDY@UVMVM	UC-Study: UVM Computing Study Forum
UCLAMAIL	UCLAMAIL@OHSTVMA	UCLAMAIL TSO MAIL Interested parties list
UCLANTBK	UCLANTBK@OHSTVMA	UCLANTBK UCLA NOTEBOOK Interested parties lis
UCP-L	UCP-L@UBVM	University Computing Project Mailing List
UCRC-L	UCRC-L@VTVM1	University Communications Resources Committee
UCSCHE-L	UCSCHE-L@UNBVM1	Undergraduate CSCHE chapters list
UDD-L	UDD-L@CEARN	LISTSERV User Directory Database discussion
UF-ITR	UF-ITR@NERVM	UF Task Force on Information Technology Resou
UFO-L	UFO-L@BRUFPB	FORUM FOR UFOLOGY
UFRJNCEN	UFRJNCEN@UFRJ	Jornal Eletronico UFRJ-NCE Noticias
UFSC	UFSC@BRUFSC	(Peered) FORUM UFSC
UG-L	UG-L@BITNIC	(Peered) Usage Guidelines List
	UG-L@DEARN	(Peered) Usage Guidelines List
	UG-L@EB0UB011	(Peered) Usage Guidelines
	UG-L@FINHUTC	(Peered) Usage Guidelines List
	UG-L@HEARN	(Peered) Usage Guidelines List
	UG-L@MARIST	(Peered) Usage Guidelines List
	UG-L@UGA	(Peered) Usage Guidelines

UGCOLL-L	UGCOLL-L@UBVM	SUNY/Buffalo Undergraduate College Discussion
UHCC	UHCC@UHCCVM	University of Hawai'i Computing Center Staff
UHNEXT-L	UHNEXT-L@UHCCVM	UHCC NeXT Computer Systems Information and Discussion
UHPCINFO	UHPCINFO@UHCCVM	UHCC PC Information and Discussion Group.
UI-PCUG	UI-PCUG@UIUCVMD	UIUC IBM PC User Group
UICMATH	UICMATH@UICVM	UIC Mathematics
UICNETP	UICNETP@UICVM	UIC Campus Network Discussions
UINCSA-L	UINCSA-L@UIUCVMD	UINCSA-L
UINOVELL	UINOVELL@UIUCVMD	UI Novell Network Administrators
UKTEX	UKTEX@FRULM11	UKTeX : UKTeX redistribution from ASTON
UKTEX-L	UKTEX-L@DHDURZ1	UKTeX-L Distribution List for German TeX User
ULDENT-L	ULDENT-L@ULKYVM	U of L Dental School Faculty/Staff Discussion
UMSUPER	UMSUPER@UMDD	Supercomputer discussion for users from U. of
UNAMUSR	UNAMUSR@UNAMVM1	Lista de los usuarios de la REDUNAM
UNC-L	UNC-L@YALEVM	University Network Committee
UNCC-L	UNCC-L@UNCCVM	UNCC LISTSERV Discussion
UNCEDDOC	UNCEDDOC@UFRJ	UNCEDDOC - Private discussion List about Envi
UNCEDGEN	UNCEDGEN@UFRJ	UNCEDGEN - Public discussion List about Envir
UNCSYS-L	UNCSYS-L@UNCVM1	UNC/ACS Systems Test List.
UNINFSEC	UNINFSEC@CUVMC	University Administrative Information Securit
UNIONLOG	UNIONLOG@UIUCVMD	CSO UNION Site Online Logbook
UNISYS	UNISYS@UBVM	SUNY Unisys Sites Discussion List
UNIT-L	UNIT-L@ULKYVM	Unit Coordinators Discussion Group
UNIX-EMACS	EMACS@BNANDP11	(Peered) UNIX-EMACS distribution list
UNIX-SE	UNIX-SE@SEARN	Swedish EARN Node

		ADministrators - Unix sys
UNIX-SRC	UNIX-SRC@NDSUVM1	Unix-Sources Mailing List
	UNIX-SRC@TWNMOE10	UNIX SOURCE discussion List
UNIX-WIZ	UNIX-WIZ@NDSUVM1	Unix-Wizards Mailing List
	UNIX-WIZ@TWNMOE10	Unix-Wizards redistribution Mailing List
UNXNAD-F	UNXNAD-F@FRMOP11	Liste des 'Node ADminis-tators' UNIX francais
UPGRADE	UPGRADE@IPFWVM	IBM UPGRADE DISCUSSIONS
UPSA-L	UPSA-L@UKANVM	"KU Unclassified Professional Staff Associati
UPSAC	UPSAC@GWUVM	UPSAC Discussion List
URANTIAL	URANTIAL@UAFSYSB	Discussion of _The_Urantia_Book_
URBAN-L	URBAN-L@TREARN	Urban Planning Discussion List
URBAREG	URBAREG@UQUEBEC	Etudes urbaines et regionales
UREP-L	UREP-L@BNLVMXA	UREP-L Mailing list
US	US@UABDPO	User Services Support List
USGA-L	USGA-L@SIUCVMB	Student Government Net
USRDIR-L	USRDIR-L@BITNIC	(Peered) User Directory List
	USRDIR-L@DEARN	(Peered) User Directory List
USRGROUP	USRGROUP@GWUVM	GWU's USERGRP Discussion List
USSR-D	USSR-D@INDYCMS	No title defined
USSR-L	USSR-L@INDYCMS	No title defined
USSRECOM	USSRECOM@INDYCMS	No title defined
UTIL-L	UTIL-L@ALBNYDH2	PLATFORM UTILITIES LIST AT ALBNYDH2
UTS-ITC	UTS-ITC@UTXVM	UT System Information Technology Council List
UTS-L	UTS-L@YSUB	Amdahl UTS discussion list
UVM-LANS	UVM-LANS@UVMVM	UVM-LANS: UVM Local Area Networks
UVNETS-L	UVNETS-L@UVVM	UVic Network Contacts
UVP-A	UVP-A@BITNIC	BITNIC Update Program Administration list
UVP-D	UVP-D@BITNIC	BITNIC Update Program development list
UVTERM-L	UVTERM-L@UVVM	UVic UVTERM users
UWDECUS	UWDECUS@UWAVM	Mailing list for UW DECUS group

UWINGRES	UWINGRES@UWAVM	UW Ingres List
UWREFLIB	UWREFLIB@UWAVM	UW Reference Library List
VAL-L	VAL-L@UCF1VM	Valentine Michael Smith's commentary
VALERT-L	VALERT-L@LEHIIBM1	Virus Alert List
VAMPYRES	VAMPYRES@GUVM	For fans of vampiric lore, fact and fiction.
VAXTOOLS	VAXTOOLS@DEARN	(Peered) The VAX Toolbox [A BITNET Magazine f
	VAXTOOLS@HEARN	(Peered) The VAX Toolbox [A BITNET Magazine f
VECSRV-L	VECSRV-L@TREARN	Ege University Remote Vector Processor Users
VECTOR-L	VECTOR-L@UNBVM1	IBM 3090 Vector Processors
VERN-USR	VERN-USR@VTVM1	VERnet Users
VETCAI-L	VETCAI-L@KSUVM	VETERINARY MEDICINE COMPUTER ASSISTED INSTRUC
VETMED-L	VETMED-L@UGA	(Peered) Veterinary Medicine
	VETMED-L@VTVM2	(Peered) Veterinary Medicine
VEVA-L	VEVA-L@VTVM2	Virginia Educational Vax Association List
VFORT-L	VFORT-L@EB0UB011	(Peered) VS-Fortran discussion list
	VFORT-L@JHUVM	(Peered) VS-Fortran discussion list
VIDEOTEC	VIDEOTEC@VTVM1	ARPA Videotech relay
VIDNET-L	VIDNET-L@UGA	Video Network Discussion List
VIRUS-L	VIRUS-L@LEHIIBM1	Virus Discussion List
VLSI-L	VLSI-L@MITVMA	BITNET part of Info-VLSI@Think.COM
VLSICAD	VLSICAD@EB0UB011	(Peered) VLSI CAD interest list (CADinterest)
VM-REXX	VM-REXX@MARIST	(Peered) VM/SP REXX Language Discussion List
	VM-REXX@OHSTVMA	(Peered) VM/SP REXX Language Discussion List
	VM-REXX@UCF1VM	(Peered) VM/SP REXX Language Discussion List
VM-SE	VM-SE@SEARN	Swedish EARN Node ADministrators - VM systems
VM-SHOW	VM-SHOW@TREARN	VM-Show- Mizah Dergisi
VM-UTIL	VM-UTIL@DEARN	(Peered) VM Utilities

		Discussion List
	VM-UTIL@MARIST	(Peered) VM Utilities Discussion List
	VM-UTIL@OHSTVMA	(Peered) VM Utilities Discussion List
	VM-UTIL@TECMTYVM	(Peered) VM Utilities Discussion List
	VM-UTIL@TREARN	(Peered) VM Utilities Discussion List
	VM-UTIL@UBVM	(Peered) VM Utilities Discussion List
	VM-UTIL@UCF1VM	(Peered) VM Utilities Discussion List
	VM-UTIL@UTARLVM1	(Peered) VM Utilities Discussion List
VMAINT-L	VMAINT-L@UIUCVMD	VM Maintenance discussions
VMARCHL	VMARCHL@GWUVM	GWU's VMARCHIVE Discussion List
VMBATL	VMBATL@GWUVM	GWU's VMBATCH Discussion List
VMCENTER	L-VMCTR@AKRONVM	VMCENTER Components Discussion List
VMCOMMS	VMCOMMS@UKACRL	TEST LIST
VMCONS	VMCONS@MIAMIU	(Peered) VM Consultants discussion list
VMESA-L	VMESA-L@UAFSYSB	VM/ESA Discussions
VMKIDS-L	VMKIDS-L@DEARN	(Peered) VM low-key Tech-staff discussion
	VMKIDS-L@EB0UB011	(Peered) VM low-key Tech-staff discussion
	VMKIDS-L@MARIST	(Peered) VM low-key Tech-staff discussion
	VMKIDS-L@UBVM	(Peered) VM low-key Tech-staff discussion
VMLAVAL	VMLAVAL@LAVALVM1	Discussion sur VM/CMS a Laval — tous bienven
VMNAD-F	VMNAD-F@FRMOP11	Liste des 'Node ADministators' VM francais
VMPROB-D	VMPROB-D@UTCVM	VMPROBE Distribution List
VMPROB-L	VMPROB-L@UTCVM	VMPROBE List
VMREL6-L	VMREL6-L@UAFSYSB	VM Release 6 (SP and HPO) Discussions
VMS-SE	VMS-SE@SEARN	Swedish EARN Node ADministrators - VMS system
VMSLSV-L	VMSLSV-L@UBVM	VAX/VMS LISTSERV Discussion List
VMSNAD-F	VMSNAD-F@FRMOP11	Liste des 'Node ADministators' VMS francais

VMSTEX-L	VMSTEX-L@UICVM	VMSTEX-L
VMSYS-L	VMSYS-L@UGA	VM Systems Programmers List
VMTAPEL	VMTAPEL@GWUVM	GWU's VMTAPE Discussion List
VMTOOL-L	VMTOOL-L@UIUCVMD	VM Tools discussions
VMUSER-L	VMUSER-L@JPNSUT00	IBM soft & hard discussion list
VMUTIL-A	VMUTIL-A@UIUCVMD	VMUTIL-A (archive files only)
VMVIRUS	VMVIRUS@PCCVM	Open Discussion forum on VM viruses and worms
VMVTAM-L	VMVTAM-L@UIUCVMD	VM VTAM discussions
VMWKSHOP	VMWKSHOP@MARIST	1991 VM Workshop - June 4-7
VMXA	VMXA@BLEKUL10	VMXA list : testing VMXA
VMXA-L	VMXA-L@DEARN	(Peered) VM/XA Discussion List
	VMXA-L@UGA	(Peered) VM/XA Discussion List
VM3800-L	VM3800-L@UIUCVMD	VM 3800 printer discussions
VNEWS-L	VNEWS-L@UBVM	VNEWS Discussion List
VNIX-L	VNIX-L@TAMCBA	Single User Unix discussion
VOLCANO	VOLCANO@ASUACAD	VOLCANO
VOLYBALL	VOLYBALL@UIUCVMD	CSO Volleyball players
VSAM-L	VSAM-L@TREARN	Virtual Storage Access Method Discussion List
VSTAT-L	VSTAT-L@ALBNYDH2	VITAL STATISTICS AT ALBNYDH2
VT-HSNET	VT-HSNET@VTVM1	VT K-12 School Network
VTLSLIST	VTLSLIST@VTVM1	VTLS users list
VTSQL-L	VTSQL-L@VTVM1	Virginia Tech Local SQL discussion
VTX-L	VTX-L@NCSUVM	DEC VideoText Discussion List
	VTX-L@RITVM	VAX VTX (Videotex) Discussion Group
VUGMAIL	VUGMAIL@UKACRL	VUGMAIL LIST
VWAR-L	VWAR-L@UBVM	Viet Nam War Discussion List
VZLA-L	VZLA-L@YALEVM	ATARRAYA (Red Venezolana)
WCETINFO	WCETINFO@UNMVM	WCETINFO - Western Cooperative Information Cl
WEIRD-L	WEIRD-L@BROWNVM	Mmytacist Mmanufacture
WGAS-L	WGAS-L@SCFVM	Working Group on As-

		tronomical Software
WG3270-L	WG3270-L@UMDD	3270 Working Group Discussion List
WG4-CONS	WG4-CONS@HEARN	CONS subgroup of RARE WG4
WG4-INT	WG4-INT@HEARN	Interworking subgroup of RARE WG4
WG4-NSAP	WG4-NSAP@HEARN	Distributionlist on NSAP-addressing (part of
WG4-NWMG	WG4-NWMG@HEARN	Network management subgroup of RARE WG4
WHIM	WHIM@TAMVM1	WHIM - a discussion list for "Humour Studies"
WIN-L	WIN-L@DEARN	X.25 - Wissenschaftsnetz (techn. Koord.)
WIN3-L	WIN3-L@UICVM	Microsoft Windows Version 3 Forum
WIP	WIP@SUVM	Teaching Tools Works in Progress List
WISCNET	WISCNET@DB0TUI11	(Peered) WISCNET interested party list
	WISCNET@IRLEARN	UCD Distribution of WISCNET
	WISCNET@TCSVM	(Peered) WISCNET interested party list
WISE	WISE@UICVM	Workshop on Information Systems Economics
WKSPHYS	WKSPHYS@IDBSU	LISTSERV LIST 'WKSPHYS - Workshop Physics'
WOMNDIVE	WOMNDIVE@UTORONTO	Women in Diving Discussion List
WORDS-L	WORDS-L@YALEVM	English Language Discussion Group
WORKS	WORKS@RUTVM1	WorkS List
WORKS-L	WORKS-L@NDSUVM1	WORKS-L Writers List Works
WOT-HELP	WOT-HELP@SUVM	What's Out There Help List
WP50-L	WP50-L@HEARN	(Peered) WordPerfect Corporation Products Dis
	WP50-L@UBVM	(Peered) WordPerfect Corporation Products Dis
	WP50-L@YORKVM1	(Peered) WordPerfect Corporation Products Dis
WRAKG-L	WRAKG-L@DCZTU1	Graphikarbeitskreis der wissenschaftlichen Re
WRITENG	WRITENG@NDSUVM1	WRITENG Writing in Engineering
WRITERS	WRITERS@NDSUVM1	WRITERS
WSLOG	WSLOG@UIUCVMD	CSO WoodShop Site On-

		line Logbook
WSULAB-L	WSULAB-L@WSUVM1	Computer Lab Management
WU-AIDS	AIDS@WUVMD	Sci.Med.AIDS Newsgroup
WUNIHG-L	WUNIHG-L@WUVMD	Washington University NIH Guide Distribution
WVGIS-L	WVGIS-L@WVNVM	WVa GIS Discussion List
WVNCSF-L	WVNCSF-L@WVNVM	WVNET Computer Science Faculty List
WWP-L	WWP-L@BROWNVM	Brown University Women Writer's Project
WX-LSR	WX-LSR@UIUCVMD	WX-LSR Local Storm Reports and other local WX
WX-MISC	WX-MISC@UIUCVMD	WX-MISC Miscellaneous WX products
WX-NATNL	WX-NATNL@UIUCVMD	WX-NATNL National Wx Summary and Selected Cite
WX-PCPN	WX-PCPN@UIUCVMD	WX-PCPN Precipitation WX products
WX-SPOT	WX-SPOT@UIUCVMD	WX-SPOT weather spotters and coordinators
WX-STLT	WX-STLT@UIUCVMD	WX-STLT Satellite interpretive messages
WX-SWO	WX-SWO@UIUCVMD	WX-SWO Severe Weather Outlooks
WX-TALK	WX-TALK@UIUCVMD	WX-TALK General weather discussions and talk
WX-TROPL	WX-TROPL@UIUCVMD	WX-TROPL Tropical Storm and Hurricane WX prod
WX-WATCH	WX-WATCH@UIUCVMD	WX-WATCH WX Watches and cancellations
WX-WSTAT	WX-WSTAT@UIUCVMD	WX-WSTAT WX Watch status and storm reports
WXMAP-L	WXMAP-L@UIUCVMD	Discussions about the wxmap program
WXSPOT-L	WXSPOT-L@UIUCVMD	WXSPOT-L weather spotters and coordinators
WYLBUR-L	WYLBUR-L@CUNYVM	WYLBUR System Maintainers Mailing List
W5AC	W5AC@TAMCBA	TAMU Amateur Radio Club
XANN	XANN@FINHUTC	Xwindows announcements
XATEST-L	XATEST-L@UKANVM	"VM/XA Test List"
XCULT-L	XCULT-L@PSUVM	International Intercultural Newsletter
	XCULT-L@TWNMOE10	International Intercultu-

		ral Newsletter
XCULT-X	XCULT-X@UMRVMB	Intercultural Communication Practicum
XEARN	XEARN@FINHUTC	X.EARN Project Information
XEDIT-L	XEDIT-L@MARIST	(Peered) VM System Editor List
	XEDIT-L@OHSTVMA	(Peered) VM System Editor List
XEROX-L	XEROX-L@TAMVM1	The Xerox Discussion List
XMAILBUG	XMAILBUG@PUCC	Mailer release 2.0 bug list
XMAILER	XMAILER@BITNIC	(Peered) The Columbia Mailer List
	XMAILER@DEARN	(Peered) The Crosswell Mailer List
	XMAILER@UGA	(Peered) Crosswell Mailer
	XMAILER@UIUCVMD	XMAILER (log files only)
XPERT	XPERT@FINHUTC	Xwindows discussion
	XPERT@TWNMOE10	XPERT XWINDOW DISCUSSION (REDISTRIBUTION FRO
XPORT	XPORT@FINHUTC	Xwindows discussion (porting Xwindows)
XYZZY-L	XYZZY-L@CMUCCVMA	XYZZY Discussion
X25-L	X25-L@UFRJ	Acesso X.25 - Discussoes e Informacoes
X400	X400@CEARN	(Peered) X400 List
	X400@EB0UB011	(Peered) CEARN X400 List
X400-L	X400-L@BITNIC	(Peered) BITNET X.400 Discussion
	X400-L@DEARN	(Peered) BITNET X400 List
	X400-L@EB0UB011	(Peered) BITNET X400 List
	X400-L@UGA	(Peered) x.400 Protocol List
YACHT-L	YACHT-L@GREARN	The Yachting, Sailing and amateur BoatBuildin
YTERM-L	YTERM-L@YALEVM	Yale Terminal Emulator Issues
YUNUS	YUNUS@TRMETU	(Peered) Turkish TeX Users Group YUNUS
Z3950IW	Z3950IW@NERVM	Z39.50 Implementors Workshop
21ST-C-L	21ST-C-L@BRUFPB	Forum about the 21ST century discussions
3COM-L	3COM-L@NUSVM	3Com User Interest

		Group Discussion List
3D-L	3D-L@ARIZVM1	A discussion of 3D-Graphics
3D-PHOTO	3D-PHOTO@UIUCVMD	3D-PHOTO (archive files only)
386USERS	386USERS@NDSUVM1	386Users
4AD-L	4AD-L@JHUVM	4ad recording artists list
5540-PC	5540-PC@JPNKISCI	5540(PC) FILES
9NOV89-L	9NOV89-L@DB0TUI11	Events around the Berlin Wall
9370-L	9370-L@HEARN	IBM 9370 and VM/IS specific topics list

7.8 The Survey Distributed to Conferencing Systems for This Study

8/17/90

Dear Conferencing System Coordinator:

I am working on a resource directory of conferencing systems and software for librarians. The directory is part of a final report to a granting agency for this exploratory work. Hopefully, it will be published, but there is no contract for publication at this time. The scope of the directory is all public conferencing systems where conferencing is something more than bulletin board activity, but includes some information about Netnews. I also have sections on the major packet switching network services, Internet, and a little Bitnet.

I may have bothered you about the directory with questions about one thing or another already. Thank you very much for all your help so far. I know you are busy.

BUT! I want to make sure I have covered all the bases with everyone, thus this survey. So, if you can get this back to me soon, I'm forever in your debt.

Name & address:

(Internet address)
(other net address)

Phone numbers:

(voice)

(data)
(fax)

Hardware system is running on (manufacturer, model, memory, storage):

Number of incoming ports and bauds:

Network access? (address if so):

Software system is using:

Date service began:

Number of Users:

Costs of access:

Do you provide private conferences (costs?):

Gateways (Can mail to internet? other systems, whatever):

Special features (database management, keyword indexing):

Permission to reproduce parts of an online session:

(Will you allow me to download and include a typical logon, a list of conferences on the system, and a help screen? I won't reproduce any material posted by an individual outside of the system organization without explicit permission.)

Bibliography (one or two good articles about the system?):

Additional info:

If there is any other info that you would like to have included in such a work, e-mail it to me or point me to it.

Please mail this back to me at the address on the header of this message or

at one of the addresses below.
Thank you very much for taking the trouble to fill this out. I'll be providing each of you with a copy of the completed project. I will finish it this fall, but have a draft deadline of September.

Brian Williams

8. Bibliography

8.1 INTRODUCTION

The following bibliography is a selected compilation of material from computerized literature searches of the ERIC, Dissertation Abstracts Online, Library and Information Science Abstracts, NTIS, Computer Database, Social Science Citation Index, and Microcomputer Index, databases plus other items as judged relevant. It is not intended to be a comprehensive bibliography of the subject. Older material, pre 1980, is mostly left out unless it is unique in some way. The material that is included is meant to reflect the scope of research and publication in the field. I began with a scan of the keywords "computer conferencing" in Easynet via Alanet. The summary follows:

Library & Computer Technology scan results for: COMPUTER CONFERENCING

PRESS	TO SEARCH	Results	Format	Source Type
1	Books in Print	4	reference	books
2	ERIC	151	abstract	journals
3	NTIS	119	abstract	gov't publ
	Buyer's Guide to Micro Software	0	abstract	multiple sources
4	Computer ASAP	69	full text	journals
5	Computer Database	102	abstract	magazines
6	Dissertation Abstracts Online	17	abstract	dissertations
7	*Information Science Abstracts	120	abstract	journals
8	Library & Information Science	85	abstract	journals
9	Microcomputer Index	72	abstract	journals
10	Social SciSearch	32	reference	journals

* Good choice for professional literature.

H Database descriptions
M Main Menu
SOS Online assistance

->

Each entry in the bibliography has four fields, or parts. The author, if there is one, is first, then the title of the piece. The name of the journal follows, if it is a journal article, then a set of keywords, for most entries. If there is no author, the entry is alphabetized by title. The format is modified ANSI. I have chosen to put each new field on a new line to facilitate transport in and out of computer files. Many of the keywords are those given to the entry in the database from which it came.

I have retained the document numbers for ERIC documents, government reports, and Dissertation Abstracts material to facilitate the acquisition of those items.

8.2 BIBLIOGRAPHY

Abrioux, Dominique A. M. X.
Computer-Assisted Language Learning and Distance Education.
Journal of Distance Education. 4(1) :20-35 ; Spr 1989.
Computer Assisted Instruction; Distance Education; Second Language Learning; Computer Assisted Testing; Computer Managed Instruction; Summative Evaluation; Teleconferencing.

Adams, Dennis; Hamm, Mary.
Telecommunications and the Building of Knowledge Networks: Here Today, Much More Tomorrow.
Educational Technology. 28(9) :51(3) ; Sept, 1988.
Trends; Outlook; Networks; On Line Inquiry; Impact Analysis; Education; Information Services.

American Geological Inst.
Design of an Experimental Cooperative Network for Sharing Information and Data Resources in Geology.
Dec 78 156p PB-296 286/8
Information Systems; Geology; Computer Networks; Teleconferencing.

Anderson, Bart; Costales, Bryan; Henderson, Harry.
UNIX Communications.
Indianapolis, Indiana: Howard Sams; 1987.
Usenet; UUCP.

Anderson, Terry; et al.
Cooperation and Collaboration in Distance Education: The Contact North/Contact Nord Experience.
RIEOCT89. ED307092.
Access to Education; Distance Education; Educational Technology; Institutional Cooperation; Nontraditional Education; Shared Resources and Services; Cooperative Programs; Foreign Countries; Postsecondary Education; Program Descriptions.

Arblaster, John R.
Contact North: The Concept, Policy, Development, and Status of the Northern Ontario Distance Education Access Network.

RIEFEB89. ED298994.
Cooperative Planning; Distance Education; Educational Technology; Institutional Cooperation; Nontraditional Education; Shared Resources and Services; Access to Education; Community Colleges; Cooperative Programs; Foreign Countries; Outreach Programs.

Arms, Caroline R.
Using the National Networks: BITNET and the Internet.
Online. 14(5):24-29;Sept. 1990.

Arms, Valarie Meliotes.
Computer Conferencing: Models and Proposals.
Educational Technology. 28(3) :43+ ; March, 1988
Computer Conferences; Guidelines; Communication; Organizations.

Arnold, George W.; Unger, Stephen H. (Columbia University New York)
A Structured Data Base Computer Conferencing System.
In Korfhage, Robert R., Ed. AFIPS Conference Proceedings. Volume 46.1977 National Computer Conference, June 13-16, 1977, Dallas, Texas. 1977.P. 461-467. 6 Illus. 19 Ref.
CBIE, a structured data base computer conferencing system.

Augsburg, Cray.
Checking into Conference.
Rainbow. 6(9) :94+ ; April, 1987.
User Groups; Computer Conferencing; Computer Bulletin Boards; Microcomputers; Communications Applications; Data Communications.

Babcock, Charles.
Remote Micros Connect for Electronic Meetings.
Computerworld. 19(42) :33+; Oct 21 1985.
Computer Conferencing; UNIX; IBM PC Compatible; Eforum; Docuform; Network Technologies Inc.; Microvax; AT&T 3B2/300; VAX.

Bacsich, P.D. (Open Univ., Walton, Bletchley, Bucks, England)
Teleconferencing for Distance Education and Training.
25 pp., Mar 1985, Pub. No: ED 273 258, 24 ref.
Information Generation, Reproduction, and Distribution Meetings, Personal Interchange; Distance Learning; Educational Technology; Teleconferences; Training

Bailey, Charles W. Jr.
Public-Access Computer Systems: The Next Generation of Library Automation Systems.
Information Technology and Libraries. 8(2) :178-85; Jun 1989.
Information Services; Information Systems; Library Automation; Library Role; Library Services; Online Systems; Computer Assisted Instruction; Expert Sys-

tems; Information Networks; Library Catalogs; Library Instruction; Microcomputers.

Baird P.M.; Borer B. (Univ Strathclyde, Glasgow)
An Experiment in Computer Conferencing Using a Local Area Network.
Electronic Library. 5(3): 162-169; 1987.

Balson, David ; Drysdale, Robert ; Stanley, Bob, eds.
Computer-based Conferencing Systems for Developing Countries : Report of a Workshop held in Ottawa, Canada, 26-30 October 1981.
Ottawa, Canada :International Development Research Centre; 1982.

Bankier, J. K. (Dalhousie Univ, Halifax, Canada)
Strategic-Planning for Computer Conferencing in Non-technological Fields - The Law - Forum Experiment
Proceedings of the American Society for Information Science, 23 :1-5 ; 1986

Barney, Clifford
Computer Conferencing With EIES.
PC Magazine. 1(9) :270-279 ; Jan., 1983
Computer Conferences; Software; Industry Analysis; Biography; Teleconferencing; Networks.

Barney, Clifford
Conferencing Compared: Face-to-Face vs. Computer vs. Video.
PC: The Independent Guide to IBM Personal Computers. 1(2) :61; Mar 1982.
Business; Management; Telecommunications; Computer Conferencing.

Barney, Clifford.
Source Bulletin Board / Conferencing / Prestel Coming for PC.
PC: The Independent Guide to IBM Personal Computers. 1(3) :80; Jun 1982.
Online Information; IBM Personal Computer; Videotex; Computer Conferencing; PC Gazette; The Source; EIES; Prestel; Wolfdata.

Barney, Clifford.
Virtual Meeting: Using Your Computer for Online Conferencing.
PC: The Independent Guide to IBM Personal Computers. 1(2) :58-60; Mar 1982.
Computer Conferencing; ARPANET; Electronic Information Exchange System (EIES); Conference Tree; Augment; Telemail; Participate.

Barney, Clifford; Cross, T.B.
The Virtual Meeting. A Report on Computer Conferencing.
Computerworld. 16(38): 48; Sep. 20, 1982.
Information Generation, Reproduction, Distribution Meetings, Personal Interchange; Computer Conferencing; Conferencing Computer.

Bates, A.W. (Open Univ., Milton Keynes (England). Inst. of Educational Technology.)
New Communications Technology and Distance Education. Implications for Commonwealth Countries of the South. Papers on Information Technology. No.239.
24 pp., Dec 1984, Open Univ., Walton, Bletchley, Bucks, England, Pub. No: ED253 215, 4 ref.
Information Generation, Reproduction, and Distribution; Education, Computer Assisted Instruction; Developing Countries; Distance Learning; Educational Technology; Media; Telecommunications.

Bates, A. W. (Open Univ., Milton Keynes (England). Inst. of Educational Technology.)
New Media in Higher Education. Papers on Information Technology No. 241.
Mar 85 17p ED-274 322
Audiotape Cassettes; Broadcast Television; Computer Assisted Instruction; Computer Graphics; Distance Education.

Bates, A.W. (Open Univ., Milton Keynes (England). Inst. of Educational Technology.)
Selecting and designing low-cost media for distance education. Papers on Information Technology. No. 138.
23 pp., Oct 1984, Open Univ., Walton, Bletchley, Bucks, England, Pub. No: ED253 216, 12 ref.
Information Generation, Reproduction, and Distribution Education, Computer Assisted Instruction; Distance Learning; Educational Technology; Media; Telecommunications.

Bates, A. W. (Open Univ., Milton Keynes (England). Inst. of Educational Technology.)
Implications for Teaching and Learning of New Informatics Developments.I.E.T. Papers on Broadcasting No. 233.
Sep 84 11p Paper presented at the Annual Conference of Higher Education International (1st, York, England, September, 1984). Available from ERIC ED-253 208
Computers; Delivery systems; Distance education; Futures(of society).

Bates, A. W. (Open Univ., Milton Keynes (England). Inst. of Educational Technology.)
New Communications Technology and Distance Education: Implications for Commonwealth Countries of the South. Papers on Information Technology No.239.
Dec 84 24p Paper prepared for Commonwealth Secretariat. Available from ERIC ED-253 215.

Bates, A. W. (Open Univ., Milton Keynes (England). Inst. of Educational Technology.)

New Technology and Its Impact on Conventional and Distance Education. Papers on Information Technology No. 237.
Oct 84 9p Available from ERIC ED-268 966.
Distance Education.

Batson, Trent.
A Selective National Survey of ENFI Real-Time Conferencing in the Composition Classroom.
IS RIEJUL89. ED303827.

Belitsos, Byron.
A Foundation for Groupware.
Computer Decisions. 20(11) :30(3) ; Nov, 1988.
Work Group Computing; Computer Conferences; Networks; Software Packages; Future Technologies

Bieber, Jacques; et al.
Common Issues in Distance Education.
European Journal of Education. 24(1) :47-78 ;1989.
Computer Oriented Programs; Delivery Systems; Distance Education; Educational Policy; Satellites Aerospace; Teleconferencing; Foreign Countries; Higher Education; Networks; Policy Formation.

Black, J.B.
Computer Conferencing: Its Potential Role in Caribbean Science and Technology Information Exchange.
24 pp., 1985, Unesco, Caracas, Venezuela
Information Generation, Reproduction, and Distribution meetings, Personal Interchange; Computers; Conferences; Developing Countries; Information Exchange; Scientific Information; Technical Information.

Black, J. B.
Reducing Isolation: Telecommunications and Rural Development. The Arkleton Lecture (6th)
6 Oct 86 16p. Paper presented at the Conference on Research on Computer Conferencing (Guelph, Ontario, Canada, October 6, 1986). Available from ERIC ED-295 608 .
Rural Development; Telecommunications.

Blankenhorn, D.
Is Computer Conferencing Finally Beginning to Mature?.
Business Communications Review. July -August 1986:18-22.

Bonner, Paul.
Computer Conferencing Leaves Lab to Find New Life in the Business World.
PC Week. 4(25) :C25(1) ; June 23, 1987.
Computer Bulletin Boards; Computer Conferencing.

Boothby Samuel Young.
The Influence of Computer-mediated Writing Conferences on Revision: Case studies of College Students.
Harvard University ED.D. 1988, 238 Pages. SO DAI V49(09), SECA, PP2566. 1988.

Boyd, G.
Appropriate Uses of Computer-mediated Communication-systems for Education
- Conferencing R-places.
Educational & Training Technology International. 25 (3) :271-275 ; 1990.

Brilliant, Lawrence B
Computer Conferencing: The Global Connection.
BYTE. 10(13) :174-175; Dec 1985.
Computer Conferencing; Case Study; International Microcomputing; Business; Seva Foundation

Brindley, Bill.
Electronic Conferencing Comes of Age.
Digital Review. 5 (14) :77(1) ; July 25, 1988.
Computer Conferencing; Electronic Mail Systems; Computer Bulletin Boards.

Britten, William A.
BITNET and the Internet: Scholarly Network for Librarians.
College and Research Libraries Newsletter. Feb 1990: 103-107.

Brochet, M.G.
Effective Moderation of Computer Conferences: Notes and Suggestions.
Proceedings of the First Guelph Conference on Computer Conferencing. pp 1-20. Guelph, Ontario, Canada: University of Guelph; 1985.

Brockenbrough, A. (San Diego State Univ., San Diego, CA); et al.
Electronic text: an amalgam of capabilities for creating, informing, and instructing (Higher education).
47 pp., 1985, Pub. No: ED 265 829
Information Generation, Reproduction, and Distribution Education, Computer assisted Instruction; Authoring; Computer Aided Instruction; Educational Technology; Electronic Libraries; Text Processing.

Buerger, David J.
Wide-Area E-mail Conferences Make the Global Exchange of Ideas a Reality.
InfoWorld .9(37) :15(1) ; Sept 14, 1987.
Computer Conferences; Computer Bulletin Boards; Networks; Information Services; Electronic Mail Systems; Information Systems.

Burke, Steven.
In-Synch Provides Interactive PC Use.
InfoWorld. 8(27) :48; Jul 07 1986.
Teleconferencing; Product Announcement; In Synch; American Video Teleconferencing; IBM PC.

Caldwell, R.L. (Univ Arizona, Tucson, AZ)
The Coming Role of Computer Conferencing.
Plant Disease. 66(3) :193-198; 1982.

Carpenter, G. C. (Air War Coll., Maxwell AFB, AL)
Computer Conferencing: An Opportunity for New Directions (Research rept.)
May 88 120p AD-A202 756/3/XAB.
Air Force; Computer communications; Conferencing (Communications)

Chandler, Doug.
Start-up Bringing Back Conference-by-Video.
PC Week. 4(24) :22; Jun 16 1987.
Teleconferencing; Computer Conferencing; Expansion Board; Product Announcement; VCE-30 PC; Concept Communications.

Chi, Uli Han Hsiang.
A Model And Notation For Specifying User Interfaces (formal Specification, Interactive Systems, Verification).
University Of Washington PH.D. 1985, 231 Pages. DAI v46(10), SECB, pp3512. 1985.

Chorafras, D.M. (UCLA, Los Angeles, CA)
Using the Network .
In Personal Computers and Data Communications. Rockville, MD: Computer Science Press; 1986.
Information Systems and Applications Networks, Regional Systems, Consortia; Automation; Computer Networks; Computer Systems; Management.

Clark, G. Christopher.
Distance Education in United States Schools.
Computing Teacher. 16(6) :7-11; Mar 1989.
Distance Education; Educational Technology; Accreditation Institutions; Audiovisual Communications; Communications Satellites; Computer Assisted Instruction; Electronic Mail; Elementary Secondary Education; Teacher Certification; Teleconferencing.

Collis, Betty.
Females and Computer Conferencing.
Computing Teacher. 15(8) :36; May 1988.
Teleconferencing; Teachers; Research; Women; Attitudinal Changes through Computer Conferencing; Second Symposium on Computer Conferencing and

Allied Technologies.
Comer, Douglas E; Peterson, Larry L.
Conversations: An Alternative to Memos and Conferences.
BYTE. 10(13) :263-272; Dec 1985.
Electronic Mail; Computer Conferencing; Programming Design.

Communicating Information. Proceedings of the 43rd ASIS Annual Meeting.Vol.17, 1980.
White Plains, NY, USA: Knowledge Ind. Publications Inc. ;1981. Xii +417 pp.
(0 914236 73 3) Conference held at: Anaheim, Ca, USA, 5-10 Oct. 1980
Information Generation, Reproduction, Distribution, Communications Techniques; Conference on Communicating Information.

Computer Conferencing and Electronic Messaging. Conference Proceedings (Guelph, Ontario, Canada, January 22-23, 1985) Guelph Univ. (Ontario).
Jan 85 219p Available from ERIC ED-255 191.
Descriptors: Computers; Design requirements; Information networks; Man machine systems; Online systems; Program descriptions; Teleconferencing

Conhaim, Wallys W.
Beyond Electronic Mail: Computer Conferencing in Business.
LINK-UP. 6(2) :14-17; March 1, 1989.
Computer Conferencing; Teleconferencing; Business; Trends; Computer Bulletin Board Systems.

Conhaim, Wallys W.
Glasnost comes to The Source.
LINK-UP. 6(2) :32; March 1, 1989.
Computer Conferencing; Russian; International Microcomputing; Promotion; Online Systems; Foreign Trade; Source Bridges '89; The Source; Source Telecomputing.

Coombs, Norman.
Computing and Telecommunications in Higher Education; a Personal View.
Educational Technology. 30(2) :46(2) ; Feb, 1990.
Education; Colleges and Universities; History; Conferences; Instructional Design; Interactive Systems.

Crickman, R. (Univ Minnesota, Minneapolis, MN); Kochen, M. (Univ Michigan, Ann
Arbor, MI)
Citizen Participation Through Computer Conferencing.
Technological Forecasting and Social Change. 14(1) :47-64 ; 1979

Crockett, Barton.
IBM Managers Curb Abuse of Computer Conferencing; Inappropriate Use of Messaging Prompts Action.

Network World. 6(18) :19+ ; May 8, 1989.
Computer Conferencing; User Behavior; Office Equipment; Employee Relations; Management; Study; Harvard University. School of Business.

Cross, T.B.
Computer Conferencing.
Computerworld .18(31A) :37-39 ; Aug. 1, 1984,

Crowley, Mary L.
Organizing for Electronic Messaging in the Schools.
Computing Teacher.16(7) :23-26 Apr 1989.
Computer Assisted Instruction; Electronic Mail; Costs; Curriculum Development; Elementary Education; Foreign Countries; Junior High Schools; Microcomputers; Modems; Student Role; Teacher Role; Teleconferencing.

Crowston, K. (MIT, Cambridge, MA); Lin, F.; Malone, T.W.
Cognitive Science and Organizational Design: A Case Study of Computer Conferencing.
In Computer-Supported Cooperative Work, p. 713-740. San Mateo, CA: Morgan Kaufmann Publishers, Inc.; 1988.
Information Generation, Reproduction, and Distribution Meetings, Personal Interchange Cognition; Electronic Communication; Information Exchange; Organizations; Teleconferences

Culnan, M.J.; Bair, J.H.
Human Communication Needs and Organizational Productivity: The Potential Impact of Office Automation.
Journal of the American Society for Information Science. 34(3) : 215-221 ; May, 1983.
Office Automation; Communication; Productivity; Information Processing; Organization Structure; Human Factors; Implementation

Dirksen, Charles J.; Ostbye, Truls.
Computer Conferencing: A Case Study in Teaching Accounting Information Systems.
Journal of Education for Business. 65(3):137-140; Dec.1989
VaxNotes

Dirksen, Charles J.; Ostbye, Truls.
Effective Computer Conferencing in University Education.
Journal of Education for Business. 64(8) :348-51; May 1989.
Computer Uses in Education; Teleconferencing; Electronic Mail; Higher Education.

Dodd, W. P.
Electronic Journal Experiment.
Data Processing. 25(5) :34-36 ; June, 1983.

Electronic Publishing; Electronic Mail Systems; Computer Conferences; On-Line; Study; Journals; Teleconferencing; Notepad; Infomedia Corporation.

Elton, M. C. J. New York Univ., N.Y. Alternate Media Center.
NATO Symposium on the Evaluation and Planning of Interpersonal Telecommunications Systems.
Mar 78 90p PB-284 361/3
Telecommunication; Meetings; Medical services; Computer networks; Information systems; Education

Ervin, Gerard.
GO FLEFO: An Electronic Network for the Foreign Language Profession.
SO CALICO Journal. 5(4) :41-46; Jun 1988.
Computer Networks; Computer Uses in Education; Databases; Language Teachers; Second Language Instruction.

Feenberg A. (Western Behav. Sci. Inst., La Jolla, Ca)
Computer Conferencing and the Humanities.
Instructional Science. 16(2) :169-186 ; 1987.

Ferguson, J. A. (Lilly Endowment , Indianapolis, IN)
Planet - Computer Conferencing System and its Evaluation through a Case-study.
Behavior Research Methods & Instrumentation. 9(2) :92-95; 1977.

Finn, T Andrew.
Process And Structure In Computer-mediated Group Communication (conferencing).
Washington University PH.D. 1983, 166 Pages. DAI v45(02), SECB, pp721. 1983.
Organizing Strategies.

Fitzgibbon, L. (UWIST, Cardiff, Wales)
Some Human-factors Issues in Computer-based Conferencing.
Bulletin of the British Psychological Society. 39: 102; 1986.

Flavin, Robert A; Williford, Jack D.
The Network Application Manager: You Can Put Any Application Involving Communications on a Conferencing System.
BYTE. 10(13) :203-216; Dec 1985.
Programming Design; Software Evaluation; Computer Conferencing

Florini, Barbara M.
Computer Conferencing: A Technology for Adult Education. Technical Report No. 1.
RIESEP89. ED305463.
Adult Education; Computer Uses in Education; Educational Technology; Tel-

econferencing; Computers; Educational Development; Instructional Materials; Material Development; Teaching Methods; Technological Advancement.

Florini, Barbara M.
Teaching Styles and Technology.
New Directions for Continuing Education. (43) :41-53 ; Fall 1989.
Computer Assisted Instruction; Information Technology; Interactive Video; Media Selection; Teaching Styles; Teleconferencing; Adult Education.

Foote, Victoria M.; et al.
The KEY Program: A University/School Partnership.
IS RIESEP89. ED306068.
College School Cooperation; Computer Networks; Distance Education; Institutional Cooperation; Program Development; Telecourses; Advanced Courses; Audiovisual Instruction; Cooperative Programs; Educational Technology; Experimental Teaching.

Foster, D.L. (National Institute of Education, Washington, DC)
Educator's Guide to Conferencing: Using Computers.
72 pp., 1985, Pub. No: ED 270 090
Information Generation, Reproduction, and Distribution Communications Techniques; Computers; Conferences; Electronic Communication; Teachers; Training.

Freeman, A. R. Melbourne Univ., Parkville (Australia).
Network Nation: The Relevance of This for Possible Educational and General Public Administrative Structures and Strategies in the 1980's and 90's.
Report No.: ISBN-0-949385-00-X May 84 192p Master's Thesis. Paper presented at the Silver Jubilee Conference of the Australian College of Education (Canberra, Australia, May 1984). Available from ERIC ED-247 936
Case Studies; Coordination; Data Processing; Decentralization; Educational Administration.

Freeman, Andrew.
Community Information Systems.
16 May 81 21p Paper presented at the National Community Education Conference (1st), Southport, Queensland, Australia, May 16, 1981. Available from ERIC ED-206 284.
Community Information Services; Information Needs; Information Networks

Freeman, Robert R.
A User's Guide to EDIS CONFER, The Environmental Data and Information-Service Computer Conference System.
Feb 79 28p PB80-130297.
Telecommunication; Computer Networks; Manuals Identifiers: Computer Conferencing; EDIS CONFER System.

Freeman, Sue C. ; Freeman, Linton C. (Lehigh Univ., Bethlehem, PA.)
The Networkers Network: A Study of the Impact of a New Communications Medium on Sociometric Structure.
(Final rept. 30 Sep 77-31 Dec 79) 1981 74p PB82-130386 NSF-DSI77-16578.
Sociometrics; Computer Networks; Telecommunication; Attitudes; Social Communication; Social Effect Identifiers: Computer Conferencing.

Galvin, Patrick F.; Bruce, Robert.
Technology and Rural Education: The Case of Audio-Graphic Telecommunications.
RIEOCT89. ED307072.
Cooperative Programs; Distance Education; Rural Education; Small Schools; Telecommunications; Advanced Courses; Case Studies; High Schools; Institutional Cooperation; Pilot Projects; Program Evaluation; Rural Schools.

Garnette, C.P. (National Inst. of Education, US Dept. of Education, Washington, DC)
Electronic Networking as a Strategy for Information Sharing.
Educational Media International (GB). 2: 25-28; 1985
Information Generation, Reproduction, and Distribution Communications Techniques; Educational Technology; Electronic Communication; Networks.

Garnette, Cheryl P. Ed.; Withrow, Frank B. Ed.
Research Notes. OERI's Regional Laboratory Technology Efforts.
Journal of Educational Computing Research. 5 (2) :253-62 ;1989.
Educational Technology; Instructional Innovation; Regional Laboratories; Computer Assisted Instruction; Computer Managed Instruction; Courseware; Decision Making; Educational Needs; Educational Research; Elementary Secondary Education.

Glossbrenner, Alfred.
New Conferencing Software for Micros: For People Separated by Time or Space.
Lotus: Computing for Managers and Professionals. 2(8) :22-23; Aug 1986.
Computer Conferencing.

Goldberg, Albert L.; Waggoner, Michael D.
A Forecast for Technology and Education: the Report of a Computer Conferencing Delphi.
Educational Technology. 26 (6) :7(7) ; June, 1986.
Forecasting; Education; Technology; Planning.

Gorin, Amy.
NASA Launches Network on UNIX Flexibility.
PC Week .5 (22) :C22(2) ; May 31, 1988.
Planning; Networks; UNIX; Research and Development; Voice Communications; Computer Conferencing; Artificial Intelligence; User Interface; User Friendliness; User Needs.

Grayson, L.P.
New Technologies in Education.
38 pp., May 26, 1981, rep. No: ED 224 458, 68 ref.
Information Generation, Reproduction, and Distribution Education, Computer Assisted Instruction; Audio; Computer Aided Instruction; Educational Technology; Evaluation; Hardware; Instruction; Surveys; Television; Uses; Video.

Guelph Symposium on Computer Conferencing Proceedings (2nd). Held in Guelph, Ontario, Canada on June 1-4, 1987 Guelph Univ. (Ontario).
323p Available from ERIC ED-302 227.
Distance Education; Electronic Mail.

Guillaume, J. (Univ. of Toronto, Toronto, Canada)
Computer Conferencing and the Development of an Electronic Journal.
Canadian Journal of Information Science/Revue Canadienne des Sciences Del'Information. 5: 21-29; May 1980.
Storing and Retrieving of Information, Computer Systems Hardware and Software; Computer Conferencing and Electronic Journal.

Hahn, H. A.
Analysis of Quantitative Data Derived from Computer Conferencing
EG and G Idaho, Inc., Idaho Falls.
Report No.: EGG-M-19987; CONF-8710101-3 1987 5p . annual Human Factors Society meeting, New York, NY, USA, 19 Oct 1987.

Haile, P. J. ; Richards, A. J.
Supporting the Distance Learner with Computer Teleconferencing.
25 Oct 84 32p Paper presented at the Annual Convocation of the Northeastern Educational Research Association (15th, Ellenville, NY, October 25, 1984). Available from ERIC ED-256 293.
College Students; Computers; Delivery Systems; Distance Education; Teleconferencing.

Hales, G. (Open Univ., Milton Keynes (England). Inst. of Educational Technology.)
Educational Technology in Distance Learning.
1985 12p Paper presented at the European Conference on Technology and Communication Impairment (1985). Available from ERIC ED-304 120.
Communication Aids(for disabled); Distance Education; Open Universities; Telecommunications.

Hancock, Chris.
Common Ground.
BYTE. 10(13) :239-246; Dec 1985.
Tutorial; Computer Conferencing; Programming Design; Education.

Hansen, C.
Computer-Mediated Communication and Other Online Applications.

In The Microcomputer User's Guide to Information Online. Hasbrouck Heights, NJ: Hayden Book Co. ;1984.
Information Generation, Reproduction, and Distribution Communications Techniques; Electronic Mail; Telecomputing; Teleconferences.

Harasim, Linda M. (Ontario Inst. for Studies in Education), ed.
Online Education: Perspectives on a New Environment.
Westport , Ct.: Praeger Pub.; 1990.
Online Education; Virtual Classroom; Bibliography.

Harasim, Linda M. (Ontario Inst. for Studies in Education); Johnson, E.M.
Computer Conferencing and Online Education: Designing for the Medium.
Canadian Journal of Information Science. 10: 1-15; 1985.
Information Generation, Reproduction, and Distribution Meetings, Personal Interchange; Canada; Computer Aided Instruction; Computer Networks; Distance Learning; Educational Technology; Teleconferences.

Harasim, Linda M. (Ontario Inst. for Studies in Education); Johnson, M.E.
Educational Applications of Computer Networks for Teachers/trainers in Ontario.
135 pp., 1986, Pub. No: ED 276 398.
Information Generation, Reproduction, and Distribution Education, Computer Assisted Instruction; Computer Aided Instruction; Computer Networks; Educational Computing; Teachers; Teleconferences.

Helal, A. H. ; Weiss, J. W. (Gesamthochschule Essen (Germany, F.R.). Library.)
International Library Cooperation. Essen Symposium (10th, Essen, West Germany, October 19-22, 1987).
Report No.: ISBN-3-922602-11-8 1988 385p Available from ERIC ED-295 678.
Information Technology; Interlibrary Loans; International Cooperation; Library Automation.

Helliwell, John.
Computer Collaboration Tools Emerge, Categories Follow.
PC Week. 4(22) :C1(2) ; June 2, 1987.
Product Development; Multiuser Microcomputers; Local Area Networks (Computer Networks); Software Packages.

Henderson, M.M.; MacNaughton, M.J.
Electronic Communication: Technology and Impacts.
AAAS Selected Symposium (52) Boulder, Co: Westview Press ; 1980. 173 p.
Information Generation; Reproduction; Distribution; Communications Techniques.

Heydinger, Richard B.
Computer Conferencing: Its Use As a Pedagogical Tool.

Presented at World Future Society Education Conference, Houston, 1978 October 20, 25 p., 1978 December.
Computer Conference Education Use; Confer.

Hiltz, Starr Roxanne.
The Computer Conference.
Journal of Communication. 28(3):157-163; 1978.

Hiltz, Starr Roxanne.
Computer Conferencing: Assessing the Social Impact of a New Communications Medium.
Technological Forecasting and Social Change. 10(3), 225-238 (1977).
Computer Conferencing.

Hiltz, Starr Roxanne.
Controlled Experiments With Computerized Conferencing:Results of a Pilot Study.
Bulletin of the American Society for Information Science. 4(5):11-12;1978.

Hiltz, Starr Roxanne.
The Impact of a Computerized Conferencing System on Scientific Research Communities. Computer Conferencing and Communications Center. Research Report # 15. Newark, New Jersey: New Jersey Institute of Technology; June 1981.

Hiltz, Starr Roxanne.
Online Communities: A Case Study of the Office of the Future.
Norwood, NJ 07648: Ablex Publishing Corp; 1984.

Hiltz, Starr Roxanne (New Jersey Institute of Technology).
The 'Virtual Classroom'. Using Computer-Mediated Communication for University Teaching.
Journal of Communication. 36(2): 95-104; Spr 1986, 12 ref.
Information Generation, Reproduction, and Distribution Education, Computer Assisted Instruction; Communications; Computer Aided Instruction; Educational Technology; Teleconferences; Training; Universities.

Hiltz, Starr Roxanne ; Kerr, Elaine B. (Upsala Coll., East Orange, NJ.)
Studies of Computer-Mediated Communications Systems: A Synthesis of the Findings (Final rept.).
Jul 81 600p PB82-107061.
Telecommunication; Systems Analysis; Social Effect; Evaluation; Computer Conferencing; Electronic Message Systems.

Hiltz, Starr Roxanne; Kerr, Elaine B.; Johnson, Kenneth .
Determinants of Acceptance of Computer-Mediated communication Systems: A Longitudinal Study of Four Systems.

New Jersey Institute of Technology. Computerized Conferencing and Communications Center. Research report # 22. Newark, N.J.:New Jersey Institute of Technology; August 1985.

Hiltz, Starr Roxanne; Scher, Julian; Turoff, Murray (New Jersey Institute of Technology).
Computerized Conferencing in Problem Solving and Decision Making.
Brenner, Everett H., Comp. The Information Age in Perspective.Proceedings of the ASIS 41st Annual Meeting. New York, November 13 to 17, 1978. Knowledge Industry Publications, Inc., White Plains, NY, for ASIS. P.159-161, 4 Ref.
Computer Conferencing in Decision Making.

Hiltz, Starr Roxanne.; Turoff, Murray.
Meeting Through Your Computer.
IEEE Spectrum.14(5): 58-64 ;1977 May.
Computer Conferencing.

Hiltz, Starr Roxanne; Turoff, Murry.
The Network Nation: Human Communication Via Computer.
ISBN 0-201-03140-x; ISBN 0-201-03141-8. Jacob Way, Reading, MA 01867: Addison-Wesley Publishing Co., Inc. ; 1978. xxxiv+ 528 p.
Information Generation; Reproduction; Distribution; Meetings; Personal Interchange; Computer Conferencing.

Hindin, Eric M.
Lotus Targets Workgroups with Notes; Uses a Different Approach, But Has a Goal Similar to IBM's OfficeVision.
Data Communications.19(3) :50(2) ; March, 1990.
Communications Software; Local Area Networks; Office Automation; Software Packages; Work group computing; Electronic mail systems.

Hough, R. W. ; Panko, R. R. (Stanford Research Inst., Menlo Park, Calif.)
Teleconferencing Systems: A State-of-the-Art Survey and Preliminary Analysis.
Apr 77 203p PB-268 455/3.
Telecommunication; Reviews; Computer Networks; Closed Circuit Television; Systems Analysis; Teleconferencing; Computer Conferencing.

Housman, E.M. (GTE Labs. Inc., Waltham, MA).
Online Communications by Computer Conferencing and Electronic Mail.
4th International Online Information Meeting, London, England, 9-11 Dec.1980. (Oxford: Learned Inf. ;1980), P.129-35.
Information Generation, Reproduction, Distribution, Communications Techniques; Computer Conferencing.

Hu, J. X. (Yunnan Prov Comp Ctr, Kunming, Peoples R China); Umpleby, S. A. (George Washington Univ, Washington, DC)

Computer Conferencing in China.
Telecommunications Policy. 13(1) :69; 1989.

Hudson, H. E. ; Boyd, C. H. (Southwest Educational Development Lab., Austin, TX.)
Distance Learning: A Review for Educators.
Mar 84 75p Available from ERIC ED-246 872.
Computer Assisted Instruction; Computers; Distance Education.

Hughes, C.; Cook, G.; McGrath, J.
A Survey of Computer Mediated Communications: Computer Conferencing Comes of Age.
Office Information Systems. November 9, 1987.
Keywords: EIES 1.0, EIES 2.0, Confer, Caucus, Participate, Notepad, E-Forum, Vax Notes.

Humphrey, Darrell.
Colorado Oracle: An Experiment Using The Dial-up Telephone Network To Provide Computer-based Message And Data Communications To Libraries.
University Of Colorado At Boulder ED.D. 1981, 177 Pages. DAI v42(11), SECA, pp 4631. 1981.
A review of the literature indicates that there is currently very limited use of computer-based message packages (CBMPs) by libraries....

Introb, Suzanne.
Video-conference Links Four Countries.
Computing Canada. 13(21) :42(1) ; Oct 15, 1987.
Videoconferencing; Communications Service Suppliers; Communications Software; Computer Conferencing; Integrated Systems.

Jaffe, L.
On-Line Services: Convenient Conferences.
Popular Computing. 4(5) :88 ; March, 1985.
Computer Conferences; Information Utilities; Electronic Mail Systems; Evaluation.

Jainschigg, John.
The Computer Cafe: Teleconferencing is the Newest Way to Hold a Meeting, Talk it Over, Get Together!
Family Computing. 3(7) :20-22; Jul 1985.
Teleconferencing; Computer Conferencing; Computer Bulletin Board Systems.

James, John.
Conference Tree: Computer Conferencing on Personal Computers.
Dr. Dobb's Journal. 6(10) :14-15+ ; Oct 1981.
Computer Bulletin Board Systems; Apple II; Online Information; The Conference Tree.

Jarvenpaa, Sirkka L.; Rao, V. Srinivasan; Huber, George P.
Computer Support for Meetings of Groups Working on Unstructured Problems: a Field Experiment.
MIS Quarterly.12(4) :645(22) ; Dec, 1988.
Decision Support Systems; Computer Conferencing; Meetings; Technology; Study; Problem Solving; Networks.

Jarvis, Bill.
Are You Ready for Computer Conferencing?
Canadian Datasystems. 20(7) :31(1) ; July, 1988.
Conferences; New Technique; Meetings.

Jennings, D.
Linking Europe's Academics.
Intermedia.12(4-5) :53 ; July-Sept., 1984.
Networks; Colleges and Universities; Scientific Research; OSI Standard.

Jennings, D.; Patel, A.
Eurokom Users Meet on Line.
Intermedia.12(4-5) :50-52 ; July-Sept., 1984.
Electronic Mail Systems; Europe; Conferences; International Organizations; Data Bases.

Jensen, Mogens.
DEUS and the DEUS TraiNet.
European Journal of Engineering Education. 14(1) :71-78 ;1989.
Computer Networks; Cooperative Programs; Engineering Education; Multimedia Instruction; School Business Relationship; Science Programs; Continuing Education; Cooperation; Engineers; Foreign Countries.

Johansen, Robert.
Telecommunications and Developmentally Disabled People. Evaluations of Audio Conferencing, Personal Computers, Computer Conferencing, Electronic Mail.
230 pp., Jul 1981, Institute for the Future, Menlo Park, CA, Pub. No: ED 227819.
Information Recognition and Description Pattern Recognition; Audio; Computers; Conferencing; Disabled; Electronic Mail; Evaluation; Telecommunications.

Johansen, Robert.
Teleconferencing and Beyond: Communications in the Office of the Future.
New York: Mc-Graw Hill;1984.

Johansen, Robert ; DeGrasse, Jr., Robert ; Wilson, Thaddeus (Institute for the Future, Menlo Park, CA.)
Group Communication Through Computers. Volume 5: Effects on Working

Patterns.
Final Report. Grant Apr 76-00512. 1978 February. Institute for the Future, Menlo Park, California. 195 P. EDRS: ED 162 615; Sponsored by National Science Foundation, Washington.
Group Communication through Computers.

Johansen, Robert (Institute for the Future, Menlo Park, CA.); Schuyler, James A. (Northwestern University, Evanston, Illinois)
Computerized Conferencing in an Educational System: A Short-range Scenario.
In Linstone, Harold A., Ed.; Turoff, Murray, ed. The Delphi Method. P. 550-562. Reading, Massachusetts.: Addison-Wesley Publishing Company Advanced Book Program ;1975. 2 Illus. 6 Ref.

Johansen, Robert ; Vallee, Jacques.
Impact of a Computer-Based Communications Network on the Working Patterns of Researchers: Design for Evaluation of Effects Related to Productivity.
Aug 76 29p Paper presented at the Annual Meeting of the American Sociological Association, August, 1976. ERIC ED-183 216.
Information networks; Organizational communication; Productivity; Research design; Teleconferencing.

Johnson-Lenz, Peter ; Johnson-Lenz, Trudy (Electronic Industries Association, Washington, DC.)
Standardization in Microcomputer/LSI Products Via Electronic Information Exchange.
30 Jun 80 145p PB82-134735.
Data processing equipment; Standardization; Computer systems hardware; Utilization; Meetings; Standards Identifiers: Computer conferencing.

Johnston, J. (Michigan Univ., Ann Arbor. Inst. for Social Research.)
Computers and the Schools: The Next Decade.
Mar 85 29p Available from ERIC ED-257 439.
Computer Assisted Instruction; Computer Software; Elementary Secondary Education; Information Networks; Information Retrieval; Information Storage; Teleconferencing; Videodisc Recordings.

Kanzler, Stephen.
Firm Offers Desktop Video-conference System.
PC Week. 3(45) :32; Nov 11 1986.
Computer Conferencing; Image Processing; Digital Video; Rembrandt Desktop Video System; Compression Labs.

Kaplan, Ray; Palmer, David.
Nota Bene.
Digital Review. 3(13) :33+ ; Aug 18, 1986.
Computer Conferences; Software Packages; Office Automation; Software Engineering; Product Development; VAX Notes; Computer Conferencing Software.

Karraker, Roger; Craig, Elinor.
Mail-and-info Network Draws Crowds at EDUCOM.
MacWEEK.3(39) :4+ ; Oct 31, 1989.
Educom; Meetings; Information Services; Networks; Electronic Mail Systems; Interface; Interactive Systems.

Katz, Mary Maxwell; McSwiney, Eileen ; Stroud, Kathryn.
Facilitating Collegial Exchange Among Science Teachers : An Experiment in Computer-Based Conferencing.
Cambridge, Mass. : Educational Technology Center, Harvard Graduate School of Education; 1987.

Kaye, T. (Open Univ., Milton Keynes (England). Inst. of Educational Technology.)
Computer Conferencing for Education and Training: Project Description.Project Report CCET/1.
May 85 13p ED-273 260.
Computer Assisted Instruction; Databases; Distance Education; Electronic Mail.

Kazlauskas, Edward John (Univ. Of Southern Ca, Los Angeles)
Kinesics in Informatic Communication.
Benenfeld, Alan R., Ed; Kazlauskas, Edward John, Ed., Communicating information. Proceedings of the ASIS 43rd Annual Meeting. Anaheim, CA, October 5-10, 1980. Volume 17. 1980. Knowledge Industry Publications, Inc., White Plains, NY, for ASIS. P. 136-138,
Informatic Communication Application of Kinesics.

Keefe, Patricia.
Lotus Releases Note-able Net Package.
Computerworld. 23(50) :7(1) ; Dec 11, 1989.
Product Introduction; Work Group Computing; Software Packages; Information management.

Kelleher, Kathleen and Thomas B. Cross.
Teleconferening: Linking People Together Electronically.
Englewood Cliffs, N.J.: Prentice-Hall; 1985.

Kelly, John N.
Technology that Supports Meetings.
Patricia Seybold's Office Computing Report. 11(9) :1+ ; Sept. 1988.
Guidelines; Meetings; Productivity; Management; Technology; Trends; Strategic Planning; Presentations; New Technique.

Kerr, Elaine B.; Hiltz, S. R. ; Whitescarver, J; Prince, S.
Applications of Computer Conferencing to the Disadvantaged - Preliminary-Results of Field Trials with Handicapped-Children.
Proceedings of the American Society for Information Science. 16:149-158; 1979.

Kerr, Elaine B.; Turoff, Murray ; Johnson-Lenz, Peter and Trudy.
Users' Manual for the Electronic Information Exchange System.
Computer Conferencing and Communications Center. Research Report # 17.
Nework, NJ: New Jersy Institute of Technology; (no date).
EIES.

Kiesler, Sara.
Thinking Ahead: The Hidden Messages in Computer Networks.
Harvard Business Review. 64(1):46-60; Jan-Feb 1986.
Kimmel, Howard; et al.
Computer Conferencing as a Resource for In-Service Teacher Education.
Science Education. 72(4) :467-73 ;Jul 1988.
Computer Networks; Computer Oriented Programs; Educational Technology; Faculty Development; Inservice Teacher Education; Teacher Improvement. Communications; Computer Uses in Education; Linking Agents. Science Education; Teacher Workshops.

Knoll, Darrel R. ; Jennings, R. Scott.
A User's Guide to the Conference Manager Subsystem of EDIS CONFER, The Environmental Data and Information Service Computer Conference System.
Feb 79 28p PB80-137359.
Telecommunication Identifiers: Computer conferencing; EDIS CONFER system; Dec System-10 Computers.

Kochen, M. (Mental Health Res. Inst., Univ. of Michigan, Ann Arbor, Mi).
Toward Medical Management Decision Support Systems.
Hum. Syst. Manage. 1(3): 247-251; Nov. 1980.
Libraries, Information Services, Medicine, Health Services.

Kowalski, Rosemary.
Computer CONFERencing in the English Composition Classroom.
Educational Technology. 29(4) :29-32 Apr 1989.
Computer Assisted Instruction; Courseware; Freshman Composition; Teleconferencing; Discussion Teaching Technique; Group Dynamics; Higher Education.

Kramer, Matt.
Computer Conferencing Gains Far-Flung Following.
PC Week.2(46) :205 ; Nov. 19, 1985.
Telecommunications; Computer Conferences; Companies; Market Penetration.

Kramer, Matt.
Computer Conferencing: The Business Meeting of the Future Will Convene as Close as the Nearest PC.
PC Week. 3(10) :59-60; Mar 11 1986.
Computer Conferencing; Teleconferencing; Network Technologies

Kramer, Matt.
Conference to Explore On-line Information Nets. (Connectivity section)
PC Week. 5(18) :C3+ ; May 3, 1988.
Electronic Networking Association; User Groups; Conferences; Computer Conferencing; Communication.

Kramer, Matt.
LANs, PCs Prowl the Campaign Trail.
PC Week. 5(30) :10(1) ; July 25, 1988.
Local Area Networks; Microcomputers; Elections; Politics; Technology; Democratic Party.

Kremers, M. (New York Institute of Technology); Haile, P.
Teaching Writing by Interdisciplinary Computer Conference.
Journal of Educational Technology Systems. 15(2): 213-219;1986-87.
Information Generation, Reproduction, and Distribution Education, Computer Assisted Instruction; Computer Aided Instruction; Educational Technology; Instruction; Teleconferences; Writing.

Kurshan. Barbara.
Educational Telecommunications Connections for the Classroom - Part 1.
Computing Teacher. :30-35;March 1990.
Online Education, Directory.

Laliberte, Stephen M.
MIX. The McGraw-Hill Information Exchange.
Learning Tomorrow. Journal of the Apple Education Advisory Council. 4 :75-92 ;Win 1988. (ED302200).
Computer Networks; Electronic Mail; Information Dissemination; Information Networks; Teleconferencing; Access to Information; Educational Cooperation; Elementary Secondary Education; Higher Education; Online Vendors; Publishing Industry.

Lancaster, F. W.
Electronic Publishing.
Library Trends. 37(3) :316-25 Win 1989.
Electronic Publishing; Publishing Industry; Databases; Electronic Mail; Futures of Society; Information Dissemination; Marketing; Photocomposition; Publications; Technological Advancement; Teleconferencing.

Lancaster, F. Wilfrid (Illinois Univ. at Urbana-Champaign. Graduate School of Library Science.)
The Role of the Library in an Electronic Society.
1980 205p Available from ERIC ED-186 043.
Information Dissemination; Information Systems; Libraries; Library Automation

Latamore, G. Berton.
GEnie: Out of the Bottle.
PC World. 4(7) :280(2) ; July, 1986.
On-Line; Communications Applications; Electronic Mail Systems; Computer Bulletin Boards; Computer Conferences; Networks.

Lauzon, Allan C.; Moore, George A. B.
A Fourth Generation Distance Education System: Integrating Computer-Assisted Learning and Computer Conferencing.
American Journal of Distance Education. 3(1) :38-49 ;1989.
Computer Assisted Instruction; Distance Education; Instructional Systems; Teleconferencing; Group Instruction; Individualized Instruction; Learning Processes; Literature Reviews.

Layne, Richard.
Computer Conferencing Lets Users Have Meetings of the Mind.
Information Week. (075) :48(3) ; July 21, 1986.
Teleconferencing; Telecommunications; Meetings; Electronic Mail Systems; Networks; Conferences.

Leet, Glen ; Leet, Mildred Robbins.
The Augmentation of International Conferences Through Computer Communications.
7 Jun 78 19p PB-297 087/9 Paper Presented at Session on Computer-Based Document Distribution, National Computer Conference, 1978, Held at Anaheim, California.
Meetings; Computer Networks; International Relations; Computer Conferencing.

Lemmons, Phil.
The Challenge of the Home Computer.
BYTE. 9(11) :6; Oct 1984.
Home Computer; Predictions; BYTEnet.
Lerch, I.A. (New York Univ. Medical Center, New York, NY)
Computer Conferencing - New Tool for Scientific Communication.
Physics Today. 36(8):9 +;1983.

Lerch, I.A.(New York Univ. Medical Center, New York, NY)
The Movable Conference.
Byte. 8 (5) :104 ; May, 1983.
Computer Conferences; Meetings.

Lerch, I.A. (New York Univ. Medical Center, New York, NY)
Electronic Communications and Collaboration: The Emerging Model for Computer Aided Communications in Science and Medicine.
Telematics and Informatics. 5 (4) : 397-414; 1988.
Information Generation, Reproduction, and Distribution Communications

Techniques; Biomedicine; Computerization; Electronic Communication; Medical Informatics.

Levinson, Paul.
Connected Education: The First Two Years.
Learning Tomorrow. Journal of the Apple Education Advisory Council. 4 :205-218 ;Win 1988. Nov 86. (ED302208.)
Distance Education; Electronic Mail; International Programs; Online Systems; Teleconferencing; Computer System Design; Electronic Publishing; Graduate Study: Higher Education; Undergraduate Study.

Levinson, Sherwin M.
Cross-system Conferencing with CLACR: Microcomputers May Offer a Way to Link Systems and Cut Costs.
BYTE. 10(13) :273-286; Dec 1985.
Programming Design; Computer Conferencing.

Levitan, Arlan R.
The Face of Things to Come.
Compute!. 8(1) :117; Jan 1986.
Teleconferencing; Software Evaluation; VMCO (Visual/Vocal MAUG Conferencing Utility); CompuServe.

Lindquist, M.G. (Paralog Ab, Stockholm, Sweden.)
3rip-com: Integrating Information Retrieval and Computerized Conferencing.
Communicating Information. Proceedings of the 43rd ASIS Annual Meeting. v 17, 1980, Anaheim, Ca, USA, 5-10 Oct. 1980 (White Plains, NY, USA: Knowledge Ind. Publications Inc. 1981), P.71-3.
Information Generation, Reproduction, Distribution, Communications Techniques; Computerized Conference.

Lindstrom Leonard Carl.
Integrating Feedback Into Teacher Inservice Training: A Potential Application for Computer Conferencing.
Texas A&M University PH.D 1987, 67 pages. DAI v49(04), SECA, pp793. 1987.
Education Teacher Training.

Lipnack, Jessica, and Jeffrey Stamps.
Networking: The First Report and Directory.
New York: Doubleday;1982 p.198.

Little, Gary B.
Diversi-DIAL: Software for Electronic Conferencing and Electronic Mail.
A+: The #1 Apple II Magazine. 5(5) :64-66; May 1987.

Love, G.; Rice, R.E.
Electronic Emotion - A Content-Analysis and Role Analysis of a

Computer-Mediated Communication-Network.
Proceedings of the American Society for Information Science. 22:266-270; 1985.

Lytle, Marilyn Jean.
Word Processors and Writing: The Relation Of Seventh Grade Students' Learner Characteristics And Revision Behaviors.
University Of Oregon PH.D 1987, 136 pages. DAI v48(11), SECA, pp2852. 1987.
Education Technology.

Mace, Scott.
Firms Find New Uses for Conferencing Software.
InfoWorld. 10(21) :11; May 23 1988.
Teleconferencing; Simulation.

Mace, Scott.
Menuing Added to Caucus Conferencing Program.
InfoWorld. 12(2) :32; Jan 8, 1990.
Mace, Scott.
Metasystems Group Unveils Computer Conference System.
InfoWorld. 8(40) :26; Oct 06 1986.
Computer Conferencing; Teleconferencing; Caucus; Metasystems Design Group.

Malone, T.W. (Massachusetts Institute of Technology, Cambridge, MA); Grant, K.R.; Lai, K.Y.; Rao, R.; Rosenblitt, D.
Semistructured Messages are Surprisingly Useful for Computer-Supported Coordination.
ACM Transactions on Office Information Systems. 5(2) : 115-131; Apr 1987.
(see next entry for descriptors.)

Malone, T.W. (MIT, Cambridge, MA); Grant, K.R.; Lai, K.W.; Rao, R.; Rosenblitt, D.
Semistructured Messages are Surprisingly Useful for Computer Supported Coordination.
In Computer-Supported Cooperative Work. San Mateo, CA: Morgan Kaufmann Publishers, Inc.; 1988. p. 311-334.
Information Storage and Retrieval Computer Systems; Artificial Intelligence; Computer Aided Performance; Design; Distributed Systems; Information Exchange; Message Systems.

Manley, J. E. (Naval Postgraduate School, Monterey, CA.)
Multimedia Computer Conferencing System (Master's thesis).
Dec 86 87p AD-A177 481/9/XAB.
Computer Communications; Conferencing (Communications); Command and Control Systems.

Mason, R. (Open Univ., Milton Keynes, England)
Computer Conferencing: A Contribution to Self-Directed Learning.
British Journal of Educational Technology (GB). 19 (1) : 28-41; Jan 1988.
Information Generation, Reproduction, and Distribution Meetings, Personal Interchange; Computer Aided Instruction; Computerization; Distance Learning; Educational Technology; Learning; Teleconferences.

Mayer, Alastair J. W.
Storage Architectures: Their Implications for Conferencing Systems.
BYTE. 10(13) :221-234; Dec 1985.
Computer Conferencing; Programming Design.
McCartt, Anne Taylor.
The Effects of Decision Conferences on the Processes and Outcomes of Group Decision-making.
State University of New York at Albany D.P.A. 1988, 229 Pages. SO DAI v49 (06), SECA, pp1575.1988.
Group Decision Support Systems.

McConnell, D. (Univ Lancaster, Lancaster, England)
Case-Study - The Educational Use of Computer Conferencing.
Educational & Training Technology International. 27(2) :190-208; 1990.

McCord, Samuel Alan.
Measures Of Participation, Leadership, And Decision Quality By Participants In Computer Conferencing And Nominal Group Technique Decision-making Exercises.
Wayne State University PH.D. 1985, 193 Pages. DAI v46(05), SECA, pp1256. 1985.
CONFER II, Nominal Group Technique.

McCreary, E.K.; Van Duren, J.
Educational Applications of Computer Conferencing.
Canadian Journal of Educational Communication. 16(2) : 107-115; Spr 1987.
Information Generation, Reproduction, and Distribution Education, Computer Assisted Instruction; Computer Aided Instruction; Distance Learning; Educational Technology; Students; Teleconferences.

McKenzie, J.A.
The Future Isn't What It Used to Be: Videotex Is on the Way.
Media & Methods. 21 (3) :8-11 ; Nov., 1984.
Videotex; Future of Computing; Interactive Video; Education; State of the Art; Electronic Mail Systems; Videoconferencing; On-Line Searching; Data Bases.

McManis, Chuck.
Local Power in a Remote Link: Conferencing Systems Can Let Micros Handle Much of the Processing Load.
BYTE. 10(13) :251-258; Dec 1985.

Programming Design; Computer Conferencing.

McQueen, R.J.
Computer Conferencing Is 'COSY.'
Computing Canada. 10 (17) :18 ; Aug. 23, 1984.
UNIX; Teleconferencing; COSY; Terminals; C Programming Language.

Meeks, Brock N.
COM1: Back to the Future Again.
Byte. 13(10): 144-147 ; Oct 1988.
Prodigy.

Meeks, Brock N.
Learning Link Helps Educators, Students.
LINK-UP. 7(1) :15, 26; January 1, 1990.
Online Systems; Education; Online Information; Learning Link; Corporation for Public Broadcasting.

Meeks, Brock N.
A Look at Two Conferencing Systems.
Profiles. 4(7) :14-15; Feb 1987.
Computer Conferencing; Teleconferencing; Software Evaluation; Whole Earth 'Lectronic Link; Byte Information Exchange; Point Foundation; Network Technologies; Byte.

Meeks, Brock N.
An Overview of Conferencing Systems: A Guided Tour Through COM, EIES, PARTI, NOTEPAD, and Others.
BYTE. 10(13) :169-184; Dec 1985.
Computer Conferencing; History; Software Evaluation.

Meeks, Brock N.
The Quiet Revolution: On-line Education Becomes a Real Alternative.
Byte. 12 (2) :183(4) ; Feb, 1987.
Education; On-Line; Teleconferencing; Computer Assisted Instruction; Colleges and Universities; Electronic Mail Systems.

Meeks, Brock N.
Regional Networks Bridge the Gap.
Pro=Files. 3(6) :14-20; Jan 1986.
Computer Conferencing; Consumer Information; Electronic Mail; Online Systems; Real Estate; Chariot; Whole Earth 'Lectronic Link (WELL); ArborNet; Electric Pages; Real Estate Information Network (REIN).
Melin, Nancy Jean.
Welcome to ALANET.
Netlink. 2(1): 8-10; Jan 86.

Melton, Emily.
ALANET: The American Library Association's Electronic Information System.
Electronic Library. 4(5):290-294;Oct 1986.

Meng, Brita.
Long-distance Control.
Macworld. 5(10) :178-180; October 1, 1988.
Teleconferencing; Computer Conferencing; Telecomputing; Software Review; Local Area Networks; Networks; Electronic Mail; Timbuktu; WOS Data Systems

Mihram, D.
A Bird's-eye View of the Present Role of Libraries and University Presses in the Dissemination of Modern Language Studies.
12 pp., Dec 29, 1983, pub. No: ED 243 480, 29 ref.
Libraries and Information Services Assistance, Reference; Libraries; Library Services; Publishing; Searching.

Miller, Holly G.
Connected for Success.
Online Today. 7 (6) :14(4) ; June, 1988.
On-Line Inquiry; Computer Conferencing; Job Search.

Miller, R.H.; Vallee, J.F. (Infomedia Corp., Palo Alto, Ca, USA)
Towards a Formal Representation of EMS.
Telecommun. Policy. 4(2): 79-95; June 1980.
Storing and Retrieving of Information, General; Electronic Message Systems; Message Systems Electronic.

Miller, Richard H.; Vallee, Jacques.
Specifications for Computer-aided and On-line Group Conferencing.
Special Report. Contract DAHC15-72-0165, Arpa order-2005. 1974 May 20.Institute for the Future, Menlo Park, California. 16 P. NTIS: AD-779064/5ga.
Computer Conferences.

Mills, M.K.
Computer Conferencing for the Third World.
17 pp., Apr 1983, pub. No: ED 233 682, 26 ref.
Information Generation, Reproduction, and Distribution Transfer of Technology and Innovation; Communications; Computers; Conferences; Developing Countries; Forecasting.

Monteau, Patricia A.
Teleconferencing.
Instructional Innovator. 29(6) :20-22; Sep/Oct 1984.
Teleconferencing; Computer Conferencing.

Moore, Jack.
Online Help from IBM.
Exceptional Parent. 18(7) :56-60 ;Oct 1988.
Computer Networks; Disabilities; Computer Software; Electronic Mail; Information Networks; Telecommunications.

Morris, S. C. ; Morgan, M. G. (Brookhaven National Lab., Upton, N.Y.)
Human Responses to Sulfur Pollutants. Proceedings of a Computer-Based Conference September--November 1974, Upton, New York
1974 103p BNL-20328.
Energy; Environmental effects ; Sulfur.

Morrison, J. L.
Personal Experience with Computer Conferencing: Problems and Possibilities.
Apr 87 9p Paper presented at the Annual Meeting of the American Educational Research Association (Washington, DC, April 20-24, 1987). ED-286 488.
Educational Research; Information Networks.

Moskaluk, P.; Moore, J.W.; Moore, E.A.
CHYMNET, a New Wave of Communication: Computerized Conferencing.
Journal of Computers in Mathematics and Science Teaching. 4(2) :37-38 ; Winter, 1984.
Education; Secondary Schools; Colleges and Universities; Computer Conferences; Teaching; Computer Bulletin Boards.

Murrel, Sharon Lynne.
The Impact Of Communicating Through Computers (Electronic Mail, Conference).
State University Of New York At Stony Brook PH.D. 1983, 159 Pages. DAI v44(12), SECA, pp 3533. 1983.
Group Performance, Synchronous Approaches.

Naidu, S.
Computer Conferencing in Distance Education.
12 Jun 88 26p Available from ERIC ED310734.
Computer Assisted Instruction; Distance Education; Teleconferencing.

Newton, James W.; Rohwedder, W.J.
Environmental Computer Networks.
E: The Environmental Magazine. 1(2):45-47; March/April 1990.
IGC; Econet.

Nichol, Tom.
The FidoNet Echomail System Echomail Provides Users with a Wealth of Information.
LINK-UP. 5(6) :14; November 1, 1988.

Nisenholtz, M. (New York University, New York, NY); Morphos, E.M.
Information Technology and New Forms of Participation in the Narrative.
In Information Processing 83. Proceedings of the IFIP 9th world Computer Congress, Paris, France, Sept 19-23, 1983, 1983, North Holland, Netherlands, Amsterdam, 4 ref.
Information Systems and Applications General; Communications; Electronic Information Systems; Information Technology; Teleconferencing; Uses; Writing.

Noor Al-Deen, Hana Salih.
Corporate Teleconferencing: Audio, Video, and Computer.
State University of New York at Buffalo PH.D 1988, 188 pages.

Norton, Robert E.;Stammen, Ronald M.
Long-Distance Learning: A Look at the Future.
Vocational Education Journal. 65(4):26+; May 1990.
Participate.

Norton, Robert E.; Stammen, Ronald M.
Using Computer Conferencing Techniques To Maximize Student Learning.
RIEAPR90. ED313034.
Curriculum Development; Distance Education; Teleconferencing; Instructional Materials; Pilot Projects; Postsecondary Education; Staff Development; Vocational Education; Workshops.

O'Flaherty, T.
Softline: Multiuser Age Raises Issues.
Computerworld.19 (5) :37 ; Feb. 4, 1985.
Multiuser Microcomputers; Applications; User Needs; Communication; Organizational Communications.

Opper, S.
Computer-Based Messaging: Keep Corporate Teams on Target.
Computer Decisions. 16 (15) :100-102 ; Nov. 15, 1984.
Computer Conferences; Management Applications.

Opper, S.
Meetings of the Minds: A Step Beyond Electronic Mail.
Data Training. 3(1) :20-22 ; Dec., 1983.
Conferences; Networks; Project Management; Future Technologies; History; Applications.

Opper, Susanna.
Computer Conferencing Adds a New Dimension to the Workplace: The Meeting Has Moved from the Board Room to the PC.
PC Week. 4(16) :57, 69; Apr 21 1987.
Teleconferencing.

Palme, Jacob. (Stockholm Univ. (Sweden). Computing Center).
Computer-Based Conferencing.
In The Application of New Technologies to Improve the Delivery of Aerospace and Defence Information. Proceedings of a Conference Held at Ottawa, Canada on 14-15 September 1983, Jan 84 7p AD-P003 100/5
Conferencing (Communications); Information Transfer; Computer Communications; Man Computer Interface Identifiers.

Palme, Jacob. (Stockholm Univ. (Sweden). Computing Center)
Distributed Computer Conferencing.
Computer Networks and ISDN Systems. 14(2) : 137-146 ; 1987.
Information Generation, Reproduction, and Distribution Meetings, Personal Interchange; Communications; Computerization; Distributed Systems; Message Systems; Teleconferences.

Palme, Jacob. (Stockholm Univ. (Sweden). Computing Center)
Survey of Computer-Based Message Systems; COM/PortaCOM Conference System:Design Goals and Principles; Computer Conferencing Is More Than Electronic Mail; Effects of the COM Computer Conference System
1984 43p Available from ERIC ED-258 557.
Information Dissemination; Information Networks; Online Systems; Social Networks; Telecommunications.

Palme, Jacob.
Conferencing Standards: The Search for a Universal Conferencing Standard Continues.
BYTE. 10(13) :187-192; Dec 1985.
Computer Conferencing; Standards; Programming Design; International Standards Organization (ISO); InternationalTelegraph and Telephone Consultative Committee (CCITT); European Computer Manufacturers Association (ECMA).

Palme, Jacob.
Database Structure in PortaCOM: A Look at the Functions that Affect Database Structures.
BYTE. 10(13) :195-200; Dec 1985.
Tutorial; Computer Conferencing; Programming Design; COM/PortaCOM; QZ; Stockholm University Computing Center.

Palme, Jacob (Foersvarets Forskningsanstalt FOA, Stockholm (Sweden)).
Experience with the Use of the COM Computerized Conferencing System.
Dec 81 55p PB82-169293.
Telecommunication; Computer Conferencing; COM System; Computer Networks; KOM System; DEC System-10 computers.

Palme, Jacob (Forsvarets Forskningsanstalt FOA, Stockholm (Sweden)).
A Human-Computer Interface for Non-Computer Specialists.
Mar 79 14p PB-296 948/3.

Telecommunication; Computer Conferencing; COM System.

Palme, Jacob (Forsvarets Forskningsanstalt FOA, Stockholm (Sweden)).
Teleconference-Based Management Information Systems.
Mar 79 13p PB-296 949/1.
Management Information Systems; Information Retrieval; Sweden Identifiers: Computer Conferencing.

Parker, L.H.
Teleconferencing in Education. ERIC Digest.
3 pp., Nov 28, 1983, Pub. No: ED 254 214.
Information Generation, Reproduction, and Distribution -Meetings, Personal Interchange; Education; Teleconferencing.

Parker, Lorne A. ; Olgren, Christine H. (Wisconsin Univ.-Madison. Center for Interactive Programs).
Teleconferencing and Interactive Media.
1980 488p Available from ERIC ED-194 045.
Audio Equipment; Business Communication; Educational Administration; On-line Systems; Organizations(Group); Telecommunications; Teleconferencing.

Parnes, Robert.
Learning To Confer: The Interplay Of Theory And Practice In Computer Conferencing.
The University Of Michigan PH.D. 1981, 353 Pages DAI v42(02), SEC A, pp 672.1981.
This dissertation presents a description and analysis of ,CONFER, a computer conferencing and multi-purpose communications system designed and developed over the past half dozen years at The University of Michigan.

Parnes, Robert; Bernstein, Maya.
The Beginners Guide to Confer II.
Ann Arbor, Mich.: Advertel Communication Systems;1986.

Petrosky, Mary.
Network Firm Encourages Low-cost Teleconferencing.
InfoWorld. 7(48) :13; Dec 02 1985.
Product Announcement; Corporate Information; Computer Conferencing; Eforum PC; Participate; Network Technologies International Inc.; Participation Systems Inc.; IBM PC.

Pfaffenberger, B.
Networking.
In The Scholar's Personal Computing Handbook. Boston, MA: Little, Brown & Co. ;1986.
Information Systems and Applications Networks, RegionalSystems, Consortia; Data Transmission; Microcomputers; Personal Computers.

Phillips, A. F.
Computer Conferences: Success or Failure.
May 83 47p Paper presented at the Annual Conference of the International Communications Association (33rd), Dallas, TX, May 1983. Available from ERIC ED-235 771.
Attitudes; Case Studies; Computer Oriented Programs; Interpersonal Communication; Man Machine Systems; Teleconferencing.

Pieper, M. (Institute for Planning and Decision-Support Systems)
Computer Conferencing and Human Interaction.
In Pathways to the Information Society. New York, NY: North Holland Publishing Company; 1982. 20 ref.
Information Generation, Reproduction, and Distribution -Meetings, Personal Interchange; Computer Systems; Conferencing; Decision Support; Human Factors; Man Machine Interfacing.

Piturro, Marlene C.
Work: Redefining Old Jobs, Creating New Ones.
Personal Computing. 13 (10) :141(3) ; Oct, 1989.
Microcomputers; Job Performance; Productivity; Career development; Telecommuting; Teleconferencing; Job Satisfaction; Social Issues.

Pompili, Tony.
Computer Conferencing Links Far-flung Pan Am Pilot Union: Pilots at Troubled Firm Use Network to Stay Informed of Contract Talks, Safety Reports; Provides 'rumor control'.
PC Week. 4(29) :C/1+; Jul 21 1987.
Teleconferencing; Computer Conferencing; Unions; Flying; Case Study.

Poor, Alfred.
In-Synch Provides Practical, Low Cost Teleconferencing.
PC Week. 4(38) :C/12-C/13; Sep 22 1987.
Teleconferencing; Computer Conferencing; Software Review; In-Synch; American Video Teleconferencing.
Pournelle, Jerry.
All Sorts of Software.
BYTE. 11(3) :269-290; Mar 1986.
Computer Bulletin Board Systems; Computer Conferencing; Data Base Management; Telecommunications; Zenith; Crosstalk; Q&A; XyWrite.

Pournelle, Jerry.
The Final Frontier: BIX is the Scene for a Discussion of an Academy for Space Cadets.
BYTE. 11(13) :291-304; Dec 1986.
Computer Conferencing.

Pournelle, Jerry.
The Real Electronic Village: There's a Conferencing System in Your Future, And it Offers a Different Kind of Communication.
Popular Computing. 4(12) :45-49; Oct 1985.
Computer Conferencing; Teleconferencing; Future; Networks; Computers and Society.

Price, Charlton R.
Conferencing via Computer: Cost Effective Communication for the Era of Forced Choice.
In Linstone, Harold A., ed.; Turoff, Murray, ed. The Delphi Method. Reading, Massachusetts: Addison-Wesley Publishing Company, Advanced Book Program:1975. P. 497-516. 48 Ref.
Computerized Conferencing.

Pyle, I.C. (University of York, Heslington, York, England)
Uses for Computer Conferencing.
Data Processing. 27(8): 30-33; Oct 1985, 4 ref.
Information Generation, Reproduction, and Distribution Meetings, Personal Interchange; Computer Networks; Telecomputing; Teleconferences.

Quarterman, John S.
The Matrix : Computer Networks and Conferencing Systems Worldwide.
Bedford, Mass. : Digital Press; 1990.

Quarterman, John S.
Somewhere Over the Network.
UNIX Review. 5(3) :50(8) ; March, 1987.
Networks; File Transfer; Electronic Mail Systems; Computer Conferences; Computer Bulletin Boards; Computer Services; Communications Service Suppliers; Market Analysis.

Ramani, S. (National Centre for Software Development and Computer Techniques); Miller, R.
A New Type of Communication Satellite Needed for Computer Based Messaging.
In Pathways to the Information Society. New York, NY: North Holland Publishing Company ;1982. 4 ref.
Information Generation, Reproduction, and Distribution; Communications Techniques; Communications; Message Systems; Satellites.

Rawson, J. A.
Simulation at a Distance Using Computer Conferencing.
Educational & Training Technology International. 27(3):284-292; 1990

Renner, Rod L. (Mathematics and Computation Lab (Fpa) Mclean Va)
Conference System User's Guide.

Nov 76 31p AD-A034 738/5
Computer Communications; Conferencing(Communications) Computer Conferencing.

Renner, Rod L. (Mathematics and Computation Lab (Oep) Mclean Va Information Analysis Div)
Conference System User's Guide.
Nov 72 29p AD-756 813.
UNIVAC 1108 Computers; Computer Conferencing.

Repo, A.J. (Technical Research Centre of Finland, Espoo, Finland)
Computer Conference in Information Service. Research Report. No. 191.
58 pp., Jun 1983, pub. No: ED 238 433, 27 ref.
Information Generation, Reproduction, and Distribution Communications Techniques; Access; Computers; Conferencing; Development; Europe; Information Services;Message Systems; Networks.

Rhine, Leonord.
Electronic Mail Journal Claiming: The Use of ALANET to Claim Missing Issues.
Serials Review 15(4):43-46 +;1989.
Rice, Ronald Eugene.
Computer Conferencing.
In Dervin, B. ; Voigt, M. (Eds.) Progress in Communication Sciences. 2:215-240. Norwood, NJ: Ablex ; 1980.

Rice, Ronald Eugene.
Human Communication Networking In A Teleconferencing Environment.
Stanford University PH.D. 1982, 360 Pages. DAI v43(04), SECA, pp959. 1982.
Computer Conferencing.

Rice, Ronald; Love, Gail.
Electronic Emotion: Sociometric Content in a Computer-Mediated Communications Network.
Communication Research. 14(1):85-108; Feb. 1987.

Ritter, Jane Marie.
The Use of a Computer-Facilitated Conferencing Technique to Encourage Revision in Children's Writing.
University of Oregon PH.D 1987, 232 pages. DAI v48(11), SECA, pp2800.1987.
Education Curriculum and Instruction.

Roberts, L.
Electronic Seminar: Distance Education by Computer Conferencing.
May 87 10p Paper presented at the Annual Conference on Non-Traditional

and Interdisciplinary Programs (5th, Fairfax, VA, May 1987). ED-291 358
Computer Assisted Instruction; Distance Education; Electronic Mail; Computer Mediated Communication.

Roderer, Nancy K. ; King, Donald W. ; McDonald, Dennis D. ; Bush, Colleen G. (King Research, Inc., Rockville, MD.)
Evaluation of the Hepatitis Knowledge Base System.
Oct 81 254p NLM-78-3 PB82-199639.
Information Systems; Hepatitis; Information Retrieval Effectiveness.

Rubin, C.
Making the Most Out of Meetings.
Personal Computing. 7(9) :76-77 ; Sept., 1983.
Business Planning; Planning; Business Graphics; Spreadsheets; Conferences; Meetings.

Ruby, D.
Terminal Behavior.
PC Week.1(45) :127-129 ; Nov. 13, 1984.
Computers; Scientific Research; Communication; Feedback; Human Factors; Terminals; Decision Making; Electronic Mail Systems; Companies.

Santo, H. (GMD, St. Augustin)
AMIGO: Advanced Messaging in Groups.
Computer Networks and ISDN Systems. 15(1): 55-60;1988.
Information Generation, Reproduction, and Distribution Communications Techniques; Communications; Computer Networks; Computerization; Distributed Systems; Message Systems; Office Automation.

Saunders, C. S. (Texas Christian Univ, Ft Worth, TX); Heyl, J. E. (Univ Colorado, Denver, CO)
Evaluating Educational Computer Conferencing.
Journal of Systems Management. 39(4): 33-37; 1988.

Schamber, Linda.
Delivery Systems for Distance Education. ERIC Digest.
RIEJUL89. ED304111.
Distance Education; Educational Television; Electronic Mail; Teleconferencing; Telephone Instruction; Videotex; Audiovisual Instruction; Cable Television; Closed Circuit Television; Facsimile Transmission.

Schnatmeier, Vanessa.
Transforming Electronic Publishing.
UNIX World. 4(7) :32(5) ; July, 1987
UNIX; Electronic Publishing.

Schneider, S.J.; Tooley, J.
Self-Help Computer Conferencing.
Computers and Biomedical Research. 19(3): 274-281; Jun 1986.
Information Generation, Reproduction, and Distribution Meetings, Personal Interchange; Communications; Computers; Healthcare; Medical Informatics; Teleconferences.

Schuler, John Kevin.
Content Analysis of a Mass Computer Conferencing System.
University of Georgia M.A. 1985, 115 Pages. MAI v24(01) pp4. 1985.
Mass communications.

Selfe, Cynthia L.; Eilola, J. Daniel.
The Tie that Binds: Building Discourse Communities and Group Cohesion through Computer-Based Conferences.
Collegiate Microcomputer. 6 (4) :339-48 ;Nov 1988.
Computer Assisted Instruction; Group Unity; Teleconferencing; Writing Laboratories; Case Studies; Community; Group Dynamics; Higher Education; Microcomputers; Social Values; Writing Composition.

Seybold, Patricia A.
Groping Towards 'Groupware'.
Patricia Seybold's Office Computing Report. 11(4) :27(2) ; April, 1988.
Office Automation; Multiuser Microcomputers.

Seymour, Jim.
Lotus Notes: A Great Way to Kick Off the New Decade.
PC Week 7 (4) :12(1) ; Jan 29, 1990.
Future of Computing; Communications software.

Sherer, Paul M.
DEC Practices What it Preaches About Networks: The Leading Seller of Networks, DEC May Also be the Leading User, Its 33-country Network Links 80, 000 Employees.
Electronic Business. 14 (18) :22(1) ; Sept 15, 1988.
Networks; Computer Industry.

Siegel, Elliot R. (Lister Hill National Center for Biomedical Communications, NLM, Bethesda, MD)
Validating and Updating the NLM's Hepatitis Data Base: the Role of Computer Conferencing.
Tally, Roy D., Ed.; Deultgen, Ronald R., Ed. Information Choices and Policies. Proceedings of the ASIS 42nd Annual Meeting. Minneapolis, Minnesota, October 14-18, 1979. Volume 16. White Plains, NY: Knowledge Industry Publications, Inc.;1979.
Computer Conferencing ; Physicians.

Simand, Bernard.
Applications and Implications of Distance Education: Manitoba.
Canadian Journal of Educational Communication. 18(1) :49-53 ;Win1989.
Distance Education; Telecommunications; Computer Assisted Instruction; Educational Radio; Educational Television; Foreign Countries; Government School Relationship; Higher Education; School Business Relationship; Secondary Education.

Simard, Ronald.
Information Services at the Nuclear Safety Analysis Center.
May 80 10p Paper presented at the Mid-Year Meeting of the American Society for Information Science (9th), Pittsburgh, PA. May 1980. Available from ERIC ED-192 802.
Clearinghouses; Data Bases; Energy; Information Centers; Information Dissemination; Information Services.

Simard, Ronald (Nuclear Safety Analysis Center, Electric Power Research Institute, Palo Alto, Ca); Miller, Richard (Infomedia Corporation, Palo Alto, Ca).
Computer Conferencing to Enhance Nuclear Reactor Safety.
Benenfeld, Alan R., Ed.; Kazlauskas, Edward John, ed., Communicating Information. Proceedings of the ASIS 43rd annual meeting. Anaheim, Ca, October 5-10, 1980. Volume 17. White Plains, NY: Knowledge Industry Publications, Inc.;1980. P. 161-162.
Notepad Computer Conference System.

Smilowitz, Michael; et al.
The Effects of Computer Mediated Communication on an Individual's Judgment: A Study Based on the Methods of Asch's Social Influence Experiment.
Computers in Human Behavior. 4(4) :311-21; 1988.
Group Dynamics; Individual Characteristics; Social Influences; Teleconferencing; Cues; Higher Education; Research Needs.

Smith, Chris.
The Educational Value of Computer-Mediated Communications.
Media in Education and Development. 21(4) :169-71; Dec 1988.
Distance Education; Computer Assisted Instruction; Dialogs Language; Electronic Mail; Questionnaires; Student Attitudes; Surveys; Teleconferencing.

Smith, Jill Yvonne.
Communication Quality In Information Systems Development: The Effect Of Computer-mediated Communication On Task-oriented Problem Solving.
North Texas State University PH.D. 1986, 189 Pages. DAI v47(04), SECA, pp1405.1986.

Smith, Tom.
New York PSC Details Plan for its Multicity ISDN Trial: Says Funding, Other

Problems May Slow Project.
Network World. 6(34) :11(2) ; August 28, 1989.
New York (State). Public Service Commission; ISDN; Pilot Projects; Cost; Negotiation; Wide Area Networks; Metropolitan Area Networks; New York.

Snyders, Jan.
Tools for the Masses: Everyday Tasks Such as Report Writing and Internal Communications.
Infosystems. 34(12) :40(1) ; Dec, 1987.

Space, J. C. (US Forest Serv, Portland, OR); Wood, G. B. (Australian Natl Univ, Canberra, Australia)
Computer Conferencing Speeds International Communications.
Journal of Forestry. 80(5) :298-299; 1982.

Spangler, Kathleen (Institute for the Future, Menlo Park, CA.)
Interactive Monitoring of Computer-Based Group Communication. Paper P-71.
Dec 78 14p Paper submitted to the National Computer Conference; Social Implications of Computerized Conferencing, New York, June 4-7, 1979. Available from ERIC ED-188 573
Information Networks; Online Systems; Teleconferencing.

Spiegelman, Lisa L.
Service Lets Telex, PC Users Conduct Electronic Meetings.
InfoWorld. 9(20) :30; May 18 1987.
Computer Conferencing; Product Announcement; Online Systems; NWI Information Systems; Networking and World Information.

Stanley, B.
Computer Conferencing - A Tool for Third-world Scientists.
International Perspectives. :s1-s3; Nov.1981.

Steele, Lisa.
Online Experience Fulfills Educators Networking Improves Teacher Morale.
LINK-UP. 5(5) :25; September 1, 1988.
Education; Networks; Teachers; Online Systems; ComputerConferencing; Networks; User Groups; McGraw-Hill Information Exchange for Educators (MIX); Science Teachers Network; McGraw-Hill; Harvard Graduate School of Education

Steinfield, C.W. (Michigan State Univ., East Lansing, MI)
Computer-Mediated Communication Systems.
Annual Review of Information Science and Technology. 21:167-202; 1986
Information Generation, Reproduction, and Distribution -Communications Techniques; Bulletin Board Systems; Communications; Computer Systems; Electronic Mail; Information Technology.Stevens, Chandler Harrison (Partici-

pation Systems, Inc., Winchester, MA).
Networking, Legitech Experiments and the Development of Politechs.
Jun 80 58p PB80-205669.

Stewart, D.
Computer Conferences Come to Order.
Business Computer Systems. 4(4) :80 ; April, 1985.
Communications Software; Telecommunications; Network Management Software; Organizational Communications; Text Communication; Cost; Teleconferencing; System Selection; Videoconferencing.

Stibic, V. (Philips Industries Ltd., Information Systems and Automation, Eindhoven, The Netherlands)
Tools of the Mind. Techniques and Methods for Intellectual Work.
Amsterdam, The Netherlands: North-Holland ;1983. 298 pp.
Information Science Documentation Professional and Organizational Aspects; Information Management; Knowledge; Productivity; Professionals; Training.

Stoll, P. F. (New York State Dept. of Education, Albany. Center for Learning Technologies.)
Telecommunications and Distance Learning in New York.
May 88 8p Available from ERIC ED-299 961.
Cable Television; Distance Education; Teleconferencing.

Strom, B.I. (Bell Labs., Murray Hill, NJ)
Computer Conferencing. Past, Present, and Future.
In Office Information Systems. Proceedings of the Second International Workshop, Couvent Royal de Saint-Maximin, France, 13-15 Oct. 1981 (Amsterdam, Netherlands: North-Holland ;1982), p. 287-315, 57 Ref.
Information Generation, Reproduction, Distribution communications Techniques; Computer Conferencing.

Strom, Bernard Ivan.
A Multi-copy Structured Database Computer Conferencing System.
Columbia University PH.D. 1980, 244 Pages. DAI V41(05), SECB, PP1833.1980.

Sweet, Patrick L.
Computer Conferencing and Technology Transfer.
BYTE. 10(13) :173; Dec 1985.
Manufacturing; Research; Computer Conferencing; Industrial Technology Institute (ITI).

Taylor, J.R. (Univ. De Montreal, Montreal, Quebec, Canada)
Computer Aided Message Systems. An Organizational Perspective.
In Office Information Systems. Proceedings of the Second International Work-

shop, Couvent Royal de Saint-Maximin, France, 13-15 Oct. 1981 (Amsterdam, Netherlands: North-Holland ;1982), p. 631-51, 14 Ref.
Information Generation, Reproduction, Distribution communications Techniques; Computer aided Message Systems; Message Systems Computer aided.

Thomas, G.S.
Electronic Campus a Reality with Computer Conferencing.
Bulletin of the American Society for Information Science. 14(4) : 23-; Apr 1988.
Information Generation, Reproduction, and Distribution education, Computer assisted Instruction; Colleges; Computerization; Educational Technology; Electronic Communication; Schools; Teleconferences.

Thompson, Diane P.
Conversational Networking: Why the Teacher Gets Most of the Lines.
Collegiate Microcomputer. 6(3) :193-201 ;Aug 1988.
Computer Assisted Instruction; Language Skills; Teleconferencing; Writing Composition; Discourse Analysis; Higher Education; Local Area Networks; Microcomputers; Models; Tables Data; Teacher Role; Writing Instruction.

Thorson, E. (Denison Univ, OH) ; Buss, T. F. (Ohio State Univ, Columbus, OH)
Using Computer Conferencing to Formulate a Computer-Simulation of Transitive Behavior.
Behavior Research Methods & Instrumentation. 9(2) :81-86; 1977.

Thrush, Emily A.; Hardisty, David.
Computer Networks for Language Learning: The Creation of Meaning through Interaction.
IS RIEOCT89. ED306780.
Classroom Techniques; Computer Assisted Instruction; Computer Networks; Interaction; Writing Instruction; Class Activities; Computer Software; Freshman Composition; Higher Education; Language Processing; Microcomputers; Program Descriptions.

Todino, Grace; Dougherty, Dale.
Using UUCP and Usenet.
632 Petaluma Av., Sepastopol, Ca. 95472: O'Reilly & Associates;1987.

Todino, Grace; O'Reilly, Tim.
Managing UUCP and Usenet.
632 Petaluma Av., Sepastopol, Ca. 95472: O'Reilly & Associates;1987.

Toner, Paul David.
Computer Conferencing In Formative Evaluation: The Development And Evaluation Of A New Model Of Tryout-revision.

Michigan State University PH.D. 1983, 311 Pages. DAI v44(03), SECA, pp650.1983.
Synchronous Conferencing, CONFER II.

Tony, K. (Open Univ., Bletchley, Bucks, England)
Computer Conferencing for Education and Training: Project Description.
13 pp., May 1985, Pub. No: ED 273 260.
Information Generation, Reproduction, and Distribution education, Computer assisted Instruction; Computers; Educational Technology; Electronic Communication; Teleconferences.

Tooey, M.J. (Univ. of Maryland, Baltimore, MD)
Getting CoSy with a Conferencing System--the UMAB Health Sciences Library's role in Educating Users.
Medical Reference Services Quarterly. 7(2) : 69-74 ; 1988.
Information Science Documentation User Training; Academic Libraries; Educational Technology; Health Sciences;Library Automation; Library Instruction; Medical Libraries; Teleconferences; Training; Universities; Users.

Tooey, Mary Joan; Wester, Beverly R.
Computer Conferencing: A Campus Meets Online.
Online. 13(4) :54-60; Jul 1989.
Online Systems; Publicity; Teleconferencing; Users Information. Higher Education.

Tracz, George. (On Institute for Studies in Education, Toronto)
Computerized Conferencing: An Eye-Opening Experience With EIES
Canadian Journal of Information Science/Revue Canadienne des Sciences de l'Information. 5(11-20); 1980 May, 6 ref.
Information Generation; Reproduction; Distribution; Meetings; Personal Interchange; Computer Conferencing Psychological Aspects.

Turoff, Murry. (Office of Emergency Preparedness,Natl. Resource Anal. Ctr., Washington DC)
Delphi Conferencing - Computer-Based Conferencing with Anonymity.
Technological Forecasting and Social Change. 3(2) :159-204 ;1972.

Turoff, Murry.
The EIES Experiment: Electronic Information Exchange System.
Bulletin of the American Society for Information Science. 4(5):9-11;1978.

Turoff, Murry. (New Jersey Institute of Technology)
Future of Computer Conferencing.
Futurist. 9(4) :182 +; 1975

Usdin, Steve.
Videoconferencing Making In-roads Companies Conduct Meetings, Interview

With People in Remote Locations.
InfoWorld. 10(38) :S1, S9-S10; September 19, 1988.
Teleconferencing; Computer Conferencing.

Vallee, Jacques.
Computer Message Systems.
New York: McGraw-Hill; 1984.
NotePad.

Vallee, Jacques.
Group Communication Through Computers. Volume 3: Pragmatics and Dynamics.
Final Report. Grant gj-35 326x. 1975 October. Institute for the Future, Menlo Park, California. 185 P. Edrs: ED 162 613;.Sponsored by National Science Foundation, Washington.
Group Communication through Computers.

Vallee, Jacques.
Group Communication Through Computers. Volume 4: Social, Managerial, and Economic Issues.
1978 January. Institute for the Future, Menlo Park, California. 182 P. Edrs: ED 162 614; Sponsored by National Science Foundation, Washington.
Group Communication through Computers.

Vallee, Jacques.
Modeling as a Communication Process - Computer Conferencing Offers New Perspectives.
Technological Forecasting and Social Change. 10(4) :391-400; 1977.

Vallee, Jacques.
Remote Viewing and Computer Communications--An Experiment.
Journal of Scientific Exploration. 2(1) :13-27 1988.
Behavioral Sciences; Computer Networks; Psychological Studies; Teleconferencing; Behavioral Science Research; Psychology;

Vallee, Jacques.
Sitting in on a Computer Conference.
PC Magazine 1(9) :256-257 ; Jan., 1983.
Computer Conferences; Software; Teleconferencing; Networks; Notepad.

Vallee, Jacques; Askevold, Gerald; Wilson, Thaddeus.
Computer Conferencing in the Geosciences.
Menlo Park, Calif: Institute for the Future; 1977.
Vallee, Jacques.; Johansen, R.; Lipinski, H.; Wilson, T.
Pragmatics And Dynamics of Computer Conferencing: A Summary of Findings From The Forum Project.
In Emerging Office Systems. Norwood, NJ, : Ablex Publishing Corp.; 1982.

11REF.
Information Generation, Reproduction, and Distribution meetings, Personal Interchange; Computers; Teleconferencing.

Vallee, Jacques ; Miller, Richard H. (Institute for the Future Menlo Park Calif)
Specifications for Computer-Aided and On-Line Group Conferencing. (Special rept.)
20 May 74 16p AD-779 064/5.
Computers; Conferencing (Communications); On-line Systems.

Vallee, Jacques. ; Wilson, T. (Institute for the Future, Menlo Park, Calif.)
Computer-Based Communication in Support of Scientific and Technical Work.
Mar 76 68p N76-28835/6
Conferences; Management Information systems; Information Dissemination; Information Management.

Vasta, B.M.; Kissman, H.M.
Toxicology Data Bank (TDB). Peer Review Augmentation via Computer Conferencing.
Chemical Information Bulletin. 36(1): 13; Spr 1984.
Information Generation, Reproduction, and Distribution meetings, Personal Interchange; Computerization; Data entry; Medical Informatics; Online Retrieval; Records Management; Teleconferences;Toxicology

Veit, S.
The Computer Network Maze: Part 1: Helpful Hints on How to Use the Various Communication Networks That Are Available on Your Microcomputer.
Computers & Electronics. 21(3) :60-62 ; March, 1983.
On-Line; Menus; Network Access Procedures.

Waggoner, Michael Douglas.
Explicating Expert Opinion Through A Computer Conferencing Delphi.
The University Of Michigan (0127) PH.D. 1987, 194 Pages. DAI v48(02), seca, pp372. 1987.

Waugh, Michael L; Levin, James A.
TeleScience Activities: Educational Uses of Electronic Networks.
Journal of Computers in Mathematics and Science Teaching. v8(2) :29-33; January 1, 1989.
International Microcomputing; Science; Telecommunications; Computer Conferencing; Educational Computing; Education; Networks.

West, Mary Maxwell; et al
Talking about Teaching, by Writing: The Use of Computer-Based Conferencing for Collegial Exchange among Teachers. Technical Report.
IS RIEJUN89. ED303363.
Computer Networks; Educational Technology; Laboratory Technology; Net-

work Analysis; Science Teachers; Secondary School Science; Communications; Computer Uses in Education; Information Transfer; Networks; Secondary Education.

West, Mary Maxwell; McSwiney, Eileen.
Computer Networking for Collegial Exchange among Teachers: A Summary of Findings and Recommendations. Technical Report.
IS RIEJUN89. ED303374.
Computer Networks; Information Transfer; Network Analysis; Science Teachers; Secondary School Science; Teleconferencing; Computer Uses in Education; Educational Technology; Secondary Education.

Wigley, Griff.
Telecommunications Planning Guide for Educators.
Computing Teacher. 16(3) :24-29; Nov 1988.
Computer Networks; Educational Planning; Telecommunications; Budgets; Computer Software; Costs; Guidelines; Information Networks; Information Services; Microcomputers; Modems; Worksheets.

Williams, Brian.
The Online Librarian's Microcomputer User Group: Teleconferencing By and For Librarians.
Proceedings of Small Computers in Libraries Conference, 1987. p 159-160.
Westport, CT: Meckler; 1987.

Williams, Brian.
Teleconferencing -- What, Why, How?
Proceedings of Small Computers in Libraries Conference, 1986. p 197-201.
Westport, CT: Meckler; 1986.

Williams, J.
Micro Meetings.
Micro Communications. 1(10) :36-40 ; Nov., 1984.
Microcomputers; Conferences; Information Storage and Retrieval; Computer Bulletin Boards; PicoSpan; Confer; Notepad.

Yates, James.
Telecommunications and Developmentally Disabled People: Evaluations of Audio Conferencing, Personal Computers, Computer Conferencing and Electronic Mail.
Educational Technology. 22(5) :47-48; May 1982.
Book Review; Handicapped; Telecommunications; Institute of the Future.

Yuen, M.
Keys To The World: Conferences Where Nobody Cares What You Look Like.
Softalk. 4 :97-99 ; April, 1984.
Computer Conferences; Guidelines; Teleconferencing.

Zientara, M.
Watch Your Words.
InfoWorld. 6(32) :33-34 ; Aug. 6, 1984.

Zimmerman, D. P. (Univ Chicago, Chicago, IL)
Effects of Computer Conferencing on the Language Use of
Emotionally-disturbed Adolescents.
Behavior Research Methods Instruments & Computers. 19(2):224-230; 1987.

Zucconi, George.
Medical Conference by Computer.
M.D. Computing. 3(2) :40-43; Mar/Apr 1986.
Computer Conferencing; Medicine.